CRI

D1765754

3

Criminology: Past, Present and Future

A Critical Overview

Ezzat A. Fattah
School of Criminology
Simon Fraser University
British Columbia
Canada

Foreword by Paul Rock

First published in Great Britain 1997 by
MACMILLAN PRESS LTD
Houndmills, Basingstoke, Hampshire RG21 6XS and London
Companies and representatives throughout the world

A catalogue record for this book is available from the British Library.

ISBN 0–333–68309–9 hardcover
ISBN 0–333–68310–2 paperback

 First published in the United States of America 1997 by
ST. MARTIN'S PRESS, INC.,
Scholarly and Reference Division,
175 Fifth Avenue, New York, N.Y. 10010

ISBN 0–312–17399–7

Library of Congress Cataloging-in-Publication Data
Fattah, Ezzat A., 1929–
Criminology : past, present, and future : a critical overview /
Ezzat A. Fattah ; foreword by Paul Rock.
p.   cm.
Includes bibliographical references and index.
ISBN 0–312–17399–7
1. Criminology.   2. Crime.   I. Title.
HV6025.F36 1997
364—dc21   96–40425
                                                      CIP

This book is printed on paper suitable for recycling and made from fully managed and
sustained forest sources.

10   9   8   7   6   5   4   3   2
06   05   04   03   02   01   00   99   98

Printed and bound in Great Britain by
Antony Rowe Ltd, Chippenham, Wiltshire

To JENNY, my life partner
and best friend

Contents

Foreword

Not all countries sustain a robust criminology. One supposes that there must be a rudimentary connection between the extent and character of a nation's criminology, on the one hand, and its wealth, traditions of independent inquiry, and public and political anxieties about risk, on the other. Barbara Wootton put one part of the matter succinctly. Social problems, she said, are what governments are prepared to spend money on. Criminology is successfully practised in only a few places, and it is to be found in one prosperous, crime-ridden and university-rich country above all, the United States of America. Criminology is almost wholly an American discipline conceived for an American audience and focused on American problems, and that has its benefits and its costs. The most impressive American criminology is very impressive indeed, and it has moulded how people throughout the world have tried to make sense of crime and its problems. Merton's *anomie* theory, the University of Chicago sociology department's early work on social ecology and the subcultures of the city, and Lemert's and Becker's anti-theory of labelling have been great motors of thought. Yet all the world is not America; neither are all criminologists American; and what works in America may not work elsewhere.

It is one of the chief strengths of this book that it has been written by a Canadian criminologist with an unusually broad and eclectic understanding of the development of crime and criminology in Europe, Britain, Canada, the United States and elsewhere. Having graduated in law from the University of Cairo, Ezzat Fattah studied the social sciences which underpin criminology at the University of Vienna; he then took further degrees in criminology at the University of Montreal. He has subsequently taught criminology in the University of Montreal and Simon Fraser University. His career is a mirror of the range of his learning: this book is important not least because Fattah is cosmopolitan enough to be able to stand at a distance from many of the domain assumptions of an Americanized criminology. Part of the substance of the book's critical overview stems precisely from his capacity to give comparative perspective, depth and context to argument. It is no small thing to be able to write authoritatively about converging trends in the politics of crime in different countries, to bring the arguments of British feminists to bear on larger debates about crime and gender, or to unravel continuities in criminological positivism over three centuries.

A second, and equally important, strength is Fattah's own personal intellectual history as a man who has worked both as a criminologist and as a victimologist. Victimology remains a fledgling discipline struggling to come into its own; it has much to say, and, having been introduced to it at an early stage in Austria, Fattah has played a significant role in nursing its progress. Fattah is an insider, one who understands the promise and limitations of victimology, and he is well-placed to marry what are all too often kept apart, the study of crimes and criminals and the study of victims. With hindsight, it is remarkable that those two enterprises should ever have been severed, and Ezzat Fattah is to be praised for tying them together so profitably in this book.

The third strength, a consequence, perhaps, of the other two, is Fattah's blend of a thoroughgoing scepticism with a humanistic morality. Crime is not accepted blithely as wrongdoing simply because legislators say it is so. To the contrary. Fattah was a critic of Egyptian political institutions under Nasser. He has worked actively for Amnesty International, and this book bears the imprint of those politics. It is a scholarly grand tour that offers a schematic, accessible and broad foundation for understanding the rudiments of a discipline. What it does not do is conceal intellectual difficulties and contradictions. It does not argue dogmatically and evangelically. Rather, it encourages an informed questioning of lay and professional ideas about crime, and that surely must be the only appropriate and responsible stance for an introductory textbook to take.

PAUL ROCK
Professor of Social Institutions
London School of Economics

Preface

Every year dozens of books are published in the field of criminology. Some truly believe that there are too many criminology books on the market. So is there really a need for yet another book that examines the historical evolution of the discipline, its present state and its possible future orientations? I dare to answer with a definite YES to this question. Most criminology books are quite similar to one another in that they devote a substantial part of their content to a review of causal explanations of crime. The same theories offering biological, psychological and sociological explanations are repeated over and over again, often with exactly the same criticisms that were made of the theories when they were first formulated. These identical reviews usually end with the same conclusion: that no theory, or a combination thereof, succeeds in adequately explaining crime. The constant repetition of the theories despite their proven inadequacies reflects criminology's long-standing obsession with the etiology of crime. There is an obvious and pressing need therefore to critically scrutinize the conceptual issues and theoretical premises underlying causal research in criminology and, if they are found wanting, to offer an alternative approach to the study of crime.

In the late sixties, Hood and Sparks (1970:11) criticized the 'cavalier approach to the problem of understanding the basic data of criminality that has so often led criminologists astray'. They were surprised that a great deal of effort in criminology is expended on the critical analysis of a theory before someone remembers to check whether the behaviour the theory is explaining actually exists! Hood and Sparks offered sound, though largely unheeded, advice to criminologists. They maintained that it is necessary to study thoroughly the phenomenon of crime before embarking on its explanations. This simple, but basic, advice, made more than a quarter of a century ago, has had a profound impact on my thinking about crime and the way I taught introductory criminology at both the university and college levels. Hood and Sparks' advice is the reason why the first part of this book is entirely devoted to a discussion of conceptual and methodological issues such as the definition of crime, the relativity of crime, the measurement of crime, and so forth.

So in what way does this book differ from other criminology texts and what distinct features, if any, does it have? Even a quick glance at the table of contents would show that this book is different from others. First, the book challenges popular views on crime, criminals and victims and exposes the concerted efforts by various interests in society to exploit the crime issue and the public's fear of crime. Second, the book also challenges many of the accepted 'truths' in criminology and questions some of the basic premises that underlie most positivist explanations of criminal behaviour. More important is the book's attempt to make a strong case against the continuing, but futile, search for the causes of crime. The book also argues against the separation of victimology from criminology, a separation dictated by an artificial dichotomy between victims and victimizers. It calls for a holistic and dynamic approach where the offender, the victim and the situation constitute a trinity of a comprehensive explanation.

The book examines recent theoretical developments in criminology and the changing views of crime. It outlines recent paradigm shifts, such as the shift from determinism to rational choice, from idealism to realism, and from male-centred criminology to feminist criminology. It also highlights some encouraging trends in criminological research, in particular the current attempts to understand conformity and desistance from crime, the growing interest in understanding and explaining crime by analyzing its motives and it extols the recent shift from dispositional theories to situational theories.

Providing a critical overview of any discipline requires a huge amount of reading and research, a great deal of reflection and contemplation over many, many years. It would not be an exaggeration to say that certain parts of this book were written, revised, rewritten, and revised again up to a dozen times.

Offering a synthesis of research carried out over more than a century in different parts of the globe is a tedious and thankless endeavour. The enormity of the task means that the job can never be perfect or complete. The final product can never satisfy all those who read the book. This is particularly the case when the book's main objective is to challenge the dominant views of the discipline's mainstream. In fact, criminology books inevitably leave the reader with a sense of frustration because many of the fundamental questions in criminology remain without answers and many of the basic problems remain without solution. After all, criminologists, as Nils Christie once pointed out, are problem-raisers not problem-solvers. I have tried, on the basis of my life-long experience studying and teaching criminology, to summarize and articulate what I believe are the major problems that criminology has had to deal with since its emergence as a scientific discipline in the second part of the 19th century and the avenues it has to pursue in the 21st century. I leave it to the reader to judge the extent to which this goal has been attained.

Ezzat A. Fattah
Vancouver

Acknowledgements

Parts of Chapters 6 and 7 of this book are based on Ezzat A. Fattah's book *Understanding Criminal Victimization* (1991), copyright Prentice Hall Canada Inc., and reproduced by kind permission of the publisher.

Quotations from R. Matthews and J. Young, *Confronting Crime* (1986) are reproduced by kind permission of Sage Publications, London. Quotations from Thomas Graber, *Everybody Does It* (1994), are reproduced by kind permission of University of Toronto Press, Toronto. Quotations from Ezzat Fattah, *Understanding Criminal Victimization* (1991), are reproduced by kind permission of Prentice Hall Canada. Quotations from Norval Morris and Gordon Hawkins, *The Honest Politician's Guide to Crime Control* (1969), are reproduced by kind permission of University of Chicago Press, Chicago and London. Quotations from Alex Comfort, *Deliquency and Authority* (1970), are reproduced by kind permission of David Higham Associates, London. Quotations from David Matza, *Delinquency and Drift* (1964), are reproduced by kind permission of the Macmillan Publishing Company, New York. Quotations from Steven Box, *Power, Crime and Mystification* (1983), are reproduced by kind permission of Tavistock Publications.

Every effort has been made to contact the copyright holders, but if any have inadvertently been overlooked the publisher will be pleased to make the necessary arrangement at the first opportunity.

Prologue

Crime: Fact and Fiction, Rhetoric and Reality

Perhaps our *worst* crime is our ignorance about crime; our easy satisfaction with headlines and the accounts of lurid cases; and our smug assumption that it is all a matter of some tough bad guys whom the tough good guys will soon capture.

Karl Menninger (1966:3)
The Crime of Punishment

Crime myths have numerous effects on our perceptions; we may not even be conscious that they are at work. Myths tend to organize our views of crime, criminals, and the proper operation of the criminal justice system. They provide us with a conceptual framework from which to identify certain social issues as crime-related, develop our personal opinions on issues of justice, and apply ready-made solutions to social problems. The organization of views through crime myths contributes to the cataloging of crime issues into artificial distinctions between criminals, victims, crime fighters, and viable social responses to crime.

Victor E. Kappeler *et al.* (1993:3)
The Mythology of Crime and Criminal Justice

WHY STUDY CRIME?

If criminology is the science of crime, then we might start this book by asking: Why study crime? What is so important or specific about crime that makes it necessary to have a distinct and specialized field of study devoted to it? The popular answer, found in most criminology textbooks, that 'crime is a major social problem' masks the enormous variations in the levels of fear of crime and concern about crime among the general population. Members of any society are not equally affected by, or equally concerned about, crime. To some, crime remains largely an abstract notion, something they hear or read about, something they see in movies or watch on their television screens. For them, crime is nothing but a means of distraction that has no impact and no bearing upon their daily routine. To others, crime is a fact of life, something they constantly have to face and to put up with and that largely affects their day-to-day activities.

3

In the United States, crime is, and has been for many years, a major political issue. And judging by the regular findings of public opinion surveys, it is generally perceived as a social problem of staggering proportions. In Canada, where violent crime rates are significantly lower than the American ones,[1] fear and concern are not as pronounced as they are south of the border. And yet, on a long list of areas of public concern, crime is likely to be rated high, probably second only to economic issues, such as unemployment, or political issues, such as, in Canada, Quebec's separation.

Crime, in one form or another, is central to the lives of many people in society. Crime control is a major sector of employment and of industrial activity. For the information media, crime is a prime news item. For novelists, playwrights, and script writers, whether they prefer fiction or real-life dramas, crime provides raw material that is extremely rich in intensity and diversity. For the television and movie industries, crime is one subject matter that allows infinite variations on essentially the same basic theme.

Crime, then, is different things to different people. It is a real threat to some but mere entertainment to others. Many are hurt by it, while others reap benefits from it. Some are busy fighting it, while others are actively exploiting it. For various groups, for differing reasons, crime is either an area of interest or a source of anxiety, an occupation or a preoccupation, something to worry about or to take advantage of.

Despite the wide coverage and publicity crime gets in the news media, crime remains largely an enigmatic phenomenon. Many of the fundamental questions about crime, such as 'How much crime is there?' 'What causes crime?' 'What should we do about crime?' remain without satisfactory answers. And as Walker (1985:5) points out, crime control policy is largely wishful thinking and most crime control proposals rest on faith rather than fact and are based on false assumptions about criminal justice.

In the dying years of the 20th century it would certainly be unthinkable to try to deal with sickness and disease using the tools and remedies of witch doctors. Yet, in another major area of public concern, CRIME, many seem to see nothing wrong in basing society's response on conventional wisdom instead of solid, empirical evidence and hard scientific facts. Metaphysical notions, such as 'free will', philosophical concepts, such as 'moral responsibility', and moral constructs, such as 'malice' and 'wickedness', continue to dominate our thinking about crime.[2] And our actions to control or reduce crime remain largely based on unverified assumptions about the possibility of changing human behaviour through deterrence, intimidation, or rehabilitation. It is not surprising, therefore, that current criminal policy has not been successful in achieving its avowed goal, namely the prevention of crime.

THE RHETORIC OF CRIME

United States

Despite past failures and present disappointments, politicians on both sides of the Atlantic continue to use the same old rhetoric and to advocate the same worn-out recipes. In his speech to the International Association of Chiefs of Police (September, 1981) Ronald Reagan, then president of the United States, declared that the 'War on Crime' will be won when an attitude of mind and a change of heart take place in America, when certain 'truths' take hold again and plant their roots deep into the national consciousness:

> Truths like: right and wrong matters; individuals are responsible for their actions; retribution should be swift and sure for those who prey on the innocent.[3]

Reagan's message was clear. What he called 'an American epidemic' of violent crime he saw as the result of lax laws, the legal safeguards provided to criminals, and the failure of the criminal justice system. The solution Reagan proposed to combat violent crime was all too familiar: Get tough with criminals! One of the get-tough measures he suggested was 'preventive detention', which would allow judges to keep suspects in jail without bail if they appeared to be a danger to the community.[4] Another measure is the abolition of the exclusionary rule, which, according to the former president:

> rests on the absurd proposition that a law enforcement error, no matter how technical, can be used to justify throwing an entire case out of court, no matter how guilty the defendant or how heinous the crime.[5]

He urged legislation to allow illegally obtained evidence gathered by police in good faith to be used in criminal trials.

Ten years later, another republican president, George Bush, delivered essentially the same message. At a Crime Summit held on 5 March 1991, Bush asked the states to follow the lead of the Federal Crime Legislation that was being considered by Congress. The legislation called for enhanced penalties against weapons offenders, more resources for police, prosecutors, and prisons, and expanded use of the death penalty.[6]

Three years later, the Democratic president, Bill Clinton, described crime as 'the great crisis of the spirit that is gripping America today' and tabled a crime bill that suggested that the most effective approach to the crime problem is to 'get tough'. The bill (*Violent Crime Control and Law Enforcement Act of 1994*) was approved and became law in September 1994 and will accelerate the expansion of the criminal justice system. A six-year, 30 billion dollar initiative, reports Sasson (1995:5), provides for massive new prison construction and the hiring of 100 000 new police officers (for a 20 per cent increase in the ranks of the nation's police). It also extends the death penalty to a range of new offences, allows for the prosecution of 13 year-olds as adults under certain circumstances, makes prison building grants to states contingent upon their compliance with a 'truth in sentencing' provision, and includes the highly publicized 'three strikes and you're out' rule.

From these repeated promises and actions one can only deduce that the continuous harshening of penalties and sanctions and the billions of dollars in increased expenditures on the criminal justice system have not made the crime situation in the United States any better. And yet, the human, social, and financial costs of the 'war on crime' are staggering. In October 1994, Associated Press[7] reported that on 30 June 1994 there were 1 012 851 people in prison in the United States (919 143 in state prisons and 93 708 in federal prisons). The number of people incarcerated was thus more than double what it was ten years earlier when it reached 462 002 on 31 December 1984. When figures are translated into rates, it turns out that one of every 260 people in the United States was imprisoned and that does not even include the approximately 440 000 in jails, many are either awaiting trial or are serving short sentences. Across the United States rates increased for both blacks and whites. The white imprisonment rate went up from 116 per 100 000 in 1984 to 203 per 100 000 in 1993. The rate for blacks almost doubled from 723 per 100 000 to 1432. Commenting on the increasing number and rates, Marc Mauer, assistant director of the Sentencing Project (a group that advocates alternatives to prison) is quoted in the same Associated Press release as saying:

> Clearly we need a prison system for people who are truly violent and dangerous, but what's happened in recent years is that we have been locking up increasing numbers of drug and property offenders and we have very little to show for it in terms of reduced rates of crime.

Projected estimates suggest that there will be dramatic increases in the prison population of the United States as a result of the newest fad, 'three strikes and you are out'. The new laws passed in some states mandate a life prison sentence for those convicted of a felony for the third time. For example, it is estimated that in the State of California alone the three strikes law will add another 85 000 prisoners over five years to the State's 1994 prison population of 120 000.[8]

The get-tough policy continues to push the US prison population to new records. In August 1996 the Associated Press reported that there were almost 1.6 million Americans behind bars the previous year. It also reported that by the end of 1995 one out of every 167 Americans was in prison or jail, compared with one out of every 320 a decade earlier (*Vancouver Sun*, August 20 1996, p. A6).

Canada

The rhetoric of right-wing parties in Canada is strikingly similar to that of American politicians. Summarizing the Reform Party's criminal policy, journalist Stephen Hume (1994) writes[9]

> Reform wants tougher judges, tougher sentences, tougher parole boards. It wants some criminals to be under state surveillance for the rest of their natural lives. (p. A21)

Populist politicians believe that they can appeal to the electorate by espousing simplistic solutions that are popular with the general public and with some interest groups, such as 'victims of violence' or 'CAVEAT' (Citizens Against Violence Everywhere Advocating its Termination).

Britain

In Britain, in the aftermath of riots that swept the slums in three British cities, the government announced in October 1985 tough new measures 'to curb crime and bolster police powers.' Canadian Press reported that the proposed legislation will make carrying a firearm punishable by life imprisonment and will also give police the power to impose conditions on crowds at sporting events or picket lines.[10]

Five years later, another Bill *The Criminal Justice Act 1991* received Royal Assent on 25 July 1991 and was implemented on 1 October 1992. And two years later another *Criminal Justice Act 1993* was given Royal assent on 27 July 1993 only to be followed by *The Criminal Justice and Public Order Act 1994*. The Home Office monitored the Criminal Justice Acts 1991 and 1993 and published the results in 1994. Among other things, there was a rise in the immediate use of custody which was most apparent among offenders found guilty of property offences. It was also reported that at magistrates' courts, among adult males sentenced for an indictable offence, those unemployed at the time they are sentenced appeared more likely to be given custodial sentences than those in employment.[11]

'*The Criminal Justice and Public Order Act 1994*' gave the police new powers such as the power to stop and search all people and vehicles for 'offensive weapons or knives', provided senior officers reasonably believe incidents involving serious violence may take place. Police were also given the power to take and retain DNA samples in a wide range of offences (Home Office News Release 89/95). Police were given the discretion to deny bail to prevent further offending while the courts were given new powers to revoke bail. The Government also introduced an amendment to the Bill to allow courts to place 12–14 year olds in secure premises while on remand awaiting trial or sentence (Home Office News Release 13/94). It was also reported that the Government was extending section 53 of *The Children and Young Persons Act* to allow long terms of detention for a wide range of 'serious offences'. And in its News Release 5/95, the Home Office reported that the Crown Court may now impose long terms of detention on 10 to 13 year olds convicted of certain grave offences, having formerly been limited to community-based sentences.

Underlying all these measures is the illusion that crime, particularly violent crime, can be reduced through tougher laws and more severe sanctions without changing or improving the social, political, and economic conditions that breed or produce violence. The suggestion that crime can be controlled or curbed by tightening procedural rules or bail laws is at best a reflection of extreme naivety and at worst an exercise in political deception.

In a sobering article published in the British magazine *The Economist* (15 October, 1994) the anonymous author draws attention to a popular misconception about crime:

> In Britain at party conferences, across America... and in many other countries around the world, politicians are fulminating against crime as though it were a peculiarly contemporary crisis of society. The public at large could be forgiven for thinking that life has never been so lawless. Yet a glance at past trends suggests they would be wrong.... And, just as there is nothing new about high rates of serious crime, so there is nothing new about supposed collapses in moral and social standards. In the past and the present alike, acts of singular brutality have provoked sudden public panics to which politicians have reacted by backing draconian new laws....
>
> Yet it must also be legitimate to wonder whether politicians in Britain, America and elsewhere are doing society a service by suggesting that a high crime rate is a peculiarly modern problem – with, presumably, peculiarly modern causes.... To some extent, the politicians are reflecting public anger; but to some extent they are also feeding it. (p. 21)

IS CRIME INCREASING?

The military terminology and metaphors often used in political speeches and public statements by law enforcement and other public officials are not apt to produce or to promote a realistic perception of the state of crime in the minds of the general public. Expressions such as 'declaring war on crime', 'waging a battle against crime', or 'intensifying the fight against crime' are bound to create an impression of a state of siege, of a crime situation that is rapidly getting out of hand, of desperate and ever-deteriorating conditions where criminals are gaining the upper hand.

In view of this rhetoric one might well ask, 'Is crime increasing?' As simple as this question may be, it is not at all easy to answer directly one way or another. First, crime, as we shall see later on (Chapter 1), is a vague concept, and under the general heading of crime one can include hundreds, even thousands, of totally diverse and heterogeneous behaviours. Second, we have no reliable measures that would enable us to do a time trend analysis of crime. Both official statistics and victimization surveys suffer from several limitations, not the least of which are those of representativeness and accuracy. As a result, official statistics are poor, or at least less than adequate, indicators of the changes in the volume and nature of crime. In addition, official statistics are subject to artificial fluctuations as well as to intentional manipulations. (See Chapter 4.)

If one goes by official figures alone, one gets the impression that many types of crimes have increased in the past three decades.[12] It is difficult to tell, however, how much of the change comes from a real increase in the incidence of these offences and how much is simply a 'paper increase' resulting from more reporting by victims, lower levels of tolerance to certain types of crime, an increase in the number of police units reporting, and so forth. Another important factor is the change in the age structure of the population. Lee (1984) provides evidence suggesting that Canadian crime rates are affected by demographic shifts, in particular, by the increase in the proportion of young people in the general population. American criminologist Alfred Blumstein has repeatedly used the proportion of young people in the American population to explain the rise in US crime rates in the sixties (when the proportion of young people reached a record high as a result of the baby boom that followed World War II) as well as their levelling off when that same proportion declined (Associated Press release in the *Vancouver Sun*, 6 May 1996, p. A8).

Victimization surveys provide a more real, though far from perfect, picture of the quantitative changes in the volume of certain crimes (see Chapter 4). Since Canadian surveys lack regularity (they are not conducted at regular intervals) and universality (the earlier one, the CUVS – the Canadian Urban Victimization Survey – did not cover the whole country but only a few selected urban centres), we may look at American surveys for some guidance.

Survey results in the United States reported by Sheley (1985:91) show that during the 1970s, rates for only one offence of those covered by the surveys, that is, household larceny, rose greatly between 1973 and 1980. Rates for assault also rose slightly while rates for other offences declined. Sheley (1985) notes that in the cases of personal theft, burglary, and motor vehicle theft, the decline was so large that even the Federal Bureau of Investigation (FBI), well known for its regular attempts to amplify the crime situation, had to admit in the Uniform Crime Reports that there was little major growth in crime during the 1970s.

According to the United States Bureau of Justice Statistics (1986), in 1984 the National Crime Survey reported more than 35 million victimizations. The 35.5 million criminal victimizations in 1984 was the *lowest* number recorded in the 12-year history of the National Crime Survey. It was about 14 per cent below the 41.5 million victimizations recorded in the peak year of 1981. Victimization rates for personal theft, household larceny, and burglary fell to 12-year lows in 1984. Crimes of personal theft were about 26 per cent below their 1977 peak. Burglary was 31 per cent below its peak in 1974. Household larceny was 26 per cent below its peak in 1979. Violent crime rates remained basically unchanged between 1983 and 1984, but they were 12 per cent below their 1981 peak. The 26 per cent of households touched by crime in 1984 was down from 32 per cent in 1975.[13]

In October 1993, the American Bureau of Justice Statistics published highlights from victimization surveys covering a 20-year period (1973–1992 inclusive). The most important finding was that overall crime rates (as measured by victimization surveys – see Chapter 4) have been stable or declining in recent years. The analysis of trends showed that the number of victimizations rose from 1973 until the early 1980s and has since declined. The 1992 estimate suggesting that 23 per cent of all households were victimized by crime was the *lowest* recorded since the measure was introduced in 1975. Rates for robbery, burglary, and for personal larceny declined. Estimates of rape rates in 1992 were significantly lower than those of 1973. The rate for simple assault increased over 1973 levels (reflecting in all probability a lower threshold of tolerance and greater willingness to report acts of domestic violence), but the rate of aggravated assaults showed a decline.

Victimization surveys in Canada reveal essentially the same trend. The *General Social Survey* (GSS) carried out by *Statistics Canada* in 1993 shows that the proportion of Canadians who were victims of at least one of the crimes covered by the survey in the previous year was the same as that observed in 1988 when the victimization survey was first conducted.

Reporting on the findings of the GSS in *Juristat*,[14] Rosemary Gartner and Anthony Doob (1994) write:

> Overall rates of victimization have either remained the same or have decreased compared with five years earlier. Canadians 15 and over in 1993 were no more likely to be victims of assaults, thefts of personal or household property, vandalism, or break and enters into households than they were in 1988. They were less likely in 1993 to have been victims of robberies or motor vehicle thefts (or attempts). (p. 1)

Three months later (August 1994) the Canadian Centre for Justice Statistics released the 1993 statistics of crimes reported to police forces across the country. They showed a decline of 5 per cent over the previous year, the largest decline in more than 30 years.[15]

One particular offence for which official statistics are relatively reliable is criminal homicide. According to the figures released by the Centre for Justice Statistics in August 1994, the 1993 homicide rate of 2.19 per 100 000 population was 15 per cent lower than the rate in 1992 (2.57 per 100 000) and represented the third largest year-to-year decrease since 1961.[16]

It is also worth noting that the 1993 homicide rate (2.19 per 100 000) is substantially lower than the 1975 rate, the year preceding the abolition of the death penalty in Canada. In 1975, the homicide rate was 3.02 per 100 000 population. In other words, contrary to the predictions made by supporters of capital punishment and contrary to public perception, the criminal homicide rate in Canada has sharply declined since the formal abolition of the death penalty (the 1993 rate is 27 per cent lower than the 1975 rate).

RISING CRIME RATES: MYTH OR REALITY?

The FBI position on the 'rising crime rate' and the popular belief of the general public that crime is increasing by leaps and bounds are not shared by criminologists. Pepinsky and Jesilow (1984) treat the so-called crime increase as a myth. They point out that, in reality, a careful study of crime statistics yields no reason to believe that overall street crime has been rising; people today are in no greater danger of being robbed or physically hurt than 150 years ago. The same conclusion was reached fifteen years earlier by Morris and Hawkins (1969:56), who suggest that:

> Looking further back to the 1870's and the late 1890's it seems clear that rates of murder, non-negligent homicide, rape, and assault have all appreciably declined with the passage of time.

Using different crime indicators can lead to varying (or even conflicting) conclusions about the crime situation and crime trends.

The discrepancy in crime trends resulting from using different measures is amply illustrated in Britain. Using the crime categories that are comparable between police statistics and the British victimization survey, Pat Mayhew *et al.* (1993) point to the following differences:

1. Recorded crime figures nearly doubled between 1981 and 1991, but the British Crime Survey (BCS) suggests a lower rise of about 50 per cent. The larger rise in recorded crime is attributed by the authors to increased reporting to the police.
2. Since 1987, recorded crime figures for this comparble subset of offences have risen particularly steeply (by 39 per cent) whereas BCS figures indicated a rise of only 14 per cent.

The popular belief that crime is increasing is not surprising. The 1980s, in particular, were years of economic insecurity and uncertainty about the future. A general feeling of malaise and scepticism seems to have permeated the public. Dissatisfaction with the present inevitably elicits nostalgia about the past and pessimism regarding the future: things were much better before, are bad now, and will get worse in the future.

Nor is this belief new. Three decades ago, the United States *President's Commission on Law Enforcement and Administration of Justice* (1967) noted that virtually every generation since the founding of the nation and before has felt itself threatened by the spectre of rising crime and violence:

> A hundred years ago contemporary accounts of San Francisco told of extensive areas where 'no decent man was in safety to walk the street after dark; while at all hours, both night and day, his property was jeopardized by incendiarism and burglary.' Teenage gangs gave rise to the word 'hoodlum'; while in one central New York City area, near Broadway, the police entered 'only in pairs, and never unarmed.' A noted chronicler of the period declared that 'municipal law is a failure... we must soon fall back on the law of self preservation.' 'Alarming' increases in robbery and violent crimes were reported throughout the country prior to the Revolution. And, in 1910, one author declared that 'crime, especially its more violent forms and among the young, is increasing steadily and is threatening to bankrupt the Nation.' (pp. 22–3)

THE FASCINATION OF CRIME

'Cops and robbers' is one of the most exciting games in childhood. Its equivalents in adult life are detective and spy stories where mystery, intrigue, chase, and confrontation climax in the death or capture of the villain. There is a pressing need for thrill and excitement in the monotonous, uneventful routine of everyday life. For some, alcohol and drugs provide an escape, albeit temporary, into a fantasy world, an artificial paradise. Watching sports events of various kinds is yet another way of alleviating the ennui of a boring existence. The dull, quiet life most people lead creates an insatiable appetite for vivid and expressive action. Hence the enormous appeal crime thrillers and real crime shockers have for a huge segment of the population. As Sykes (1978:22) points out

> The persistent popularity of the detective story, the countless portrayals of crime in the movies and on television, and the time and space devoted to crime in the news media attest to widespread interest in wrongdoing in a world where most men and women must conform.

The millions of crime novels, true crime accounts, detective stories, and magazines sold every year confirm the immense popularity of crime as an entertainment subject. It is also attested by the enormous success of movies that have crime as their central theme. Many of the greatest box-office hits of all time and many of the highly acclaimed pictures in the history of Hollywood are films depicting ghastly and sanguinary crimes: *The Godfather, Bonnie and Clyde, Butch Cassidy and the Sundance Kid, Rambo, Cobra, The Terminator, Silence of the Lambs,* not to mention the ever-popular films of Alfred Hitchcock. It seems obvious that had it not been for the popularity of crime, the history of the film industry and of television would have been very different. To movie-goers, crime is apparently a more appealing and entertaining subject than art or sex.

Crime appears to draw readers, listeners, and viewers from all walks of life. Whether this interest in crime is normal and healthy or morbid and harmful is debatable. One thing seems certain: the fascination with crime cuts across class, age, gender, and race boundaries. For those who own or manage the press or the electronic media, reporting and sensationalizing crime seem to be sure ways of increasing circulation, regaining audiences, improving sagging popularity, and securing a higher ranking on the Nielsen ratings.

Sacco and Kennedy (1994:25) suggest that while some audience members may view crime news as an important source of information about the 'facts' of crime, others may be caught up in the dramatic and sometimes lurid nature of the events reported.

To Katz (1987:72), reading crime news is some kind of a 'ritual moral exercise'. He believes that for many readers such reading 'appears to serve a purpose similar to the morning shower, routine physical exercise and shaving'.

THE SENSATIONALIZATION AND DRAMATIZATION OF CRIME

How Accurate are Public Perceptions of Crime?

The discrepancy between subjective beliefs about crime and an objective analysis of the crime situation casts doubts on the accuracy of public perceptions about crime. A Government of Canada working paper, *The Criminal Law in Canadian Society* (1982), gives some idea about Canadians' perceptions (or misperceptions) about crime. In February 1982, more than 2000 adult Canadians were asked a series of questions about the extent of violent crime and about sentencing and conditional release practices in Canada. The results indicated that, generally, Canadians vastly overestimate the proportion of crime which involves violence, believe murders have increased since Parliament abolished the death penalty (when they have in fact declined), and think people released on parole are far more likely than in fact they are to commit violent crimes soon after release (*ibid.*, p. 16).

Because violent victimization is a relatively rare phenomenon, perceptions of, and opinions about, crime are not usually based on actual personal experience but on secondary sources of information. Since the mass media seem to play a major role in the construction of the crime picture, one might wonder whether the sensationalization of crime by the media is responsible for the distorted perceptions the general public seems to have.

A few decades ago, before the advent of radio and television, the knowledge of any given crime was usually confined to the locality where it had been committed. Nowadays, thanks to the modern techniques of mass communication, news about far distant crimes travels wide and fast. The print and electronic media daily give detailed accounts of gruesome crimes and reserve prominent space and prime time for crime news.

The killings in the 'house of horrors' in Britain, of Jeffrey Dahmer in Milwaukee, of Paul Bernardo in Ontario, and of Clifford Olson in British Columbia are but a few examples of horrible crimes that were prominently displayed on the front pages of most newspapers for weeks. Hardly a day passes without millions of people being exposed, in the privacy of their homes, to scenes of bloody crimes depicted on their television screens.

The media's apparent obsession with crime and its sensationalization and overdramatization of crime news, though understandable, are disturbing. Mundane, average, or typical crimes do not make headlines and are not, by any account, big news. What makes the news are the atypical, the abnormal, and the extraordinary. The more unusual the crime, the more newsworthy it is. The selection, the filtering, and the dramatization mean that the public is presented with an uncharacteristic and unrepresentative image of crime. Wright (1985:20–1) suggests that:

> One need not closely scrutinize media reports to find numerous examples of distortions and exaggerations in crime reporting. Newspaper and magazine articles, as well as the evening news, offer illustration after illustration... overdramatization is the norm rather than the exception in modern crime reporting. The media distorts its presentation of crime patterns by selecting particular incidents to report. Unusual, bizarre, violent, and macabre incidents receive more media attention.

A historical analysis of crime reporting reveals a consistent tendency in the press to ring alarm bells about a rise in crime, particularly youth crime.

Twenty years ago, on 1 September 1976, the biggest headline in *The Province*, one of the two leading newspapers in British Columbia, read 'JUVENILE SYSTEM SPAWNS YOUNG SAVAGES: THEY KILL – THEY

RAPE – THEY BURN.' The same day, the newspaper had several pages full of carefully selected stories of juvenile crime presented in a highly dramatic fashion.

The tone and contents of the articles were not very different from what had been reported half a century before in another Canadian newspaper, the *Regina Daily Post*. On Tuesday 22 April 1924, the paper had a huge headline reading 'Juvenile Crime Assumes Alarming Proportions.' The story was followed the next day (Wednesday 23 April 1924, p. 4) by an editorial under the title 'Youthful Criminals'. Agreeing with the statement of the police that juvenile crime in the city has 'assumed proportions formerly unknown in Regina', the editorialist wondered why it is 'that the young people of the present day are getting out of the hands of their parents and into the hands of the Police.' The editorial offered the 'breakdown of home discipline' as one of the primary causes of the alarming increase in juvenile crime in Regina – in 1924!

The Distortion of Crime News

It seems, therefore, that press coverage of crime news has not changed much over the years. And it is conceivable that members of the public who rely heavily or exclusively on the written press for their information about crime are likely to unquestioningly accept the alarmist views presented by the reporters and the editorialists. And yet, there is a growing body of empirical research findings pointing to a considerable selection and filtering in crime reporting (Fishman, 1978; Mathiesen, 1990; Ericson, Baranek and Chan, 1991; Lotz, 1991; Surette, 1992; Barak, 1994).

In a study of the selection of crime news by the British Press, Roshier reported, as early as 1973, that newspapers do give a distorted impression of crime and criminals through their process of selection. Moreover, the distortions showed remarkable consistency both over time and between newspapers. Ten years later, another study by Ditton and Duffy (1983) of how newspapers covered crime in a Scottish city revealed that stories about violent crime in general, and sexual offences in particular, were over-reported.

An American study by Fishman (1978) showed how the media create crime waves. Fishman reported how a major 1976 'crime wave against the elderly' in New York City, was constructed in the media. Analyzing data from participant observation, interviews, and content analysis of crime news, Fishman was able to show that crime waves are heavily reported themes in crime which journalists perceive as they select news. These crime waves, he concluded, result from processes internal to a news production system involving the overlap of news judgements among media organizations, a 'crime wave dynamic', and journalists' reliance on police for accounts of crime.

According to Fishman, only a restricted class of crime themes – those dealing with street crime – ever become crime waves.

Chermak (1995) identified five factors that greatly influence the news media selection of newsworthy stories: (a) seriousness of the offence; (b) incident participants, that is, characteristics of the victim or defendant; (c) incident producers, these are the individuals who produce crime stories; (d) uniqueness, how out of the ordinary the crime is; and (e) salience of the event determined by its location and the frequency of its presentation. Chermak concluded that:

> The news media's portrait of the crime problem in society is narrow and distorted because of the way news is constructed. The majority of events that occur are excluded from public preview. The media may not find out about particular crimes, they may be exposed to crimes they do not consider newsworthy, or time limitations may preclude or limit their presentation of crime. What ultimately gets presented in the news is determined by a filtering process. The need to satisfy organizational objectives and the interrelationships between news and source organizations determine which crimes are considered for presentation, which survive the newsmaking process, and how much space is given to a story. (p. 170)

Criticism of the way crime news is covered by the media is not limited to those from outside; it is also voiced, though infrequently, by insiders as well. Writing in the *Globe and Mail* (Monday 26 October 1992), reporter Timothy Appleby cites the example of a Toronto newspaper that ran a front-page story about Canada's 'soaring' increase in arson in 1991. The story began with figures showing a 40 per cent increase followed by a long piece about 'recession-battered property owners torching buildings and speculation about higher insurance rates.' The story was inaccurate for reasons pointed out by Appleby: first, arson, in fact, only rose by 20 per cent (wrong figures had been supplied, the paper said the next day); second, even this increase was partly the result of Criminal Code changes broadening the definition of arson, a fact that was overlooked the first time around.

Appleby (1992) gives several reasons why crime gets hyped in the media. One of the reasons he cites is the absence of a restraining mechanism:

> With any other hot topic – a labour dispute, a controversial medical breakthrough, a contentious court judgement – there will be at least two sides scrutinizing what gets written and aired, and reporters walk on eggs in trying to be both accurate and fair. With crime, however, the statistics almost seem to beg, 'Massage me, massage me,' and there is little to prevent it happening. Indeed, all kinds of groups have an interest in perceptions of rising crime....

When reporters go over the top in recording [rising] trends, and we do, there's no one to put on the brakes, no one to say, 'Wait, credit-card fraud has increased, but so has the population, and you didn't mention that.' (*Globe and Mail*, 26 October 1992)

The Impact of Media Coverage on Public Views

Public exposure to the media is quite extensive or to use the words of Skogan and Maxfield (1981:140) 'most residents of American cities are hooked on the media'. And since most people do not have direct personal exposure to crimes that cause the most concern, it is important to know where people get their information about crime and how they form their views on, and attitudes to, crime. Studies by Doris Graber (1980, 1984) shed some light on both issues. Ninety-five per cent of the respondents surveyed cited the mass media as their primary source of information about crime and criminal justice. Despite this massive reliance on the media for information about crime, Graber believes that the media do not have a great impact on people's views. She points out that members of the public have fixed ideas about crime and criminals that are not readily altered or replaced by current media coverage. Graber's view echoes that of Roshier (1973:39) who found little evidence to suggest that 'the biased impression of crime and criminals consistently presented by the press is very influential on public perceptions of, and opinions about, these phenomena.' This conclusion is similar to the one reached by Hubbard, Defleur and Defleur (1975:33) who reported that mass media emphasis does little to shape public opinion about the relative incidence of established social problems.

In a study of mass media and crime (Sacco, 1982:487–8) no evidence was found that could be interpreted as supporting the hypothesis of a direct causal relationship between patterns of media consumption and perceptions of crime. Sacco interpreted his findings as indicating that 'public perceptions of crime are diffuse phenomena that reflect generalized anxieties concerning the social and political environment' (p. 490).

Studies by Richard Ericson (1991:221) led him to conclude that the mass media have diverse and conflicting influences. These influences, he suggests, are a function not only of mass media organization, content, and mode of presentation, but also of the broader social networks of which they, their sources, and their readers are a part. Ericson insists that the mass media are not always the main source of people's knowledge about crime, law, and justice, but a source interpreted along with other sources in terms of practical contexts and purposes. According to Ericson (1991:242)

The mass media do not distort reality, but rather provide a discourse – an institutional mode of classifying and interpreting reality – that helps people to construct their own organizational realities. Mass media stories are therefore not accepted by people directly and uncritically, but rather are part of people's strategies, struggles, and pleasures in the production of meaning in various contexts. Exposure to mass media is therefore not a source of distorted thoughts and bad behaviour, as the 'evil causes evil' fallacy has it, but a means of constituting and articulating attitudes to and versions of crime, law, and justice.

The best that could be said then of the various attempts to gauge the impact of the news media on public perceptions, public views of, and public attitudes to crime is that they are inconclusive. Knowledge of how crime reporting affects the public psyche, people's feelings of safety, their mutual trust, and how it influences their willingness to help strangers, to intervene, remains fuzzy. What is certain is that the printed media are rapidly yielding their position as the primary source of information about crime to the electronic media. The growing influence of television at the expense of the written news is well demonstrated by Postman (1985). He points out that we are in the midst of a crucial change from an emphasis on the written message to an emphasis on the picture, and on the picture as that which defines what is true and what is false. This shift has brought about a significant transformation in the presentation of news by the press, a trend which Mathiesen (1990) calls the 'tabloidization' of the newspapers, with large 'on the scene' pictures, large punchy headlines and brief texts. Mathiesen also suggests that the primary function of newspapers, namely information, is changing into one of entertainment where even the most serious and most violent of reported events are given an 'entertaining slant'.

The study by Lotz on the reporting and portrayal of crime by the American press documents the declining impact of the written media. Lotz (1991:16) cites four reasons for this trend:

1. citizens can now turn to other fare (notably television) that is much more exciting and evocative than news items;
2. nowadays, newspapers rarely break the news. While they generally have one edition, radio and television can bring listeners the latest developments;
3. newspaper readers nowadays tend to be more educated, influential, and well-to-do adults, that is people whose taste does not usually run to crime and violence;
4. usually, crime coverage is assigned to the least able reporters and this results in dull and pedestrian reporting.

As permeant as television might be, its impact remains questionable. Based on their study of newspaper and television coverage of crime news in New Orleans, Sheley and Ashkins (1981) offered some explanations of television's lack of impact on public opinion about crime. They feel that the public is more sophisticated in its analysis of media reports than is often assumed:

> At least with respect to local crime news, television may be viewed by the public as a summarizing and highlighting medium while newspapers are seen as providing broader coverage. The mature viewer may understand that there is more to the crime picture than the few murders and robberies reported on television. If this is so, however, public sophistication seems to stop short of a healthy skepticism of newspapers as distorting crime news (p. 504).

THE GLAMORIZATION OF CRIME

For thousands of years crime has been a source of fascination and inspiration for men and women of letters. Crime is an integral part of the literary heritage of the human race from the tragedies of ancient Greece to Shakespearian plays to present-day novels and dramas. Over the years, real and fictitious criminal deeds have been described, analyzed, and sometimes glamorized and glorified in poems, plays, novels, films, and television dramas. One of Hollywood's most successful movies, *The Sting*, starring Paul Newman and Robert Redford, is a highly glamorized account of the criminal exploits of two Chicago con artists who try to put 'the sting' on a bigwig from New York City after he has one of their pals killed. The film won seven Oscars, including Best Picture, Director, and Screenplay.

The glamorization of crime is more common in the United States than it is in Europe. Until World War II, there was a widely accepted rule in British literature that required authors to end their crime stories in a way that clearly demonstrates the triumph of good over evil, and affirms that crime receives the punishment it deserves. Novels and plays deviating from this unwritten rule drew sharp criticism, particularly from the Church. Angiolillo (1979) reports that *The Beggar's Opera*, by John Gay, enjoyed great popularity in eighteenth-century England when it was first presented. As the play toured the country, it was criticized by some clergymen for glamorizing a criminal and for not showing that he was hanged in the end. It was feared that the play would incite to crime which was rampant at the time. Angiolillo (1979:28) notes that although the play itself probably had no effect on the crime rate of the times, it does 'bear some responsibility for establishing the highwayman as a glamorous figure.'

Fear of such criticism probably induced the German dramatist and poet Schiller to defend his choice of an outlaw-hero by the name of Karl Moor as one of the central characters for his famous play *The Robbers*. In the preface to the first edition, Schiller goes to considerable length to defend his choice of such an unlikely character as hero (see Angiolillo, 1979:33). Schiller's play, however, is more an attack on political tyranny than mere glamorization of outlaws and robbers.

James Hadley Chase's novel *No Orchids for Miss Blandish*, a successful British novel of the 1940s, was seen as an important departure from the unwritten rule against glamorizing crime. George Orwell (1969:52) was obviously disturbed by the book and its popularity as may be seen in the following comment he made on it:

> In a book like *He Won't Need it Now* the distinction between crime and crime-prevention practically disappears. This is a new departure for English sensational fiction, in which till recently there has always been a sharp distinction between right and wrong and a general agreement that virtue must triumph in the last chapter. English books glorifying crime (modern crime, that is – pirates and highwaymen are different) are very rare. Even a book like *Raffles*, as I have pointed out, is governed by powerful taboos, and it is clearly understood that Raffles's crimes must be expiated sooner or later. In America, both in life and fiction, the tendency to tolerate crime, even to admire the criminal so long as he is successful, is very much more marked. It is, indeed, ultimately this attitude that has made it possible for crime to flourish upon so huge a scale. Books have been written about Al Capone that are hardly different in tone from the books written about Henry Ford, Stalin, Lord Northcliffe and all the rest of the 'log cabin to White House' brigade. And switching back eighty years, one finds Mark Twain adopting much the same attitude towards the disgusting bandit Slade, hero of twenty-eight murders, and towards the Western desperados generally. They were successful, they 'made good,' therefore he admired them.

Orwell does not explain why and in what way modern criminals are different from pirates and highwaymen. He offers nothing to support his claim that Americans' tendency to tolerate crime and to admire the criminal is ultimately responsible for the flourishing of crime upon so huge a scale in the United States. Orwell obviously considers Stalin, on whose orders millions were exterminated, to be different from, and superior to, Al Capone. In this respect, he differs from Lombroso, who reminded us a century ago that 'even less different from overt criminals are these latent criminals, high in office, whom society venerates as its chiefs.'[17]

THE POLITICIZATION OF CRIME

For various reasons, crime in Canada is not as hot a political issue as it is in the United States. American crime rates are higher than the Canadian ones, and crime is much more violent south of the forty-ninth parallel.[18] More important still is that access to many political and judicial offices is by appointment in Canada and through elections in the United States. South of the border, governors, attorney-generals, district attorneys, prosecutors, and judges run for office, prepare more or less elaborate electoral campaigns, publicly discuss issues, and make electoral promises. In states, cities, counties, and precincts where concern about crime is high and fear of criminal victimization is widespread, crime is bound to surface as an electoral issue and to be exploited by some or all of the candidates. Candidates lacking in new political ideas and imaginative social policies as well as those trying to appeal to right wing voters are likely to capitalize on public's fear of crime to get elected. According to Conklin (1975:25):

> Crime has been effectively employed by politicians – including a number of ex-policemen – to gain public support. . . . Deep-seated fears and concerns are aroused by crime, and the promise to reestablish law and order and to make the streets safe is an effective way to mobilize support. Crime is an even better target than communism because it affects everyone. It is both a realistic threat and a symbol of the breakdown of the social order.

Since the Criminal Code of Canada is under federal jurisdiction, matters related to changes in criminal law are usually debated during federal rather than provincial or municipal elections. In recent federal campaigns, some candidates either tried to use the death penalty issue to their advantage or were forced to take a public stand in the debate. By and large, however, crime has not yet become a major political issue in Canada whereas it has been part and parcel of American federal, state, and local politics for many years.

Conklin (1975:26) believes that when street crime was limited to the lower class, the disenfranchised, and the ethnic minorities, it was not an important or effective political issue, but when it spread to middle-class communities and claimed middle-class victims, it caused greater fear and concern. Conklin traces the emergence of 'crime in the streets' as a major domestic issue to the 1968 Presidential election when the Republican candidate, Richard Nixon, adopted the law and order stance, forcing the Democratic candidate, Hubert Humphrey, to go on the defensive. According to Conklin, crime in the streets was of somewhat less significance in the elections of 1970 and 1972.

Several political commentators attribute George Bush's victory over Michael Dukakis in the American presidential elections of 1988 to the 'Willie Horton' television advertisements, which were meant to portray Governor Dukakis to the American people as a politician who is 'soft' on crime, who allows convicted killers like Willie Horton to be released on parole.[19]

Crime was again a central issue in the political campaigns in 1994 where candidates nationwide, reports Sasson (1995:165), engaged in schoolyard-like contests over who was tougher and more capable of standing up to criminals. Sasson believes that the salience of the issue in the campaign was responsible for Republican victories in congressional, gubernatorial and other elections. He also predicts that conservative politicians will try hard to keep the issue on the public agenda.

Sasson (1995:6) suggests four reasons to explain why crime, as a political issue, is so beneficial to conservatives:

1. crime provides conservatives with an enemy against whom they can rally middle Americans in a common fight;
2. the presence of crime on the public agenda tends to crowd out issues such as poverty, health care and education, issues which call for income redistribution or governmental initiatives;
3. as white Americans tend to associate criminality with blackness, crime can be used effectively by Republican politicians to drive a wedge through the democratic Party's inter-racial coalition;
4. from a strictly ideological standpoint, conservatives seem to be closer than liberals to the views of most Americans on crime and its remedies.

All this tends to suggest that the issue of crime is the subject of manipulative exploitation by many politicians. Scheingold (1991:1) maintains that the political will to tackle the problem of street crime is more apparent than real. He adds:

> For all of its attention to street crime, the political process tends to divert and to dilute rather than to mobilize purposeful political energy. This is not primarily a matter of manipulation and deception, although they do play a prominent role. More fundamentally, our responses follow a path of least resistance through a complex tangle of criminological uncertainty, social cleavage, cultural truths, and political prudence.

The politicization of crime in the United States is by no means confined to presidential and other electoral campaigns. Many constituencies, including the police, use crime to buttress their demands for more money and manpower. Pepinsky and Jesilow (1984:24) point out that there are few enterprises in which people can hope to be supported more for accomplishing less:

> Police are hired in the hope they will prevent and contain crime, and yet it is by demonstrating their failure to do so – by showing that the crime problem is larger than ever – that they can best argue for expansion.

J. Edgar Hoover, who headed the Federal Bureau of Investigation for several decades, was able to convert increases in crime rates into successful requests for greater Congressional appropriations for the FBI. According to Mitford (1974), Hoover was constantly trying to create an impression of a 'new all-time high' in the rate of crime increase, for the higher the crime rate, the easier it was to get Congress to approve ever-larger appropriations.

Hoover is usually credited with having invented 'the US crime clock', a highly questionable technique designed to highlight the seriousness of the American crime problem. Aggregate daily data on index crimes for the whole country are divided by time units and the frequency of each crime, such as homicide, rape, or robbery, is presented in terms of minutes or seconds. As a result of the enormous variations in the rates of crime between regions, states, and cities and between areas within cities, the message to the American public – for example, that there was a homicide every 23 minutes or a robbery each minute in the United States – is totally devoid of any informational value.[20] Its sole aim is to heighten anxiety and to raise the level of concern about crime to still higher levels.

THE COMMERCIALIZATION OF CRIME

The police are only one of several agencies in society that have an obvious vested interest in painting a gloomy crime picture and in emphasizing and capitalizing on whatever real or apparent increase may take place in crime rates. In addition to the social agencies that stand to gain from a worsening crime situation, there are numerous industries that clearly benefit from a growth in crime and a rising fear of victimization. Among the most visible of these industries are:

1. *The gadget industry:* primarily engaged in the manufacture, marketing, sale, rental, maintenance, and monitoring of mechanical and electronic protective or alerting devices, such as burglar, hold-up, and fire alarm systems, sensors, metal detectors, locks, chains, safes, vaults, bullet-proof vests and glass, helmets, whistles, chemical sprays, automatic light and sound switchers, armoured vehicles, and so on.
2. *The personal safety training industry:* engaged primarily in training potential victims (and other members of the public who for one reason or another may feel threatened by crime) in how to avoid attacks and how to defend themselves in case they are attacked.
3. *The insurance industry:* Another industry that reaps considerable economic benefits from a worsening crime situation is the insurance industry. Home and business insurance against a wide variety of criminal risks constitutes a substantial chunk of the industry's revenue. And the

greater the perceived risk, the wider the coverage and the higher the premiums.

4. *The private security industry:* primarily engaged in providing personnel for detective, investigative, patrolling, night watching, or protection services for businesses and/or individuals.

The private security industry is one of the largest growth industries in both Canada and the United States. In both countries, the number of private security personnel has increased dramatically and at a very rapid pace in the last 25 years.

Shearing and Stenning (1982) estimate the number of private security guards and investigators in Canada to be about the same as the number of public police officers. They also estimate that specialized private security has been growing more rapidly than both the population and the public police. They point out that

> Although there is some evidence to suggest that this growth rate has levelled off over the past few years, figures available for 1971 and 1975 indicate that specialized private security was still growing faster than the public police .... While more recent figures are unavailable, it seems likely that in the years ahead private security will continue to expand at a time when the public police strength seems likely to remain stable and perhaps even decline slightly. It thus seems probable that the 1980s will see private security outstrip the public police in size. (pp. 3, 5)

Crime, then, is big business. It generates profits not only for the criminal but also for a host of private industries and service delivery businesses. These businesses and industries reap benefits from an increase in the threat of crime and in the risks of criminal victimization. Like other goods and services, services related to the threat of crime need to be marketed using a variety of strategies. The following are some of these marketing strategies:

1. creating, fostering, or reinforcing an impression that certain types of crime are rampant or are rapidly increasing;
2. emphasizing or exaggerating the threat and the dangers of victimization by crime. The greater the threat and the higher the risk, the greater is the need for protection, security, prevention, and so on;
3. stressing 'the pressing need' to take specific and effective measures to prepare and to protect oneself, one's home, and one's business against crime;
4. highlighting some of the available techniques and new, modern devices for protection against criminal and 'terrorist' attacks as well as publicizing the available security systems, designs, and procedures aimed at reducing or minimizing the risks of victimization and the losses from crime.

NOTES

1. According to the Canadian Centre for Justice Statistics, in 1993 the American homicide rate was more than four times that of Canada (9.5 per 100 000 compared to 2.19 per 100 000 population) (*Juristat*, 14, No. 15 [1994]: 3).
2. See Fattah, F. (1992).
3. See Pepinsky and Jesilow (1984:1).
4. Associated Press report published in *Vancouver Sun* on September 29 1981.
5. See K.N. Wright (1985).
6. *Bureau of Justice Statistics National Update*, Vol. 1, No. 2, Oct. 1991, p. 1.
7. *Vancouver Sun*, 29 October 1994.
8. *Vancouver Sun*, 3 June 1994, A16.
9. *Vancouver Sun*, 15 October 1994.
10. *Vancouver Sun*, 10 October 1985.
11. *The Howard Journal*, Vol.33, No. 1, February 1994, p. 87.
12. According to *Statistics Canada*, the total number of all offences in Canada in 1970 was 1 576 843 and in 1984 it was 2 713 986; the number of Criminal Code offences in 1970 was 1 112 686, and in 1984 it was 2 147 697; violent offences increased from 92 416 in 1970 to 175 655 in 1984 (Crime and traffic enforcement statistics, Catalogue 85–205 annual, several years). In 1994, the Canadian Centre for Justice Statistics (*Juristat*, 14, No. 14, [1994]) reported that the 1993 crime rate (9516 incidents per 100 000 population) was 13 per cent higher than the rate a decade ago (8440) (p. 3).
13. *Crime and Justice Facts*, 1985 (Washington, DC: Government Printing Office), pp. 2–3.
14. *Juristat*, June 1994, Vol. 14, No. 13.
15. *Juristat*, 1994, Vol. 14, No. 14, p. 1.
16. *Juristat*, 1994, Vol. 14, No. 15.
17. Quoted after Alex Comfort (1970:15).
18. As mentioned in note 1, the American criminal homicide rate, for example, is almost four times the Canadian rate, and the total number of criminal homicide victims in Canada in a given year is slightly less than the number of those criminally killed in one US city: Detroit.
19. See Gordon, D. (1990) *The Justice Juggernaut* and Anderson, David C. (1995) *Crime and the Politics of Hysteria: How the Willie Horton Story Changed American Justice*.
20. These were the figures released by the FBI for 1980 and reported by Associated Press (*Vancouver Sun*, 10 September, 1981, p. A16).

PART I
Unresolved Conceptual and Methodological Issues

1 The Thorny Issue of Defining Crime

...crime is not a single simple phenomenon that can be examined, analyzed and described in one piece. It occurs in every part of the country and in every stratum of society. Its practitioners and its victims are people of all ages, incomes and backgrounds. Its trends are difficult to ascertain. Its causes are legion. Its cures are speculative and controversial.

The President's Commission on Law Enforcement and Administration of Justice (1967:1)

WHAT IS CRIME?

The term 'CRIME' is as central to criminology as the term 'SOCIETY' is to sociology. Criminology may be loosely defined as 'the study of crime' or as 'the science of crime', and a definition of crime is therefore essential for our understanding of what criminology is all about. A definition of crime is also necessary for determining who is a criminal, and for delineating the subject-matter of criminology.

But the problematic nature of the concept of crime seems to deter many criminologists from the thorny task of defining it. Despite the crucial importance of defining and explaining what crime is, most textbooks devote no more than a few lines to the issue, and the majority content themselves with citing the legal definition of crime. Since it will be argued below that criminality is neither an inherent nor an intrinsic quality of any given behaviour but simply a definition given by others to that behaviour, we will pay much more attention to the definitional issues than is usually the case. This is necessary in order to provide background for an attempt to show that there is no such thing as a 'natural' or 'universal' crime, and to prove that no human behaviour, whether killing, kidnapping, rape, or theft, has at all times in all societies been defined as crime (see Chapter 3).

The frequent and indiscriminate everyday use of the term 'crime' might give the false impression that the meaning of the term is obvious or that the term is self-explanatory. The fact that the term is very difficult to define is illustrated by the following two quotations. As early as 1933, Michael and Adler highlighted the unsuccessful attempts to reach a satisfactory definition of crime. They wrote:

Attempts have been made to define crime in moral terms and in social terms. The definition of crime as behavior which is immoral lacks precision and clarity... . The definition of crime as anti-social behavior is hardly more precise or less ambiguous although it does shift the emphasis somewhat from what is thought of as the intrinsic quality of conduct to its social consequences... . The most precise and least ambiguous definition of crime is that which is prohibited by the criminal code. (pp. 1–2)

Four decades later, the same problems were outlined by Henry Hart, Jr. in his essay on the aims of the criminal law. Hart (1971:65), declared that:

[Crime] is not simply anything which a legislature chooses to call a 'crime.' It is not simply antisocial conduct which public officers are given a responsibility to suppress. It is not simply any conduct to which a legislature chooses to attach a 'criminal' penalty. It is conduct which, if duly shown to have taken place, will incur a formal and solemn pronouncement of the moral condemnation of the community.

And a quarter of a century later, Sack (1994), insisted that the simple question 'What is crime?' is still an embarrassing and intricate question for criminology despite its routine and pragmatic handling in the empirical workshops of the discipline. He explains:

The reason and source of this embarrassment became clear when criminologists did not succeed in finding another answer to this question than that which is given by the penal code. All attempts that were made by sociologists and criminologists to arrive at a law-free, independent, scientific, and authentic definition of crime have failed in the past and are doomed to fail in the future. (p. 10)

The elasticity of the term 'crime' has led some to claim that crime does not exist. In a lengthy radio interview on the CBC program *Ideas* (10, 17, 24, March 1993), Nils Christie flatly stated that 'crime doesn't exist.' The point Christie was trying to make is that crime is simply a matter of definition. He said:

So theft is not a theft. A theft is an act; in certain situations it is natural to see it as a criminal activity. But the more you know the parties in detail, and the more they live in a communal setting where everybody knows a lot about them, the less are the chances that at least minor acts, on a scale of severity, will be seen as criminal. (p. 9)

Christie's claim is a reiteration of Louk Hulsman's (1986) assertion that 'there is no ontological reality of crime.' To stress that crime is simply a matter of definition, Nettler (1984:16) claimed that 'crime is a word, not a deed.'

Sacco and Kennedy (1994) view crime as synonymous with lawbreaking. They insist that terms like 'crime', 'offender', and 'victim' are legal concepts. And rather than studying crime as a legal category, they offer an analytical framework they call 'the criminal event.' They argue that while the traditional approach has attempted to understand crime in society largely in terms of the actions of criminal offenders, a criminal event can best be understood as having precursors and aftermaths that influence its occurrence. In other words, the criminal event is an integrated approach to the analysis of crime. Sacco and Kennedy explain their proposed framework as follows:

> What is meant by a conceptualization of crimes as social events? To characterize crimes as *events* is to recognize that as incidents that occur at particular times in particular places. Like any other type of social event – a dinner party, a corporate board meeting, or a car accident – they are more likely to happen under particular circumstances and to involve particular types of people. (pp. 114, 116)

LEGAL DEFINITIONS

There are two popular legal definitions of crime:

1. According to the first definition, 'crime is what the law says it is.' This simple but evasive definition neither enhances our knowledge nor understanding of crime. It is similar to the one some psychologists use to explain intelligence: 'intelligence is what intelligence tests measure.'
2. The second legal definition defines 'crime' as 'an act or omission punishable by law.'

The second definition has the advantage of being objective, clear, and concise. It does not suffer from the ambiguity that characterizes most sociological definitions of crime, but it raises a number of problems:

(a) If crime is simply an act or omission punishable by law, then it would be possible to pass all kinds of laws to fit what we want to call crime. Would the existence of a certain law decreeing punishment for a certain conduct automatically convert such conduct into crime? In other words, is the term 'crime' synonymous with the term 'illegal act'? Is every illegal behaviour a crime? Does the mere prescription of penalties suffice to confer criminal character on acts otherwise not regarded as such? Could a punishable act be considered a crime if it is committed daily by a large majority of the population? For example, many traffic rules (and the rule governing the speed limit is only one example) are daily violated by a substantial number of motorists. According to the legal definition, these violations are crimes and the perpetrators are criminals.

(b)   According to the legal definition, any act punishable by law is a crime. Yet there is a wide variety of behaviours for which the law prescribes some kind of penalty (a conservative estimate puts the number in Canada at 70 000 offences). Could it be said that each and everyone of these prohibited, punishable behaviours is a crime?

In Canada, there is a federal criminal code that applies throughout the country; there are also federal statutes of general applicability regardless of geographic location or boundaries. In addition, there are provincial laws, municipal bylaws, and so forth. Is any violation of any of these statutes, laws, or bylaws a crime? Furthermore, acts punishable by law are not of equal seriousness or gravity. There are major offences, minor offences, and offences in-between. Should all of these offences be defined as crimes because they all carry some penalty? Accepting the legal definition of crime, would, in fact, mean extending the criminal epithet to the whole population since there is hardly anyone who has not violated some or several of these legal prohibitions. If, on the other hand, the definition of crime is limited to offences carrying a heavy penalty, the dilemma would be: where to draw the line between major and minor offences. Any line would inevitably be arbitrary!

(c)   To accept the legal definition of crime, one would have to agree with authors such as Michael and Adler (1933), who argued that the criminal law is the 'formal cause' of crime and that crime could be eradicated simply by abolishing the criminal code since 'without a criminal code there would be no crime.' Although this argument may appear convincing, its sophistry can be easily demonstrated. Hermanus Bianchi (1956) is, in my opinion, right when he argues that the objective semantic function of the term 'crime' is, as much as the phenomenon itself, independent of any legislative operation, that both the term and the phenomenon are evidently *pre-legislative* that they exist independently of, and in spite of any legislative use of the terms (see also Hermann Mannheim, 1965:31).

Several arguments can be advanced in support of the claim that crime is a *pre-legislative* phenomenon that exists independently of any legislative operation:

(i)   Crime is a social, not a legal phenomenon. It does exist in societies that do not have formal criminal laws (written or customary) defining what acts are criminal and decreeing sanctions for such acts.

(ii)   The origin of crime can be traced to the origin of society, not to the origin of the criminal law. Criminal law originated as a way of dealing with crime. Crime is not created by criminal laws; it is simply recognized by them, and it can, therefore, be defined independently of those criminal laws. Rules making certain behaviours punishable succeed rather than precede the existence of these behaviours. The criminal code designates certain acts as criminal because those acts generate a specific social reaction. The criminal law recognizes and formalizes such reaction. It would, therefore, be incorrect to claim that those acts evoke this social reaction because they are made criminal by the law. In Durkheim's words 'We must not say that an action shocks the common conscience because it is criminal, but rather that it is criminal because it shocks the common conscience. We do not reprove it because it is a crime, but it is a crime because we reprove it.'[1]

(d) The legal definition of crime does not explain why certain types of behaviour are singled out, defined as criminal, and made punishable by law while other similar or even identical forms of behaviour are left uncriminalized and consequently unpunishable. It does not explain why the same conduct may be treated as criminal for some purposes but not for others. Violent acts and aggressive behaviours are not invariably 'criminal' or punishable. Why is it that the criminal law punishes certain types of violence but not others? Why is it that certain forms of gambling or certain modes of cheating are made punishable while other forms of gambling or cheating are not? Why is it that the use of certain psychoactive drugs is legal while the use of others is forbidden, illegal, and punishable? The legal definition does not provide answers to any of these questions.

(e) If crime is simply defined as an act punishable by law, what would happen if society abandoned punishment in favour of other forms of justice? If restitution to the victim or community service orders are substituted for punishment for some offences, will these offences still fit the legal definition of crime?

The problems discussed above show that the legal definition of crime is both too broad and too narrow and that it is, therefore, inadequate as a basis for determining who is a criminal or for delineating the subject matter of criminology. It is too broad because it extends the term 'crime' to behaviours that, despite being punishable, neither transgress social norms nor violate social rules, to acts that are neither harmful nor anti-social, to conducts that are neither condemned by the community at large nor regarded as warranting social intervention of any kind. On the other hand, the definition is too narrow because it excludes from the study of criminology behaviours that are not punishable by law even though they are similar or identical to those that are. Would it be possible to understand aggressive behaviour if the study was limited to those forms of violence that are punishable by law? Would it be possible to comprehend compulsive or addictive behaviour if the research was restricted to those types made illegal by the law? Would it be possible to understand, explain, and treat sexual deviance if the investigation was confined to those deviations that have been criminalized?

As Henry and Milovanovic (1994:118) point out, the legal definition of crime merely provides closure where robust debate must begin.

The inadequacy of the legal definition of crime for the purposes of criminology has been underlined by many sociologists and criminologists. Sellin (1938) advised criminologists who are interested in developing a science of criminal behaviour, to get rid of the shackles forged by criminal law. In Sellin's view, the categories set up by the criminal law do not meet the demands of scientists because they are of 'a fortuitous nature' and do not 'arise intrinsically from the nature of the subject matter'. He adds:

> The unqualified acceptance of the legal definitions of the basic units or elements of criminological inquiry violates a fundamental criterion of science.... . Confinement to the study of crime and criminals and the acceptance of the categories of specific forms of 'crime' and 'criminal' as laid down in law renders criminological research theoretically invalid from the point of view of science. The data of the criminal law and the data about crimes and criminals now subservient to legal categories must be 'processed' by the scientist before he can use them. (p. 30)

Sellin suggests that the study of conduct norms would afford a sounder basis for the development of scientific categories than a study of crimes as defined in the criminal law. Such study would involve the isolation and classification of norms into *universal categories*, transcending political and other boundaries, a necessity imposed by the logic of science. (p. 30)

POLITICAL DEFINITIONS

Several political considerations intervene in the process of defining certain acts as criminal. The political dimension in making certain behaviours illegal and punishable has been forcefully stressed in recent years by radical and critical criminologists (Quinney, Chambliss, Taylor, Walton, and Young, among others) who regard the criminal law as an instrument of social control in the hands of powerful interest groups. Radical criminologists argue that defining a particular behaviour as criminal is invariably an act of authority by people or groups who have the power or the means to use the law to protect their own interests and to impose their own values, ideas or beliefs on society as a whole. In their view, there exist in every society powerful pressure groups, groups of 'elites,' or 'moral entrepreneurs', as Howard

Becker (1963) prefers to call them, who use their own value systems, their own social and economic interests, to define what should and what should not be punishable.

An example of the political definitions of crime is given by Quinney (1970): 'Crime is a definition of human conduct that is created by authorized agents in a politically organized society.'

One advantage of this definition is its affirmation that 'criminality' is not an intrinsic quality or an inherent character of the behaviour; it is a 'label' that is attached to that behaviour. It also emphasizes the roles of authority and coercion in defining certain acts as criminal. This definition, however, does not explain when and why an act becomes a crime. How do the authorized agents in society define a certain conduct as crime? By means of criminal legislation? By prescribing a certain punishment for the behaviour? Why do the authorized agents in society define certain acts as criminal and leave other identical acts uncriminalized? The definition makes no mention of the sociological criteria necessary for qualifying an act as crime: the transgression of a social norm, the violation of a social rule, social harm, societal reaction, and so forth. Like the legal definition, which stipulates that 'crime is what the law says it is,' this definition, in fact, stipulates that 'crime is what the politically authorized agents say it is.'

SOCIOLOGICAL DEFINITIONS

Durkheim's definition of crime according to which 'An act is criminal when it offends the vigorous and well defined states of the collective conscience' is popular among sociologists. This definition may be useful in defining crime in small, harmonious, and homogeneous societies, but is less suitable when the task is to define crime in large, pluralistic, multicultural, and heterogeneous societies. In small, non-state societies it may be possible to discern a state of 'collective conscience' and to detect a fair degree of 'consensus' regarding social norms and values. This is impossible, however, in complex industrial societies, characterized as they usually are by heterogeneity and cultural diversity. In such societies, very few acts would shock the collectivity or the whole community. An act may be offensive to a certain social group but quite acceptable to another; it may be shocking to a certain class but tolerated by another. This lack of consensus, this absence of agreement regarding basic values and norms, can easily be seen in controversies surrounding acts that put an end to human life (euthanasia, assisted suicide, abortion, capital punishment) or acts involving sex (incest, homosexuality, prostitution) or morality (gambling, drug addiction, pornography).

Many other sociologists have attempted to formulate a definition of crime. In his book entitled *Criminology* (1918:31), Maurice Parmelee suggests that

A crime is usually an anti-social act of such a nature that its repression is necessary or is supposed to be necessary to the preservation of the existing system of society.

Although this statement contains elements not found in other definitions, it still raises some questions. What is an anti-social act? According to what criteria may an act be considered anti-social? Why is it that the criminal law punishes many acts that cannot be regarded as anti-social? Sociological definitions that define crime as a 'socially harmful act' or as a 'socially injurious act' share many of the problems of Parmelee's definition. What are the characteristics of a socially harmful or a socially injurious act? Why is it that certain acts that are not socially harmful are punishable (for example abortion in an overpopulated society) while others that are harmful are left unpunishable.

The notion of harm is essentially relative. An act may be *harmful* to one social group but useful to another. Theft is harmful to those who have, but it *does not harm the have-nots*. Some economists consider certain property offences where the goods are not destroyed but simply change hands as economically useful since they lead to a more equitable distribution of goods and/or an increase in the economic value of certain wares (for example a television set is stolen from a family that possesses three sets and ends up in the home of a family that has none).

Conflict theorists maintain that the various segments of society do not share common interests and that the interests of different groups are quite often in conflict. They claim, therefore, that the criminal law is likely to protect the interests of the powerful groups and to define as crimes those acts that are harmful to the interests of those groups. The social history of the criminalization of vagrancy and mendicity shows that laws against vagabonds and beggars were passed in 16th-century Europe to protect the interests of capital suffering from labour shortages caused by the Black Death.[2] According to Reed (1978), the suppression of birth control information in the United States in the late 19th and early 20th centuries through federal and state legislation was the result of the fear of American men that middle-class women would become dissatisfied with their traditional role as well as their concern about the high fertility of the foreign born in comparison with those from genteel backgrounds.

PSYCHIATRIC AND PSYCHOLOGICAL DEFINITIONS

Whereas legal and moral definitions concentrate on the normative aspects of crime, psychiatric and psychological definitions stress the behavioural aspects of criminal conduct and/or the characteristics of the perpetrator. The late Swedish psychiatrist/criminologist, Olof Kinberg (1960:140) defined crime as:

> a form of social maladjustment which can be designated as a more or less pronounced difficulty that the individual has in reacting to the stimuli of his environment in such a way as to remain in harmony with that environment. (Author's translation.)

Unlike legal definitions of crime, which emphasize the legal proscription and the punishment the law provides for the act, and unlike sociological definitions, which stress the social harm or injury resulting from the behaviour, Kinberg defines crime by referring to the characteristics of the perpetrator. He does not refer to the act itself but to the actor. But Kinberg does not explain the difference between crime and other forms of social maladaptation or maladjustment. Is every form of social maladjustment a crime? Is everyone who has difficulty in reacting adequately to the stimuli of the environment and who is unable to remain in harmony with that environment a criminal? Kinberg's definition seems to fit mental disease more than it does crime. Are the two identical? If not, what is the difference? Finally, the definition makes no mention of society's reaction to the behaviour or the form such reaction takes.

As may be seen from the above, definitions of crime are varied. There is no universal or agreed upon definition. Different definitions reflect the multidisciplinary background of students of crime and suggest that the term 'crime' does not have a single, consistent meaning. It means different things to different people. Each scholar has his/her own conception of what crime is. For this reason, working out a generally satisfactory definition of crime is not as simple as it might appear. One wonders whether it will ever be possible to formulate a definition that integrates the various views and does not place the emphasis on any one aspect of crime to the exclusion or to the neglect of others, or whether Fritz Sack (1994) is right when he predicts that all attempts are doomed to fail.

WHAT CONDUCT OUGHT TO BE CRIMINALIZED?

The Boundaries of Criminalization

> It became the civilized custom to attempt to legislate morality and to coerce virtue by law. The law took over not only the great destructive sins – murder and mayhem and rape – it took over the Ten Commandments, then it took over the lesser sins and vices. They were all made into crimes and were constantly augmented. They were prosecuted by clumsy machinery which has become more and more unusable; it commits more

crime than it punishes. Most of the crimes involve acts that do not injure anyone but the offender through self-destructiveness.

Karl Menninger, (1973:78)
Whatever Became of Sin?

The question 'what conduct ought to be criminalized?' is a very important policy question. It is also a question that is not easy to answer. The liberal answer is usually based on the principle enunciated by John Stuart Mill in his famous essay on liberty (see below). Braithwaite and Pettit (1994:65) cite two major attacks on this liberal position: one comes from legal moralism and the other from legal paternalism:

> Legal moralism would allow that an activity may be criminalized just because it is immoral or is at least regarded as immoral in the community at large. Legal paternalism would allow that an activity may be criminalized because it is likely to cause harm to the agent herself. The legal moralist questions the harm restriction in the harm-to-others constraint; the legal paternalist questions the restriction to others.

In the past, crime was more closely linked to morality than it is now. The criminal law was often used to impose specific standards of morality. Needless to say, those standards were the moral standards of the upper and middle classes. The present trend in many Western countries is to separate morals from the criminal law and to decriminalize acts that do not cause tangible social harm (Aspelin, 1975) and do not generate any forceful reaction from the majority of people even though they are considered immoral according to prevailing standards.

There are many reasons for the separation of morals from the criminal law:

1. In modern, ethnically heterogeneous societies, characterized by cultural and religious diversity, there exist different moral standards. In line with the basic principles of democracy and freedom, no social group, no social class, no matter how powerful or influential it may be, has the right to impose its religious beliefs or moral standards on other groups by means of force, the criminal law, or the threat of penal sanctions. Free adults living in a democratic society are entitled to their own moral beliefs, standards and rules.

2. It is becoming increasingly recognized that in a free, democratic society, the state has no right to interfere with the private lives of adult members of society and their behaviour as long as such behaviour does not cause harm to, and does not violate the rights of, others. To quote the words of the former Prime Minister of Canada, Pierre Eliott Trudeau, 'The state has no business in the bedrooms of the nation.'

3. It is becoming increasingly recognized that not all moral values need to be, or can be, protected by the criminal law. Criminal concepts, though

greatly influenced by moral concepts, should be distinct. The criteria for criminalizing specific types of behaviour should, therefore, be other than the mere immorality of those behaviours. As Ernst Freund said, 'Not every standard of conduct that is fit to be observed is also fit to be enforced' (see Morris, 1973). The extension of the arms of the criminal law to all kinds of immoral behaviour has led to excessive repression of behaviours that were neither harmful nor dangerous to society. Historically, human sexuality has been a prime domain for suppression through the criminal law. Until very recently, in many countries, including Canada, the criminal law regulated and punished every form of sexual behaviour other than masturbation and conventional sexual intercourse between legally married couples. The situation is best described by Norval Morris (1973) in his paper 'The Law is a Busybody':

> It is improper, impolitic and socially harmful for the Criminal law to act the moral busybody, to intervene in or attempt to govern the private conduct of the citizen.... Indeed, it is as if the sex-offense laws were designed to provide an enormous legislative chastity belt encompassing the whole population and proscribing everything but solitary and joyless masturbation and normal coitus inside wedlock.

4. The regulation of morality through the criminal law inevitably leads to many inconsistencies (not to mention the injustices resulting from selective and haphazardous application of the laws). For example, according to current laws in Canada, two consenting adults can engage in private in almost any type of sexual activity or practice. Is it not inconsistent for the law to set standards for what they can purchase to read or watch in the privacy of their homes?

5. Morality is undergoing a rapid social evolution. What may have been considered immoral and made punishable in previous years may be decriminalized this year or next year, and what is condemned as vice today may not be considered as such tomorrow. Attitudes to moral issues, such as mercy killing, assisted suicide, artificial insemination, homosexuality, pornography, prostitution, gambling, lottery, abortion, premarital sex, and birth control, have changed considerably in recent years. This means that people are being punished for acts that are likely to be decriminalized in the near future. Before changes were made to the Canadian Criminal Code in 1969, most forms of public lottery were illegal. At present, not only are they legal, but also the federal and provincial governments are in conflict over which level should reap the lion's share of the profits. James Reed's (1978) study of the history of the birth control movement in the United States clearly shows that what is

considered a vice today may be a virtue tomorrow. The title he chose for his book is particularly revealing: *From Private Vice to Public Virtue: The Birth Control Movement and American Society Since 1830.* In his book, Reed shows how social reformers were arrested, tried, and punished for acts that receive high praise nowadays.

In recent years, criminologists have offered three general principles that should govern the domain of criminalization and be used as criteria in deciding what type of behaviour ought to be criminalized in a democratic, secular society:

Immorality as such is not enough to make an act criminal. This principle is hardly new and was forcefully stated by A.C. Hall (1902:19) in his book *Crime in Its Relations to Social Progress*: 'No depth of moral heinousness is sufficient in itself to make an action criminal.' More recently, Norval Morris (1973:2) expressed the view that the criminal law should not be used 'to lead men away from vice and sin, including those vices and sins that injure only the sinner.' It should not be employed to prevent 'going to hell in one's own fashion.' It is argued that a behaviour should not be made criminal simply because some people or, for that matter, the majority of people find it disgusting, improper, or repulsive. In a free democratic society the law is not supposed to criminalize behaviour simply because the behaviour, in the view of some, is wrong, blameworthy, abnormal, or aberrant, unless it has been unequivocally proven that the behaviour is socially harmful or infringes upon the rights of others.

The criminal law should not be used to punish immoral or sinful behaviour unless the behaviour in question is clearly anti-social or socially injurious. Three decades ago, Mannheim (1965:67) explained this principle as follows:

> No form of human behavior which is not anti-social should ever be treated as crime... the reverse, however, is far from true. There are many types of anti-social behaviors which are not, and many others which should not be crimes... . The lawgiver [should] not penalize acts whose anti-social character could not be clearly seen. Crime should not be produced unnecessarily and artificially by a body of criminal law which interferes with acts not clearly anti-social.

In Canada, *The Canadian Committee on Corrections* (1969:12), advocated this principle in its report:

> No conduct should be defined as criminal unless it represents a serious threat to society, and unless the act cannot be dealt with through other social or legal means.

The Committee also recommended that 'No act should be criminally pro-scribed unless its incidence, actual or potential, is substantially damaging to society.'

The act must be actually or potentially harmful to others, or, at least, it must violate the basic rights of others.   As mentioned above, neither the immor-ality of a given behaviour nor its repulsive or aberrant character is sufficient grounds for invoking criminal sanctions or for mobilizing the criminal justice apparatus. Unless an act is apt to cause actual (or potential) harm to others, the state's intervention to regulate the incidence of such behaviour by means of the criminal law seems unwarranted.

Most criminologists question the appropriateness of the state's most ser-ious form of intervention – punishment   and the wisdom of using a costly and already overburdened criminal justice system to regulate or suppress acts that cause no harm to anybody except, perhaps, to the participants them-selves. They point to a wide variety of behaviours (for which the terms 'crimes without victims' or 'victimless crimes' have been coined (Schur, 1965)) that are currently, or were until recently, prohibited by the criminal law under threat of criminal sanctions. Examples of such behaviours are: loitering, gambling, disorderly conduct, vagrancy, public drunkenness, homosexuality, drug addiction, and so forth.

One argument in favour of the decriminalization of these so-called victim-less crimes is based on Mill's principles stated in his book *On Liberty* (1859) in which he affirmed that

> The only purpose for which power can be rightfully exercised over any member of a civilized community against his will is to prevent harm to others. His own good, either physical or moral, is not a sufficient warrant.

A government document entitled *The Criminal Law in Canadian Society* (1982:52–3) refers to the doctrine of restraint, according to which the crim-inal law should be an instrument of last resort or ultimate recourse. The document proposes that the criminal law

> should be employed to deal only with that conduct for which other means of social control are inadequate or inappropriate, and in a manner which interferes with individual rights and freedoms only to the extent necessary for the attainment of its purpose.

The document adds that

> the purpose of the criminal law is to contribute to the maintenance of a just, peaceful and safe society through the establishment of a system of prohibitions, sanctions and procedures to deal fairly and appropriately

with culpable conduct that causes or threatens serious harm to individuals or society. (p. 52)

The former Law Reform Commission of Canada advocated the same approach in its report *Our Criminal Law* (1976). The Commission urged that 'the real criminal law should be confined to wrongful acts seriously threatening and infringing fundamental social values.' The principle of restraint was to be applied at every stage, including that of defining criminal offences in the first place. The Commission suggested a set of 'tests' for determining what are, and are not, crimes:

1. Does the act seriously harm other people?
2. Does it in some other way so seriously contravene our fundamental values as to be harmful to society?
3. Are we confident that the enforcement measures necessary for using criminal law against the act will not themselves seriously contravene our fundamental values?
4. Given that we can answer 'yes' to the previous three questions, are we satisfied that criminal law can make a significant contribution in dealing with the problem?

These 'tests of criminality' clearly indicate that the primary criterion for criminalization is *harm*, actual or threatened. The Law Reform Commission refers to serious harm to other people; the government of Canada document talks about 'culpable conduct that causes or threatens serious harm to individuals or society.'

While calling for a clear-cut distinction between crime, vice, and sin and while advocating the secularization of the criminal law and its separation from religion and morality, criminologists are aware that criminal concepts will always be influenced, and in some cases will be determined, by moral and religious concepts. For example, in the Roman imperial period, perfidy and breach of trust were regarded as highly immoral; in fact, they were received with a greater degree of moral condemnation than violence. In response, some of the early criminal codes treated theft (in which the victim's property is perfidiously stolen) more severely than robbery (in which the perpetrator is face to face with the victim thus giving the latter a chance to defend their property). The evolution in our thinking and moral concepts has led us to view violence much more seriously than perfidy. Consequently, our present Criminal Code, like that of most Western nations, punishes violent crimes more severely than perfidious crimes and punishes robbery more harshly than theft, embezzlement, or trust violation.

While violent crimes are presently regarded as the most serious of all crimes, it is not unthinkable that this attitude will change in the future as a result of further evolution in our moral and social thinking. It is quite possible that in the not-too-distant future certain 'non-violent' behaviours, such as the pollution of the environment, will be treated by the criminal code more severely than the violent offences of robbery, rape, or assault. In fact, certain white collar crimes may be regarded as extremely harmful and may be punished with penalties harsher than those prescribed for less harmful, but more physically aggressive, offences. Such a trend prevails in several socialist countries where some economic crimes are ranked by the criminal code as more serious than most violent crimes. In certain cases, these economic crimes are punishable by death.[3]

Present moral attitudes dictate that intentional crimes are more serious and should, therefore, be punished more severely than unintentional crimes. In the future, we may realize that certain unintentional crimes or certain negligent offences (for example, drink driving) cause more loss of lives, injuries, financial losses, and so forth than the intentional crimes of murder, assault, or theft. At such a point of evolution in our penal thinking, we may decide that these negligent offences are more serious and more dangerous and should be dealt with accordingly.

NOTES

1. Durkheim, E. (1965 reprint) *The Division of Labor in Society*. NY: The Free Press (p. 81). In another book, *The Rules of Sociological Method* (1938), Durkheim also writes: 'Non certes, ce n'est pas la peine qui fait le crime, mais c'est par elle qu'il se révèle extérieurement à nous et c'est d'elle, par consequent, qu'il faut partir si nous voulons arriver à le comprendre' (p. 42).
2. See Chambliss, W. (1964) A sociological analysis of the law of vagrancy. *Social Problems, 12*, 335–52.
3. Rod Mickleburgh (1996:A10) reports on a recent wave of executions in China where people guilty of offences ranging from stealing communication cables and wire, rustling oxen, stealing large quantities of rice, passing counterfeit money, forging value-added-tax receipts, running a brothel and so forth, are put to death.

2 The Relativity of Crime in Time and Space

In view of the diversity of moral systems in the world, it is difficult to understand why the presumption of universality could endure so long without being seriously questioned. The answer lies in the psychological predisposition of human beings to generalize from their own perspective. Western philosophers in particular seem to be prone to projecting their moral categories on others. As a consequence, the presumption of universality is deeply ingrained in Western moral philosophy.

> Alison D. Renteln (1990:49)
> *International Human Rights:*
> *Universalism Versus Relativism*

Mainstream criminologists are generally criticized for accepting the criminal law and the legal definitions of crime as givens and for paying little attention to the historical origins of the criminal law or to the social processes by which the criminal law is made and changed. In contrast, critical criminology questions the raison d'être of the criminal law and challenges the need for a criminal code (separate from the civil code) that uses punitive sanctions such as imprisonment and, in some countries, the death penalty (see Chapter 7). The need for a specific criminal (or penal) code is predicated upon the premise that CRIME is a unique or exceptional category of behaviour that is more serious and more harmful than other behaviour. The primary purpose of this chapter is to test the validity of these assumptions.

THE CRIMINAL LAW: A RETROSPECTIVE LOOK

Introductory texts on criminal law usually trace how the criminal law emerged as a separate branch of public law. There is no need to repeat or summarize this history. What follows is a cursory glance at how the criminal law evolved. The origins of criminal law can be easily traced to the attempts by the kings and feudal lords to consolidate their authority, to enhance their powers, and to generate revenue for themselves and their estates by imposing fines and by seizing the lands and property of convicted persons. The process is related by the Law Reform Commission of Canada (1974:8–9) in its working papers 5 and 6 as follows:

In Anglo-Saxon England there was no criminal law as we know it. Disputes were dealt with by a process greatly resembling our civil law. When an individual felt that he had suffered damage because of another's wrongful conduct he was permitted either to settle the matter by agreement or to proceed before a tribunal. Restitution was the order of the day and other sanctions, including imprisonment, were rarely used.

As the common law developed, criminal law became a distinct branch of law. Numerous antisocial acts were seen to be 'offences against the state' or 'crimes' rather than personal wrongs or torts. This tendency to characterize some wrongs as 'crimes' was encouraged by the practice under which the lands and property of convicted persons were forfeited to the king or feudal lord; fines, as well, became payable to feudal lords and not to the victim. The natural practice of compensating the victim or his relatives was discouraged by making it an offence to conceal the commission of a felony or convert the crime into a source of profit. In time, fines and property that would have gone in satisfaction of the victim's claims were diverted to the state. Compounding an offence (that is, accepting an economic benefit in satisfaction of the wrong done without the consent of the court or in a manner that is contrary to the public interest) still remains a crime under the Canadian Criminal Code and discourages private settlement or restitution.

It would now seem that historical developments, however well intentioned, effectively removed the victim from sentencing policy and obscured the view that crime was social conflict. (pp. 8–9)

IS CRIME QUALITATIVELY DIFFERENT FROM TORT?

Parker's (1977:28) account of the historical development that led to the emergence of the criminal law shows that the differentiation between crimes and torts is of relatively recent origin. Parker states:

At this stage of legal development there was no differentiation between what we know as crime or criminal law and tort or civil liability for damage inflicted. All injuries to persons or property were considered as 'wrongs.' The seriousness of the wrong depended upon the disruption caused to the community or the actual or perceived affront to the injured parties. Slowly, a distinction emerged between wrongs which were private disputes and required payment to the injured party or his kin and wrongs which had a public quality and required compensation to the whole group.

This historical fact is often ignored by those who claim that crime is a unique, exceptional, or distinct category of harmful behaviour. In the not-too-distant past, all harmful injurious behaviours were civil torts treated in more or less the same manner. The emergence of the criminal law saw the creation of a new category of behaviour believed to be deserving of punishment. The selection of behaviours to be brought under the realm of the criminal law was guided by political, historical, and religious considerations and not by the unique qualities of the behaviours that came to be defined as crimes. As a result, the distinction between crime and tort, between the criminal and the civil code, is both artificial and arbitrary and the demarcation line separating the two is blurred. As Morris and Hawkins (1969:46) point out, very frequently the same act is both a crime and a tort. They add that a large part of criminal behaviour is perfectly 'normal', both in the statistical sense and in the sense that it occurs naturally. They write:

> ...the truth is that almost all adults have at some time in their lives committed criminal acts and it is those who have not who are abnormal. Almost all the acts which are defined as criminal in our society have at some time in some society been tolerated and even socially approved. The line between legitimate and illegitimate means of acquiring property is both arbitrary and difficult to define precisely. There are wide differences between states in regard to what sexual behaviour is criminal, and considerable variation in the same state at different historical periods. There is no evidence that the bulk of criminal behaviour is the result of some pathological mental or somatic condition which distinguishes criminals in general from noncriminals. (p. 48)

IS CRIME UNIQUE?

Is Criminal Behaviour Qualitatively Distinct?

Dependent primarily on social assessments of appropriate time, place, and participants, behaviorally identical phenomena (e.g. killing a person) can be considered on a continuum from justifiable and necessary to reprehensible and wanton. The failure to recognize such social processes at the assumptive level forces *a priori* consideration of 'criminal acts' and their perpetrators as qualitatively distinct phenomena from that considered conventional. Such a distinction necessarily restricts subsequent formulations by granting ontological status to pretheoretical categories.

Steiner, J.M., Hadden, S.C. and Herkorner, L. (1976:173)
'Price Tag Switching', in *Criminology Between the Rule of Law and the Outlaws*

Society disapproves of a wide variety of human behaviours, and spares no effort in displaying its disapproval. Obviously, society cannot formally control or regulate every form of unacceptable or undesirable behaviour, and most of these behaviours are, therefore, left to informal means of social control. Certain unacceptable behaviours are singled out, criminalized, and subjected to the control of formal agencies, the most important of which is the criminal justice system.

Society's disapproval of behaviours that do not conform to social, moral, or religious norms is amply illustrated in the rich vocabulary used to designate or to condemn such behaviour. I was able to compile a list of more than a hundred adjectives used in English to describe various types of censurable behaviour. A somewhat arbitrary classification of these adjectives appears in Table 2.1.

One can easily see from the list that some of the adjectives imply value judgements of the behaviour and carry with them a pejorative connotation. Examples of these value-laden adjectives are repulsive, wicked, bad, odious, atrocious, and so forth. Some adjectives are objective, neutral, or value-free. They merely indicate that the behaviour in question deviates from a certain norm or diverges from acceptable standards. They may refer to the fact that the behaviour violates legal prescriptions or proscriptions or to its aggressive or violent nature. Examples of these are illegal, unlawful, deviant, aberrant, violent, and aggressive.

In view of this wide variety of reproved behaviours, it is necessary to search for specific characteristics that distinguish or differentiate criminal behaviour from other reprehensible behaviours. Why are certain acts singled out and made punishable by the criminal law? Is the difference in the nature or in certain qualities of the behaviour? Is it a difference in degree, or is it just a difference in definition?

Positivist theories are based on the assumption that crime is a distinct category of human behaviour. Wilson and Herrnstein (1985:22), for example, contend that predatory crime, on which they chose to focus, 'is condemned in all societies, and in all historical periods, by ancient tradition, moral sentiments, and formal law.' They further claim that certain acts, such as murder, theft, robbery, and incest, are regarded as wrong by every society, nonliterate as well as literate. This contention, made in 1985, is not too different from the one made a century earlier by R. Garofalo (1885), who claimed that there are 'natural crimes' that offend the fundamental altruistic sentiments of pity and probity in the average measure possessed by a given social group. Rather than using Garofalo's term natural crimes, Wilson and Herrnstein (1985) prefer to call them universal crimes. Both claims fly in the face of incontrovertible historical, anthropological, and sociological evidence that shows that all the examples used by Garofalo or Wilson and Herrnstein were at one time or another not norm violations but cultural imperatives. In his book, *Comparative Criminality*, Gabriel Tarde (1886) demonstrates over and over again the fact that crime is relative both in time and space. More

Table 2.1 Adjectives used to designate behaviour disapproved of by society

Deviant character of the behaviour	Immoral character of the behaviour	Harmful character of the behaviour	Illegal or violent nature of the behaviour	Others' reactions to the behaviour	
Aberrant	Abominable	Abrasive	Aggressive	Annoying	Intolerable
Abnormal	Atrocious	Abusive	Assaultive	Blameworthy	Irritating
Anti-social	Bad	Destructive	Belligerent	Brazen	Naughty
Bizarre	Corrupt	Disorderly	Brutal	Censurable	Objectionable
Criminal	Debauched	Disruptive	Cruel	Contemptible	Obnoxious
Criminaloid	Deceitful	Dysfunctional	Culpable	Detestable	Provoking
Delinquent	Despicable	Harmful	Guilty	Disgusting	Reprehensible
Deviant	Dishonest	Hurtful	Hostile	Disrespectful	Repulsive
Eccentric	Dirty	Injurious	Illegal	Distasteful	Rude
Erratic	Evil	Insensitive	Illicit	Embarrassing	
Impudent	Heinous	Mischievous	Offensive	Grotesque	Unacceptable
Irrational	Immoral	Negligent	Riotous	Immodest	Unbecoming
Irregular	Improper	Noxious	Unlawful	Impolite	Undesirable
Kinky	Indecent	Pernicious	Violent	Inconsiderate	Unpleasant
Neurotic	Irreligious	Reckless		Indecorous	Unreasonable
Non-conforming	Lascivious			Inopportune	Unseemly
Peculiar	Lewd			Insolent	Unsound
Perverse	Lustful			Insulting	Untoward
Psychopathic	Malicious				Vexatious
Senseless	Mean				
Sociopathic	Misbehaviour				
Unruly	Odious				
	Promiscuous				
	Sinful				
	Vicious				
	Wanton				
	Wicked				
	Wrongful				

recently, Wilkins (1964:46) noted that 'at some time or another, some form of society or another has defined almost all forms of behaviour that we now call criminal as desirable for the functioning of that form of society.'

Many contemporary criminologists argue that 'criminality' is neither an intrinsic quality of the behaviour nor an innate character of the act. According to this view, no act is inherently criminal, but certain acts are defined as criminal by a given culture. Crime, therefore, is seen as culturally defined and culturally variable. One of the strong advocates of this view is Howard Becker (1963:9), who affirms that:

> Deviance is *not* a quality of an act the person commits, but rather a consequence of the application by others of rules and sanctions to an offender. The deviant is one to whom the label has successfully been applied; deviant behaviour is behaviour that people so label.

A comparison of acts made illegal by the Criminal Code or by statutes with similar behaviours that are unregulated by the criminal law suggests that there is no qualitative difference between criminal and non-criminal behaviour.

For every behaviour defined as criminal and sanctioned by law, there are identical or similar types of behaviour that are neither illegal nor punishable. Even acts that may, at first glance, appear to be morally heinous, socially harmful, and, therefore, condemnable are generally condoned in certain circumstances and are required or encouraged in specific conditions. The act of killing is not invariably criminal. Killing the enemy in war is not a crime (in fact, refusal to do so may be a criminal offence); it is an act of courage and heroism. The killers are not punished; they receive medals, decorations, awards, and citations. Executing a convicted murderer is considered by many as an act of 'justice' or a 'proper' measure of social protection. It enjoys the support of a majority of the population and was once so popular that public executions drew huge crowds to the places where hanging or beheading took place. Killing a prison inmate trying to gain freedom or a hold-up man attempting to escape is considered a justifiable or excusable homicide in many jurisdictions. But killing in most other circumstances is regarded as a very serious, perhaps the most serious, crime. The difference does not lie in the nature of the act itself. Killing is killing. But killing is only defined as a crime if it is committed under certain conditions or against certain victims. This point is well made by Pfohl (1985:284) who writes:

> Homicide is a way of categorizing the act of killing, such that taking another's life is viewed as totally reprehensible and devoid of any redeeming social justification. Some types of killing are categorized as homicide. Others are not. What differs is not the behavior but the manner in which reactions to that behavior are socially organized. The behavior is

essentially the same: killing a police officer or killing by a police officer; stabbing an old lady in the back or stabbing the unsuspecting wartime enemy; a black slave shooting a white master or a white master lynching a black slave; being run over by a drunken driver or slowly dying a painful cancer death caused by a polluting factory. Each is a type of killing. Some are labeled homicide. Others are excused, justified, or viewed, as in the case of dangerous industrial pollution, as environmental risks, necessary for the health of our economy, if not our bodies. The form and content of what is seen as homicide thus varies with social context and circumstance. This is hardly the characteristic of something which can be considered naturally or universally deviant.

Shooting and killing East Germans trying to flee to the West by crossing the Berlin wall was a legal act under the laws of the former German Democratic Republic. After the reunification in 1989 and the replacement of the East German Code by the Criminal Code of the Federal Republic of Germany, these killings are being prosecuted as murders, and the shooters are now charged with the deliberate taking of a human life.

Until a few years ago, the Canadian Criminal Code and many others did not define forcible sexual intercourse with one's own wife as a crime. But the same act perpetrated on a woman who is not the man's wife did qualify as a serious crime punishable by imprisonment for life.[1]

Although the behaviour in the two cases is identical, in one case it is criminal; in the other, it is not, depending on whether the two parties are bound by marriage or not. The same can be said of statutory rape where an arbitrarily determined age is the deciding factor whether the behaviour is criminal or not, is punishable or not.

Not all types of violent, aggressive, or assaultive behaviour are made criminal by the law. Many forms of violence are condoned and tolerated to the extent that they become culturally legitimate. Until recently use of the strap in school for misconduct, using violence to discipline or control the behaviour of inmates in penal institutions, and flogging offenders guilty of certain crimes were all seen as legitimate forms of violence, and those on whom such punishments were inflicted were seen as deserving targets. Milder forms of violence within the family are not criminal in most jurisdictions. Children are considered legitimate targets for the use of physical force in the process of training and control,[2] and for a long time, husband–wife violence was regarded as legitimate by both the police and courts.

The absence of a qualitative difference between behaviour defined as criminal and behaviour that is not can also be observed in the areas of property and traffic offences where the line between what is legal and what is illegal is often quite arbitrarily drawn. Offences like speeding and impaired driving are determined by speed limits and blood-alcohol levels set up in an arbitrary fashion. And the line separating the criminal offences of theft and fraud from what are normally referred to as 'sharp business practices' is exceptionally thin. Many would argue that profiteering or the realization of excessive gains by companies and corporations is not qualitatively different from consumers' attempts to exaggerate their losses when claiming from insurance companies. Yet, the former is often regarded as 'good business', while the latter is defined as fraud.

Recapitulation

A comparison between acts defined by the law as criminal and those that are not, reveals some interesting facts. Criminal behaviour is not qualitatively different from non-criminal behaviour. For every behaviour defined as criminal and made punishable by law, there are identical or similar behaviours that are not. The absence of a qualitative difference between criminal and non-criminal behaviour raises serious doubts about the validity and utility of the traditional classification of crimes into acts that are *mala in se* and *mala prohibita*.

This classification, popular for a long time, divides punishable acts into two categories:

1. Acts that are *mala in se*: those are offences that are also moral wrongs, behaviours deemed bad in themselves, irrespective of the prohibition of the criminal law;
2. Acts that are *mala prohibita*: those are offences that are not contrary to the basic moral values. They are bad simply because they are forbidden by law, such as traffic or regulatory offences,

The former Canadian Law Reform Commission's working paper No. 2, *The Meaning of Guilt* (1974), discusses a similar distinction between (1) 'crimes' or 'real crimes' and (2) 'offences' or 'mere offences' or 'regulatory offences'.

1. According to the working paper, 'real crimes are acts that are both forbidden by law and revolting to the moral sentiments of society. They contravene fundamental rules, constitute wrongs of greater generality, and involve harm of a far more obvious kind than do acts of the second category.' The obvious example of a real crime is murder.
2. Mere offences, on the other hand, are acts forbidden by law. They are not revolting to the moral sentiments of society, nor do they contravene fundamental rules. These are regulatory offences, such as illegal parking, fishing out of season, the unlawful sale of liquor, and so forth.

As will be argued when discussing the *relativity of crime*, the notions of 'good' or 'bad', 'right' or 'wrong', 'moral' or 'immoral', 'useful' or 'harmful' are all relative, both in time and space. It cannot be said, therefore, that certain acts are intrinsically wrong or bad in themselves, which is basically what the distinction between *mala in se* and *mala prohibita* implies.

Leslie Wilkins (1964:46–7) is undoubtedly right in his assertion that human actions, even as interpreted within a society at a fixed time, do not divide into black and white, good and bad, functional and dysfunctional:

> The divisions into crime and no crime, into what are regarded as health and ill health, are cutting-points on a continuum. It is, then, possible to picture these concepts as forming a continuous distribution. For example, a continuum of human acts ranging from very saintly to the most sinful may be imagined. In our society there are very few acts which are regarded as extremely saintly or extremely helpful to the society, and there are very few acts which are regarded as extremely sinful or seriously criminal. The majority of actions of ordinary people in our present culture are regarded as 'normal'.

IS VICTIMIZATION BY CRIME MORE HARMFUL THAN OTHER VICTIMIZATIONS?

There is no doubt that deaths, injuries, and losses from victimization by crime are relatively minor in comparison to those caused by other forms of victimization. Unfortunately, there are no accurate statistics for several victimization types. Lady Wootton (1963) insists that the category of strict liability offences illustrates vividly the fact that in the modern world in one way or another as much and more damage is done by negligence, or by indifference to the welfare or safety of others, as by deliberate wickedness. Snider (1993:1) reports that every year in the United States 30 000 people are killed and an estimated 20 million receive serious injuries from buying unsafe consumer products. Industrial accidents, she asserts, claim another 14 000 lives per year while an additional 100 000 deaths are estimated to result from occupationally induced diseases. The numbers, compared with those of criminal homicide (20 000 a year) are staggering. Reiman (1984:51) reaches a similar conclusion regarding property crime:

> The general public loses more money *by far*...from price-fixing and monopolistic practices and from consumer deception and embezzlement, than from all the property crimes in the FBI's index combined. Yet these far more costly acts are either not criminal, or if technically criminal, not prosecuted, or if prosecuted, not punished, or if punished, only mildly.

A major study of medical malpractice in the US released in 1990 (*Vancouver Sun*, 1 March 1990) and reported by Reuters, provides some startling figures on one minor type of victimization, namely victimization resulting from medical malpractice. The study, conducted by researchers at the Harvard Medical School, reports that in 1984 there were about 7000 hospital deaths and 27 000 injuries caused by the negligence of doctors or hospital staff at 51 hospitals in the state of New York alone. The study further found that 99 000 patients out of 2.7 million in New York hospitals in 1984 suffered injuries during their hospital stay, and 28 per cent of those suffered injuries caused by negligence. The study shows that only 2 per cent of the patients who suffered malpractice injuries that year sued a doctor or a hospital.

With the exception of a few rare types (such as murder, rape, or serious injury), most victimizations, even the ones usually termed serious, are actually trivial in nature, as well as consequence. That is why they are easily forgotten. One of the major problems of victimization surveys, which by their very nature rely on the memory of the respondents, is that people forget. Even when the recall period is shortened to six months, the interviewers have to work hard to get the respondents to remember what criminal victimization they have suffered (Chapter 4). It is also the trivial nature of most criminal victimizations that accounts for the extremely low reporting rates characteristic of most offences. Fewer than half of personal crimes – such as household burglary and personal robbery – are said in most surveys to be reported to the police (Sparks, 1981). The most common reason given in surveys for not notifying the police is that the victimization was too trivial. As Hulsman (1986:28) points out:

> If we compare criminal events with other events, there is – on the level of those directly involved – nothing intrinsic which distinguished those 'criminal events' from other difficult or unpleasant situations. Nor, as a rule, are they singled out by those directly involved to be dealt with in any way which differs radically from the way other events are dealt with. It is therefore not surprising that a considerable proportion of the events which would be defined as 'serious crime' within the context of the criminal justice system remain completely outside the system. They are settled within the social context in which they take place (the family, the trade union, the associations, the neighborhood) in a similar way as other 'non-criminal' conflicts. All this means that there is no *ontological reality of crime*.

THE RELATIVITY OF CRIME

One age has pronounced martyrs and worshipped as saints the criminals that another age has put to death . . . . It is quite as possible that another generation will look with the same horror on the subjects of our laws as we look upon those of the years that are gone.

Clarence Darrow (1902:53)
Resist not Evil

Crime is culturally defined. An act cannot be regarded as criminal or non-criminal in the abstract but only with reference to a specific culture. Since crime is culturally defined, it changes with cultural evolution and varies significantly in time and space. It follows that what is defined as criminal in one society may not be so defined in another society. And with the continuous process of criminalization and decriminalization, new types of behaviour come to be defined as crimes (for example, pollution), while others are taken out from the criminal code (like vagrancy, homosexual practices between consenting adults in private). In a country such as the United States, where every state has its own criminal code, the concept of the relativity of crime is quite obvious. Adultery is punishable in some states but not in others. Gambling and prostitution are legal in some states but outlawed in others. Possession of small quantities of marijuana for personal use has been decriminalized in some states but still carries heavy penalties in others. These few examples clearly show that there are no absolute standards by which a certain behaviour can be judged to be anti-social, immoral, or criminal. As Jeffery (1956) has pointed out, all standards of conduct are 'relative and impermanent.'

The relativity of crime can be clearly shown through a historical survey of acts that were considered crimes by ancient and more recent cultures. A good illustration is given by Gabriel Tarde (1886) in his book on comparative criminality, *La Criminalité Comparée*. He notes that ten crimes were punished by lapidation according to Hebraic laws, namely: idolatry, incitation to idolatry, consecration to Moloch (a Canaanite god), sorcery, evocation of spirits, obstinate disobedience to parents, profanation of the Sabbath, blasphemy, rape of another man's fiancée, unchastity of an unmarried girl attested by the absence of virginity on her wedding day. Of these, nine have ceased to be criminal in most modern societies, while the tenth, that is, the rape of another man's fiancée, remains a crime but in a different context and for a different reason. It is no longer the violation of the man's property right on his fiancée that is being punished but the violence against the female victim and the serious violation of her right to choose her male sexual partner.

The cultural variability and temporal relativity of crime clearly indicate that social definitions of crime and deviance are not static, but dynamic. They are subject to constant transformation. To illustrate the dynamism of 'crime' definitons, Barnes and Teeters (1959) note that in 1931, 76 per cent of all the inmates of federal and state prisons in the United States were incarcerated for committing acts that had not been crimes 15 years earlier. They point out that 500 000 new state laws were enacted in the first half of the 20th century. The dynamic process of criminalization and decriminalization has important implications for criminology:

1. The relativity of crime contradicts notions such as 'natural law' or 'natural crime' because it shows the absence of universal, transcendental, absolute, permanent, and immutable standards of morality necessary for the existence of a natural law. It proves that there are no universal moral standards and no universal code of morals. Morality is relative. This view is shared by many criminologists including Maxwell (1914) and Mannheim. Mannheim (1965:47) points out that:

> There is no single and unchanging concept of natural law. While its underlying idea is the longing of mankind for an absolute yardstick to measure the goodness or badness of human actions and the law of the State and to define their relations and morality, the final lesson is that no such yardstick can be found.

2. The relativity of crime and morals and the constantly changing concepts of crime and morality, or vice and virtue, indicate that human beings are not born with an 'innate moral sense' or an 'inborn sentiment' of what is good and what is bad. Notions of good and bad, of right and wrong, are essentially relative and depend on the geographic, economic, social, cultural, and political conditions in which the person's group has developed.

It is easy to give several examples that testify to the lack of an *innate* moral sense in human beings:

1. The abhorrence and repulsion we feel at the thought of eating human flesh are neither innate nor inborn. They are culturally built and culturally developed. In some societies, human flesh is a delicacy and is eaten with great enjoyment on occasions such as cultural and religious feasts. The following story, related by Sumner (1906:331), illustrates well this point:

> Spix and Martius asked a chief of the Miranhas why his people practiced cannibalism. The chief showed that it was entirely a new fact to him that some people thought it an abominable custom. 'You whites,' said he, 'will not eat crocodiles or apes, although they taste well. If you did not have so many pigs and crabs you would eat crocodiles and apes, for hunger hurts. It is all a matter of habit. When I have killed an enemy, it is better to eat him than to let him go to waste. Big game is rare because it does not lay eggs like turtles. The bad thing is not being eaten, but death, if I am slain, whether our

tribal enemy eats me or not. I know of no game which tastes better than men. You whites are really too dainty.'

2. Parental affection for children, which is regarded by many as quasi-instinctive, is not universal; nor does it have everywhere the same intensity. In some societies, babies are regularly killed and even eaten by their progenitors (see Maxwell, 1914). Even the desire to have children, which for a long time was thought to be common to all human beings, does not seem to be as universal as originally thought. In his historical survey of the birth control movement in the United States, Reed (1978:ix) makes reference to the findings of many anthropologists corroborating this:

    > Anthropologists studying human reproduction in premodern cultures have found that the desire for children is not an innate human drive but an acquired motive which must be reinforced by social rewards and punishments sufficient to overcome the wish to avoid the pain of childbirth and the burdens of parenthood.

3. In the sphere of human sexuality, an area that in most societies is closely associated with morality, we can find great differences between cultures, indicating once more the absence of absolute moral standards and a universal moral code. In some societies, pre-marital sex is encouraged; in other societies, it is strongly condemned. In some societies, extra-marital relations for the male, female, or both is the established norm; in other societies, it is a serious crime. For 90 per cent of the world's cultures, polygamy is the norm; for the remainder of the world's cultures, it is a taboo (Harris, 1975:312). Sociologists and anthropologists have revised their belief about the 'incest taboo.' In his comprehensive cross-cultural study of incest, Sumner (1906) concluded that 'the instances show that the notion of incest is by no means universal or uniform, or attended by the same intensity of repugnance. It is not by any means traceable to a constant cause.' Forward and Buck (1983) give several examples of societies where various forms of incest (father–daughter; mother–son; brother–sister, etc.) are widely practised.

    Not only do sexual norms vary greatly from one culture to the other, but they are also reported by social and cultural anthropologists to be absent in some societies, particularly those that escaped the European influence mediated by the missionaries or the colonial administration. Anthropologist Aster Akalu (1985), for example, affirms that the Ethiopian Nuer, whom she studied, do not have a sexual morality and make no ethical assessment of human conduct, sexual or otherwise. Akalu reports that the Nipnip have no word meaning 'incest'. And while sexual encounters do occur between brother and sister or between parent and descendant, the Nipnip speak about such affairs without condemnation (p. 76). She adds that sexual intercourse between kindred people is commonplace, particularly in the dry season camp and is not taken seriously (p. 69).

Akalu further reports that 'youth have sexual freedom and that married women often have love affairs with other men and do not try much to hide them from their husbands' (p. 77). 'Wives who have given birth to two children are officially free and are expected to have love affairs' (*ibid.*). Akalu also reports that the Nipnip have no word for 'being naked', that they have no feeling about running around naked, and, in fact, always do so (p. 74).

4. The relativity of crime is incompatible with the notion of born criminals or the existence of a criminogenic gene. It contradicts the belief that criminal traits or criminal propensities are inherited. Physical traits are no doubt inherited, but the same cannot be said of morals. Moral degeneration can only be the product of the cultural environment. If there is no natural moral law and if moral standards are neither absolute nor universal, how could it be said that some individuals are born good and that others are born bad? If we admit that crime is relative, if criminality is not an intrinsic quality of the behaviour, there can be no born criminals, but only society-made and culturally defined criminals. A criminal in a given society may be a hero in another society. He might have been a hero in the same society if he were born at a different period of history. Che Guevara was 'wanted' as a criminal in some South American countries but glorified as a hero in others. History shows that many so-called criminals and terrorists later became political leaders. Fidel Castro, Nelson Mandela, Yasser Arafat and Menahem Begin are a few recent examples.

THE ELASTICITY OF TERRORISM

St Augustine tells the story of a pirate captured by Alexander the Great. 'How dare you molest the sea?' asked Alexander. 'How dare you molest the whole world?' the pirate replied. 'Because I do it with a little ship only, I am called a thief; you, doing it with a great navy, are called an emperor.'
Noam Chomsky (1987:9)
Pirates and Emperors

Terrorism, like crime, is a relative, pejorative, value-laden, emotionally loaded and ideologically tainted term. With crime, there is at least the criminal code, which singles out certain behaviours and defines them as criminal. There is no equivalent to the criminal code in the area of terrorism, and people have to rely on their own conceptions and perceptions to designate certain activities as terrorist. In other words, terrorism is in the eye of the beholder. Labelling a certain act as 'terrorist' is a value judgement, a subjective construction of social reality.

The selective use of the word terrorism in the media, in the literature, and in public statements and private conversations provides a clear illustration of how definitions of the same activity may vary according to one's political views and ideological leanings. Wardlaw (1982) points out that the 'slippery nature of the concept of terrorism is illustrated well by its selective use, particularly its selective, pejorative use.' He believes that a major stumbling block to the serious study of terrorism is that, at best, terrorism is a moral problem. Wardlaw insists that definitions of terrorism are frequently based on the assumption that some classes of political violence are justifiable whereas others are not. He adds:

> These confusions, together with the use of the word 'terrorism' almost entirely as a pejorative term to refer to the actions of some opposing organization makes problems of definition almost insoluble...the problem is further complicated by the unwillingness of many to acknowledge that terrorism, whatever the definition may be, is as much a tool of states and governments as of revolutionaries and political extremists. (p. 9)

Terrorism comes from terror, which in turn comes from the Latin word 'terrere', meaning to frighten. Originally, the word 'terror' was used to designate a mode of governing, and the word 'terrorism' was employed to describe the systematic use of terror, especially by governments, as a means of coercion to force the governed into submission. According to *Webster's New 20th Century Dictionary*, terror is a period characterized by political executions, as during revolution, especially such a period (also called the Reign of Terror) during the French Revolution, from May 1793 to July 1794. And according to the *Oxford Dictionary*, 'terrorism' is to fill with terror, to rule or to maintain power by terrorism. It seems clear, therefore, that there has been a change in the usage of the term since it was first employed at the end of the eighteenth-century. At the time, it was applied almost exclusively to acts and policies of government intent upon spreading fear and anxiety among the population for the purpose of ensuring submission, compliance, subjugation, and conformity with the will of those who governed. Nowadays, the term is mainly applied to actions by individuals or groups against governments. A century ago the talk was of incumbent terrorism; at present it is being increasingly confined to insurgent terrorism.

The subjective, relative, and ideological nature of terrorism is, in my view, responsible for the absence of a satisfactory definition. After a decade of endless debates, the United Nations General Assembly offered in December 1985 a loose definition referring to acts of international terrorism in all its forms which endanger or take innocent lives, jeopardize fundamental freedoms and seriously impair the dignity of human beings.

The vagueness and limitations of this definition are obvious. The restriction of the definition to acts of international terrorism and the omission of any direct reference to acts committed by states and governments against their own subjects is, to say the least, perplexing.

One definition that recognizes the subjective and elastic determination of terrorism is formulated by H.H.A. Cooper (1977) according to which:

> Terrorism is ... an easily recognized activity of a bad character, subjectively determined and shaped by social and political considerations.... . This highly elastic category will suffice to contain all the activities which the political dictates of the moment deem appropriate or expedient. Terrorism ... is anything we choose it to be, neither more nor less.

The political dictates of the moment, referred to by Cooper (1977), explain why identical acts may be defined differently depending on who perpetrates them. Thus, the same acts of political violence that are designated as acts of 'intelligence', 'counterintelligence', or 'national security' when carried out by Western liberal democracies (such as the sinking of the Greenpeace ship off the coast of New Zealand by French government agents or the American CIA operations in Central and South America), are labelled 'terrorism' when committed by revolutionary or nationalistic groups against the West or by totalitarian and fascist regimes of the left. Seizure and diversion of aircraft by Palestinians or other Arab nationals were invariably called *hijacking* in the Western media as well as in official statements, in public and private utterances. But when the Egyptian airplane carrying the suspected hijackers of the cruise ship Achille Lauro was forced by American aircraft to change its route and land in Italy, the incident was reported as a case of *interception*. The same term was used a few months later when a Libyan civil aircraft was forced by Israeli jets to deviate from its course and land in Israel. In neither incident was the term hijacking used. This clearly illustrates the different social meanings assigned to words such as hijacking, air piracy, terrorism, and so forth.

THE CULTURAL RELATIVITY OF VICTIMIZATION

> To regard one class of persons as victims and another not as victims is thus an appeal to one's own morality.
>
> Richard Quinney (1972:322)
> *Who is the Victim?*

Like crime and criminals, victims and victimization are social and cultural constructs. As mentioned in Chapter 1, crime cannot be defined in abstract terms but only with reference to a given society or a specific culture. The same is true of victimization. Nevertheless, mainstream victimology continues to presuppose 'that some persons or groups are objectively victims without explicitly considering the interpretive definitional processes implicated in assignment of victim status' (Holstein and Miller, 1990:104).

Even violence, which is usually the basis for claiming that some categories of victimization are universal, has a strong cultural content. Hence the marked differences in the meaning of violence and the great difficulty of developing an objective, universal definition of what violence is.

What is often overlooked is that people may be subjected to serious acts of violence resulting in terrible pain and suffering, sometimes even permanent injury or infirmity, without experiencing them as victimization. We may call those who are injured in battle 'victims of war', while they, seeing themselves as heroes may be offended or feel insulted by the label. Although the rites of passage that mark the transition from childhood to adulthood are quite violent and painful in many societies, they are not experienced as victimization (Herdt, 1982; Heald, 1986). In most cases, they are eagerly awaited and despite the pain and the violence are joyfully endured. The same is true of the initiation rites for freshmen in college or the hazing [subjecting to ridicule] of new recruits in the army or the navy. Although these initiation rituals involve, most of the time, acts of violence, humiliation, and degradation, those who are subjected to them do not feel victimized; they do not define themselves as victims.

Applying the definitions of victimization across cultures is even more problematic because the norms and standards used by the observer to interpret and judge the behaviour are often different from those of the people being observed. Anthropologists studying societies that are very different from ours are becoming more and more sensitive to this dilemma. Paul Heelas (1989), for example, points out that attention to context has the great virtue of dispelling 'myths' generated by essentialism. In support of his contention, Heelas quotes Chagnon's study of the Yanomamo Indians of the Venezuela jungle (1983). The study clearly shows that what may be defined or viewed by the researcher as aggression might not be experienced as such by the 'victims'.

In our society, abortion is viewed by many as 'victimization', as an act that deprives the fetus of the chance to be born and to live. In other societies, where people die from hunger, the same practice is regarded as an act of pity and charity, that saves the unborn from a life of misery, poverty, suffering, and starvation. The same is true of euthanasia. For those who oppose it, it is the ultimate victimization, a premeditated murder. For those who favour it, it is an act of mercy, a humanitarian gesture that puts an end to the unbearable pain and suffering of a terminally ill person. For them, the real victimization is to let the sick individual suffer, to deny him/her the choice and the means to put an end to the suffering, to seek permanent relief from acute or chronic pain.

The relativity of the definition and the subjectivity of the victimization experience mean that the subjects' perceptions, their assessment, and their definition of what happened, their self-labelling, do not always coincide, and may even be at odds, with those of the external observer or the law. As Bilsky and Wetzels (1994) point out, victimization defined according to the normative standards or ideological values of the researcher (or according to the law) may not be defined as such by those involved. Inversely, people may define and perceive themselves as victims although what they suffer does not fit the legal definition of victimization. The discrepancy is well described by Bilsky and Wetzels (1994.5–6).

> Obviously, individual thresholds come into play that reflect the ability and readiness to tolerate distressing or harmful events without feeling victimized. The harmfulness of an event, the probability of its occurrence, and the personal vulnerability as perceived by the afflicted person may differ significantly from a bystander's point of view. Consequently, categorization of an incidence may fall apart and people may consider themselves victims of crime although this judgement neither fits the perception of others nor bear legal examination.

Bilsky and Wetzels further write:

> there are cases in which people have definitely been victimized according to normative (legal) standards although they do not understand their situation this way. The discrepancy in judgement can be attributed to different reasons, depending on the respective situation. (p. 6)

These few examples of the cultural relativity of victimization – and one can give many others – are meant to emphasize the extreme variability in the definitions within one society or from one society to another. They are also intended to show how difficult it is to measure victimization across cultures and to do meaningful cross-cultural quantitative comparisons of the incidence and rates of victimization.

THE RELATIVE NATURE OF ABUSE AND NEGLECT

The term 'abuse', as in 'child abuse', 'wife-abuse', or 'elder-abuse' is frequently encountered in the criminological, victimological, psychological, and gerontological literature, and it seems to be gaining greater popularity with the passing of each day. There are even scholarly journals with the word in

their title, such as *Child Abuse and Neglect*. It seems that this vague, ambiguous, highly subjective, and elastic concept has become, since it was first
used in the 1960s in the context of mistreatment of children, one of the
staples of criminological and victimological terminology (see Fattah, 1994b).

Surprisingly, the terms 'child abuse', 'wife abuse', and 'elder abuse' do not
denote a legal category or a homogeneous class of behaviour. For example,
despite the widespread use of the term 'elder abuse', it is not possible to find
in the voluminous research literature one objective definition that lends itself
to adequate operationalization. The lack of a standardized definition, in
turn, has rendered both fruitless and frustrating any attempt to compare
the findings of the studies whether at a national or an international level.
Thus, while many studies have been conducted to assess the frequency of
child abuse or elder abuse, there is still no reliable estimate of their incidence
or prevalence in any country. The elasticity of the term 'abuse' is such that it
makes it possible for any researcher to downplay or blow up the incidence of
abuse simply by adopting a narrow or a broad definition of the concept. One
has to wonder whether the term 'abuse' has any research or practical utility,
whether it should continue to be used, or whether it should be erased from
the language of criminology! When every effort is made in criminology to
break down broad categories of behaviour into smaller, homogeneous units
that allow meaningful analysis, generalization, and theory construction, one
has to question the need for, and the utility of, a generic or umbrella term
such as 'abuse' (see Fattah, 1994b:115).

Where abuse can be objectively established and measured, such as in cases
of 'physical', 'sexual', or 'financial' abuse, one finds that the types of victimization involved already constitute offences under the provisions of 'assault',
'assault and battery', 'aggravated assault', 'sexual assault', 'indecent assault',
'theft', 'fraud', 'forgery', and 'breach of trust', among others. So what is
gained by grouping such concrete but varied offences under a catch-all
category called 'abuse'?

When the types of behaviour included under the general term 'abuse' are
not criminal but are simply forms of conduct that people disapprove of, or
disagree with, such as addressing elderly people in a rude, impolite, or
insulting manner, shouting at, teasing, or interrupting them, the question is
then whether these inappropriate behaviours should be lumped together with
the more serious offences in one general category.

The same applies to the concept of 'neglect' and to behaviours that are
labelled 'abuse' simply because they do not meet, or fall short of, the
standards of good care that should apply to the elderly. Surely, everything
should be done to ensure that old people live in decent, healthy, comfortable,
and tidy conditions. However, failure to provide such conditions by reason
of poverty, stinginess, or greed is not the same as intentional physical or
sexual assault or as deliberate acts of fraud or misappropriation. Inadequate,

improper, insufficient, or substandard care is a matter for social services, but it has little, if anything, to do with criminology (Fattah, 1994b:116).

THE CONCEPT OF EVOLUTIVE CRIMES

The history of religion and science amply indicates that acts deemed criminal at a given time in a given community often turn out to be of the greatest value for human life.

Morris Raphael Cohen (1971:42)
Moral Aspects of Criminal Law

The relativity of crime indicates that crime is not always regressive, retrograde, or atavistic in nature. Some criminals are progressive and their crimes could lead to positive change, social evolution, reform, and social justice.

The idea that crime has evolutive, innovative, and adaptive social functions was advanced by Durkheim, who argued that crime prepares social change and enables society to adapt to such change. Yesterday's criminals may, therefore, be today's moral precursors, and today's criminals may be tomorrow's moral pioneers.

In *The Rules of Sociological Method*, Durkheim writes (1938:71–2):

Crime implies not only that the way remains open to necessary changes but that in certain cases it directly prepares these changes. Where crime exists, collective sentiments are sufficiently flexible to take on a new form, and crime sometimes helps to determine the form they will take. How many times, indeed, it is only an anticipation of future morality – a step toward what will be! According to Athenian Law, Socrates was a criminal, and his condemnation was no more than just. However, his crime, namely, the independence of his thought, rendered a service not only to humanity but to his country. It served to prepare a new morality and faith which the Athenians needed, since the traditions by which they had lived until then were no longer in harmony with the current conditions of life. Nor is the case of Socrates unique; it is reproduced periodically in history. It would never have been possible to establish the freedom of thought we now enjoy if the regulations prohibiting it had not been violated before being solemnly abrogated. At that time however, the violation was a crime, since it was an offence against sentiments still very keen in the average conscience. And yet this crime was useful as a prelude to reforms which daily become more necessary. Liberal philosophy had as its precursors the heretics of all kinds who were justly punished by secular authorities during the entire course of the Middle Ages and until the eve of modern times.

As Durkheim said, the case of Socrates is by no means unique. Humanity and science are clearly indebted to Galileo (1564–1642), the Italian astronomer and physicist whose observations and ideas were ahead of his time and who was intellectually in opposition to the theologians of the period. His correct observations and his courage in iterating them brought him into conflict with the Inquisition, who compelled him to repudiate the Copernican theory. It took the first non-Italian pope in 455 years to offer an apology to the man he referred to as 'the founder of modern physics.' Pope John II told scientists of the *Pontifical Science Academy* in the Vatican that 'the greatness of Galileo, like that of Einstein, is known to all. But the former had to suffer greatly, we cannot hide it, from church institutions and men.'

Another Italian philosopher, Lucilio Vanini (1585–1619), a precursor of modern materialism was burnt alive in Toulouse, France, in 1619 after being accused and convicted of atheism and magic. The famous 'Monkey Trial' in the United States and the 'Morgentaler Case' in Canada are examples of crimes paving the way for much needed social reforms. More than anything else, the latter case showed dramatically and emphatically the urgent need to reform abortion laws in Canada. In December 1955, Rosa Parks, a black working woman from Montgomery, Alabama, who later became a symbol, refused to surrender her seat on a bus to a white man. Her arrest spurred black civil disobedience that helped wipe out segregation laws. Reed (1978) shows how Margaret Sanger's and others' persistent violations of federal and state laws (outlawing the mailing of birth control information and the practice of family limitation) were influential in changing social attitudes towards birth control and in preparing the much needed law reform.

Maurice Parmelee (1918:455) coined the term 'evolutive crimes' which he defines as 'illegal acts committed in accordance with, and in defence of, fundamental human rights, and in the course of various movements for bringing about more or less extensive social and economic changes in society.' Parmelee gives several examples to illustrate the concept of *evolutive crimes*, among which he includes offences in defence of the right to freedom of thought and belief, in defence of the right to express one's self in words in free speech, in defence of the right to dispose of one's life as in suicide, illegal acts committed by conscientious objectors to military service, offences of labourers in strikes and other labour disturbances, and violations of law committed by those who are trying to achieve the equality of sexes or to eliminate other forms of discrimination.

Evolutive crimes, according to Parmelee, have particular significance in relation to social evolution as they underline the presence of serious problems of readjustment in any social system:

Custom, public opinion, religious beliefs, moral ideas, and laws at any given time and place prescribe certain forms of conduct, and a more or less fixed mode of living. These forces maintain the prevailing regime, and invariably present much opposition to change. Consequently, in order to bring about change it frequently becomes necessary for some individuals to defy these forces for permanence, and in some cases this defiance involves violation of the law, so that evolutive crime is an inevitable concomitant of social change and progress. (1918:469)

It is easy to see the affinity between Parmelee's thinking and that of Durkheim. But although Parmelee was familiar with Durkheim's writings on crime, he makes no reference to him when discussing evolutive crime.

That certain criminal laws are specifically intended to deter change is a fact that has been recognized for many years. Wines (1895:23) pointed out that 'The conservative instincts of people, which are allied to authority in church and state in the form of established governmental institutions, oppose the radical and revolutionary tendencies of the political and social innovators whose respect for the past is limited by the intensity of their aspirations for the future.'

Haskell and Yablonsky (1974:28) give examples of laws enacted to deter social change together with examples of statutes used for the same purpose. Consequently, systematic violations of these laws and statutes are organized by individuals or groups who want to bring about social changes they deem necessary. They explain the process as follows:

In order to deter social change, statutes forbidding trespass have been employed to outlaw protest marches, demonstrations, and certain types of picketing. These forms of protest are considered essential to civil rights groups, student groups, anti-war protesters, other dissenting groups, and labour unions in their efforts to bring about social change. When the political authority employs the criminal law or law enforcement personnel to prevent marches and demonstrations, the objective is to reinforce the power structure by reducing and minimizing all forms of resistance and maintaining the status quo. Although formal sanctions may be applied to those who violate these statutes by agents of the society, violators are likely to be considered heroes by their respective groups.

NOTES

1. Before the Canadian Criminal Code was changed in the 1980s, Paragraph 143 stipulated that 'A male person commits rape when he has sexual intercourse with a female person who is not his wife, a) without her consent, or b) with her consent if the consent (i) is extorted by threats or fear of bodily harm, (ii) is obtained by

personating her husband, or (iii) is obtained by false and fraudulent representations as to the nature and quality of the act.'

2. Paragraph 43 of the Canadian Criminal Code stipulates that 'Every school teacher, parent or person standing in the place of a parent is justified in using force by way of correction toward a pupil or child, as the case may be, who is under his care, if the force does not exceed what is reasonable under the circumstances.' And in England caning was abolished by a margin of just one vote in July 1986. *Agence France Presse* reported that the vote to outlaw corporal punishment in British schools came after three and half hours of debate in which Education Minister Chris Patten called for retention of caning – 'the vigorous application of a cane to the posteriors of recalcitrant students' – saying the abolition would weaken the position of headmasters. Some Conservative MPs were reportedly angered by the vote and one of them described the result as a tragedy (*Vancouver Sun*, 23 July 1986).

3 Criminology's Traditional and Persistent Bias

In spite, therefore, of the extent and seriousness of delinquency as a social problem, its most serious aspect for humanity to-day is the prevalence of delinquent action by persons immune from censure, and by established governments.

The government of a modern industrial state, backed by the police, the army, the media of communication, wields powers undreamed of one hundred years ago. The abuse of these powers by political opportunists, gangsters, psychopaths and authoritarian cliques pose a far more serious threat to society than the ordinary criminal.

Alex Comfort (1970:11–12; back cover)
Delinquency and Authority
A Study in the Psychology of Power

THE BIAS DEFINED

Since it emerged as a scientific discipline in the 19th century, criminology has exhibited and continues to exhibit a clear bias. Research and theory have focused on crimes by the powerless, not the powerful; crime in the streets, not crime in the suites; conventional crime, not white collar crime; crime by individuals, not crime by governments and corporations; disorganized crime, not organized crime. Mainstream criminological theories are the product of this slanted attitude. They are based on behaviours that are not necessarily the most injurious, most harmful, or most deleterious; and on offenders who are not necessarily the most vicious, most serious or most dangerous.

Criminology's traditional bias, namely to regard corporate and business crime as less serious than conventional street crime, is exemplified in James Q. Wilson's (1975:xix) statement in the introduction to his book *Thinking About Crime* where he states that he is convinced, a conviction he believes is shared by most citizens, that 'predatory street crime is a far more serious matter than consumer fraud, antitrust violations,... because predatory crime... makes difficult or impossible the maintenance of meaningful human communities.'

It is fair to claim that Wilson's view reflects that of mainstream criminology. Box (1983:17) is critical of this position and maintains that Wilson and similar-minded authors fail to substantiate their position. In responding to Wilson's argument, Box (1983:17) insists that

> ...the absence of public apprehension over corporate crime does not justify it being ignored by criminologists; rather, it should justify creating a publicity campaign to create an awareness of corporate crime. If the bulk of the community are being criminally victimized in ways they do not understand or realize, surely that too is sufficient reason for prioritizing the study of corporate crime.

Studying, researching, powerful criminals, gilded criminals, white collar criminals, is bound to shatter the popular view that serious criminals are 'pathological'. This popular explanation of positivistic criminology, argues Box (1983:4), could only be plausible if crimes were committed by a majority of individuals living in conditions of relative deprivation:

> However, if we look up rather than down the stratification hierarchy and see serious crimes being committed by the people who are respectable, well-educated, wealthy, and socially privileged then the imagery of pathology seems harder to accept. If these upper- and middle-class criminals are also pathological, then what hope is there for any of us! Wanting to avoid this pessimistic conclusion, we might instead entertain the idea that these powerful persons commit crimes for 'rational' – albeit disreputable – motives which emerge under conditions that render conformity a relatively unrewarding activity. Having rescued the powerful from 'abnormality,' we might do the same for the powerless. Maybe they too are rational rather than irrational morally disreputable rather than organically abnormal, overwhelmed by adversity rather than by wickedness.

The end of the 1980s and the beginning of the 1990s witnessed many positive political changes. Totalitarian regimes in Eastern Europe and some South American countries were replaced by more democratic ones. The apartheid system in African countries like Zimbabwe and South Africa came to an end. All this created a wave of optimism, a hope for a new world order in which governments would be accountable to international bodies and where there is more respect for fundamental human rights. Recent events in the former Yugoslavia, in Chechenia, and many other parts of the world have shattered this rosy dream. Amnesty International's report 'Getting Away with Murder – Political Killings and Disappearances in the 1990s' (1993:2), shows that the promises of the new era were hollow, that tens of thousands of people are still being killed every year by government agents or are 'disappearing' without trace. What is even more shocking is AI's claim that some of the worst violations are taking place in countries ruled by governments which are ostensibly accountable to their own people and the international community, and which proclaim the sanctity of human rights.

Amnesty International (1993:5) reports that many governments rely on sophisticated cover-ups, blatant lies and covert methods of repression in order to perpetuate the terror while presenting a respectable face to the international community.

According to AI (1993:5) 'governments use methods of murder aimed at concealing the crime. For example, killings are carried out by night when the victims are alone. Bodies are mutilated and hidden to avoid identification and discovery.' AI reports that 'governments distort the truth to blame others for political killings. They may try to blur the status of the killers, claiming they are civilian forces acting beyond their control. Governments often present political killings as the legitimate result of law enforcement when, in reality, the action taken goes far beyond the limits of the law' (p. 6). Executions that are carried out after secret, summary trials – or no trials at all – are presented as lawful executions. In many countries, reports AI (1993:7) the police and security forces routinely use grossly excessive force in response to demonstrations and in many cases they deliberately kill unarmed civilians in order to make a political point. AI insists that official accounts of such incidents often blame the protestors for starting the violence!

CRIMES BY GOVERNMENTS

Criminologists interested in political crimes have traditionally concentrated on acts by individuals and organizations against the government, namely, attempts to change the political system through violating the law. While these political acts are important to understand, this exclusive focus neglects those crimes perpetrated by the government against the people.
Simon, D.R. and Eitzen, D.S.
Elite Deviance (1986:199)

1. Killings by Governments

Mass murderers are still on the loose.
They are called governments and the
scale of their crimes defies belief.
Amnesty International (1993:1)

Democide, Genocide, and Politicide
When compared to crimes by individuals or groups, crimes by governments are far greater in their scope and have a much stronger impact. Comparing the two, Dr Clyde Snow (AI,1993:1), a forensic anthropologist who analyzed skeletal remains to expose crimes committed by state officials in several

countries, noted that 'the great mass murderers of our time have accounted for no more than a few hundred victims whereas states that have chosen to kill their own citizens can usually count their victims by the carload lot.'

Rummel (1994:36) coined the term democide (from the Greek *demos*, or people and the Latin *caedere*, to kill) to describe the intentional killing by governments of an unarmed person or people, a term which, he suggests, includes genocide, politicide, and mass murder by governments. Rummel also calls these killings 'megamurders' because the victims are sometimes in the millions. He estimates that in the 20th century alone over a hundred million people were killed by political regimes in different parts of the world.

Murder of unarmed civilians by government forces, militia, police, public officials, groups operating on behalf of the government, can take many forms and may be committed in different circumstances. Nsereko (1983), who was commissioned by the United Nations to study murder by governments, talks about arbitrary killings that go unpunished. Nsereko defines these arbitrary deprivations as:

> ... the taking of life by or at the instigation, connivance or condonation of the government or those acting under its authority in a manner that contravenes the principles of natural justice or domestic law or International Human Rights law.

Summary Executions
Summary execution is defined by Nsereko as 'the practice of imposing and carrying out the death penalty in a manner which disregards the rules of natural justice or the due process of law. The proceedings leading to the execution may have a semblance of legality, but they fall far short of the international minimum standards of procedural justice as recognized under the international human rights instruments and under the reasonably developed legal systems of the world.' According to Nsereko, the sentence is usually handed down by a special court, a 'people's court', 'revolutionary court' or 'military tribunal', which is not bound up by the ordinary rules of procedure. Nsereko, (1983:7) adds:

> At most times the special courts sit in camera, emerge only to announce the sentence or the fact that it has already been carried out. They thus violate a cardinal rule of procedural justice that requires Judicial tribunals to open their proceedings to public scrutiny so that justice is not only done but also manifestly appears to be done... .

Extrajudicial Executions
The term 'extrajudicial executions' is used by Amnesty International (1993:10) to describe 'unlawful and deliberate killings carried out by order of a government or with its complicity or acquiescence.' Nsereko (1983)

notes that extrajudicial executions 'are acts of murder par excellence, committed by the State against its own inhabitants. They are political in nature, used to eliminate insecure regimes' adversaries, real or imagined, and to cow the population into submission.' According to Nsereko, the killings are often directed against targeted individuals, but may, and often are, directed against entire groups, be they ethnic, racial, religious or social, sometimes to genocidal proportions (Nsereko, 1983).

Nsereko adds that homicidal acts are also often employed against government opponents in exile. But not all extralegal executions are politically motivated. Police killings of criminals are common occurrences in many countries. Death squads composed of former or active policemen have been operating in many countries for many years.[1] In particular, the Brazilian death squad has gained notoriety for its liquidation of known offenders.

Involuntary or Enforced Disappearances

According to Amnesty International (1993:13), the term 'disappearance' (*desaparecido*) first entered the human rights vocabulary in Guatemala in 1966, when the government began disposing of political opponents in secret. The practice was then adopted in several Latin American countries only to be copied by governments of many other countries. The phenomenon of involuntary or enforeced disappearances is not a new one. However, it has gained much publicity in recent years following the mass disappearances that took place in Chile and Argentina under the rule of their military governments. Most of those who disappear are killed by Government agents.

The shocking revelations made in Argentina following the ousting of the military regime and the return to democratic rule provide a shocking picture of the phenomenon of disappearances. In January 1984, the Argentinian weekly newspaper *Siete Dias* (Seven Days) reported that more than 1000 prisoners were anaesthetized, tied together, and thrown into the sea from aircraft by Argenina's military authorities during the 'dirty war' against leftist guerrillas in 1975–79. 'Terrorists' or 'suspected terrorists' were kidnapped, tortured, then anaesthetized. Once they were asleep, they were undressed, tied together, and thrown out of planes.[2]

The fate of those who disappeared was back in the news when Reuter reported in March 1995 (*Vancouver Sun*, 4 March 1995) that Commander Adolfo Francisco Scilingo was suing his superiors over the 'dirty war' against leftist guerrillas. He admitted having crewed two flights in June and July 1977 and described in graphic detail how the victims, many so weak from torture and detention they had to be helped aboard the plane, were injected with a sedative by a navy doctor. Commander Scilingo confessed to having, together with another officer, undressed the victims and to throwing their unconscious bodies into the ocean. Few weeks later, (*Vancouver Sun*, 26 April 1995) a second former member of the armed forces acknowledged having thrown prisoners out of airplanes in the late 1970s. Ironically, neither officer can be prosecuted for what they did as Argentina has pardoned all those who participated in the dirty war between 1976 and 1983.

Ethnic Cleansing

Ethnic cleansing is a term that has become associated with the ethnic strife in former Yugoslavia. Bassiouni and McCormick (1996:5) point out that 'ethnic cleansing is a strategy that uses concentration camps, torture, sexual violence, mass killings, forced deportations, destruction of private and cultural property, pillage and theft, and the blocking of humanitarian aid to kill, terrorize and permanently force non-Serb populations out of areas targeted to become part of a "Greater Serbia".' Bassiouni and McCormick (p. 5) report that sexual violence is a particularly effective tool of ethnic cleansing. Most of the victims of sexual violence are women and when they are rendered unfunctional they are unable to take care of themselves, their families, or the communities. The authors estimate that as many as 20 000 women in the former Yugoslavia may have been raped; in many cases, by men and boys of their own villages and neighbourhoods – sometimes close relatives were forced to rape them, and family members were forced to watch.

2. Abuse of Political Power

Canadians and Americans generally believe that the phenomenon of abuse of power is alien to Western democracies, that it occurs only under totalitarian regimes, or in third world countries. This is, of course, not true. Although abuses in democratic societies may not be as widespread as they are under other political systems, they are by no means rare. The annual reports of Amnesty International are bound to shatter any illusion that violations are confined to developing nations or nations under some form of dictatorship.

To the average North American citizen, disappearances are events that happen in Chile or Argentina. Political killings by governments are crimes committed by dictators in Asian or African countries, and torture is associated with the former regimes of Duvalier in Haiti, the Shah in Iran, or Marcos in the Philippines. The public might simply not be aware of the nature and extent of illegal practices by governments or government agencies at home or close to home. How many Americans, for example, are aware of the CIA's involvement in assassination plots and coups against foreign governments or of the CIA's use of American (and Canadian) citizens as guinea pigs?

Simon and Eitzen (1986) cite several examples of CIA murder plots based on a report by the *Senate Select Committee on Intelligence*. The report covering the CIA activities over a 13–year period was published over the objections of former President Ford and former CIA director William Colby. According to Simon and Eitzen, between 1960 and 1965, the CIA initiated at least eight plots to assassinate Fidel Castro. In 1975, the *Senate Select Committee* found strong evidence that CIA officials had planned the assassination of Congolese (Zaire) leader Patrice Lumumba and that President Eisenhower had ordered his death. The authors also claim that the United States was implicated in the assassination of Dominican dictator Rafael Trujillo, South Vietnam's President Ngo Dinh Diem, and General Rene Schneider of Chile.

On February 22 1987, the *New York Times Magazine* carried a report by investigative reporter Seymour Hersh saying the real aim of the April 1986 American raid on Libya was not to strike at guerilla and military bases as the Reagan administration had claimed but to assassinate Libyan leader Moammar Gadhafi. Hersh said he interviewed more than 70 US officials and servicemen, and he quoted one US Air Force intelligence officer as saying, 'There is no question they were looking for Gadhafi.'

Even countries with a long democratic tradition are not immune to serious abuses of power. In her book on abuse of power in Britain, Patricia Hewitt (1982:*xi–xii*) challenges the myth 'that Britain is a tolerant country, respectful of the rights of minorities, watchful of the principles of justice, ever-ready to challenge and restrict the growth of state power.' The reality, asserts Hewitt, is drastically different. She illustrates her point with three examples. First, she shows that *habeas corpus*, which is the most famous symbol of British liberty, has failed to protect black migrants settled in Britain from arbitrary power. They could be arrested without warrant, imprisoned on suspicion of being illegal entrants, be denied bail, detained for an indefinite period, and deported without ever being brought before a court. Hewitt maintains that in 1980 alone, over a thousand people were the victims of this abuse of power.

Second, she cites the system of exclusion orders created by the 1976 *Prevention of Terrorism Act*, under which 'a citizen of the United Kingdom born in Northern Ireland may be arrested, detained, deported to Belfast, and banned from ever re-entering Great Britain – all without any criminal charge being made against him and with no right to a court hearing.' Over two hundred people, she claims, have been exiled through the use of this power.

The third example she cites is the impotence of elected representatives and the courts to ensure that the police are answerable to the law that they are meant to enforce. She points to serious cases where a police officer who has broken the law has escaped with impunity. She also notes 'the massive development of the police surveillance capability has taken place with no legal restraint and no public supervision whatsoever and the police have denied to the public the information about their activities which could make such supervision effective.'

Acts of democide, genocide, and politicide claim millions of lives. While other forms of abuse of political power may not cause as many deaths, they can have disasterous effects on those victimized, their families, their communities, and society at large. The traumatic effects of 'disappearance' on the families of those who vanish are far deeper and much longer lasting than the effects of a loss of one of their members to an act of outright killing or legal execution.

Other types of abuse of power such as torture, internment, violations of human and civil rights, while less traumatic, do cause an enormous amount of human pain and suffering. Yet the pain and sufferings of the victims and their families are but one aspect of the total picture. The impact of acts of abuse of power on the social fabric itself can never be over-estimated. The psychological effects of living under conditions of political oppression or under a reign of terror have been all too well described in the literature. In particular, the randomness with which many acts of abuse strike members of racial, religious, or political minorities generate not only feelings of fear, anxiety, and insecurity but outright terror.

The general, long-term effects on society's development, cohesiveness, values, political, and economic stability can never be measured. The frustration, the injustices, the loss of confidence in the ability of the law to protect, the loss of faith in government and in public institutions, and in the impartiality of the justice system, do not lend themselves to quantification or accurate measurement.

Torture

Torture is an ancient way of extracting information and confessions that has survived the test of time. Over the years, methods of torture have changed from the crude to the sophisticated, from the raw to the subtle, from the bloody to the refined.

In the Declaration of Tokyo, adopted by the 29th World Medical Assembly in October 1975, torture is defined as

> ...the deliberate, systematic, or wanton infliction of physical or mental suffering by one or more persons acting alone or on the orders of any authority, to force another person to yield information, to make a confession or for any other reason. (Genefke, 1995:97)

Amnesty International's report 'Torture in the Eighties' (1984) covers 'a wide range of abuses and cites cases including systematic torture during interrogation – electric shocks, severe beatings, and mock executions – harsh prison conditions, the involvement of doctors in the process of torture, and punishments such as floggings and amputations decreed by law.' The report covers every continent but Australia, and makes allegations of torture and ill-treatment of prisoners in more than 90 countries.

It is worth noting that as of June 1993, the UN's Convention against Torture has been ratified by only 71 governments, that is less than half of the nations of the world (Genefke, 1995:98).

Internment of Civilians

Another common form of abuse of political power is the internment of civilians, who have committed no offence, in concentration camps or in remote isolated areas. A lot has been said and written about the Nazi concentration camps in Europe during the Second World War and about the Siberian labour camps. Amnesty International report (1975) on 'Prisoners of Conscience in the USSR: Their Treatment and Their Conditions', talked not only of internment in labour camps but also of the systematic torture to which the prisoners were subjected.

Again these abuses of power are by no means limited to totalitarian, military, or racist regimes, they do take place occasionally in democratic countries, especially during times of external or internal crisis. In Canada, demands for compensation of victims of acts of abuse of power have prompted the publication of vivid accounts of the injustices to which Canadians of Japanese origin were subjected during the Second World War, their internment, the confiscation and sale of their property, and so on. As Canada declared war on Japan, the persecution of Japanese Canadians began. In February 1942, mass evacuation started and by 1943 they had all been transferred from the British Columbia coastline to the interior of the province. Almost 21 000 Japanese Canadians in British Columbia were stripped of their farms, businesses, and homes that were later sold to the highest bidder (Bohn, 1983; see also Ujimoto, 1976).

The fate of Japanese–Americans was not much different. 10 000 were removed from Washington State alone – 7000 of them from Seattle. They were sent to camps in Idaho, some with barbed wires and soldiers. The confinement took over 5 months to complete. Families were given only days to pack belongings and sell homes. They were only allowed to take what they could carry.[3]

Another recent example of the deprivation of liberty of innocent civilians in Canada occurred during the October 1970 crisis which involved the kidnapping of a British diplomat (James Cross) and the kidnapping and subsequent killing of a Quebec Government minister (Pierre Laporte). Once the War Measures Act was passed by the federal Parliament, hundreds of members of the outlawed organization: Fédération de la libération de Québec (FLQ) were rounded up, arrested, and detained. The arrests were made in conjunction with a law that retroactively made the membership in the federation a punishable offence. The law was a clear violation of the fundamental democratic principle of the non-retroactivity of criminal laws.

Another form of internment popular in some countries is the holding of political dissidents in psychiatric hospitals. This was a common practice in the former Soviet Union where members of the psychiatric profession collaborated with the police to have political dissidents committed to mental institutions under the pretext that they are mentally disturbed.[4]

Psychiatric suppression of politically troublesome or threatening individuals is not uncommon in the United States. According to Turk (1982:52) 'such individuals have frequently been neutralized by being treated as mentally incompetent rather than as authentic political resisters'. He points out that 'the standard official and public view is that there is no "physical oppression" in a democracy, therefore serious – especially violent – individual or collective political resistance is symptomatic of mental disorder'.

Turk also cites examples given by psychiatrist Thomas Szasz, who voiced strong criticism of the readiness with which many psychiatrists have facilitated American governmental suppression of political dissidents such as the poet Ezra Pound (who was kept in St Elisabeth's Hospital, Washington, DC from 1945 to 1958) and General Edwin Walker.

The Use of Humans as Guinea Pigs

Use of convicted offenders for human experimentation.   In the aftermath of the Second World War, 15 German doctors were convicted by the Nuremberg war criminal tribunal for cruel and often murderous 'medical experiments' performed on concentration camp inmates. In their defence, the accused doctors cited comparable experiments carried out on prisoners by American physicians (Mitford, 1974:151). Mitford reports that the standards established by the Nuremberg trial did not stop a huge expansion of medical research programmes in many prisons in the US sanctioned by federal health agencies and state prison administrators. In 1961, the World Medical Association declared that prisoners, 'being captive groups, should not be used as the subject of experiments'. However, according to Mitford, the recommendation was never formally adopted, largely because of the opposition of American doctors. She quotes one American scientist as saying 'criminals in our penitentiaries are fine experimental material – and much cheaper than chimpanzees.' She also points out to those large pharmaceutical companies with high financial stakes in experimental testing on human subjects because of FDA regulations requiring that all new drugs be tested on humans before being marketed.

Use of patients for human experimentation.   Some years ago Canadians were shocked by some startling revelations about Canadian psychiatric patients at the Allan Memorial Institute (a renowned psychiatric hospital in Montreal) who in the 1950s were used as guinea pigs in covert psychiatric experiments partly financed by the CIA. According to reports published in the press,[5] the patients were subjected to a variety of techniques including: brain electro-shock, LSD, curare poison, weeks of drugged sleep, and sensory deprivation extending sometimes to five weeks. Once in a state of stupor, the patients were then bombarded with tape-recorded messages, designed to programme new patterns of behaviour into their brains. A CIA front organization, 'The Society for the Investigation of Human Ecology', reportedly gave the psychiatrist who conducted the experiments $19 000 a year during the late 1950s and early 1960s to finance the brainwashing experiments (*Vancouver Sun*, 17 January 1984).

Use of unsuspecting citizens as guinea pigs. Chambliss (1989:200) relates how the CIA conducted experiments during the 1970s on unknowing subjects by hiring prostitutes to administer drugs to their clients. CIA-trained medical doctors and psychologists observed the effects of the drugs through a two-way mirror in expensive apartments furnished to the prostitutes by the CIA. According to Chambliss, at least one of the victims of these experiments died and others suffered considerable trauma.

Use of the poor for human experimentation. In an article on the use of steroids published in *Sports Illustrated* (1 August 1983) the magazine re-ported a shocking story. It revealed a grandiose plan announced by the founder and president of Nautilis Sports/Medical Industries Inc. at a strength-coaching conference at the University of Virginia. The President declared that

> Next week I am going south of the border to institute a 10 year study using thousands of subjects. Why south of the border? Because we can get the subjects at a price we can afford, and we can get subjects who are motivated, who will train. When you take starving subjects you can motivate them, believe me. We're going to take about 1000 subjects and give them massive doses of steroids, and we're going to take another 1000 and give them no steroids. You can't do that in this country. But you can do it down there. When they sign up for this program they will be told in advance, 'Look, what we give you may be a drug, or it may not be. Even if it is you won't know it. The drugs might be dangerous and they might ruin your liver. Now if you don't want to sign up, there's the door, leave!'

On 13 July 1987, the *Vancouver Sun* reported from London that Britain's Ministry of Defence had acknowledged testing nerve gases on human volun-teers for the previous 25 years to assess the possible results of exposure to enemy weapons but said the doses were too small to be dangerous! Volun-teers were paid the equivalent of $225 each.

3. State-Organized Crime

> There is a form of crime that has heretofore escaped criminological in-
> quiry, yet its persistence and omnipresence raise theoretical and methodo-
> logical issues crucial to the development of criminology as a science. I am
> referring to what I call 'State-organized crime.'
>
> W.J. Chambliss (1989:183)

Under what he calls 'state-organized crime', Chambliss (1989:184) describes
'acts defined by law as criminal and committed by state officials in the
pursuit of their job as representatives of the state.' The examples he
gives include a state's complicity in piracy, smuggling, assasinations,
criminal conspiracies, acting as an accessory before or after the fact, and
violating laws that limit their activities. In the latter category Chambliss
includes the use of illegal methods of spying on citizens, diverting funds
in ways prohibited by law (for example, illegal campaign contributions,
selling arms to countries prohibited by law, and supporting terrorist activities).

Chambliss excludes from this category of state-organized crime
criminal acts 'that benefit only individual officeholders, such as the acceptance of bribes or the illegal use of violence by the police against individuals, unless such acts violate existing criminal law and are official
policy.'

In an attempt to explain the phenomenon of state-organized crime, Chambliss (1989:201) points to the contradictions inherent in the formation of
states, contradictions which create conditions under which there will be a
tendency for state officials to violate the criminal law. He writes:

> State officials inherit from the past laws that were not of their making and
> that were the result of earlier efforts to resolve conflicts wrought by
> structural contradictions.... . The inherited laws nonetheless represent
> the foundation on which the legitimacy of the state's authority depends.
> These laws also provide a basis for attempts by the state to control the acts
> of others and to justify the use of violence to that end.

CRIMES OF THE POWERFUL

> Law has created many crimes of the powerless, and too few crimes of the
> powerful. The key concept here is power: who has power, and who
> doesn't: who uses power, and who are its victims.
>
> M.J. Lynch and W.B. Groves (1989:40)
A Primer in Radical Criminology

1. Crimes by Legitimate Corporations

Literature on corporate crime contains several definitions of the term. Schrager and Short (1977:409), define corporate crime or organizational crimes as

> ... illegal acts of omission or commission of an individual or a group of individuals in a legitimate formal organization in accordance with the operative goals of the organization which have a serious physical or economic impact on employees, consumers or the general public.

Despite the tangible and intangible harm caused by corporate crime, despite the loss of life, the injuries, the damage to human health, the pollution of the environment caused by it, and despite the economic depredations that result from it, corporate crime is usually regarded, like other types of white collar crime, as less serious, less vicious, and less of a problem than conventional street crime. Most even fail to see it as violent crime. The reasoning underlying this common view is that the acts are committed without a willful intent to kill, maim or injure. Even when the corporate acts or omissions causing the death, injury or harm are deliberate and calculated, the ensuing result is seen as unintentional and thus less culpable than deliberately inflicted injury or harm. This attitude is well described by Reiman (1990:52)

> Because we accept the belief – encouraged by our politicians' statements about crime and by the media's portrayal of crime – that the model for crime is one person specifically intending to harm another, we accept a legal system that leaves us unprotected against much greater dangers to our lives and well-being than those threatened by the Typical Criminal.

Reiman (1990:51) insists that this popular model of the Typical Crime 'keeps us from calling a mine disaster a mass murder even if 26 men are killed, even if someone is responsible for the unsafe conditions in which they worked and died'.

The view that corporate crime is less evil or wicked than conventional crime is due to the failure to acknowledge that the harmful outcomes are quite often a direct result of lax safety measures, violations of safety regulations, deliberate failure to correct known irregularities, and so on. The leak of toxic gas from the Union Carbide Plant in Bhopal, India, in December 1984 was responsible for the death of at least 1500 persons. Another 100 000 inhabitants of the city (that is one-eighth of the population) became serious candidates for developing severe respiratory and vision problems. Thousands became totally or partially blind. In January 1985, the *New York Times* reported that its team of investigators at the disaster site was able to establish no less than ten irregularities and attributed the leak to operational errors, design defects, maintenance failures, shortcomings in the training of employees, and so on. Thirteen years later the death toll climbed to more than 15 000 according to a report by the Associated Press (*Vancouver Sun*, November 27 1996, p. A12). The same report indicated that India's Supreme Court has set aside a lower court's ruling charging eight company executives with manslaughter and reduced the charges to criminal negligence claiming that the executives did not know that methylisocyanate gas produced in the factory could kill humans.

The Bhopal disaster is just one of many cases that have highlighted the enormous death and destruction that can result from corporate wrongdoing, illegal actions and statute violations. Three widely publicized cases, summarized by Hills (1987:6–7) illustrate well the concepts of 'corporate crime' and 'corporate violence'.

(1)   *The Dalkon Shield intrauterine device for birth control.*   Hills cites US District Judge Miles Lord, who presided over a court settlement of seven 'product liability' cases, and who accused top executives of the A.H. Robins Company of putting profits above the health of women and causing 'catastrophic harm' to women who used the Dalkon Shield IUD. During the trial, Justice Lord described the Dalkon Shield as 'an instrument of death, mutilation and disease' by which thousands of users had become infertile, had involuntary abortions, or developed pelvic inflammatory disease (p. 6).

Hills points out that after the death of 17 women, the Robins Company finally took the Dalkon Shield off the market though it continued to export millions of unsterilized IUDs overseas, still marketing them as 'modern, superior and safe' (p. 6).

(2)   *The near melt-down at Three Mile-Island nuclear plant.*   According to Hills, the operators of the nuclear plant, Metropolitan Edison, falsified test data on water leaking from the reactor's primary cooling system for at least five months prior to the accident. Convicted of falsifying records, an action that put the lives of thousands of people in the area in danger, Metropolitan Edison agreed to pay the modest sum of $45 000 fine in a plea bargain in which the utility pleaded guilty to one count and *nolo contendere* (no contest) to six other charges (pp. 6–7).

(3)   *The Ford Pinto automobile case.*   Hills cites here the now infamous internal Ford Company memorandum that revealed callous indifference to human life and suffering. Once Ford engineers discovered that the fuel tank on the Pinto ruptured upon rear-end impact at speeds as low as 25 miles per hour exploding into flames from any spark of scraping metal, a cost-benefit analysis of the problem was ordered by company executives. Projecting millions of car sales, Ford decided it was not worth making an $11 alteration per car to save several hundred lives, and for several years con-

tinued to manufacture and sell a car they knew could become a rolling incinerator (p. 7).

Hills reminds us that Ford is not the only automobile manufacturer to engage in deceptive practices or to allow defective vehicles to continue to cause life and health hazard. He points out to a criminal action filed in 1983 by the Justice Department against General Motors for deliberately concealing problems with its front-wheel-drive 1980 X-cars. He reports that documents released in another civil suit against GM, revealed that test drivers and internal company documents repeatedly warned key company executives just prior to general production that the rear wheel brakes had a tendency to lock prematurely, causing the car to spin dangerously out of control. Despite more than 1700 complaints, and at least 71 known injuries and 15 deaths, GM fiercely resisted the government's attempt to force a recall to repair, at no charge to the owners, over one million 1980 cars (p. 7).

Other crimes by corporations might not cause physical harm but can have devastating effects on the economy, economic stability, public confidence, social and moral values, and so on. For obvious reasons, it is impossible to put a dollar value on the economic costs of corporate crime. As Edelhertz (1970) points out

> How does one set a dollar value on food and drug violations which may permanently disable or kill? What is the true dollar cost of a fraudulent banking operation without valid deposit insurance which destroys the life savings of the elderly and makes them a burden on their children or on the state?... (pp. 8–9)

> The social and economic costs of tax violations, self- dealing by separate employees and bank officials, adulteration or watering of foods and drugs, charity frauds, insurance frauds, price fixing, frauds arising out of government procurement, and abuses of trust are clearly enormous even though not easily measured. (p. 4)

Schur (1980:170) reports that direct and indirect physical costs of corporate violations are huge even though it is difficult to adequately document or measure them. He cites violations such as: marketing of inadequately tested drugs, which result in illness or even death; unsafe work conditions that lead to injuries and death; environmental pollution that produces long-term health hazards; and marketing harmful food products. 'Additional social costs in terms of widespread public cynicism and a generalized hostility among the poor and the exploited are likewise incalculable' (p. 170).

Despite the difficulty, several estimates of the financial costs of white-collar crime in the United States have been made. Sutherland and Cressey (1978:24) state that the financial losses from fraudulent business transactions are probably many times greater than the financial losses from burglary, robbery, and ordinary larceny.

Bosworth-Davies and Saltmarsh (1995:13) report that during the year 1992–93, the British Serious Fraud Office was investigating fraud cases whose total losses exceeded £5300 million. Over a third of the cases involved allegations of theft or false accounting within corporate entities. They add that in the year 1993–94, the figures had risen and the aggregate value of the alleged frauds under investigation was £6000 million, of which 31 per cent of the cases involved frauds on companies.

The potential impact of certain acts or omissions, such as nuclear plant accidents (for example, the Chernobyl disaster in Russia) or industrial pollution, the dumping of hazardous waste, and so on, is horrendous. But there is a surprisingly sharp discrepancy between the substantial impact of abuse of economic power and the weakness of official responses to it. One reason advanced to explain such discrepancy is the non-violent and therefore non-threatening, nature of most white-collar crimes. Yet, as Edelhertz (1970) points out, 'the impact of white-collar crime on people and on their physical and psychological integrity and security is not so different from that of common crime – except that its effects are longer lasting.'

2.   White-Collar Crime

> Now as through this world I ramble,
> I see lots of funny men,
> Some rob you with a six gun,
> And some with a fountain pen.
> > Woody Guthrie
> > *Pretty Boy Floyd*

Definitions of white-collar crime vary. Sutherland's (1949:2) original definition as 'a crime committed by a person of respectability and high social status in the course of his occupation' was later revised and modified by different authors. Newman (1977:52) asserts that the chief criterion for a crime to be 'white-collar' is that it occurs as a part of, or a deviation from, the violator's occupational role.

Laureen Snider (1993:14) suggests that current definitions of white-collar crime include some combination of the following characteristics:

1) they are offences committed as part of a lawful occupation; 2) a violation of trust is involved; 3) there is no direct physical force, although physical harm may well result; 4) the goals are money, property, power, or prestige; 5) there is a specific intent to profit by the act; and 6) there is an attempt to conceal the crime or use power to prevent the application of sanctions.

Snider draws attention to an important distinction that needs to be made within the broad category generally labelled white-collar crime. She distinguishes occupational (or employee) crime from corporate (or organizational) crime. According to Snider (p.14) *occupational crimes* are 'white-collar offences committed by an individual or group of individuals exclusively for personal gain. The victim is an organization, public or private, business or government, often though not necessarily the offender's employer.' She gives the examples of embezzlement of corporate funds, expense account fraud, commercial bribery, tax evasion and most computer crimes. *Corporate crimes*, on the other hand, according to Snider's distinction, 'are white-collar crimes committed by legitimate formal organizations, through the individuals inside them, with the aim of furthering the interests of the corporation as well as those of the individuals involved. They are committed by companies or individuals on the company's behalf, and they are punishable by law' although quite frequently they go unpunished (p. 14).

As examples of these crimes, Snider cites the conspiracies among oil companies to restrict the supply and raise the price of gasoline; dumping hazardous wastes into landfills or nearby lakes and oceans; paying kickbacks to retailers to attain prime display space on supermarket shelves; or paying workers less than the minimum wage.

White-collar crime continues to be a controversial topic in criminology. The controversy centres around three major issues identified by Newman (1977:51) as follows:

1. whether the law violations in question are really crimes;
2. whether the behaviour involved could be equated with the conceptual meanings of criminal behaviour when the perpetrators themselves do not think of themselves as criminals and are not commonly perceived as such;
3. whether anything could be gained by reformulating the definitions of crime to include behaviour customarily punished civilly or by administrative action rather than by the conventional criminal procedures

3. Crimes by Professionals

> I'm walking about a prison,
> What do you think I see?
> A lot of dumb-bells doing time,
> While all the crooks go free.
> Quoted by Albert Morris (1941)

Crimes by professionals are among the most difficult to study. For one thing, they have an extremely high 'dark figure' (see page 96), and for another thing, those that come to light are mostly dealt with by professional bodies (such as medical associations, dental associations, bar associations, teachers' federations, and so on) outside the criminal justice system. Many end up in administrative sanctions (suspension, erasing name from professional register, compensation, and so on) rather than criminal sanctions.

The growing concern over the escalating costs of certain government subsidized systems (medicare, legal aid, pharmacare, and so on) has led to increasing scrutiny and attempts to crack down on cases of fraud and abuse of the system by the professionals involved. Enhanced awareness of sexual victimization that might take place in the context of privacy in which professional and client usually meet, (physician/psychiatrist/dentist and patient; psychologist/lawyer and client; teacher and student; and so on) has led to more cases being reported by the victims, either to the criminal justice system or to the body governing the profession. Several highly publicized cases have highlighted the seriousness of the victimization and the lasting trauma suffered by the victims. Despite all this, the number of studies that have researched these types of crime remains relatively small.

Crimes by Members of the Legal Profession
Crimes by members of the legal profession are not phenomena of recent origin. However, the sharp increase in the number of lawyers, judges, prosecutors, notaries, and so forth in recent years, the growing competitiveness, and the increasing pressures mean that the crimes and illegal practices will only increase. Already in 1938, Frank Tannenbaum wrote about the shady activities of some lawyers. He said:

> Thus the professional crook seeks out the professional criminal lawyer. Every large professional criminal gang has its trusted mouthpiece, the lawyer who can be depended upon to arrange things. He is on hand with the bail bond or the habeas corpus writ to 'spring' the members of the gang who have had the misfortune to be arrested. If the case can be fixed, the lawyer will find the ways and means to fix it. If, for some reason, it cannot be fixed, the lawyer can be depended upon to arrange for a perjured defense or for the bribery or intimidation of jurors and witnesses. 'There is a group of criminal lawyers,' wrote the Chicago City Council, 'whose work includes dealing with the police, furnishing professional alibis and professional witnesses, jury fixing, spiriting away of witnesses, exhaustive continuances, and all the underground activity of all around 'fixers.' (p. 265)

In his book on occupational crime, Green (1990:196) points out that lawyers, as professionals, have abundant opportunities to commit crime in the course of their occupation and that there are several aspects of service delivery related to the practice of law which offer tremendous opportunity for abuse and fraud. Green suggests that lawyers can commit crimes for their own enrichment (such as overbilling clients for time, embezzlement of funds entrusted to them, and so forth) or for the benefit of their clients (for example, falsification of documents). Green cites several examples of violation by lawyers of their fiduciary duties. In addition to these clearly illegal practices, Green lists a number of ethical violations often perpetrated by lawyers.

Physician Fraud and Abuse
Wilson *et al.* (1986:130) estimate that medical abuse in Canada is costing the taxpayers between Can$ 300–400 million annually and that in Australia approximately Aus$ 200 million is illegally taken annually by practitioners from the national Medicare scheme.

Medical fraud and abuse take many forms and encompass a wide variety of practices. Wilson *et al.* (1986:130) claim that some physicians are billing for services never rendered, or for services more extensive and expensive than those actually provided, as well as carrying out medically unnecessary treatments and operations in order to obtain additional fees. The authors distinguish between fraud which is based on fact – whether a treatment was performed or not; and abuse which is largely a matter of medical judgement and relates to the overutilization of medical services.

Wilson *et al.* (1986) describe five specific types of medical fraud and abuse: extra time, extra money, extra treatment, extra referrals, and phantom treatment. But the fraud and abuse examined by Wilson *et al.* (1986) are not the only crimes that are committed by physicians. Attention to criminal activities in the medical profession was drawn by Sutherland in his original paper on white-collar crime (1940:2) in which he wrote:

> In the medical profession, because it is probably less criminalistic than some other professions, are found illegal sale of alcohol and narcotics, abortion, illegal services to underworld criminals, fraudulent reports and testimony in accident cases, extreme cases of unnecessary treatment, fake specialists, restriction of competition, and fee-splitting.

Sexual abuse of patients is an old, but largely hidden, criminal activity committed by some doctors, psychiatrists, dentists (as well as clinical psychologists, therapists, teachers and so on).

4.   Crimes by the Police

Police Brutality
Police brutality, usually hidden from the public eye, made a dramatic appearance on American national television when millions of viewers watched members of the Los Angeles Police Force brutally kick and beat a black citizen named Rodney King. Police brutality refers to the use of excessive and unnecessary force by the police in the exercise of their duties.

It takes many forms and most of it occurs while the victim is in police custody or under police control. The extreme form of police brutality is the unnecessary shooting and killing of fleeing suspects or suspects who are in no position to cause serious harm to the arresting officer. Simon and Eitzen (1986:211) report that in cases where there is a confrontation with the police resulting in the discharge of a firearm, five times as many citizens as police are killed in the US.

Police killings do not seem to be random. Members of certain groups appear more likely to be shot at than others. In Toronto and Montreal there have been several incidents in recent years suggesting that the police may be using their guns more frequently against black suspects. Simon and Eitzen (1986:211) report that in the US, a disproportionately large proportion of those killed by the police are non-white males (49.6 per cent of all males killed by the police). This, they claim, translates statistically into a shooting death rate of blacks and chicanos by police that is ten to 13 times higher per 100 000 population than that of whites.

Simon and Eitzen (1986:211) cite three instances of police brutality that received wide publicity in the US: The Chicago Police's treatment of civil rights demonstrators at the 1968 Democratic Convention, the Ohio National Guard's firing of 61 shots that killed four college students and wounded nine at Kent State University in 1970, and the killing of 43 inmates at Attica Prison in the State of New York in 1971. One may add to this the horrible tragedy caused by police intervention at the Davidian Sect Compound in Waco, Texas, that resulted in the death of several persons, many of whom were children.

Police Violations of Citizens' Rights

Police violations of civil and human rights are legion and yet they go most of the time undetected and unnoticed. Occasionally, they are brought to light through some highly publicized cases which serve to highlight the level to which the police can sink in their zeal to fight terrorism, organized crime, or even victimless crime. The list of outright criminal and deviant practices is rather long and includes incidents such as planting evidence, fabricating confessions, bribing and intimidating witnesses, committing perjury, falsifying documents, wire tapping, spying, secret surveillance, intercepting and opening mail, to name but a few. The case of the Birmingham six in Britain provides clear evidence that, even in a democracy, police often adhere to the principle 'the end justifies the means.'

In Canada, the abuses of power by the RCMP security service, the fore-runner of CSIS (Canadian Security Intelligence Service), were exposed in several books: Mann and Lee (1979); Sawatsky (1980); Dion (1982). Mann and Lee as well as Dion relied, among other sources, on testimony before, and the findings of, two government commissions. The first is the Keable

Commission (1981) which investigated police operations on the territory of the Province of Quebec (Commission d'Enquête sur des Opérations Policières en Territoire Québécoise). The second is the 'Royal Commission of Inquiry into Certain Activities of the Royal Canadian Mounted Police' commonly known as the MacDonald Commission (1977). Testimony before the two commissions revealed a wide range of crimes and illegal activities by the RCMP. Ellis (1987:126) reports that these crimes included:

> ... arson, kidnapping, obstructing justice, perjury, blackmail, burglary, theft, bombing, disseminating information known to be false, entering premises without a search warrant and intimidation. In addition, the Mounties have illegally intercepted and opened mail and have obtained confidential unemployment, health insurance, and income tax infor mation.

Police Corruption

Police corruption, documented by several commissions of inquiry in the US, Canada and other countries, is not, despite claims to the contrary by police associations and organizations, limited to a few bad or rotten apples. In some forces it is endemic and can reach as high as the top of the organization. Sherman (1974:13) insists that corruption is 'a given feature of every police system in the world.' He also asserts that 'virtually every urban police department in the United States has experienced both organized corruption and a major scandal over that corruption.' (1978:xxiii)

Punch (1985:8) notes that there is no unanimity on defining police corruption and there is a paucity of good, analytical material on the subject. Descriptive typologies can offer guidance when definitions are difficult to formulate. Barker and Roebuck (1973) identify eight types of corruption: corruption of authority; kickbacks; opportunistic theft; shakedowns; protection; the fix; direct criminal activities; and internal pay-offs.

Punch (1985:13–14) elucidates four types of police corruption:

1. *Straightforward corruption*: something is done or not done for some form of reward.
2. *Predatory (strategic) corruption*: the police stimulate crime to extort money and actively organize graft.
3. *Combative (strategic) corruption*: this type of corruption is poised on using illicit means for organizationally and socially approved ends. It includes 'flaking' (that is planting evidence on a suspect); 'padding' (that is to add to drugs or evidence to strengthen a case); falsifying testimony; 'verbals' (where words attributed to a suspect are invented by policemen to help incriminate him); buying and selling drugs; 'scoring' (where

police take money, drugs or goods from suspects or prisoners; and paying informants with illegally obtained drugs).

4. *Corruption as perversion of justice*: lying under oath, intimidating witnesses, planting evidence on a suspect, and so forth. Here the motive is to use one's power and position to ensure that justice does or does not get done for reasons that are not mercenary and not 'idealistic.'

One of the most extensive investigations into police corruption was the Knapp Commission investigation into alleged police corruption in New York City. The commission was established in May 1970, worked for 2 1/2 years and submitted its final report in December 1972. Some of the conclusions of the commission, reproduced below, tell the story:

> We found corruption to be widespread. It took various forms depending upon the activity involved, appearing at its most sophisticated among plainclothesmen assigned to enforcing gambling laws. In the five plainclothes divisions where our investigations were concentrated we found a strikingly standardized pattern of corruption.... Evidence before us led us to the conclusion that the same pattern existed in the remaining divisions which we did not investigate in depth. (p.1)
>
> Corruption in narcotics enforcement lacked the organization of the gambling pads, but individual payments – known as 'scores' – were commonly received and could be staggering in amount. (p. 2)
>
> Corruption among detectives assigned to general investigative duties also took the form of shakedowns of individual targets of opportunity. Although these scores were not in the huge amounts found in narcotics, they not infrequently came to several thousand dollars. (p. 2)
>
> Sergeants and lieutenants who were so inclined participated in the same kind of corruption as the men they supervised. In addition, some sergeants had their own pads from which patrolmen were excluded. (p. 3)
>
> Of course, not all policemen are corrupt. If we are to exclude such petty infractions as free meals, an appreciable number do not engage in any corrupt activities. Yet, with extremely rare exceptions, even those who themselves engage in no corrupt activities are involved in corruption in the sense that they take no steps to prevent what they know or suspect to be going on about them. (p. 3)
>
> The problem of corruption is neither new, nor confined to the police.... On the contrary, in every area where police corruption exists it is paralelled by corruption in other agencies of government, in industry and labor, and in the professions. (p. 5)
>
> The Commission found that corruption within the Department was so pervasive that honest rookies joining the police force were subject to strong pressures to conform to patterns of behavior which tended to make cynics of them and ultimately led many of them into the most

serious kinds of corruption. This situation was the result of an extremely tolerant attitude toward corruption which had flourished despite the efforts – sometimes vigorous and sometimes not – of police commissioners and various law enforcement agencies. (p. 260)

5. Organized Crime/Criminal Organizations

One reason for including organized crime under crimes of the powerful is that members of organized crime, particularly those on the top or who are high in the organizational hierarchy can wield enormous power and can literally have high ranking politicians, public officials, members of the judiciary and the legal profession, and so on, under their thumb. In countries such as Columbia and Italy, organized crime is considered a state within the state. The recent revelations about former Italian prime ministers who allegedly were on the mafia's payroll, were protecting its members and maintaining secret contacts with them, indicate the extent to which such criminal organizations are able through corruption, threats or blackmail, to secure the cooperation of politicians and government officials. In the United States, revelations about the late president J.F. Kennedy's connections to certain organized crime figures came as a shock to those who for years considered Mr Kennedy to be one of the finest presidents in American history. In his book on former FBI Chief, J. Edgar Hoover, Summers (1994:5) claims that the man who ruled the national law enforcement agency for nearly 50 years had 'an understanding' with top organized crime figures. According to Summers, this understanding was behind Hoover's long neglect to pursue 'the most insidious criminal force of all – the Mafia.'

So what is organized crime? Like many other criminological concepts, the concept of organized crime is an ambiguous and problematic concept, hence the absence of any uniform definition. The synonymous use of the term with several others such as 'the Mafia', 'Cosa Nostra', 'the Syndicate' only adds to the confusion. As one author (Albanese, 1985:4) put it, '...there seem to be as many descriptions of organized crime as there are authors.'

When the New York State legislature wrote the *Organized Crime Control Act* in 1986, it stated that because of its 'highly diverse nature, it is impossible to precisely define what organized crime is' (Ryan, 1995:4). Cressey (1969:299) points out that 'organized crime' is merely a social category, rather than a legal category. This makes it difficult for police and other governmental agencies to routinely compile information on it as they do for other categories of crime, such as larceny, burglary, and automobile theft, thus rendering the scientific study of the phenomenon rather difficult.

In the Task Force Report on Organized Crime, the *US President's Commission on Law Enforcement and the Administration of Justice* (1967:8) concluded that organized crime can be distinguished from other kinds of criminal activity by the 'element of corruption' and the 'element of enforcement.' The difference is explained as follows:

> There are at least two aspects of organized crime that characterize it as a unique form of criminal activity. The first is the element of corruption. The second is the element of enforcement, which is necessary for the maintenance of both internal discipline and the regularity of business transactions. In the hierarchy of organized crime there are positions for people fulfilling both of these functions. But neither is essential to the long-term operation of other types of criminal groups.... Organized crime groups... are believed to contain one or more fixed positions for 'enforcers', whose duty it is to maintain organizational integrity by arranging for the maiming and killing of recalcitrant members. And there is a position for a 'corrupter', whose function is to establish relationships with those public officials and other influential persons whose assistance is necessary to achieve the organization's goals. By including these positions within its organization, each criminal cartel, or 'family', becomes a government as well as a business.

Ryan (1995:5) argues that organized crime is best defined by its structural features. He insists that all types of organized crime have certain definitive characteristics in common: durability, continuity, hierarchy, multiplicity, violence or the threat of it, and political corruption. Ryan (p. 3) suggests that today's definition of organized crime 'not only includes the Mafia, but also Jamaican posses; Nigerian drug smugglers; Chinese triads and tongs; Columbian drug cartels; Chicano and African–American organizations; motorcycle gangs; Russian, Middle Eastern, and West Indian gangs; and a host of other criminals banded together in criminal pursuits.' Ryan maintains that the economic toll taken by all these organizations operating in the US is estimated to approach a half trillion dollars each year.

Organized crime's main operations are concentrated on profit-making illegal activities. The rise of organized crime is generally traced to the era of prohibition in the US. Present day activities have as their focus the provision of illicit goods and services for which the demand is high: gambling, prostitution, drugs, pornography, loan sharking and so on. Ryan (1995:6) notes that

> Such criminals also control many legal entrepreses such as restaurants, trucking firms, and entertainment establishments, using them as cover for their illegal practices. They have infiltrated labor unions and businesses, using the facade of legitimacy as fronts to conceal money or for other criminal purposes.

POWERFUL CRIMINALS AND CRIMINALS IN POWER

Studies of conventional criminals abound. But relatively little has been written on those criminals who hold the strings of power, on whose orders or behalf atrocious crimes are committed. Comfort, (1970:59) points out that:

> The practical difficulties of verifying any hypothesis about the criminology of power are particularly forbidding. It is relatively easy to study the mentality of any type of delinquent other than the delinquent in office. Lawbreakers in prison, or psychiatric cases referred to clinics, provide material for study which is either relatively docile or relatively defence-less.... Personal study is, however, one source of information about modern political and executive leaders which the form of society today effectively limits.... With the politician, it is not only inadequate to base long-range guesses about motivation upon public utterances or policies, but any interpretation of abnormality would be unlikely to fall within the legal definition of privilege or public interest.

The idea that those who commit crimes while holding political office can fit under specific criminological or psychological types is probably false. As Lord Acton once said 'power corrupts and absolute power corrupts absolutely.'

Silberman (1978:45) notes that 'well-bred people steal far larger sums than those lost through street crime.' Geis and Meier (1977:208) report that after its study of the United States Senate and the House of Representatives, the Ralph Nader investigative group offered the observation that 'it could probably be shown by facts and figures that there is no distinctly American criminal class except Congress.' Geis and Meier also noted that Americans expect their political leaders to be devious; and the leaders tend not to disappoint them.

Comfort (1970:25-7) believes that democratic societies offer the prospect of entry into public affairs to many aggressive personalities whose ambitions might otherwise have been limited to local affairs.

> There is, therefore, in centralized societies, a tendency for the personnel of these occupations to be drawn increasingly from those whose main pre-occupation is a desire for authority, for powers of control and of direction over others. In the case of would-be politicians, these impulses may spring from a highly developed political and social sense; they may equally well spring from maladjustment and a deep-seated impulse toward self-asser-tion and dominance... the centralization of power attracts inevitably to-wards the administrative centre those for whom power is an end in itself.

There is no reason to believe that politicians and government officials who commit serious crimes in the course of exercising their functions also do so in other contexts. Comfort (1970:29) believes that 'the intense strain and the other incidentals of modern political office have an observable effect in evoking delinquent conduct in persons who would probably not otherwise exhibit it.'

Neither the traditional approaches to the etiology of crime nor the conventional theories of criminal behaviour provide an adequate explanation for criminal acts linked to abuse of political and economic power. To quote the well-known words of Sutherland (1949:257–8):

> The current tendency is to advocate emotional instability as the trait which explains ordinary criminal behavior and this explanation has been emphasized particularly by psychiatrists and psychoanalysts. Even these advocates, however, would suggest only in a jocular sense that the crimes of the Ford Motor Company are due to the Oedipus Complex, or those of the Aluminum Company of America to an Inferiority Complex, or those of the US Steel Corporation to Frustration and Aggression, or those of du Pont to Traumatic Experience, or those of Montgomery Ward to Regression to Infancy.

Another difficulty in theoretically explaining criminal acts linked to abuse of power stems from the fact that the manifestations of abuse arise in a wide variety of conditions and in extremely diverse situations. No political system seems immune, whether it is democratic or totalitarian; no economic system seems to be exempt, whether it is capitalist, socialist, or communist. The chances, therefore, of coming up with a general explanatory theory encompassing the various types of power and the various manifestations of abuse are extremely remote. A much more promising approach to a better understanding of the phenomenon of abuse of power would be to try to identify some of the criminogenic factors that contribute to abuse and some of the criminogenic situations that are conducive to or facilitate abuse.

1. A New Typology of Criminals

Most typologies of criminals use as classifying criteria the personal characteristics of the offenders or their behaviour. These traditional typologies can only be applied with great difficulty, if at all, to powerful criminals and criminals in power. It is necessary, therefore, to develop a different kind of typology. The proposed typology uses not the qualities and attributes that characterize the various types, but the attitudes and social reactions to different groups of offenders. Based on these criteria one can classify conventional and non-conventional criminals into four categories:

The sacrificeables. These are the poor wretches so well described in Victor Hugo's famous novel *Les Misérables*. They are the scapegoats of society, the poor, the have-nots, the powerless, the underprivileged who commit conventional crimes, who are targeted by the organs of the criminal justice system and who form the bulk of those prosecuted, punished and imprisoned.

The undesirables. These are the deviants and the marginal types. They are neither dangerous nor harmful in a strict sense. Their real crime is that they have opted for a lifestyle which is deemed immoral, unconventional, or threatening by some other members of society. They are the prostitutes, the pimps, the alcoholics, the drug addicts, the vagrants, the vagabonds and so on.

The unreachables. These are the delinquents who cannot be reached by the arm of the law except with great difficulty and in exceptional circumstances. Those who, because of their political power, socio-economic status, remain sheltered from the law and shielded from criminal sanctions. They are the delinquents capable of escaping detection, prosecution, or conviction, thanks to their ability to take advantage of the lacunae which exist in the laws, to obstruct the course of justice, to circumvent the criminal justice process, to avoid the laying of criminal charges, or the administration of penal sanctions.

The untouchables. These are the delinquents who are truly above the law, such as the heads of state (Stalin, Hitler, Nixon, Idi Amin, Bokassa, Pol Pot, to mention but a few examples), and others who enjoy legal immunity from prosecution such as foreign diplomats, and various other categories (Fattah, 1980).

2.   Implications for Criminology and Criminological Theories

The primary purpose of this chapter is to show that crime and deviance are not confined to the lower strata of society, that the criminals and delinquents who have been the central focus of criminology for over a century are not necessarily the most serious, most dangerous or most vicious. It was meant to present a more balanced picture by highlighting the deaths, the injuries, the harm, the depredations that result from non conventional types of crime. Several conclusions can be drawn from examining crimes by governments, crimes of the powerful, powerful criminals and criminals in power and contrasting this criminality with ordinary conventional criminality. First, it could easily be seen that a much better understanding of these crimes and why they occur could be achieved not by searching for their causes but by analyzing the motives behind them. As Barnes and Teeters (1959:49) point out, 'white-collar crime flows from a competitive economy and a philosophy that reveres success based almost exclusively on money and material consumption.' Secondly, an examination of these types of unconventional crimes reveals the inherent weaknesses of criminological theories that are based on notions of pathology or abnormality. According to Newman (1977:55) 'research on upper-strata criminality has to be viewed as a challenge to those particularistic theories which explain crime in terms of personal inadequacies or essentially lower-class characteristics, such as poverty or poor home life.' This echos Geis and Meier's (1977:19–20) opinion:

> White-collar crime challenges the more banal kinds of explanations of criminal activity. To say that poverty 'causes' crime, for instance, fails utterly to account for widespread lawbreaking by persons who are extraordinarily affluent.

And is very similar to the view expressed by Quinney (1977:283):

> Most important to the field of criminology, use of the concept of white-collar crime has led to the reexamination of the grounds on which generalizations about crime and criminals are made.

NOTES

1. On 2 January 1984, Reuter reported that Indonesia's shadowy death squads were continuing their liquidation of known criminals. A Jakarta lawyer claimed that these so called 'mystery killings' may have claimed about 4000 victims. The same report quotes the founder of the Indonesian legal aid institute who claimed that the campaign is a joint military–police operation. The bodies of the victims are usually found bullet-riddled and bearing tattoos which are the mark of underworld gangs.
2. In a magazine interview published in *La Semana* (The Week) a former Argentine navy petty officer admitted that he helped kidnap 200 political detainees and witnessed their torture. The detainees had their heads placed under water and received electric shocks. Some were thrown alive out of aircraft into the River Plate after being drugged. The officer was part of a paramilitary group based in the Navy Mechanics School in Buenos Aires, a notorious secret prison and torture centre in the late 1970s.
3. *Vancouver Sun*, 21 September 1983.
4. Peter Brain, a British author of a book on Soviet psychiatric practices, told the US Congrssional subcommittee that he had documented cases of 500 Soviet individuals against whom politically motivated use of psychiatry was used.
5. *Vancouver Sun*, 17 January 1984.

4 The Formidable Challenge of Measuring Crime

The state of statistics and information on the nature of crime and the administration of justice in Canada is simply deplorable. There is a clear agreement on this situation even by those charged with the collection and dissemination of data... . The public, legislators, administrators and judges are largely at the mercy of hunches in assessing the total picture of crime, and are forced to rely on their personal or work experience.... Even where data are available they are not published in a form or with sufficient speed to check assumptions, mitigate exaggerations, or even more important, indicate pressure points and identify reasons for crises.

Law Reform Commission of Canada (1976:52)
Dispositions and Sentences in the Criminal Process

How Much Crime?

The general public is generally under the impression that crime can be easily and reliably counted in much the same way that inches of rainfall or snow, hours of sunshine, traffic or labour accidents, are counted. And although people may occasionally exhibit some scepticism regarding crime figures or crime rates they are usually unaware of how difficult it is to measure the real incidence of crime and have little or no knowledge of the wide gap that separates official crime statistics from true crime figures.

Obviously, it is utterly impossible to know the actual number of criminal offences and law violations committed by all members of a given community in a determined geographical area during a specific period of time. Many crimes are never detected, others are detected but not reported, and some of those detected and reported are not formally recorded. The impossibility of knowing how much crime there is often leads to estimates which, for rather obvious reasons, cannot be trusted. No one has yet found a way of accurately estimating the incidence of incest or sexual molestation of children, the number of violations of speed limits, drug offences, or illegal abortions that take place in any given year.

Official or Recorded Criminality

Crime statistics are not measures of real criminality but of official criminality. 'Official' criminality refers to the total number of criminal offences and law violations reported or known to the official agencies of social control and recorded by those agencies during a given time period. These figures are usually published in various government documents and in certain catalogues commonly called 'criminal statistics'. These catalogues contain data gathered at various stages of the criminal justice process: police, courts, penal institutions, parole, and so forth. The volume of recorded criminality is obviously smaller than that of actual criminality. The size of the gap between the former and the latter varies widely from one community to the other and from one offence to the other, depending on a host of variables affecting the rates of detection, reporting, and recording. Not only does the gap between official and real criminality vary according to offence and locality, but it also may increase or decrease from year to year. Actually, there is no reason to assume that the proportion of registered criminality to that of actual criminality remains constant. As Sellin (1951) points out

> ... recorded criminality is only a *sample* of the total criminality, the latter being an unknown quantity. The early statisticians always assumed that the sample maintained a constant ratio to the total criminality, no matter what offence or time period was involved, and drew their conclusions on that assumption. The modern criminologist realizes that this was an error.

The Dark Figure

The dark figure is a common criminological term used to refer to the difference between real and recorded criminality. The dark figure of crime totals the amount of hidden criminality, in other words, all offences committed but which for one reason or another remain undetected or unreported, and unrecorded.

SOURCES OF DATA ON CRIME

1   Criminal Statistics

Many crimes are not reported to the police, and some that are reported go unrecorded. Police statistics are thus an unreliable guide to the extent of crime. They can also be misleading about trends, as readiness to report crimes to the police varies over time.

> Pat Mayhew *et al.* (1993:vii)
> *The 1992 British Crime Survey*

It is uncontestable that UCR rates for most crimes are not an accurate indication of the absolute amount of crime.

> Robert M. O'Brien (1985:34)
> *Crime and Victimization Data*

Three decades ago, official statistics constituted the main source of quantitative data on crime. These official statistics suffer from several shortcomings, some of which are caused by problems inherent in the methods used to collect, compile, and process them. The quality, and consequently the usefulness, of these official statistics are further lessened by the existence of the dark figure. To solve, at least partially, the problem of the dark figure and to obtain better and more extensive information than is provided by official statistics on the real volume of crime, criminologists looked at possible alternative sources of quantitative data. Two additional sources, namely *victimization surveys* and *self-reported delinquency studies* were explored. Data obtained from these sources can be contrasted with the official statistics, and together they could provide a more realistic picture of the crime situation.

Some Limitations of Official Statistics on Crime and Offenders

As mentioned above, official criminal statistics suffer from several shortcomings and limitations. What follows is a brief summary of some of these limitations:

1. Crime statistics are limited to offences detected, reported, and recorded. Court and correctional statistics are even less extensive. Data included in judicial statistics report only those who have been charged and brought before the courts while institutional statistics are restricted to offenders who receive a custodial sentence. For these reasons, court and correctional statistics are of limited value in general crime trend studies since they only describe a small sample of the universe of offenders or offences. Police statistics, despite their deficiencies, are closer to the real numbers of crimes than court or correctional statistics are.

2. Official statistics on crime and criminals are highly dependent on the diligence and accuracy of the different organs of the criminal justice system. Their quality is subject to the limitations and biases of such organs.

3. Official criminal statistics are subject to several artificial fluctuations and may show upward and downward trends without any actual changes in the offences concerned (see below).

4. Owing to wide regional variations in police practices, in the collection, compilation, and recording of data and because of differences in legal definitions and interpretations of the law, official criminal statistics are not a suitable basis for national and international comparisons. Changes in practices over time also limit the value of official statistics for trend studies, especially those extending over a long time period.

5. Since official criminal statistics use legal rather than criminological classifications of offences, they are, at least in their crude form, of

limited use to the social scientists unless they are able to group or reclassify them according to criminological criteria into more or less homogeneous categories.

Use and Misuse of Criminal Statistics

To maintain that criminal statistics are an essential and valuable legislative, administrative, and scientific tool is not to say that their use is free of dangers and pitfalls. They are a delicate and subtle instrument that has to be used with the utmost care and in full knowledge of its limitations and short-comings and of the factors that are likely to produce upward and downward fluctuations.

Criminal statistics, as Hood and Sparks (1970) once noted, are notoriously easy to misinterpret. We often hear from members of the general public that statistics can be made to say whatever one may want them to say. Scepticism regarding statistics in general, and criminal statistics in particular, is rein-forced by frequent misuse of these statistics. For instance, when they are used in support of demands for money and manpower for the police, higher *figures* may be cited regardless of whether the *rate* itself has increased or declined and without mentioning that the upward figures may be the result of increased police activity or improved reporting and recording practices. On the other hand, when criminal statistics are used to demonstrate major political or social achievements or to bolster a higher level of police effect-iveness, the emphasis is placed on decline rather than on growth. For example, during the Nixon years, the FBI tried to amplify the growth in crime while the politicians tried to play it down by emphasizing 'the decreas-ing rate of increase.'

Deliberate Manipulations of Crime Statistics

Despite their limitations and shortcomings, official crime statistics, particu-larly police statistics, continue to be used extensively for policy purposes and for budget and resource allocation. They are frequently used to measure the effectiveness of law enforcement agencies and of police action and to evalu-ate crime control programs and crime prevention measures. Since the alloca-tion of funds is often contingent upon these measurements and evaluations, there is a strong temptation (and sometimes pressure) to manipulate the statistics to influence the outcomes. As Seidman and Couzens (1974:484) point out:

> Each of these uses of crime statistics creates pressures to have the statistics show certain things. Sometimes the pressure is to show that crime is being reduced. Sometimes the pressure is to increase the number of crimes. These pressures impinge upon the data generating system, the police depart-ments, and in some cases affect the statistics, entirely apart from the effects

of the number of crimes which are actually committed. Consequently, those indicators almost invariably used for these purposes – the Index crimes of the Uniform Crime Reporting System – are highly misleading for what they are said to measure, in part simply because they are used as measures.

Artificial Fluctuations in Crime Statistics
Increases or decreases in crime *figures* or crime *rates* or both, which regularly appear in crime statistics, do not necessarily reflect an actual change in the incidence of crime. Quite often, such fluctuations are caused by one or several factors known to influence the levels of detection, reporting, or recording of criminal offences. *Statistics Canada* usually caution the user of criminal statistics against the flaws and imperfections in the data. They also advise the reader that changes over the years have been geared toward increasing efficiency, toward more complete recording, and toward universal coverage. Because of these factors, it is usually difficult to say when the statistics show a rise in the general crime rate or in the rate of a particular offence whether the increase is real or merely due to the improvements in data gathering and data processing. Similarly, when statistics show a downward trend, it may be caused by lower reporting or to a relaxation in the enforcement of the law(s) pertaining to that offence. Such declines are most common when the offence in question is one of those commonly detected not through a victim's complaint but as a result of police observation and intervention.

Factors Leading to Fluctuations in Crime Figures
Several factors are known to produce artificial fluctuations in crime figures. Some have to do with the collection and processing of data. Others pertain to the process of law enforcement, while a third category comprises factors related to the demographics and attitudes of the population.

Structural Differences and Structural Changes
Variations in crime rates, whether between regions, provinces, cities, or municipalities, may partially result from differences in reporting and recording practices or in the methods of collecting and processing crime data.

Hahn (1977) reports that when the New York Police instituted revised procedures for reporting and storing information, the number of robbery occurrences reported rose over 150 per cent in one year, while clearance rates fell by more than 50 per cent. Hood and Sparks (1970:38) report from England that a change in the method of recording crimes of violence in 1949 combined with a tightening up of recording procedures led to a purely statistical (that is, paper) increase of 13 per cent in recorded crimes between 1949 and 1960.

Silverman (1980) was intrigued by the differences in crime rates in two otherwise comparable Canadian cities: Calgary and Edmonton. He set out to examine the coding and information processing by the two police departments. It became clear that the police in the two cities process information differently, which, in turn, affects crime statistics. Silverman explains:

> The nature of policing practices affects crime rates. In this case the reporting or recording of crime reflects different styles of policing in the two cities. Calgary's police officers have more discretion to settle disputes on the streets than do Edmonton's police officers. This discretion clearly affects the recording of crime and, as a result, affects the gross criminal statistics generated in the two cities. (p. 273)

Changes in the Size of the Dark Figure
The dark figure of many criminal offences is neither constant nor stable, and it may undergo a considerable change in a relatively short period of time. A large number of variables (see below) pertaining to the police, the victims, and the public at large are usually responsible for the fluctuations in the dark figure of a given offence. Rape (or aggravated sexual assault[1]) is a good case in point. There are reasons to believe that the dark figure of rape in Canada, and in several other countries, has been shrinking in recent years. This change is a result of growing willingness of victims to report, the creation of several rape crisis centres, a more enlightened attitude towards those who are victimized, and an improved treatment of the complainants at the hands of the criminal justice system.

Changes in the Number of Reporting Units
Crime statistics (Police) are a collection of criminal offences reported to *Statistics Canada* by various police forces: municipal, provincial, national, specialized, etc. Judicial statistics on crime are in the main a collection of data reported by different courts across the country. The failure of certain police forces or certain courts to report is likely to produce a decline in the figures while an increase in the number of reporting units (police or courts) is likely to cause the figures to rise. *Statistics Canada* conducts a continuing program to reduce the number of non-reporting units, and this program is no doubt responsible for at least some of the increases that have been reported in crime statistics in the 1960s and early 1970s.

Changes in the Size of Police Forces
Substantial increases in police manpower are likely to raise official crime figures considerably. When, for example, the number of officers on the drug squad or vice squad in a certain city is doubled, the number of known drug, gambling, and prostitution offences can go up substantially. The dramatic

increase in drug offences reported by *Statistics Canada* in the 1970s can be directly traced to the vast growth in the number of law enforcement officers assigned to this type of activity. Even the figures of offences usually reported by the victim or another member of the public are likely to go up as a result of the increase in police manpower since increased police visibility and police presence usually lead to more reporting.

Changes in Police Efficiency and Effectiveness
It may seem paradoxical that official crime rates go up with improved police efficiency, but this is usually the result of better detection and a higher level of reporting by the victims and the public at large. One major reason why many victims do not report the offence to the police is their scepticism about the ability of the police to arrest the culprit or to recover the stolen goods. A more efficient police force is likely to raise the level of confidence in the community it serves and to receive a larger number of reports and complaints.

Changes in Levels of Tolerance of the Police and the Public
Not every offence detected or reported to the police is officially recorded and processed. The police exercise a great deal of discretion in the execution of their daily duties (see Silverman's study, 1980, cited above). A high level of tolerance on the part of the police leads to low rates of many minor offences and, in particular, of those offences where detection is largely dependent upon police initiative (drugs, gambling, prostitution, and so forth). A high level of tolerance to marijuana offences or to public drunkenness is likely to result in the recording of only a few cases of such incidents, while a low level of public tolerance is likely to lead to the opposite result. As a result of a lower level of tolerance to family violence, more incidents of domestic violence are being reported and recorded than used to be the case before.

Changes in Levels of Enforcement
The level of enforcement of many laws does not remain constant. For one reason or another, the police might decide to relax enforcement of certain laws, or they might crack down on certain offences and offenders. These changes in the level of enforcement lead to strong fluctuations in crime statistics even though the actual incidence of these offences might not have changed. Changes in municipal administrators following municipal elections often lead to great shifts in the enforcement of certain laws. An administration elected on a promise of 'cleaning up' the city may require the police to accelerate the enforcement of the laws governing prostitution, gambling, or drugs. During a given year, police may decide to crack down on drink driving or on teenage drinking, and a much higher number of such offences subsequently appears in official statistics. Comparisons between cities

regarding these offences and similar ones may reflect differences in law enforcement rather than real differences in the frequency with which these particular offences are committed.

Changes in Definitions of Crime by the Police

Police enjoy considerable latitude in deciding whether or not to define any particular act as a crime. Changes in such definitions over time, in response to changes in police views or in public attitudes, result in upward and downward fluctuations in crime statistics. In England, McCabe and Sutcliffe (1978) found evidence, notably in the area of domestic violence and offences by those who are thought to be mentally ill, that incidents brought to the notice of the police in the belief that there was in them some criminal ingredient are redefined in a way that avoids police action or even police record. In Canada, Clark and Lewis (1977) claim that a significant number of complaints about rape in Toronto were dismissed by the police as unfounded. This is a classical example of police discretion in defining an incident as not being a crime.

Changes in Population Size

Crime figures are usually meaningless unless they are linked to population size, environmental opportunities, or both. Comparisons between regions, provinces, cities, or municipalities can be particularly misleading if they are based on absolute figures that do not take into account the differences in population size, population age, or environmental opportunities. For this reason, rates based on total population are usually computed before comparisons are made. Because of changes in population size over the years, crime figures may show certain fluctuations even if the rates have not experienced any or only a slight change.

Rates would be more meaningful if they were calculated on the basis of the population at risk rather than the total population. The statistical picture of rape would be more revealing if the rates were calculated on the basis of potential victims – the female population – rather than the total population as is usually the case. Relating crime rates to environmental opportunities is particularly useful for geographical comparisons and for the study of temporal and spatial trends. Unfortunately, very few rates are calculated on this basis. One exception is motor vehicle theft, the rate of which is calculated by *Statistics Canada* both on the basis of total population and on the number of registered vehicles. The latter rate provides a much better data set for statistical comparisons both in time and space.

Changes in Public Attitudes Towards Crime and the Police

Most criminal offences are brought to the attention of the police either by the victim or by the public. McCabe and Sutcliffe (1978:4) found that about

70 per cent of all recorded crime is reported by the victim or another member of the public while 30 per cent or less is the result of police observation or intervention. In view of these facts, changes in the degree of reporting can usually be traced to changes in public attitudes towards certain offences, to upward or downward shifts in public tolerance, to changes in the degree of public confidence in the police, in police–community relations, and so forth. Several examples show that fluctuations in the degree of social toleration of crime do result in increased or decreased reportability. One such example comes from Denmark. The liberalization of sexual attitudes and the legalization of pornography were followed by a sharp drop in sexual offences (see Kutschinsky, 1970, 1973). While several factors may have been responsible for such significant decrease, there is no doubt that the level of tolerance vis-à-vis minor sex offences was raised, which led to reduced reportability.

2 Victimization Surveys

Crime surveys are also prone to various forms of error, mainly to do with the difficulty of ensuring that samples are representative, the frailty of respondents' memories, their reticence to talk about their experiences as victims, and their failure to realise an incident is relevant to the survey.

Mayhew *et al.* (1993:vii)
The 1992 British Crime Survey

The introduction of victimization surveys is without doubt one of the most exciting developments in criminology in the past 30 years. When carefully conducted, victimization surveys are apt to yield data on crime that are superior in some respects to official statistics. A comparison of data obtained by means of victimization surveys with official figures allows an approximate estimate of the size of the dark figure for the offences covered by the survey.

History of Victimization Surveys

Victimization surveys, which have become a major source of data in criminology, owe their existence to an article published in *Excerpta Criminologica* three decades ago. In that article on 'The Criminological Significance of Unregistered Criminality', Finnish criminologist Inkeri Anttila (1964) explained how it would be possible by means of surveys to establish how many individuals have been victimized and how many have reported their victimization to the police. It was this original idea that led Biderman and Reiss to suggest to the US President's Commission a pilot survey designed according to Professor Anttila's conception. This survey was the beginning of what has become a standard measurement tool in criminology.

The first large-scale victimization survey was carried out in the United States in 1965 for the *President's Commission on Law Enforcement and Administration of Justice*. The survey, usually referred to with the abbreviation NORC (*National Opinion Research Center*) used a national sample of 10 000 American households. The findings of this first survey were, to say the least, startling since the volume of unreported crime revealed by the survey was far beyond expectations and previous estimates. The survey revealed that rates of victimization exceeded those officially reported by 50 per cent for robberies, by 100 per cent for aggravated assault and by nearly 300 per cent for forcible rapes. There were also twice as many larcenies and three times as many burglaries as shown in the FBI's Uniform Crime Reports. Although subsequent American surveys used improved methodology and better and larger samples, their findings were not substantially different from those reported in the NORC study.

Following the NORC study of 1965, researchers in some other countries conducted similar, though sometimes more limited, victimization surveys. Among those are the ones conducted in Scandinavia (Aromaa, 1974, 1984; Hauge and Wolf, 1974; Reino, 1980), in England (Sparks, Genn, and Dodd, 1977; Home Office, 1983; Mayhew *et al.*, 1993), in Holland (Fiselier, 1978; Van Dijk and Steinmetz, 1984), in Switzerland (Clinard, 1978; Killias, 1989), in France (Levy, Diaz, Robert and Zauberman, 1986) and in Australia (Braithwaite and Biles, 1980, 1984). All these surveys revealed high percentages of unreported and unrecorded victimizations. The degree of non-reporting and non-recording varied, needless to say, according to the nature and seriousness of the offence.

In Britain, the British Crime Survey has become a major source of data and information about crime. The BCS has been carried out in England and Wales in 1982, 1984, 1988, 1992 and 1996 with each survey measuring crime in the previous year. In each sweep a representative sample of over 10 000 people aged 16 and over were interviewed (see Mayhew *et al.*, 1993; Hough, 1995).

In Canada, victimization surveys have not been conducted on the same regular basis as in the United States. In 1973, Waller and Okihiro conducted a small survey in Toronto that dealt only with the offence of burglary. They published their findings in 1978. In British Columbia, a victimization survey using a mail questionnaire was carried out by sociologist Daniel Koenig (1974, 1977). In collaboration with *Statistics Canada*, the Ministry of the Solicitor General conducted two pilot surveys, one in Edmonton (1977) and the other in Vancouver (1979). Only parts of the findings of the latter survey have been published (Corrado *et al.*, 1980). The first extensive Canadian survey was carried out early in 1982 by the Ministry of the Solicitor General, again with the assistance of *Statistics Canada*. The survey was conducted in seven major urban centres: Greater Vancouver, Edmonton, Winnipeg, Toronto, Montreal, Halifax-Dartmouth, and St. John's. Findings of this survey are published in ten issues of the *Canadian Urban Victimization Survey Bulletin*.

Two national victimization surveys have been conducted by *Statistics Canada*. Findings of the first survey (conducted in 1988) were published in 1990 in the General Social Survey Analysis Series (catalogue 11–612E). Highlights of the second national survey (conducted in 1993) appeared in *Juristat* (Vol. 14, No. 13, June 1994).

Problems of Victimization Surveys
Although victimization surveys can provide a wealth of information unavailable through official crime statistics, they are not without their problems. The following are some of the major problems of victimization surveys, particularly national ones.

The Sample
Unless the sample used in the survey is representative of the total population, no reliable estimates or generalizations could be based on the results. Experience shows that it is difficult to get a truly representative sample, and victimization surveys in the United States, particularly the early ones, suffered from overrepresentation of certain groups and underrepresentation of others. For example, many surveys limit participation to household members 18 years and over. They exclude businesses as well as citizens under 18 years of age. Because interviews are usually conducted at home during the day, there is always the danger that homemakers and pensioners will be overrepresented in the total of those actually interviewed. And since serious criminal victimizations of the kind usually covered by victimization surveys are relatively rare, it is necessary to use a large sample so that reliable estimates could be extrapolated from the findings.

The Attrition in the Sample
Even when a good, representative sample is constructed, it is practically impossible to reach and to interview all members of the sample. If members are designated in person, there are always some who have moved and cannot be traced. If the sample is constructed on the basis of residences rather than persons, there are always those found vacant, demolished, or temporarily closed. Furthermore, there are members of the sample who refuse to cooperate, to be interviewed, to answer all or some of the questions asked, and so forth. There are also those who do not take the survey seriously enough and who do not make any serious effort to provide accurate information or to answer the questions correctly.

The Costs
The costs of victimization surveys, especially national ones, can be prohibitive. The costs stem largely from the need for a large sample and because the technique most frequently used to collect the data is the personal or

telephone interview, an expensive method. For the sake of economy, it is possible to reduce the sample size, but such a reduction is likely to compromise, sometimes quite seriously, the representativeness of the sample and consequently the reliability of estimates based on the findings.

Faced with the high costs of personal interviews, researchers have used one of two alternatives: the mail questionnaire and the telephone interview. The advantages and disadvantages of the mail questionnaire are well described by Garofalo (1977:23). It minimizes expenses, makes it possible to reach more people than through personal visits (the problem of finding anyone at home being eliminated), affords more privacy to the respondents, and gives them more time to think about replies to the questions. In addition, it ensures that the presentation of the questions is uniform from respondent to respondent, that is, there is no bias introduced through variability in interviewer performance. The major disadvantages of the mail questionnaire are also outlined by Garofalo (1977:24). Response rates are generally low and the instrument must be shorter and less complex than for interviews since there is no interviewer to clear up misunderstandings and to probe for answers. Add to that the total lack of control over the quality of data, the questions left unanswered, inaccurate and incorrect replies resulting from lack of comprehension, misunderstanding, or misinterpretation of the questions, and so forth.

Canadian surveys were conducted by telephone using the technique known as *random digit dialling* (RDD), that is using a sample of telephone numbers generated completely at random (see Tuchfarber and Klecka, 1976).

There are three major difficulties associated with the use of telephone interviewing in victimization surveys.

1. Telephone interviewing excludes those who do not have a telephone. Since there is a strong correlation between income, social class, and having a telephone at home, any sample so constructed is likely to be seriously biased through an underrepresentation of the poor, the homeless and the members of the lower income classes. Moreover, this technique can hardly be used in countries where telephones are not as widespread as they are in the United States, Canada or Switzerland.

2. A sample constructed on the basis of telephone book listings automatically excludes those who have a telephone but whose number is, for some reason, unlisted. Unlisted numbers include confidential ones and those of new telephones installed after the printing of the telephone guide. While random digit dialling does avoid such bias in the construction of the sample; it is reasonable to expect that individuals maintaining a confidential, unlisted number will not be very cooperative when called by an unknown interviewer dialling at random.

3. Contrary to person-to-person interviews, telephone interviewing does not allow a lengthy, in-depth interrogation of the subject. Telephone interviewing has to be brief and superficial. The quality, the truthfulness, and the accuracy of information communicated on the telephone are more difficult to control than those in a personal interview. By contrast, telephone surveying allows a better control of the quality of the interview since it makes it possible to observe, supervise, and evaluate the interviewers themselves. It is also probable that more detailed and more personal information may be obtained over the telephone than in a personal interview because the situation is less threatening both for the interviewer and the interviewee. This is the case, for example, of hostile homes in which the interviewer may feel grossly uncomfortable. (Garofalo, 1977:23) It is also true of embarrassing information such as that on sexual victimization or family violence.

In an attempt to improve the quality of telephone interviewing researchers are now using a new technique called CATI or 'Computer Assisted Telephone Interviewing'. This technique is described by Lynch (1993:167) as telephone interviewing in which the instrument is presented to the interviewer on a computer display. The computer is programmed to guide the interview in a manner determined by the skip pattern of the instrument and the responses of the respondent. The interviewer reads the question from the display to the respondent. When the respondent answers, the interviewer types the response (or codes it) into the computer. On the basis of that response, the computer displays the next screen containing a question to be asked of the respondent.

Quality of the Information
Since victimization data are collected either by a mail questionnaire or in a personal/telephone interview, they are subject to all the limitations and shortcomings of these two methods. The accuracy of the information depends naturally and before everything else on the sincerity of the subjects, their goodwill, and their ability to understand the questions and to provide the required answers. Even when all these conditions are met, the respondent may not want, for one reason or another, to divulge incidents in which he or she was a victim or may report the incident without wanting to provide any details about it. It is also conceivable that some respondents might be tempted, for various reasons, to either exaggerate the frequency, the extent, and the seriousness of their victimization or the reverse.

It can be reasonably expected that victimization types that usually have a high dark figure (such as intrafamily violence and sexual offences) will still be underreported in victimization surveys. Some techniques have been developed to check the information provided by respondents. One is *reverse record checking*. In reverse record checks, victims who appear in police files are sampled and subsequently interviewed. Under ideal conditions, such studies are conducted so that neither the victim nor the interviewer is aware that the respondent has been selected for study in this way (see Garofalo and Hindelang, 1977:12). This condition, as Garofalo and Hindelang point out, is very difficult to achieve in practice, and none of the three reverse record checks conducted by the Census Bureau in the USA attained the ideal. Reverse record checks revealed that a number of confirmed victims failed to report their victimization to the interviewer and suggested at least two reasons for the failure of victims to report these known victimizations. First, there was evidence of forgetting. Second, there was some indication that for face-to-face personal crimes, especially rape, victimizations committed by persons known to the victim were less likely to be mentioned to survey interviewers than were victimizations committed by strangers (see Garofalo and Hindelang, 1977:14).

Memory Gaps

Forgetfulness is not restricted to the elderly or the sick. It affects all categories of respondents, though to varying degrees. It is not surprising, therefore, that many members of the sample will have difficulty remembering events, particularly minor ones, that occurred sometime in the past. Even when the recall period is reduced to six months, it is conceivable that many incidents will not be mentioned in oral or written responses, not because of bad faith but simply because they were forgotten. The problem is even more serious when the subjects are being asked not about their own victimization experiences but about those of other members of the household.

Telescoping

Another source of bias mentioned by Garofalo and Hindelang (1977), is telescoping. Telescoping is a problem common to all victimization surveys regardless of the technique used. It refers to a memory mechanism by which respondents misplace victimizations in time (see Garofalo and Hindelang, 1977:14). Many victims, especially those who do not report their victimizations to the police, do not record the date or the time of the incident. When asked about it months or weeks later, they have to rely on their memory. Their recall is subject to distortions, and one of the most frequent errors is to misplace the victimization incident in time. A confusion about the exact date of the incident may result in some victimizations occurring outside the reference period being included and others taking place within the recall period being omitted.

Garofalo and Hindelang (1977:14) distinguish between *backward telescoping* and *forward telescoping*. The former is 'the reporting of a victimization incident as having taken place during the reference period when in fact it occurred after the period, during the days or weeks separating the end of the period from the actual interview.' The problem of backward telescoping can be partially overcome when interviews are conducted immediately or very soon after the end of the recall period. The latter, that is, forward telescoping, refers to 'victimizations that occurred prior to the beginning of the reference period being "telescoped" forward into that period'.

The Problem of Defining the Incident
Incidents reported to the police are subject to scrutiny at various levels to ascertain that they meet the definition of the offence as specified by the law. Yet, in victimization surveys, it is left to the respondent with the help of the interviewer to decide whether these elements are present or not. The problem is particularly acute when it comes to borderline cases or to incidents that are not clear-cut offences. Acts that may not qualify as crimes in a legal sense may be reported to the interviewer, while others that do qualify may not. In other words, the respondent's perception of what took place may be at variance with the legal point of view. Victimization survey data may, therefore, contain acts that are not crimes but are perceived as such by the respondents. The reverse also occurs, that is crimes are not reported in the interview because they are not perceived as such.

Limitations of Victimization Surveys
Although victimization surveys represent a distinct progress over traditional criminal statistics, they too have limitations:

1. They do not provide information on victimizations of which the victim is not aware. A money purse may disappear as a result of misplacement, loss, or theft. Young children who are victims of sexual offences may not understand the nature of the acts and may not be aware that they have been sexually victimized. As a result they may not tell their parents. And since in many cases the parents are themselves the abusers, incidents of physical and/or sexual abuse of children are not likely to be revealed or reported in victimization interviews.
2. Victimization surveys cannot be used to gather information on any kind of offence. High costs and memory problems require that the survey be limited to a small number of serious offences that can be easily remembered. Restricting the number of offences is also necessary if the interview is to be kept within reasonable time limits. It is unthinkable that national surveys be used to collect data on minor or petty offences. In addition, there are offences which by their very nature do not lend themselves to this type of inquiry. Among these are victimless crimes, white collar crime, organized crime, and so forth.
3. It is difficult, practically impossible, to include in the sample all categories of victims. As mentioned earlier, the first victimization survey,

the NORC study, did not include businesses in the sample, and interviewing was restricted to members of the household 18 years and over. Even at present, children under 12 years are usually excluded from the sample, and no information is obtained directly from them.

4. Like official statistics, data gathered by means of victimization surveys cannot be easily used for transcultural comparisons. Differences in sampling techniques, in the methods and instruments used to collect the data and variations in cultural and legal definitions of crimes make international or crosscultural comparisons fraught with dangers of error.

International Crime Surveys

A recent attempt was made to collect standardized victimization data from a number of countries (including Canada and the United States) using the same questionnaire in each country. The main purpose was to avoid the problems of comparing data collected by means of different instruments using different methodologies. Field data for this international crime survey were gathered in January 1989 and published in 1990 (Van Dijk, Mayhew, and Killias, 1990). The size of each nationally representative sample varied between 1000 and 2000, though most participating countries opted for the larger size sample; the Federal Republic of Germany even chose 5000 interviews.

Telephone interviewing was chosen because of its relatively modest costs, and it was decided to use the computer-assisted telephone interviewing method (CATI method), which allows for much tighter standardization of questionnaire administration. Respondents were asked about their victimization experience with nine types of crimes over the previous five years, though victimization in 1988 was highlighted to give up-to-date annual risks. The nine crimes covered were theft of motor vehicles (cars, motorcycles, and mopeds); theft from moter vehicles; vandalism to motor vehicles; burglary and attempted burglary; robbery and attempted robbery; other thefts of personal property; sexual assault (women only); and assault. Victims were then asked short questions about the nature and material consequences of crime; whether the police were involved (and if not, why not); and their satisfaction with the police response and any victim assistance given.

A second round of the International Crime Survey was carried out in 1992. Some of the countries that participated in the first survey such as Switzerland, Norway and Northern Ireland did not take part in the second one. But the survey included some countries from Eastern Europe which did not participate in the first one such as Poland and the former Czechoslovakia (see Del Frate *et al.*, 1993).

What do Victimization Surveys Really Measure?

As mentioned earlier (Chapter 2), victimization is a personal, subjective and relative experience. The feeling of being victimized does not always coincide with the legal definition of victimization. So what exactly are victimization surveys trying to measure? Despite the proliferation of these surveys in recent years, it is far from clear whether their objective is to measure those criminal victimizations that meet the criteria set by the criminal code, or whether they are meant to measure the subjective victimizations experienced by the respondents. These, needless to say, are two different realities. Or to put it bluntly, are the surveys designed to measure crime or victimization? The titles 'crime survey' and 'victimization survey' continue to be used interchangeably.

Rape is a good case in point because of the enormous gap that may exist between the legal definition and the subjective experience of the female. Also because the sexual act can be experienced in very different ways by different women.

To Report or Not to Report to the Police?

One of the most important reasons, perhaps the most important, for not reporting certain victimizations to the police is the trivial nature of the events in question. The 1992 British Crime Survey (Mayhew *et al.*, 1993) asked victims of incidents that went unreported why the police had not been involved. The reason most often given for non-reporting (55 per cent) was that the incident was too trivial or involved no loss – as, for example, in cases of low-value criminal damage or attempted offences. Other common reasons were that the police could do nothing (25 per cent of cases), that they would not be interested (13 per cent), or that the incident was not a matter for the police or better dealt with privately (12 per cent); 6 per cent of incidents had been reported to another authority. Rarely cited overall, was the inconvenience of reporting, dislike of the police, or fear of reprisals. These results are consistent with previous BCS findings, and they are closely in line with results from other surveys (see, for example, Skogan, 1984; Gottfredson and Gottfredson, 1988; van Dijk and Mayhew, 1993).

The reason for not reporting varied by offence. A higher than average proportion of personal thefts – often taking place at work – were not reported to the police because they were reported to someone else (20 per cent). In a higher proportion of assaults, respondents said that it was inappropriate to report the incident or that they had dealt with the matter themselves (40 per cent of unreported assaults) (Mayhew *et al.*, 1993:25).

Mayhew *et al.* (1993) point out that over the last three surveys there has been some increase in the proportion of incidents going unreported because of 'police-related' factors: principally, because it was felt the police could do nothing or that they would not be interested. The view that the police's hands were tied was cited more in 1992 than in earlier surveys by victims of burglaries and thefts; lack of interest on the part of the police was mentioned more often for most types of offences. The increase in 'police-related' reasons for not reporting, the authors note, does not suggest any improvement in attitudes among victims as to the ability or commitment of the police to deal with the relatively less serious incidents, which typically go unreported (Mayhew *et al.*, 1993:26).

If the primary reason for not reporting the victimization to the police is that the incident was too trivial, one may ask whether victims should be encouraged to report or not to report.

There seem to be no tangible benefits to having minor conflicts brought before the criminal justice system just because they happen to be defined as criminal offences. In the case of civil torts, people are encouraged to settle their claims outside the court system and to try to solve the matter privately or with the help of a mediator or an arbitrator. The ever-increasing civil litigation in countries such as the United States has been the source of major complaints. One has to wonder why it is that while attempts are made to curb and restrict civil litigation, everything is being done to promote criminal litigation. The firmly entrenched belief that criminal conflicts belong to the state, not to the parties involved, creates this seemingly insatiable desire to have them dealt with by the state's official agencies. This desire has gone so far that in many criminal codes (such as those of Canada and of Cyprus) it is a crime to compound a criminal offence, that, is to hide it from the authorities and deal with it privately (see Chapter 2). And yet, at a time when there is a renewed interest in mediation, in victim–offender reconciliation, in alternative mechanisms of dispute settlement and conflict resolution, it might be wise to encourage the offended parties in minor conflicts not to report.

At a time when legislation is being passed to give victims more say in the criminal justice process, there is a need to allow victims to use more discretion and to give them the final say about what should be done. After all, if those who suffer the harm, the injury, or loss judge it to be trivial or are able to settle the matter amiably without resorting to the criminal justice system or simply want to claim the insurance, why not let them do that? People use their discretion all the time. They do not rush to the hospital emergency room whenever they scratch their knee or hurt their finger. They do not run to the doctor everytime they suffer from a slight cold or a stomach upset. They use their discretion to decide when the problem is serious enough to require professional treatment. Efforts to reduce the use of the health system could be extended to the criminal justice system. Unfortunately, the trend in recent years has been in the opposite direction, towards a more extensive use of the justice system. This is so even though victimization surveys repeatedly show that the major reason for non-reporting is the victim's judgement that the offence is too trivial. In the 1970s and the 1980s, criminologists, worried about the size of the dark figure, were trying to devise ways and means to induce victims to report more victimizations to the police. State compensation to crime victims and victim assistance programs were promoted as vehicles to encourage more victims to go to the police (see Fattah, 1993a).

Reporting the incidents became a requirement for applying for compensation or benefiting from the service. And there are some reasons to believe that private insurance companies might be behind a part of the 'paper increase' in some property offences. In Canada, it is now standard practice for companies to require a police report of the victimization prior to processing any claim for damages. Victims who might otherwise have gone directly to their insurers to recoup their losses are now forced by this rule to report their victimization to the police. And private businesses that are run for profit are thus using an overburdened justice system to screen out fraudulent claims.

Since most criminal justice systems are working at overcapacity, an increase in case flow through the system can exacerbate the current problems of response and response time and cause delays in the handling of cases. It can result in shorter time being devoted to each case, more pressure on the correctional and prison systems, and so forth. Since no significant increases in resources can be foreseen in current economic conditions, shouldn't an effort be made to stop mobilizing the system for every petty offence or minor dispute? Preaching tolerance and raising its threshold is one of the best and surest ways of achieving this goal. The advantages lie not only in reducing crime rates and alleviating the system's workload, but also in enabling the police to devote more time and resources to serious types of victimization. They are similar to the advantages of decriminalization and depenalization that are strongly favoured by most criminologists.

Despite this, the suggestion that victims of minor victimizations should be encouraged not to report is always met with shock and disbelief. The naive and exaggerated faith in the efficacy of general deterrence leads people to reject offhand any measure that might weaken the threat of incurring punishment or might result in some offenders getting away with 'crime'. Nor does the shock wear off when they are presented with the empirical evidence indicating that the majority of victims do already deal with their victimization by other means without soliciting the help of the criminal justice system (see Hulsman, 1986).

A re-examination of the dominant view of the dark figure of crime might be in order. The conventional view is that the dark figure is, in every respect, a negative feature of crime, and thus everything should be done to bring it down. Actually, the dark figure might be a blessing in disguise, and the higher it is, the better things might be for the criminal justice system and for society. R.K. Merton (1957), for one, suggests that there is a functionally optimum degree of visibility of various social structures, a degree that never coincides with complete visibility. Merton believes that 'full visibility of conduct and unrestrained enforcement of the letter of normative standards

would convert a society into a jungle. It is this central idea which is contained
in the concept that some limits upon full visibility of behaviour are functionally required for the effective operation of a society' (p. 345).

Merton cites George Orwell and Aldous Huxley as literary figures who
were able to portray the horror of full observability of conduct. He also
quotes the Victorian novelist and essayist William Makepeace Thackeray
(1869) who was able to portray a horrendous society in which all deviations
from social norms were promptly detected and punished. In his essay 'On
Being Found Out', Thackeray writes:

> Just consider what life would be, if every rogue was found out, and
> flogged.... What a butchery, what an indecency, what an endless swishing
> of the rod.... Just picture to yourself everybody who does wrong being
> found out, and punished accordingly.... The butchery is too horrible.
> The hand drops powerless, appalled at the quantity of birch which it must
> cut and brandish. I am glad we are not all found out.... To fancy all men
> found out and punished is bad enough; but imagine all women found out
> in the distinguished social circle in which you and I have the honour to
> move. Is it not a mercy that a many of these fair criminals remain
> unpunished and undiscovered?...I say it is best, for the sake of the
> good, that the bad should not all be found out.... Ah me, what would
> life be if we were all found out, and punished for all our faults? (pp. 126–7)

Attrition in the Legal Process

One of the first and most important findings of victimization surveys was to
highlight the attrition in the legal process. The non-reporting of an offence
by the victim is only one step in a long process of attrition that takes place at
the various stages of the legal ladder from the commission of a crime to the
conviction of the offender. The first victimization survey in the United States
(NORC study) gave a vivid illustration of this attrition. Victims who reported an offence were asked how the police reacted and how far the case
proceeded up the judicial ladder: arrest, trial, sentencing, and so forth. Out
of an initial total of 2077 victimizations, only 120 reached the trial stage, and
slightly more than half of the latter (52 per cent) ended in a conviction
considered appropriate by the victim. The startling revelation of these figures
is that less than 5 per cent of all reported incidents ended up with a criminal
conviction.

The attrition in the legal process has serious implications for the system of
penal sanctions. First, the chances of incurring the punishment prescribed by
law for criminal offences are extremely low, while the chances of escaping
detection, arrest, and conviction are very high. Since certainty of punishment
is the most important factor in deterrence, the attrition in the legal process
means that in the present conditions punishment does not attain the min-

imum level of certainty necessary to achieve deterrence. Second, changes in the degree of severity of sanctions meted out by the courts to the small percentage of offenders who are convicted are not likely to have any significant impact on the incidence of offences they punish. If nine out of ten offenders are likely to escape conviction, dealing more harshly or more leniently with the few who are convicted is not likely to influence the frequency with which any particular offence is committed and is unlikely to increase or decrease its occurrence.

3 Hidden Delinquency Studies/Self-Report Studies

> Oh, I was like that when a lad!
> A shocking young scamp of a rover.
> I behaved like a regular cad;
> But that sort of thing is all over.
> I am now a respectable chap
> And shine with a virtue resplendent,
> And therefore I haven't a rap
> of sympathy for the defendant.
> > Gilbert and Sullivan
> > *Trial by Jury* Operetta

Hidden delinquency studies, or self-report studies as they are sometimes called, provide an additional source of data on crime and delinquency. Hidden delinquency studies and victimization surveys may be considered as two sides of the same coin. In victimization surveys, a sample of the population is requested to provide information on incidents of victimization and whether they have reported those incidents or not. In hidden delinquency studies, a sample of young people is asked whether they have committed delinquent or criminal acts, and if so, whether they were detected and arrested or not. Hidden delinquency studies have been carried out in the US, the UK, and the Scandinavian countries as well as in Canada. One of the earliest studies is the one done by Wallerstein and Wyle (1947), who sent a mail questionnaire to 1800 men and women in New York State, asking them to tick any of 49 criminal law violations that they had committed. Most hidden delinquency studies use samples of relatively young people. In Stockholm, Elmhorn (1965) used school children as his subjects, while in Norway and Finland, entrants to the armed forces were used (Anttila and Jaakkola, 1966; Christie, Andenaes and Skirbekk, 1965). In England, Belson, *et al.* (1970) used a sample of 1400 London boys aged 13 to 16. Among the Canadian studies, the ones by Edmund Vaz in a small town in Ontario and those by Marc Leblanc and his team in Montreal are worth mentioning (Vaz, 1965, 1966, 1967; Leblanc, 1975a, 1975b, 1977).

Although hidden delinquency studies have not been conducted on the same scale as victimization surveys, they have yielded some important findings, and have made a significant contribution to criminology. For one thing, they shattered some of the erroneous beliefs firmly and widely held about the frequency and distribution of delinquency, and, for another, they indirectly helped the development of the labelling perspective (see below).

Problems of Hidden-Delinquency Studies

Hidden delinquency studies face problems similar to those of victimization surveys, and they suffer from most of the same limitations. Problems of sampling and lack of co-operation are common. Concerns about the truthfulness and accuracy of the information can be stronger in self-report studies because the respondents are usually asked to report their own illegal behaviour. Researchers have usually tried to minimize this problem through the use of anonymous questionnaires. Nevertheless, many respondents may still be reluctant to reveal violations of the law or illegal activities in which they were involved. Others may feel tempted to exaggerate the frequency and/or seriousness of delinquent acts they have committed. Memory decay is as much of a problem in self-report delinquency studies as it is in victimization surveys.

General Findings of Self-Report Studies

Despite the geographical and cultural differences between the countries in which hidden delinquency studies have been conducted, the studies have yielded some common information:

1. Delinquency is by no means exclusive to the lower classes of society as previously thought. It cuts across class boundaries and is more related to age than to social class.
2. The great majority of people have, at one time or another, perpetrated acts that qualify as criminal offences (some of which are rather serious) according to existing laws.
3. Only a tiny minority of those who violate the law are detected, arrested, charged, and convicted. Therefore, 'the criminal justice system expends most of its resources on a relatively small group of offenders whose offences are not necessarily the most serious or the most widespread.' (Doleschal, 1970; Doleshal and Klapmuts, 1973.)
4. Most young people who commit delinquent acts and are not formally processed through the official agencies of the criminal justice system grow up to become 'law abiding citizens' and lead a 'normal' life, free from crime.

To summarize, it can be said that self-report studies have demonstrated that delinquency in one form or another, is a 'normal', 'developmental', and 'transitory' phase in the life of most male teenagers (Doleschal, 1970).

Theoretical Implications of Self-Report Studies

Although the findings of self-report studies have not had a major impact on the criminal justice system and have not significantly changed the practices, operations, and procedures of the system, they do have far-reaching theoretical implications.

1. They showed that studies based on, and limited to, convicted criminals are unproductive and futile in the search for the causes of crime and delinquency. Studies of 'official' criminals may, however, be useful in shedding some light on the process by which certain offenders are labelled by the official agents of society.

2. Findings of self-report studies lead us to believe that there can be no basic biological or psychological differences between those officially labelled as criminals or delinquents and those who are not labelled as such. The labelling process may, however, be biased along ethnic, cultural or class lines.

3. Findings of self-report studies led to a reformulation of some of the basic questions that had preoccupied criminologists since the birth of modern criminology. For decades, criminologists have asked, and tried to find answers to one burning question: why do some people commit crimes while others do not? As a result of the revelations of self-report studies, this classical question has been replaced by three more relevant ones.

(a) Why do certain individuals commit offences that are far more *serious* than those committed by others. For example, why do some people perpetrate a serious property offence, such as robbery, while others may not go beyond petty larcenies or shoplifting; or why do certain husbands kill their wives while others never go beyond verbal or physical assault?

(b) Why do certain individuals *persist* in their delinquent activities while others do not? What are the effects of official labelling on the continuation of delinquency?

(c) Why are some law violators officially *labelled* as delinquents or criminals while others are not? What are the factors that lead to or favour official labelling?

Findings of self-report studies led many criminologists to reformulate their definition of the criminal from 'a person who has committed a crime' to 'a person who has been labelled as such.' According to the definition, a criminal is anyone who has been convicted of a crime, whether or not he has actually committed it (Doleschal and Klapmuts, 1973: 621–2).[2]

The findings of self-report studies seem to have had a great deal of influence on the development of what is now known as the *labelling perspective* or the *labelling approach*, a perspective that draws on earlier writings of

George Mead, C. Wright Mills, Frank Tannenbaum, and others. This perspective views deviance 'not as a static entity but rather as a continuously shaped and reshaped *outcome* of dynamic processes of social interaction' (Schur, 1971:8).[3]

Combining Self-Report Delinquency and Victimization Questions in the Same Survey

Some victimization surveys, particularly in Britain (Sparks, Genn, and Dodd, 1977; Chambers and Tombs, 1984; Gottfredson, 1984; Mayhew and Elliott, 1990), included questions about the delinquency of the respondents. Combining victimization and delinquency questions yielded extremely interesting results. In their London, England, survey, Sparks, Genn, and Dodd (1977) found victims of violent crime to be significantly more likely than non-victims to self-report the commission of violent crimes. Gottfredson (1984) analyzed the 1982 British Crime Survey data and was struck by the relatively strong interrelationship between offending and victimization. For persons with at least one self-reported violence offence, the likelihood of victimization was 42 per cent, or seven times the likelihood of personal victimization for persons reporting no self-reported violent offences. The British Crime Survey Scotland (Chambers and Tombs, 1984), revealed that 40 per cent of respondents admitting an assault had themselves been the victim of an assault during the survey period. Only one per cent of those who did not admit an assault were themselves assault victims during that period.

NOTES

1. In a recent amendment to the Criminal Code of Canada, the traditional offence of rape was abolished. Forcible rape is now qualified as sexual assault or aggravated sexual assault (sections 246.1, 246.2 and 246.3).
2. As B. Kutchinsky (1971) puts it, 'What makes a person "criminal" is not the fact that he has committed a crime (because non-criminals have done that also) but the fact that he was caught, tried, convicted and punished.'
3. The essence of the *labelling approach* is that the criminal justice system labels certain individuals as criminals through a biased, selective, and discriminatory process. Those who are officially labelled are not so labelled because of bad luck or through mere chance; rather, they become labelled through systematic biases acting against society's underdogs: the poor, the powerless, the underprivileged, members of lower social classes, members of minority groups, and so forth. These systematic biases do not usually operate at a conscious level. Quite often, there is no deliberate attempt to discriminate against particular social classes. In many cases, formal action leading to official labelling is taken because other alternatives, which are easily available to the upper social classes, are not available to people

from the lower social strata. Labelling theorists insist that labelling an individual as a criminal, an alcoholic, or a drug addict does, in fact, aggravate the problem it is supposed to help solve. It leads through social stigmatization and self-identification to a continuation and possibly to an aggravation of deviance or of delinquent activities. Many criminologists (Lemert, 1951) believe that the explanation of 'secondary deviance' and the persistence of certain delinquent patterns can be found in the labelling process and the social stigma attached to, or resulting from, it.

PART II
Criminals and Victims, Criminology and Victimology

5 The Criminal: Conventional and Unconventional Views

The criminal produces an impression now moral, now tragic, and renders a 'service' by arousing the moral and aesthetic sentiments of the public...the criminal interrupts the monotony and security of bourgeois life...he protects it from stagnation and brings forth that restless tension, the mobility of spirit without which the stimulus of competition would itself be blunted...crime, by its ceaseless development of new means of attacking property calls into existence new measures of defence and its productive effects are...great...in stimulating the invention of machines.

Karl Marx, quoted in Steven Box (1971:28)
Deviance, Reality and Society

WHO IS THE CRIMINAL?

The term *criminal*, as currently used, has a strong pejorative connotation. It is a value-laden term, which conveys, more than most other terms used to designate those who violate the law, society's hatred, contempt, and disapproval. In recent years, there has been a tendency in criminological literature to replace the term 'criminal' with more neutral terms such as 'offender', 'perpetrator', 'law breaker', 'law violator', 'transgressor', and so forth.

As mentioned earlier, a definition of crime is essential to the definition of who is a criminal. Since there is no universal definition of crime, there is no agreed definition of a criminal. The traditional definition, which says that 'a criminal is someone who commits a crime', is clearly unsatisfactory not only because of the difficulty in defining what crime is, but also in view of what hidden delinquency studies have revealed, namely, that nearly everyone, has at one time or another committed some kind of criminal offence.

Needless to say, the question 'who is the criminal?' is of extreme importance both to theoretical and applied criminology. Tappan (1960:20) summarizes the need and the problems as follows:

It should be clear at the start that to understand and treat the criminal we require as sharp a delineation as possible of those who are criminals. This involves other and, in some respects, more difficult issues than defining crime itself. It is easy enough to describe the criminal, as the dictionaries do, as 'one who commits a crime, especially one who is discovered and convicted', but this leaves a host of problems to be resolved. In an abstract sense the criminal is one who has committed a crime, as defined . . . above, whether or not he is discovered, convicted, or treated as a criminal. It would be desirable to learn the distinguishing characteristics of a representative sample of criminals so defined, but it would be quite impossible to do so. Obviously this abstractly defined population differs to a significant extent from those violators who are discovered by the police, those who are convicted by the courts, and those who are treated through correctional measures.

Tappan (1960:21) goes on to note that while the general definition of the criminal (as one who violates the criminal law whether or not he is discovered or convicted) is conceptually accurate, its value for empirical research is seriously limited by the impossibility of securing a representative sample of such criminals. Tappan suggests that criminals who are convicted and sentenced are the most accurately selected sample of offenders that our procedures of policing and trial can provide among the total universe of individuals who are criminal.

Toward a More Rational Definition of the Criminal

If, in the light of what was said in the previous chapters, we accept that the term 'criminal' is nothing other than a label that society, through its official agents, sticks on certain individuals who break the law, then it is necessary to determine the type of individual who best fits this label. In doing so, we may be guided by other labels society frequently uses to designate other deviants and outcasts. In labelling certain deviants as alcoholics, drug addicts, gamblers, prostitutes, homosexuals, and so forth, a distinction is usually made between a person who drinks and an alcoholic, between a person who uses drugs and a drug addict, between someone who gambles and a gambler, a person who accepts a gift in exchange for sexual favours and a prostitute, a person who has had some sexual experience with a member of his/her own gender and a homosexual. In the same way, it seems only logical to distinguish between a person who steals and a thief, a person who commits a criminal offence and a criminal. Deviancy labels seem to be intimately related to the frequency of the deviant behaviour, its regularity, its persistency, and its centrality to the life of the deviant. This seems to indicate that for a person to be stereotyped as an alcoholic, drug addict, gambler, prostitute, or else, at least three criteria have to be present:

1. a reasonable frequency of the deviant behavioural pattern;
2. a reasonable regularity and persistency with which the person engages in the deviant behaviour; and,
3. the dominance of the deviant behavioural pattern in the life of the subject.

The three criteria are obviously interrelated. Regularity and persistency imply frequency, and dominance requires frequency, regularity, and persistency. If the three criteria are applied to criminal behaviour in an attempt to reach a definition of the person who fits the label 'criminal', we might say that 'The term criminal is a label that designates a deviant way of life characterized by frequent, regular, and persistent criminal law violations.'

As such, the label fits, though not exclusively, those who make crime their occupation and/or those whose major activities revolve around crime and/or whose major income is derived from criminal activities. Contrary to abstract and legal definitions, this one is operational and suitable for empirical research. It delineates a specific population that may be the subject of etiological, behavioural, and prophylactic studies. This definition purposely excludes those who once or occasionally commit (or have committed) one type or another of criminal offences. On the other hand, it does apply to the professional, whether he or she is a professional thief, swindler, forger, counterfeiter, burglar, safecracker, fence, or anything else.

The Myth of the Criminal Type

The criminal type is an artificial type, manufactured in prison by the prison system...the type is not one of the accidents of the system, but must be produced by imprisonment no matter how normal the victim is at the beginning, or how anxious the authorities are to keep him so. The simple truth is that the typical criminal is a normal man when he first enters a prison, and develops the type during his imprisonment.

George Bernard Shaw (1946:108)
The Crime of Imprisonment

In the second half of the 19th century, Lombroso (1876) claimed that criminals are 'not a variation from a norm but practically a special species, a subspecies, having distinct physical and medical characteristics' (see Wolfgang, 1965). Later studies comparing large groups of criminals with the general population or with control groups demonstrated that the so-called stigmata Lombroso thought were characteristic of the 'criminal type' were no more frequent among offenders than among others. One of the researchers, Charles Goring, wrote in his book *The English Convict* (1913:173):

We have exhaustively compared, with regard to many physical characters, different kinds of criminals with each other, and criminals, as a class, with the law-abiding public.... Our results nowhere confirm the evidence of a physical criminal type, nor justify the allegation of criminal anthropologists. They challenge their evidence at almost every point. In fact, both with regard to measurements and the presence of physical anomalies in criminals, our statistics present a startling conformity with similar statistics of the law-abiding class. Our inevitable conclusion must be that there is no such thing as a physical criminal type.

Despite some attempts to revive the Lombrosian theory under different labels (such as chromosomal aberrations), criminologists are almost unanimous at present that criminals do not exhibit any physical or anatomical characteristics that distinguish them from 'law-abiding' citizens.

The Stereotype of the Criminal

...there is indeed a criminal type – but he is not a biological, anatomical, phrenological, or anthropological type; rather, he is a social creation, etched by the dominant class and ethnic prejudices of a given society.

Jessica Mitford (1974:62)
Kind and Usual Punishment

While most criminologists agree that there is no such thing as a criminal type, there seems to be little doubt that there exists a stereotype of the criminal. This stereotype exists not only in the mind of the public at large but also in the mind of many social scientists. British sociologist Dennis Chapman (1968:239) warns social scientists against operating 'with a stereotype of the criminal rather than with a definition derived from an objective appraisal of the attributes of the variable with which the study is concerned.' Chapman insists that such a definition must be an operational definition, that is, one that directs the investigator in his identification of his data. Chapman goes so far as to accuse sociologists and criminologists of contributing to the creation and maintenance of the stereotype of crime and the criminal, a 'stereotype asserting that crime is a distinctive kind of behaviour and that criminals are created by special physical, psychic, social, or environmental factors'. Chapman (1968:244) adds:

Such theories are maintained and diffused by researches that are based on socially determined groups, generally chosen without controls, often by criteria which prejudge the issue.The literature of crime and delinquency quoted in earlier chapters abounds with examples of the way in which authors prejudge their subjects and treat them as a class of 'untermensch' in much the same way as nineteenth-century sociologists, economists, and politicians regarded the poor, or early anthropologists and missionaries considered 'primitive' peoples.

According to Chapman, the present system of justice and punishment has the effect of making a small number of persons, drawn mainly from the poor, the ill-educated, and the unskilled, into designated criminals.

The majority of the public rely only on secondary sources to form their opinions on crime and criminals. It is not surprising then that the general public holds a distorted image of the criminal. This portrait is largely based on a body of stereotyped misinformation, notorious cases sensationalized by the mass media, widely shared prejudices, and built-in biases. The public, Menninger (1966:183) points out, generally thinks of rapists 'as raging, oversexed, ruthless brutes', yet 'most sex crimes are committed by undersexed rather than oversexed individuals, often undersized rather than oversized, and impelled less by lust than by a need for reassurance regarding an impaired masculinity.'

The public generally thinks of killers as violent, tough, and sadistic monsters. Yet, most killings are committed within the family or the circle of friends and work associates by frustrated individuals suffering from a sense of helplessness, hopelessness, or both.[1]

There is a strong tendency to view those who are different as dangerous, as potential, even as actual criminals. Since white Americans have always associated crime with blacks, every black stranger is, therefore, viewed suspiciously as a would-be attacker. Earlier this century, the stereotyping and the suspicious attitude that goes with it were by no means confined to blacks but extended to other ethnic groups as well. Brown, quoted by Sarbin (1969:20), betrays the racist stereotyping that prevailed at the time. He writes:

> In the poorer quarters of our great cities may be found huddled together the Italian bandit and the bloodthirsty Spaniard, the bad man from Sicily, the Hungarian, Croatian and the Pole, the Chinaman and the Negro, the cockney Englishman, the Russian and the Jew, with all the centuries of hereditary hate back of them.

Another popular stereotype during the 1930s and 1940s was that of the 'dope-crazed killer' and the 'dope fiend rapist'. Lindesmith (1940) took it upon himself to challenge this mythology. He noted that opiate addicts rarely commit violent or sex crimes since opiates inhibit rather than stimulate the sex function. As a result, the overwhelming proportion of offences committed by drug users is made up of violations of the narcotic laws and petty offences against property perpetrated to maintain their habit. Deploring the fact that 'addiction is called a disease when applied to the wealthy and a vice when referring to the underworld addict', Lindesmith ends his article on the following note:

> The 'dope fiend' mythology serves, in short, as a rationalization of the status quo. It is a body of superstition, half-truths and misinformation

which bolsters up an indefensible repressive law, the victims of which are in no position to protest. The treatment of addicts in the United States today is on no higher plane than the persecution of witches of other ages, and like the latter it is to be hoped that it will soon become merely another dark chapter of history. (p. 208)

It is interesting to see that the same stereotype described half a century ago by Lindesmith has now been transposed to crack addicts!

Are Criminals Fundamentally Different from Others?

The False Dichotomy Between 'Criminals' and 'Non-Criminals'
Positivist criminology takes as its point of departure that criminals are fundamentally different from the rest of the population. Hence the primary goal of scientific inquiry is to identify those distinguishing characteristics that differentiate criminals from other law-abiding citizens. In Matza's words (1964:11–12):

Differentiation is the favored method of positive explanation. Each school of positive criminology has pursued its own theory of differentiation between conventional and criminal persons. Each in turn has regularly tended to exaggerate these differences. At its inception positive criminology revolted against the assumption of the general similarity between criminal and conventional persons implicit in classical theory. In rejecting the obviously untenable classical conception of similarity, positive criminology characteristically proceeded to the other extreme – radical differentiation – and in a variety of guises has persisted in this caricature.

Wilson and Herrnstein (1985:459), for example, explain that their book is chiefly concerned with the individual differences between criminals and non-criminals. Cornish and Clarke (1986) are critical of criminologists' repeated attempts to identify differences between criminal and non-criminal groups that could explain offending. Such attempts, they feel, 'have reinforced assumptions that offenders are similar to each other and different from everybody else.' The well established tendency of positivist criminology to 'overpathologize' offending and offenders and to focus on their supposedly abnormal personalities, deviant characters, or irrational modes of thinking discounts the fact that most criminal behaviour is of a mundane, opportunistic, and rational nature. It is neither irrational nor purposeless. Senseless crimes are the exception not the rule, and they are often committed by individuals suffering from some mental imbalance or disorder. But these individuals are only a very small minority of the offender population. The Japanese criminologist Hiroshi Tsutomi (1991:14) said it best when he wrote:

'People commit crimes not because they are pathological or wicked, but because they are normal.'

The vast majority of criminals are normal people driven by the same motives that drive all of us. Criminals' pursuit of illegal profitable activities is not very different from the pursuit of other risky, dangerous, lustful activities. In many cases, such pursuit is motivated by the search for pleasure, thrill, adventure, excitement, or fun. Motives for criminal behaviour are therefore essentially the same as those behind everyday legal activities. The quest for pleasure, profit, gain, status, and power are the principal driving forces behind everyday activities: criminal and non-criminal, legal and illegal. As Sutherland and Cressey (1978:82) point out, both criminal and non-criminal behaviours are expressions of the same needs and values: 'Thieves generally steal in order to secure money, but likewise honest laborers work in order to secure money.' Whatever difference there may be lies not in the goals being pursued but in the *means* used to achieve those goals. The common saying 'the end justifies the means' is an effective technique of rationalization used by criminals and non-criminals alike. It played a major role in the Watergate affair and the 'crimes' of Colonel Oliver North. It is also the justification used by police officers who falsify evidence or commit perjury and by individual terrorists and terrorist groups.

Nobody maintains that people are biologically, or socially different from others just because they earn their living by performing stunts in movies, through boxing, car-racing, and so on, or because they get their kicks from bungee-jumping, killing animals in hunting, shooting birds, climbing mountains, and so forth.

Positivist criminologists' assertion that 'people who break the law are often psychologically atypical' or that 'offenders are...atypical in personality' (Wilson and Herrnstein, 1985:173) is contradicted by the observation that anyone placed in certain situations, under certain conditions, and subjected to certain pressures and constraints is capable of committing acts of extreme atrocity, cruelty, cupidity, dishonesty, and so on. The experiments of Milgram (1969) and of Zimbardo (1972) prove it. So does Christie's (1952) study of Norwegian guards in concentration camps during the Nazi occupation of Norway, and Christopher Browning's (1992) study of the reserve police battalion 101, to name but a few. The so-called folk crimes, such as lynching or the looting by the masses during civil disturbances or blackouts or in the aftermath of natural disasters, are proof that it does not take an atypical personality to commit the predatory crimes that seem to be singled out by Wilson and Herrnstein (1985) as the trademark of 'real' criminals. On the contrary, these crimes illustrate the preponderant importance and role situational factors play in crime causation. The assumption that criminals are inherently different from non-criminals is further contradicted by the findings of self-report studies.

Most theories of positivist criminology, starting with those of Lombroso, were based on unrepresentative samples or populations of convicted offenders. Furthermore, the studies serving as the basis for these positivist theories rarely include those committing white-collar crime or corporate crime or those whose crimes are committed mainly through abuses of political and economic power.

Surprisingly, the erroneous belief that offenders arc abnormal or have atypical personalities continues to persist despite recent surveys showing that family violence, for example, is extremely widespread[2] and studies showing that 'so-called respectable citizens account for a large proportion of many kinds of crime' (Gabor, 1994).

Ordinary Citizens as Criminals

As mentioned in Chapter 3, criminology has paid relatively little attention to corporate crime and white-collar crime. Even more neglected are the crimes committed by ordinary citizens, by members of the general public. And yet folk crimes or crimes by the public have a long and infamous history. They range from extreme acts of violence, such as lynching, destructive acts, such as massive looting, vandalism and arson that accompany riots (for example, the 1994 Stanley Cup riot in Vancouver) or in the aftermath of natural disasters, disorderly conduct, such as football (soccer) hooliganism, to acts committed for financial motives, such as tax evasion, customs violations, pilfering, and so forth. Since this is a neglected area of research in criminology, Thomas Gabor's book *Everybody Does It! Crime by the Public* (1994) is an important attempt to fill this gap in our knowledge about the crimes that ordinary people commit. This original book should be required reading for every criminology student. To illustrate the extent of criminal behaviour and dishonest practices that are commonly committed by ordinary citizens and to document the fact that everyone has at one time or another violated provisions of the criminal code or criminal statutes and committed illegal, unlawful, dishonest, immoral, and unethical acts, Gabor (1994:7–8) writes:

> How many of us have taken home linens, silverware, art, and other 'souvenirs' from hotels in which we have stayed or from restaurants in which we have dined? How many of us have relieved our employers of office supplies, materials, tools, or merchandise, or redirected our travelling and telephone budgets, or other privileges, for personal use? How many people have deliberately failed to report some income when filing tax returns, made deductions that were not legitimate, or otherwise misrepresent their economic situation to lessen their tax burden? Many of us have also done one or more of the following:
> – made inflated insurance claims following a fire or theft;

- driven while legally impaired by alcohol in a manner endangering others;
- used prohibited drugs or abused prescription drugs;
- failed to inform a store, customer, or bank of a financial error in our favour;
- engaged in dishonest business practices;
- failed to make truthful declarations at a border crossing;
- destroyed or damaged property maliciously;
- physically struck another person intentionally;
- exhibited disorderly conduct in public;
- illegally copied computer software or videos;
- abused the environment through dumping trash in an inappropriate place or by some other means;
- violated the human rights of others through sexual harassment or discrimination on the basis of race, disability, age, or sexual orientation;
- demonstrated cruelty to animals or hunted without a permit, out of season, or in excess of that permitted by law.

Most of these acts contravene criminal law, federal statutes, or local by-laws. At the very least, they violate moral prohibitions against dishonesty and the requirements of good citizenship.

Aside from the general transgressions listed above, people violate numerous laws, rules, and moral or ethical codes relating to their personal situations and occupations. It is not only blue-collar workers (e.g., taking home tools and materials) and clerical workers (e.g., stealing office supplies and applying office machinery for personal use) who commit illegalities and behave unscrupulously on the job.

Stuart Henry (1978) used the term 'borderline crime' to describe rule violations and various other illegal acts by people who otherwise are law abiding. One area studied by Henry is that of participation in the 'black economy' or hidden economy. Participation in such illegal activities is widespread in countries where the economy is strictly controlled: China, Cuba, former socialist countries of Eastern Europe, and so on. In such controlled economies, breaking the rules becomes a daily activity of a large part of the general population.

Ellickson (1991:260) pays particular attention to 'lawless academic photocopying' and cites it as an example of academics' rejection of a law that restricts their freedom to copy material protected by copyright law. Ellickson suggests that there is abundant, if unsystematic, evidence that university instructors engage in rampant unconsented photocopying when preparing class materials. Law professors he questioned almost invariably admitted to the unconstrained copying of articles for class use, although most noted that they would decline to duplicate major portions of books. Ellickson concluded that

> 'Professors' substantive norms seem to permit the unconsented copying for class use, year after year, of articles and minor portions of books. Professors apparently allow this informal rule to trump copyright law. (p. 260)

DIFFERING VIEWS OF THE CRIMINAL

A. Dysfunctional Role Theories

The Criminal as an Abnormal or Subnormal Being
Probably the oldest view of the criminal regarded him as someone instigated by the devil, a creature succumbing to the blandishments of evil spirits. This view was widely held in early societies. One way of driving out the evil spirits was to exorcise or chasten the possessed individual. Such beliefs persisted until the past century. Sutherland and Cressey (1960:51) point out that the English indictment used as late as the nineteenth century not only charged the criminal of violating the law but also of 'being prompted and instigated by the devil and not having the fear of God before his eyes.' They also cite the Supreme Court of North Carolina which as late as 1862 declared: 'To know the right and still pursue the wrong proceeds from a perverse will brought about by the reductions of the evil one.'

With the development of medicine and psychiatry during the second half of the 19th century and the first half of the 20th century, the focus shifted from the evil forces dominating or influencing the criminal's mind and soul to the pathological peculiarities of the criminal's physique and brain. Many of the early criminologists, physicians and psychiatrists themselves, believed that criminals suffer from hereditary genetic abnormalities and/or impaired mental and moral faculties. In the criminological literature of that period, the criminal is portrayed as sick, mad, or bad. The Italian Positivist School described the criminal as a biologically inferior being carrying the burden of bad heredity. The School of Mental Testers (Goddard, 1920) claimed that criminals are mentally defective suffering from imbecility, feeble-mindedness, or low intelligence. The Psychiatric School propagated the belief that criminals suffer from severe or mild forms of mental illness (epilepsy, psychoses, neuroses, and so on), minor brain injuries, cerebral instability of some kind, or some other neurological impairment.

Following the development of the electroencephalograph, some psychiatrists claimed that certain categories of criminals, particularly murderers, have readings that exhibit abnormal brain rhythms. More recent variations of these views of the criminal stress glandular imbalance or dysfunctions, chromosomal aberrations, physical anomalies, physical ailments, deformities, defective physical conditions, and so forth. Criminals have not escaped the recent trend to attribute behavioural problems to nutritional and dietary habits. A study conducted by the Biosocial Research Institute in the State of Washington (1980) has purportedly found that delinquents drink too much milk and eat too few fruits and vegetables. The head of the research institute, Dr Schauss, was quoted as saying that there is an apparent relationship between heavy milk drinking and anti-social behaviour since delinquents consume ten times the 'normal' amount of milk![3]

Despite their variety, all these medical and psychiatric explanations share the view that criminals are in one way or another abnormal, inferior, or defective mentally and/or physically.

Moral views regard the criminal as an evil being, as immoral, morally defective, or morally insane. He is seen as an individual suffering from a lack of conscience, an underdeveloped or a weak super-ego. He is characterized as selfish, insensitive, impulsive and destructive, a creature who displays lack of foresight, sympathy, and guilt.

Theories of criminality advanced by psychologists invariably stress the psychological abnormalities of offenders and insist that delinquents and criminals do suffer from some personality and/or emotional disorders. These abnormal personality traits criminals are said to suffer from are believed to result mainly from unhealthy parental attitudes during the process of development and/or major perturbations in parent/child relationships, in particular, maternal deprivation. They are likely to grow up in unhealthy family environments, such as conflict-ridden homes and homes characterized by violence, abuse, rejection, neglect, indifference, and lack of affection. As Gabor (1991:472) points out

> The impression of criminals the public is fed, and largely subscribes to, is of sinister people who are clearly discernible, by their characteristics from the rest of society. The actions of this 'fringe' element of society are seen as being qualitatively different from what law-abiding people are capable of committing. Criminals are often thought to be vicious characters, inclined toward the commission of heinous acts inconceivable to the rest of us....
>
> The view that the world can be divided into good and evil or the dangerous and endangered is a popular one, perpetuated by the media, politicians, corporations, and even by criminologists.

The Criminal as a Dysfunctional Social Agent

In medieval Europe, as in many non-industrial societies, the criminal was regarded as an enemy and treated as such. Chapman (1968) tells us that 'historically the Saxon villain in Norman society lost status, and the revolt of 1381 created the identification of the villain as the enemy in class conflict.' The practice of outlawry is a further illustration of how the criminal was treated like an enemy. According to Mary McIntosh (1975:30), 'an outlaw was turned out from ordinary society; it was forbidden to give him aid or comfort; he was to be hunted like the wolf.'

Moral and theological beliefs that prevailed during the Middle Ages and later on the evolutionist theories of Lombroso that portrayed the criminal as a savage, a throw-back, a representative of an early species of the human race, helped perpetuate the view that criminals are purveyors of evil, sturdy rogues, agents of violence, public enemies, and so forth. Certain categories of criminals, such as vagrants, beggars, and robbers, were regarded as social parasites whose presence in society is as detrimental to social hygiene as the presence of a parasite in a healthy human body. It is not surprising, therefore, that they were often described as a plague or as a social epidemic. As Schmidt (1895) put it:

> It had become a matter of paramount importance to suppress the bands of vagabonds, beggars, and robbers who were becoming a plague on the land. In one place after another the sluice gates would open and release a new and poisonous flood into the muddy sea of crime.
>
> Quoted in Rusche and Kirchheimer (1939:18)

Only a few voices were raised to contradict or challenge the view that criminals were the refuse of society. Among them was the French criminologist Corré, who in his essay on criminality ('Essai sur la criminalité') pleaded that:

> Criminals must not be regarded as the refuse of society, they are rather a part of it as a wound is a part of the body.
>
> Quoted in Aschaffenberg (1913:5)

To the politicians, the landowners, the wealthy merchants, and the emerging class of industrialists, criminals were neither poor misguided sinners nor victims of the deep rooted social inequities, economic injustices, and the unfair distribution of power and wealth. Political and economic interests were very influential in reinforcing the view that criminals are disruptive elements who threaten social stability and social harmony and who by their actions endanger not only peace and order but also the social fabric itself. Criminals were thus portrayed as challengers to established authority and rebels against social control. This view of criminals was gradually extended to the proletariat as a whole. Since criminals, at least arrested and convicted criminals, were almost exclusively members of the poorer classes, it was not uncommon to view not only them but the poor as a whole as *dangerous classes* that pose a threat to established social institutions and to the existing social order. Rather than blaming crime on the subhuman socioeconomic conditions of the proletariat, the proletariat was blamed for crime, and a new concept, the concept of the dangerous classes, emerged. The concept was in vogue in the nineteenth century, particularly in England, as explained by Radzinowicz (1966:38):

> The concept of the dangerous classes as the main source of crime and disorder was very much to the fore at the beginning of the nineteenth century. They were made up of those who had so miserable a share in the accumulating wealth of the industrial revolution that they might at any time break out in political revolt as in France. At their lowest level was the hard core of parasites to be found in any society, ancient or modern. And closely related to this, often indistinguishable from it were the 'criminal classes.' ... It served the interests and relieved the conscience of those at the top to look upon the dangerous classes as an independent category, detached from the prevailing social conditions.

B. Functional Role Theories

The Criminal as a Folk Hero

The King and the condemned wrong-doer are, at some points in social history, interchangeable.

Alex Comfort (1970:23)
Authority and Delinquency

In the history of every society, presumably, some of its culture heroes have been regarded as heroic precisely because they have had the courage and the vision to depart from norms then obtaining in the group. As we all know, the rebel, revolutionary, nonconformist, individualist, heretic or renegade of an earlier time is often the culture hero of today.

Robert K. Merton (1957:183)
Social Theory and Social Structure

The criminal is a curious being who stirs love and hate, respect and contempt, admiration and indignation, pity and vindictiveness. At times, he is heralded as a folk hero, at others, he is denounced as a public villain. History is full of tales of criminals who were venerated and others who were crucified. The writers of the ancient literature of Israel make a hero out of David, who slew the Philistine and who later was an outlaw and did not hesitate to live off the country (see Gillin, 1926:4). And Robin Hood, the thief of Sherwood Forest, is nothing less than a legend. Angiolillo (1979:1) points out that:

One of the most universal and enduring of legendary figures is that of the variously named romantic highwayman, social bandit, noble brigand, or robber-hero .... Epitomized in the stereotypical character of Robin Hood, he has over the years often changed his dress, his habitat, and, superficially, the manner of performing his lawless deeds ... but essentially the myth remains the same: the fearless, independent outlaw, dedicated more or less to the defense of the helpless, the righting of wrongs, the humbling of the rich and powerful, and the dauntless display of extraordinary courage, deemed to be beyond the ken of the common run of men. Likewise, the public's fascination with his exploits, as recounted through either the oral or literary tradition, seems to be based upon a rather constant emotional and quasi-intellectual enjoyment of thrilling adventures vicariously experienced.

Kooistra (1983:214) points out that the Robin Hood outlaw

... is a man who violates the law but still represents justice of a higher sort; he robs from the rich to give to the poor and only harms others in self-defense or in 'just' revenge. He does not challenge the legitimacy of the state, only the corrupt oppressors of the people.

American and Canadian Outlaw Heroes

The list of American outlaw heroes is a long one, containing legendary names such as Billy the Kid, Jesse James, and Butch Cassidy, to mention but a few. Billy the Kid, a convicted murderer who allegedly sent 21 people to their graves, was described by one of his biographers, Pat Garrett (1954:8) as

Bold, daring, and reckless, he was open-handed, generous, frank and manly. He was a favorite with all classes and ages, especially was he loved and admired by the old and decrepit, and the young and helpless. To such he was a champion, a defender, a benefactor, a right arm. (quoted by Kooistra, 1989:7)

Another outlaw, Butch Cassidy, was blessed, according to Lula Parker Betenson (1975), with a winning personality: 'His friendly, singular charm and his interest in people – the struggling people – won him their protection from the law .... I can honestly say that I have not found one person who knew him personally who will say a bad thing about him' (cited after Kooistra, 1983:215).

No Canadian outlaw has achieved the notoriety nor the popularity of American outlaws. There are, however, criminals who have become famous in the Canadian annals of crime not only because of their daring exploits but also because of the attitudes of sympathy, admiration, and fascination they evoked among the Canadian people. One of these was Betsy Bigley who was born in 1857 in Eastwood, Ontario, and who after a life in crime, died in an Ohio penitentiary on 10 October 1907. Her life and exploits were the subject of a 1985 CBC TV-movie called *Love and Larceny*. Another well-known Canadian outlaw is Red Ryan, the Toronto gangster of the 1930s whose shadow, according to Ted Honderich (1957), still hangs over every Canadian prison yard. According to Robin (1982:70), Ryan was called the Jesse James of Canada by the Hearst Press, and at one of his trials the crown attorney deplored the fact that 'certain newspapers have seen fit to picture him as a glorified hero' (p. 72). Robin (1982:86) reports that after Ryan was shot and killed during the course of robbery, his body was exhibited in a Sarnia funeral parlor where an estimated six thousand curious people filed by to have a glimpse of the criminal hero.

Another famous name in the annals of Canadian crime is Bill Minor, whose illustrious career spanned the entire west for over half a century. Although Minor was born in Bowling Green and buried in Georgia, he has secured himself a place in the history of crime in Canada. According to Robin (1976:189), Minor marauded throughout the Southwest and Rocky Mountain States, robbed scores of stage coaches and trains, and mouldered in prisons from San Quentin to New Westminster. Robin reports that

> Among his nicest prey was Canada's national dream, the Canadian Pacific Railway Company, whose transcontinental train was halted and robbed in 1904 by a gang of hooded bandits as polite as they were efficient.

Robin (1976) cites several editorial writers of the era who speculated on the motives of the sympathizers and admirers of the wanted robber. He suggests that some believed that what the sympathizers lacked or suppressed in their inner selves, the outlaw possessed and displayed in abundance:

> As men admire contrasts ... these foolish ones admire Miner. He is clever; they are conscious that they are not; he is possessed of a certain courage; they know they have not got it; he can conceive a plan and carry it through to completion; but these men know that they could not do such a thing to save their lives. (p. 214)

Theoretical Explanations of the Heroic Criminal
Despite a well-documented history of criminals becoming public idols, no one has yet been able to explain adequately the excessive admiration and fascination some criminals generate. Is it their audacity and their bold disregard of consequences? Gillin (1926:5) claims that in the criminal, people vicariously experience the thrill of danger met with active purpose. Is it their defiance of authority, their willingness to stand up against oppressive regimes or unjust laws? Is it because we view them as the victims and not the aggressors? Is it because we admire perversity or courage, because we are

attracted to the notorious, the odd, and the non-conforming? Speaking of brigands and pirates, Mary McIntosh (1975:32–33) notes that there has been a tendency, especially in popular tales, ballads, and folklore, to exaggerate the noble qualities of bandits. This tendency arises to some extent because they often represent important social aspirations of the people, avenging oppressors and 'robbing the rich to help the poor.' It is also because, as Shakespeare put it, 'it is an honourable kind of thievery.' McIntosh points out that 'brigands and pirates are open about what they are; they are not sneaking or deceitful, they take enormous personal risks – so that the odd instance of gentlemanly behaviour is recorded with admiration as superrogatory – and they can seldom retire in comfort to live on their spoils.' Furthermore, 'these brigands have many attributes that are universally admired: foresight, wisdom, decisiveness, resourcefulness, daring, determination, and physical prowess.'

Do Notorious Criminals Have a Special Appeal?

Killers, in particular, seem to attract a great deal of love and sympathy. It is well known that some of the most notorious killers got an incredible number of letters expressing positive rather than negative feelings towards them. Gary Gilmore, the Utah killer who in 1977 became the first convict to be executed in the United States after a ten-year period free of executions, is reported to have had trouble handling the flood of mail he received. Jean Harris, the school mistress who in 1980 killed her lover Dr Herman Tarnower, creator of the Scarsdale diet, got more than just mail. A Jean Harris defence fund was set up to help defray the costs of her defence. To many American women she became a symbol; she represented all women wronged by their lovers.

Love for criminals is nothing new. It is so common that a special term was coined to designate this particular kind of passion: *enclitophilia*, a word with a Greek etymological origin. The term was used for the first time by the French criminalistics expert Dr Edmond Locard in 1938 and then served as the theme for a doctoral thesis by Yvon Samuel. Samuel (1939) cites Dr Corré who in his book *Crime and Suicide* (1891) speaks of a mysterious sexual instinct that unconsciously pushes well-bred women to become carried away or even obsessed by a bizarre sympathy for the heroes of crime.

In the January 1995 issue of *Chatelaine Magazine*, Michael Posner tries to answer the question 'Why do some women fall for notorious men?' For his story, he uses a lengthy interview with L.B., a 27-year-old woman who seems to have a special fondness for Paul Bernardo, who was charged with the sex killings of two teenage girls in Ontario and with more than a dozen sexual assaults committed in the Toronto area between 1987 and 1992. According to Posner, L.B. spends hours every week drafting long letters to Bernardo and keeps a framed 8–by-10 inch photograph of him in her apartment, one which she had specially enlarged (p. 48).

Posner refers to what he calls 'the bizarre but undeniable attraction that some women feel for murderers, rapists and other violent criminals' and cites as examples the case of Ted Bundy (who was found guilty of killing several women, including two Florida State University female students) and the woman, Carole Boone, who married him and bore his child before he was executed in 1989. He also mentions John Wayne Gacy who was executed in May 1994 for killing more than two dozen Chicago-area youths and who got letters from dozens of women during the more than 14 years he spent on death row (p. 48).

The Criminal as a Functional Social Agent

Many sociologists and criminologists do not share the conventional view that regards the criminal as a disruptive element or as a social parasite who has to be eliminated, segregated, or reintegrated. In accord with the view of the French sociologist, Emile Durkheim (1858–1917), they believe that the criminal is an agent who plays a needed role in social life and who performs a useful social function. Society, they insist, needs crime and criminals for a wide variety of reasons:

1. Crime, or at least certain types of crime, is useful because it is indispensable to the normal evolution of morality and law. Crime and deviance keep the path open for progress and social change. This is the essence of the sociological dictum: 'conform to norm and all stands still, non-conformity drives the mill.' In some cases, as Durkheim puts it, the criminal is an innovator, the precursor of a new morality.

2. In our discussion of evolutive crime (Chapter 2) several examples were given of 'criminals' who through their criminal, deviant or non-conforming behavior paved the way for much needed social change. By violating the law they drew attention to the need for reform and served as agents of social change.

3. The criminal performs a useful social function since he promotes, through his behaviour, social integration, social solidarity, and norm reinforcement. When a serious crime is committed, the community becomes united in its indignation and its condemnation of the offender. And through the punishment of the offender, society reaffirms its adherence to the social norm that was violated. The norm is thus reinforced every time society reacts to its violation.

4. The commission of the crime and the punishment of criminals that follows serve to reassure law-abiding citizens and to reinforce their sense of justice. It demonstrates the virtues of conformity and reasserts the rewards associated with citizens' respect for the law.

5.   The criminal performs yet another useful social function by serving as a scapegoat for society. Every society needs scapegoats, that is, individuals or groups on whom sentiments of fear, hate, hostility, anger, and frustration may be projected. Criminals have always served this function. They are ideal scapegoats – killed, tortured, and maimed with little or no remorse, qualm, guilt, or compunction.

The Criminal as a Scapegoat

We need criminals to identify ourselves with, to secretly envy, and to stoutly punish. Criminals represent our alter egos – our 'bad' selves rejected and projected. They do for us the forbidden, illegal things we wish to do and, like scapegoats of old, they bear the burdens of our displaced guilt and punishment – 'the iniquities of us all.'

Karl Menninger (1966:153)
The Crime of Punishment

Since the time of Freud, psychoanalysts have claimed that vicarious punishment has salutary cathartic effects. According to this view, punishing criminals helps release vindictive feelings and serves as outlet for unconscious sadistic impulses and repressed antisocial tendencies. Weihofen (1956) sees it as 'a weapon in our struggle against trends and drives which we do not admit to consciousness, against our repressed instinctual drives.'

Psychoanalysts argue that we are unconsciously jealous of criminals, that we secretly envy them for having dared to do what we unconsciously want but are unable or unwilling to do. To see them punished helps ease our guilt and shows us that our virtue has been rewarded. In his book *The Crime of Punishment*, psychiatrist Karl Menninger (1966:154) explains how the displacement mechanism works:

The vicarious use of the criminal for relieving guilt feelings of 'innocent' individuals by displacement is no recent theory, but it constantly eludes public acceptance. The internal economics of our own morality, our submerged hates and suppressed aggressions, our fantasied crimes, our feeling of need for punishment – all these can be managed in part by the scapegoat device. To do so requires this little maneuver of displacement, but displacement and projection are easier to manage than confession or sublimation.

Psychiatrists also claim that punishment of criminals further acts as an outlet for inhibited aggression and suppressed violent impulses. When legal executions were carried out in public, an enormous amount of vicarious enjoyment seemed to be felt by the crowds watching them. This sense of pleasure confirms what anthropologists have observed in non-industrial societies, where executions and human sacrifices are regarded with bloodthirsty

enjoyment by the natives who seem to derive immense pleasure from obser-
ving acts of cruelty 'righteously' inflicted (see Dollard *et al.*, 1957). Although
the scapegoat theory, like other psychoanalytic theories, is difficult to test
empirically, it has, as Chapman (1968) points out, a high degree of plausi-
bility and is supported by many observations. Noting that Christianity as an
ethical system is heavily involved in the scapegoat culture (the crucifixion
being the supreme case of the sacrifice of the innocent for the sins of a whole
society), Chapman (1968:246–7) writes:

> It is surely not implausible to see here one more ambivalence in the
> culture, the practice of the sacrifice of the scapegoat as solving the emo-
> tional maladjustment of the great mass of society and theories of crime
> and punishment as providing a 'rational' basis for the practice.... There is
> some evidence, therefore, that the identification and punishment of crim-
> inals do provide satisfaction for many people. What is not proved is that
> there is widespread guilt or aggression which is released or discharged
> when a criminal is punished. It would be possible to test such a hypothesis,
> but the results, if positive, might prove unacceptable. If it was found that
> the punishment of offenders relieved guilt in others, and, if guilt acts to
> inhibit amoral or antisocial behavior, it could be argued that punishment
> of scapegoats functions to allow crime in others and that, without such
> punishment, the general level of social behavior would conform more
> closely to the mores.

Reiwald (1949) affirms that the criminal, whose punishment discharges the
guilt of the reader and the onlooker, is needed by society. He doubts whether
modern societies could forego this particular form of projection without
finding others more destructive. One strong point Reiwald makes in support
of his argument is his reference to the practice that persisted until the last
century in England of disguising the condemned man as an animal by
wrapping him in a cow-hide.

Alex Comfort (1970:22–3) insists that the idea of the condemned man as
saviour long precedes its use in Christian symbolism:

> The lawbreaker in primitive societies has a distinct magical status. The
> criminal yields in fact to impulses which most members of his culture
> entertain in fantasy, and which are a source of guilt. By doing so he offers
> himself as a sacrificial victim on behalf of the less impulsive or better-
> repressed members of society, who are duly grateful. In this sense the idea
> of the condemned man as saviour and exorcist long precedes its use in
> Christian symbolism.

NOTES

1. Homicide statistics for 1993 released by the Canadian Centre for Justice Statistics (*Juristat*, 14, No. 15 [August 1994]) show that only 15 per cent of the homicides for which an accused was identified were committed by strangers, the same as in 1992. Slightly more than one-half (51 per cent) of homicide victims in 1993 were killed by an acquaintance, and one-third (33 per cent) by an immediate family member or relative. The centre reports that 'many domestic homicides are a tragic outcome of continued domestic violence: 43 per cent involved a history of domestic violence known to police' (p. 13).
2. In an American survey cited by Steinmetz (1986:56) spanking, the most prevalent form of family violence, was reported to occur in between 84 and 97 per cent of all American families.
3. *Bulletin of the Canadian Association for the Prevention of Crime, 9*, No. 4 p. 6. See also Schauss, A. (1981) *Diet, Crime and Delinquency*. Berkeley, CA: Parker House.

6 The Victim: Beyond Popular Stereotypes

Not only does considerable overlap exist between populations of victims and offenders as demonstrated by the substantial proportion of violators having also been victims, but considerable evidence exists that the experience of being victimized increases the propensity for offending and that populations of victims and offenders have homogeneous characteristics.... Clearly any theory that assumes no overlap exists between populations of victims and offenders or that they are distinct types of persons distorts the empirical research.

Albert J. Reiss, Jr. (1981a:710–11)
Towards a Revitalization of Theory and Research on Victimization by Crime

WHY STUDY THE VICTIM?

Since the dawn of scientific criminology, criminologists have tried to find out why some individuals become criminal while others do not. They conducted countless studies to discover whether criminals are different in any respect from non-criminals. An equally interesting and thought-provoking question is 'Why do some individuals become victims of crime while others do not?' Is criminal victimization a random occurrence? Is it due simply to chance factors, misfortune, or bad luck? Do victims of crime constitute a representative sample, an unbiased cross-section of the general population? Do victims of crime differ in any way from non-victims? How do offenders select their targets; how do they pick their victims? There are many other questions for which research is seeking answers. The following are just a few examples:

1. Why are certain individuals or groups of individuals more frequently victimized than others? Why are certain targets (individuals, households, businesses, and so on) repeatedly victimized? How can the differential risks and rates of victimization be explained?
2. Are certain persons (or targets) more prone and more vulnerable to victimization than others, and if so, why? What is the nature of this proneness; what are the elements of this vulnerability?

143

3. Are there born victims, predestined victims, predisposed victims? Are there recidivist victims? Are there victim stereotypes just as there are criminal stereotypes?

4. Are there specific characteristics or specific behaviours that enhance the risks and chances of criminal victimization, that are responsible for, or conducive to, becoming a victim? And if so, what are these characteristics and these behaviours?

5. Is there such a thing as victim-invited, victim-induced, victim-precipitated, victim-facilitated criminality? Do some victims promote, provoke, or trigger their own victimization? Do potential victims emit non-verbal signals, signalling their vulnerability to would-be assailants through gestures, posture, and movements?[1]

These questions and many others raise a number of issues and research topics that are quite different from those that have been the focus of mainstream criminology. Although the scientific study of the criminal is more than a century old, the systematic study of the victim is still in its infancy. And yet, it seems axiomatic that to analyze the crime phenomenon in its entirety and in all its complexity, equal attention has to be paid to the criminal and his victim. There are several reasons that render the study of crime victims essential, indeed, indispensable, for a better understanding of the phenomenon of crime (Fattah, 1991):

1. Motives for criminal behaviour do not develop in a vacuum (von Hentig, 1948). They come into being through drives and responses, reactions and interactions, attitudes and counter attitudes. In many cases, the victim is involved consciously or unconsciously in the motivational process as well as in the process of mental reasoning or rationalization the criminal engages in prior to the commission of the crime (Fattah, 1976). In some instances, the motives for the criminal act develop around a specific victim. An examination of the place the victim occupies or the role the victim plays in these processes is necessary to understand why the crime was committed and why a particular target was chosen.

2. The commission of a crime is the outcome of a process where many factors are at work. In most cases, crime is not an action but a reaction (or an overreaction) to external and environmental stimuli. Some of these stimuli emanate from the victim. The victim is an important element of the environment and of the criminogenic situation.

3. Often, the criminal act is not an isolated gesture but the denouement of a long or brief interaction with the victim. In such cases, it is not possible to understand the act fully without analyzing the chain of interactions that led to its perpetration. It is scientifically unsound to examine and analyze the offender's act in isolation from the dynamic forces that have prepared, influenced, conditioned, or determined it or to dissociate it

from the motivational and situational processes that led to its commission.

4. Current theories of criminal and deviant behaviour, whether attempting to explain causation or association, offer only static explanations. Since criminal behaviour, like other forms of human behaviour, is dynamic it can be explained only through a dynamic approach, where the offender, the act, and the victim are inseparable elements of a total situation that conditions the dialectic of the victimizing behaviour (Fattah, 1976).

5. The traits approach, seeking the genesis of criminal behaviour in the characteristics and attributes of the offender, is simplistic. It needs to be replaced by a complex model of total interactions. Theories of offenders' attributes, personalities, or social background do not explain why other individuals who have the same traits or personality type or who grow up in identical or very similar conditions do not commit crimes or do not persist in a criminal career. They fail to explain why the offender committed the crime in a particular situation, at a given moment, against a specific victim. The traits approach either ignores or deliberately minimizes the importance of situational factors in actualizing or triggering criminal behaviour.[2] The study of the victims, their characteristics, their relationship to, and interactions with, the victimizer, their role and their contribution to the genesis of the crime, offers great promise for transforming etiological criminology from the static, one-sided study of the qualities and attributes of the offender into a dynamic, situational approach that views criminal behaviour not as a unilateral action but as the outcome of dynamic processes of interaction.

6. As Anttila (1974) points out, the study of the victim has a general informational value. It provides information on the frequency and patterns of victimization, thus making possible the measurement of risk probabilities and the establishment of risk categories (high, low, medium). It also provides valuable information on proneness to victimization, fear of victimization, response to victimization, consequences and impact of victimization. Such knowledge is essential for the formulation of a rational criminal policy, for the evaluation of crime prevention strategies, and for taking social action aimed at protecting vulnerable targets, increasing safety, and improving the quality of life.

7. The victim has a strong impact on criminal justice decisions, particularly those of the police and the courts.[3] In most cases, it is the victim who decides whether or not to mobilize the criminal justice system by reporting or not reporting the offence. Furthermore, the characteristics, attitude, and behaviour of the victims and their relationship to the offender have a significant bearing upon the decision of the police to proceed in a formal or an informal way (see Black, 1970). In the latter case, victim-related factors can greatly affect the final outcome. The study of the

victim leads not only to a better understanding of the functioning of the criminal justice system but also to improving the decision-making process. Enhancing victims' involvement in the process and establishing the modalities of such involvement require a better understanding of the role victims currently play in criminal justice.

8. To better fulfil society's obligations to the victims of crime – in order to help, assist, and make the victim whole again – it is necessary to gain a thorough knowledge of the consequences and impact of the crime on those who are victimized. Moreover, an adequate knowledge of the various needs of victims of different types of crime is a prerequisite for setting up efficient victim services, victim assistance, and compensation programs. A better understanding of victims' perceptions of, and attitudes to, the criminal justice system, their reasons for not reporting victimization and refusal or unwillingness to co-operate with the system, are essential to improving attitudes and enhancing co-operation.

9. Modern criminology is paying more attention to the concept of opportunity (see Mayhew *et al.*, 1976). The commission of many crimes is believed to be largely a function of the opportunities to commit those crimes (see Chapter 11). Opportunities, in turn, are viewed as being greatly influenced by the behaviour of potential victims. The collective behaviour of potential crime victims may have a strong impact on crime rates, and variations in those rates may be explained, at least partially, through differences or changes in victim behaviour. For this reason, a better understanding of the attitudes and behaviour of victims holds great promise for crime prevention. Victim-based prevention strategies have several advantages over offender-based ones. The former aim at hardening the targets, making the commission of crimes more difficult and less profitable. The role potential victims are called upon to play in this environmental/situational approach is a primary one.

10. The medieval paradigm of 'retributive justice' seems to have reached its terminal phase and attempts are already underway to have it replaced by another paradigm of 'restorative justice'. Restorative justice is based on the principles of mediation, conciliation, restitution and compensation. Its primary aim is healing, not punishment. In a restorative justice system, the victim ceases to be a secondary or peripheral player and assumes an active role. He/she becomes a full party in the process. The study of the impact of victimization on the victim, the attitudes and the needs of the victim are thus essential to a system of restorative justice (Fattah, 1995).

As useful as the study of crime victims may be, it is not without dangers. Anttila (1974:9) points to two potential dangers in victim-centred research:

1. A real danger is the possibility that interest will simply shift from the individual offender to the individual victim.... Individual-centred research in its narrowest sense takes into account offender and victim independently. More sophisticated research also considers the interaction process and the general situational factors. But even then, if the problems related to society in general and to the volume of criminality are left aside, the research results tend to be of little importance for decision-making.

2. The growing interest in victim-centred research may lead to over-emphasis on types of criminal behaviour where there is an easily identified individual victim. This implies a concentration of research efforts on traditional types of crimes, such as assaults, larcenies, and sexual offences. Some large groups of crimes seem to be neglected altogether, only because there are no easily identified victims.

Problems with the Concept of 'Victim'

The answer to 'who is a victim of crime?' may seem obvious. But it often isn't as easy to describe victims as one might suppose. For some crimes, such as rape or murder, of course, it is quite clear who has been victimized. But for other crimes, such as welfare or insurance fraud, embezzlement, public corruption, or vagrancy, the victim is less clearly defined. A crime in which corporation funds are taken may ultimately be paid for by shareholders. Welfare fraud is absorbed by taxpayers. Public corruption may affect the trust of the general public toward officeholders.... For crimes of property, in general, the economic loss involved may be absorbed by the crime victim or may be covered partially or entirely by insurance. Defining the victims of crime can be more difficult than one might assume.

Victims of Crime
Bureau of Justice Statistics Bulletin (1981:1)

The word 'victim' comes from the Latin word 'victima', which, according to its etymological origin, was used to designate a creature (a human being, a bird, or an animal) sacrificed to the gods. As with many other words, over the years the use and meaning of the word changed quite considerably. Its scope was broadened to a great extent. Today, the word victim is used in almost every possible context to designate anyone who suffers a negative outcome or any kind of loss, harm, or injury, whether the harm is material, physical, or psychological. We thus talk about victims of crime, accidents, war, natural disasters (tornadoes, hurricanes, earthquakes, floods, volcano eruptions, draught, famine, and so on). We talk about victims of diseases: AIDS, cancer, strokes, heart attacks, and so on; victims of society, such as those who suffer from poverty, injustice, inequality, oppression, discrimination, exploitation, and prejudice. Obviously, the generic term victim is vague and imprecise and is of little use to scientific and research purposes (Fattah,1994).

As Quinney (1972:321) suggests, 'the victim' is only a social construction. He points out that 'we all deal in a conventional wisdom that influences our perception of the world around us, and it is this wisdom that defines for us just who the victim is in any situation, which also means that alternative victims can be constructed.'

Although the word 'victim' is a staple of the criminological language and although it was used to coin the term 'victimology', its real criminological meaning remains unclear and its utility remains in doubt. Just what does the term, as used in criminology and victimology, mean? Is it a label, a stereotype? Is it a state, a condition? Is it meant to assign a status, a role to the one so described? Is it a self-perception, a social construction, an expression of sympathy, a legal qualification, a juridical designation? (Fattah, 1991:90).

If the victim designation is a label, and a debasing one at that, then we may ask about the utility of such label. The label 'criminal' has been widely criticized, yet the label 'victim' seems to generate few, if any, objections or criticism. Labelling theorists have decried the stigma, degradation, and stereotyping attached to the label 'criminal' and have pointed to the danger of the person identifying with the label. Victimologists, on the other hand, seem all too willing (even eager) to use the label 'victim' in a wide variety of contexts. It might well be that the designation is useful (or necessary) for legal purposes. However, the utility of the label, like that of other labels, for research and policy purposes is doubtful (Fattah, 1991:91). 'The dichotomized nature of the criminal law requires that acts be divided into crimes and non-crimes and that the participants be assigned the status of criminal or victim' (Christie, 1977). More neutral, objective, and value-free terms (such as those used in civil or tort law, for example, litigants) seem more appropriate and more useful for social science research. It is certain, for instance, that the concept of precipitation would have escaped a great deal of the criticism it received had it not had the emotional term 'victim' attached to it (Fattah, 1991:91).

In a paper on critical victimology, Walklate (1990) suggests that 'the concepts of criminal and victim might not be the most useful ones with which to proceed in the policy arena.' We should also question the utility of these concepts for research purposes. One negative consequence of the present indiscriminate use of these labels is to perpetuate the popular stereotypes of the crime protagonists and to reinforce the notion that criminals and victims are as different as night and day. The readiness with which these labels are currently applied ignores the complementarity and the interchangeability of the roles of the victim and offender. Using these labels overlooks the reality that today's victims may be tomorrow's offenders and that today's offenders may be yesterday's victims (Fattah, 1991:91). Yet any call to abandon these firmly entrenched labels and to replace them by more neutral designations, such as 'participants to the conflict', 'parties to the dispute', 'protagonists', and so forth (Fattah, 1991) is bound to encounter fierce resistance and will even require changing the name of the discipline 'victimology' itself.

And yet this neutral terminology has several advantages over the pejorative labels of 'criminal' and 'victim'. First, it represents a much needed return to the notion of crime as a conflict (Christie, 1977; Kennedy, 1990) and the notion of conflict as an interaction. The criminal law is interested in action; criminology should be more concerned with interactions. As Kennedy (1990:35) points out:

> Fundamentally, penal law looks more into acts than into interactions – which removes the negotiated feature of civil disputes from penal or criminal ones. Claiming becomes a process of defining an offender and a victim. But this transformation of the dispute does not deny its origins in conflict or the negotiation over punishment that occurs after the criminality is established.

Second, the proposed judgment-free terminology re-emphasizes the artificial nature and the arbitrariness of the distinction between crime and tort and between criminal and civil law. A third benefit is that it avoids the negative consequences (particularly the stigma) of labelling and the real danger of the participants' self-identification with their labels. Fourth, as sciences of observation and explanation, criminology and victimology need to use a guilt- and blame-free language and to abstain from using terms or labels that imply *a priori* value-judgments. The normative designations of 'criminal' and 'victim' pre-empt a thorough and objective investigation into the real and actual roles each party played in the genesis of the crime (Fattah, 1991).

WHO ARE THE VICTIMS OF CRIME?

Victimization surveys provide empirical support to criminologists' claim that criminality and victimization are clustered within certain groups and certain areas and that there is much greater affinity between offenders and victims than is commonly believed.[4] The idea that victims of crime share common characteristics with their victimizers runs counter to popular perceptions and to the generally held stereotypes of victims. As Singer (1981:779) points out:

> The idea that victims and offenders are part of the same homogeneous population runs contrary to the public's popular impression that criminals are distinct from their innocent victims.

Without the information now available from victimization surveys, few would have accepted Anttila's statement, made in 1974, in which she declared that 'both victims and criminals, particularly in violent crime, appear to be odd people, inclined to unlawfulness, provocative and easily provoked.' She noted that 'the same individuals may alternatingly or even simultaneously turn up as offenders and victims, while the majority of society's ordinary citizens are safely outside' (p. 8).

This is not to say, of course, that *all* victims of crime share the attributes of their victimizers. It is simply to emphasize that the two populations have several common characteristics as has been shown by victimization surveys conducted in the US, Europe, Canada and Australia.[5]

The *Canadian Urban Victimization Survey Bulletin* (1983:4) reports that the profile of the victim of crime against the person is similar to that of the offender:

> When we examine the categories of people most likely to be victimized, many popular myths are exploded. Using the victimization data we can draw a profile of the victim of crime against the person: young unmarried male, living alone, probably looking for work or a student, and with an active life outside the home – not very different from the profile we might draw of the offender.

Studies in Europe, the US, Canada, and Australia show that offenders involved in the types of crimes covered by victimization surveys are disproportionately male, young, urban residents, of lower socioeconomic status, unemployed (and not in school), unmarried, and, in the US, black. Victimization surveys reveal that victims disproportionately share these characteristics and that the demographic profiles of crime victims and of convicted criminals are strikingly similar (Gottfredson, 1984).

Analyzing crimes of violence in Finland, Aromaa (1974) reported that the victims had much in common with the offenders and in Australia, Braithwaite and Biles (1984) declared that the findings provide strong support for the proposition that victims and offenders share many characteristics.

In the US, the similarities between victims and offenders were stressed by Hindelang *et al.* (1978). Their conclusion is the same as that reached by Singer (1981), who found that in crimes of assault victims and offenders were related in their demographic characteristics and in terms of certain shared responses to perceived situations of physical or psychological threat. Singer's conclusion is worth noting:

> A key question then in explaining personal victimization as a consequence of the victim's exposure to an offender is the extent to which violence reflects a lifestyle that leads victims to alternate as offenders in the same

social environment. If victims and offenders share certain understandings and misunderstandings supporting their use of physical force, then both populations are not distinct, but rotate in a web of subcultural relationships. (p. 780)

It is understandable that the frequency with which some individuals become involved in violence-prone situations will affect both their chances of using violence and of being recipients of violence, of attacking and being attacked, of injuring and being injured, of killing and being killed. Who will end up being the victim and who will be legally considered the offender depends quite often on chance factors rather than deliberate action, planning, or intent. Thus, victim/offender roles are not necessarily antagonistic but are frequently complementary and interchangeable (Fattah, 1994d). This situation is particularly true of brawls, quarrels, disputes, and altercations. In many instances, dangerousness and vulnerability may be regarded as the two sides of the same coin. They often coexist since many of the factors that contribute to dangerousness may create or enhance a state of vulnerability. One such factor is alcohol consumption, which may act simultaneously as a criminogenic and as a victimogenic factor, enhancing the potentiality of violent behaviour in one party and of violent victimization in the other (see Fattah and Raic, 1970).

Similarities Between the Victim and Offender Populations

The homogeneity of the victim and offender populations can be easily seen by looking at some of the general socio-demographic characteristics of the two populations.

Age
When young children, who according to the law cannot commit crime, are excluded, it becomes clear that delinquency and victimization rates for the different age groups follow an identical pattern. Younger age groups (15–25) who commit the largest portion of delinquency and crime are the ones most victimized, while elderly groups (65+) who commit the least crime are also the ones least victimized. Intermediary age groups have intermediary rates of both crime and victimization.

Gender
Males commit more crimes and with certain exceptions are criminally victimized more frequently than females. This is also a consistent pattern observable in official crime statistics and in the findings of victimization surveys. Sexual offences are the most glaring exception since they are predominantly committed against women. A national crime victimization survey

report (US Bureau of Justice Statistics, 1995:2) based on the redesigned
survey and devoted to violence against women reveals that *per capita* rates
of reported rapes and other sexual assaults against women were about 10
times higher than equivalent rates against men. The rates of robbery and
aggravated assault against men were about double those against women. The
rate for simple assault against men was one and half times higher than the
equivalent rate against women (38.8 and 26.7 per 1000 persons age 12 or
older respectively).

Marital Status
Victimization surveys in the UK, United States, Canada, Australia and
others show that unmarried persons (single, separated and divorced) are at
higher risk for personal victimization than those who are married, living
common-law, or widowed. This is the same pattern that prevails among
offender populations.

Race and Ethnicity
Because crimes of violence are, to a large extent, intraracial, races and ethnic
groups with high violent crime and delinquency rates (such as blacks and
hispanics in the US) also have high violent victimization rates. The American
white population, on the other hand, registers lower rates on both counts.

Unemployment
Unemployed persons are overrepresented among convicted offenders and
among victims. As with differences associated with marital status, age and
lifestyle are probably responsible, at least partly, for this pattern. In Australia, for example, Braithwaite and Biles (1979) found the unemployed to
have significantly higher rates of victimization for theft, break and enter, and
assault. Most striking is the difference with respect to assault, where the
unemployed were more than twice as likely to report victimization than those
in full-time jobs.

Income
The relationship between income and victimization is not as clearcut as the
relationship between income and crime. Low-income categories are greatly
overrepresented among convicted offenders. Concerning victimization, the
situation is far more complex. The *Canadian Urban Victimization Survey*
(1983) found, as one might expect, that the higher the family income of
urban residents, the more likely they will experience some form of household
victimization of personal theft. Needless to say, the differences among income groups in their levels of tolerance for and awareness of some types of
incidents are likely to affect the level of reporting to the interviewers. The
survey found, however, that lower-income individuals are as likely or more

likely than others to suffer a personal violent victimization – sexual assault, robbery, or assault.

The picture that emerges from American surveys regarding violent victimization by crime is a clearer one. According to the Bureau of Justice Statistics (1985), for both whites and blacks there was a direct relationship between family income and the likelihood of violent victimization: the lower the income, the greater the victimization. While the pattern was consistent for both races and the differences between the lowest and highest income categories were statistically significant, not all differences between adjacent income categories were statistically significant.

Involvement in Delinquency

Committing a crime increases the chances of further involvement in delinquency. For example, if someone commits an armed robbery, a burglary, or an act of shoplifting, the chances that the same person will commit a second offence are much higher than for the rest of the population. The same is true for the risks of victimization. Thus, victimization in one event increases the risk of a second victimization and so on (Fattah, 1989a, 1991).

There is evidence suggesting that criminals are more frequently victimized than non-criminals and that victims of violent crime themselves have considerable criminal involvements.[5] There is also evidence showing that marginal groups are more involved in crime and more often victimized than non-marginal groups. Typical examples of those prone to victimization are persons implicated in illicit activities or those who have opted for a deviant lifestyle: gang members, drug pushers, drug addicts, prostitutes, persons involved in illegal gambling, loan sharks, and so forth.

Canadian homicide statistics for 1991 (*Juristat*, 1992) reveal that almost half of homicide victims (45 per cent) have a criminal record. And in an American study of gunshot victims, Paul Friday (personal communication, March 1995) found that 71 per cent of the victims had their own criminal histories.

Of the 92 assault victims in the hospital-based sample interviewed by Cretney and Davis (1995:32) 24 (26 per cent) told the researchers that they themselves had a criminal record, while 16 (17 per cent) had at least one previous conviction for assault. Other offences committed by the sample of 'victims' included: shoplifting; theft; robbery with violence; and possession and dealing in drugs. Cretney and Davis argue that

> If allowance is made for the fact that some informants might be reticent about their possession of a criminal record, it can be inferred that a high proportion of assault victims are themselves convicted offenders. (p. 32)

The data reviewed above leave little doubt that offender and victim populations, particularly in violent crime, are homogeneous populations that have similar characteristics. The affinity between the victim and offender popula-tions should not come as a surprise. Crimes of violence, particularly those not motivated by sex or financial gain, are interpersonal crimes or crimes of relationships. Since the motives for violence do not develop in a vacuum, it is understandable that these crimes are frequently committed between people who know each other, who interact with each other, and who are bound by family, friendship, or business ties. The typical contexts in which criminal homicide, attempted murder, or assault occur are domestic fights, family disputes, quarrels between non-strangers, or other altercations where insult, abuse, or jealously are present. The interpersonal character of crimes of violence, particularly criminal homicide, is well documented in several stud-ies carried out in different cultures (Svalastoga, 1956; Driver, 1961; Wolf-gang,1958).

The similarities between the victim and offender populations may there-fore be due to the social and geographical proximity of victims and victimi-zers. Proximity and accessibility are important factors in family violence. Geographical proximity is also evident in certain types of property offences. There is a well-established distance decay pattern in human spatial beha-viour. Brantingham and Brantingham (1984) point out that people interact more with people and things that are close to their home location than with people or things that are far away. Interactions decrease as distance increases (distance decay). Some of this decrease in activity as distance increases is the result of the 'costs' of overcoming distance. They further note that the bias of greater density of interaction close to home is also the result of biased spatial knowledge. People have more experience of and are more aware of what exists around them:

> Searching behaviour starts from home and first covers likely areas that are 'known.' Criminals probably follow a similar searching pattern. Although specific studies have not been done on the spatial searching patterns of criminals, the results of other studies show strong traces of such patterns. Crimes generally occur *close* to the home of the criminal. The operational definition of close varies by offence, but the distance-decay gradient is evident in all offenses.... Generally, violent offences have a high concen-tration close to home, with many assaults and murders actually occurring in the home. The search pattern is a little broader for property offences, but these are still clustered close to home. (1984:345)

The Artificial Dichotomy Between Victims and Offenders

Criminals and victims, in the public's view, are as different as night and day. They are perceived as two distinct and mutually exclusive populations who have nothing in common. Positivist theories of criminal behaviour depart from a very similar viewpoint, thus creating an artificial dichotomy between offenders and victims. This dichotomy is coming under increasing criticism as a result of a growing body of evidence pointing to a strong link between victimization and offending (see Thornberry and Figlio, 1972; Singer, 1981, 1986; Johnson *et. al.*, 1973; Lauritsen, Sampson, and Laub, 1991).[6]

The positive association observed between violent offending and violent victimization apparently extends to property offences as well. In two studies of Dutch juveniles, Van Dijk and Steinmetz (1984) discovered a substantial overlap between being a victim of various theft offences and admitting to having committed them. One of the explanations they offer for the observed overlap is the possibility that theft might result from normative curbs being weakened by victimization or because it is a convenient way of recouping losses.

Commenting on the findings of the British Crime Survey, Mayhew and Elliott (1990:20) conclude that:

> In the broadest terms, the self-report evidence from the BCS, especially Gottfredson's (1984) analysis, bears on thinking about victims insofar as it highlights the inappropriateness of seeing victims and offenders as distinct groups.... The fact that men and the young face higher risks of personal crime, especially violence, has been one of the most significant findings of victimization surveys, countering the idea that it is the weakest and most vulnerable who are uniformly sought out by offenders.

One problem with victimization data in their present form is their inability to reveal the chronological order and the time sequence of offending and victimization, thus making it difficult to tell which occurs first. Does offending precede or succeed victimization? It is quite possible that becoming a victim of violence creates the motivation (and justification) for offending (revenge, retaliation, getting even). Van Dijk and Steinmetz (1984) seem to lean toward this explanation for property victimization/offending. But the reverse chronological order is also plausible. That is, violent offending may increase the chances of becoming a victim of retaliatory violence. It could also be that involvement in delinquency and adoption of a delinquent lifestyle do enhance the likelihood of violent (or property) victimization in other ways (Fattah, 1991).

That victimization creates the motives and rationalizations for offending and that offending provides the reasons for victimization means that the two activities are closely linked. To look upon them as separate and unrelated activities or to look upon victims and offenders as two distinct or mutually exclusive populations is in direct contradiction to the available empirical evidence (Reiss, Jr., 1981).

If it is true that prior victimization is a primary or a major factor in offending or if victims and offenders are constantly moving between the two roles, then it seems necessary to revise the tenets of positivist criminology (as well as the theories based on those tenets) to take into account the role victimization plays in the process of primary or secondary offending. Moreover, if the traits and attributes claimed by positivist theories to be characteristic of offenders are common to both offenders and victims, their criminogenic role and their explanatory value as causes of delinquency would be greatly diminished.

Another problem is the current practice of categorizing (and labelling) offenders and victims on the basis of a single event instead of the totality of their life experiences. By so doing, the frequent link between victimization and offending is often missed. With the exception of birth cohort studies, few researchers have used a longitudinal analysis to explore the existence and the nature of the link between victimization and offending experiences.

And since dispositional theories (whether of the biological, constitutional, psychological, or even sociological variety) exclude situational variables from their explanatory models, they naturally fail to come up with a satisfactory explanation of crime. As Kinberg (1960) points out, when analyzing the genesis of an action to determine its causes, it is not possible to regard certain facts or groups of facts as separate entities. The logical intellectual process requires that the researcher take an overall view of the intricate web of factors that form a tight causal chain, the last link of which is the action being analyzed.

Gibbons (1971:271) also observes that in many cases criminality may be a response to nothing more temporal than the provocations and attractions bound up in the immediate circumstances. He adds:

> It may be that, in some kinds of lawbreaking, understanding of the behavior may require detailed attention to the concatenation of events immediately preceding it. Little or nothing may be added to this understanding from a close scrutiny of the early development of the person.

SOME VICTIM TYPES

Classic typologies of victims (von Hentig, 1948; Mendelsohn, 1956; Fattah, 1967) have been repeatedly discussed and critically evaluated in the victimological literature. Instead of repeating these typologies we will discuss some types of victims who were either missing or were dealt with in a fleeting manner in the earlier typologies (see Fattah, 1991).

The Born Victim

In the early days of criminology, Lombroso claimed that criminals are born. And in the early days of victimology, some claimed that there are born victims. In 1941 von Hentig suggested that:

> If there are born criminals, it is evident that there are born victims, self-harming and self-destroying through the medium of a pliable outsider.

Another pioneer in victimology, Ellenberger (1955:277), a psychiatrist, also believed that born victims exist. He wrote:

> In summary, we contend that there are individuals, probably in great numbers, whom one could consider as 'born victims', in the sense that they attract criminals, not so much by external circumstances or fleeting event, but by reason of a permanent and unconscious predisposition to play the role of victim.

These views might have been acceptable at a time when determinism was still in vogue. At present, however, the concept of the 'born victim', in the sense of an individual doomed by birth to become the target of criminal victimization, is, like the concept of the born criminal, universally rejected. In contemporary victimology, the fatalistic notion of the 'born victim' is replaced by other probabilistic concepts, such as predisposition, propensity, proneness, and vulnerability to victimization. It is argued that while few individuals may become victims by pure chance or through chance encounters, others tend by reason of structural or behavioural characteristics (such as lifestyle) to get themselves in situations or interactions likely to lead to criminal victimization. Others still may invite, induce, provoke, precipitate, or attract victimization.

Cultural Types

The Ideal Victim

Each culture creates its own popular stereotypes of offenders and victims. Society's attitudes and reaction to actual offenders and actual victims are shaped by the extent to which they fit these images and stereotypes. The 'ideal victim' is one such stereotype.

As used by Christie (1986), the term 'ideal victim' does not refer to the person (or category) most perceiving him-or herself as a victim. Nor does it describe those who are in the greatest danger of being victimized or most often victimized. By 'ideal victim' Christie means a person (or category of individuals) who – hit by crime – most readily are given the complete and legitimate status of being a victim. The 'ideal victim', writes Christie, is, in my use of the term, a sort of public status of the same type and level of abstraction as that for example of a 'hero' or a 'traitor.' It is difficult to count these ideal victims. Just as it is difficult to count heroes. But they can be exemplified...the little old lady on the way home in the middle of the day after having cared for her sick sister. If she is hit on the head by a big man who thereafter grabs her bag and uses the money for liquor or drugs – in that case, we come, in my country, close to the ideal victim. (pp. 18–19)

The Culturally Legitimate Victim

The concept of the culturally legitimate victim was first used by Weiss and Borges in 1973 to describe victims of rape. They point out that socialization and, especially, sex-role learning exploit males and females and produce victims and offenders. The authors suggest that a male-dominated society, in which most positions of power and influence are occupied by men, tends to establish and perpetuate the woman as a legitimate object for victimization. In such a society, Weiss and Borges maintain, social processes prepare the woman for her role as a potential victim and provide the procedures to make her a socially approved or legitimate victim for rape.

The culturally legitimate victim is a broad type, and it is possible to identify several subtypes, that is, groups whose victimization is encouraged, condoned, tolerated, or not condemned by the culture. Below are some types that are culturally regarded as appropriate targets for victimization.

Appropriate Victims

Cultural as well as subcultural norms designate certain individuals or groups as appropriate targets for victimization. In non-industrial societies, in youth gangs, and in other self-contained groups marked by inner solidarity, violence against members of the out-group is tolerated and sometimes encouraged, while violence against members of the in-group is strongly condemned. The normative system governing these societies or groups designates the out-group members as legitimate targets for victimization. A national survey of attitudes towards violence in the United States found that excluding people from groups to which one feels related can serve as a rationalization justifying violence toward them or make violence inflicted on such people more easily acceptable (Blumenthal *et al.*, 1972; Conklin, 1975).

In most jurisdictions, including Canada (until the law was changed), forcible sexual intercourse with one's wife is not a criminal offence and is excluded from the criminal code's definition of rape. The wife 'raped' by her husband is a culturally legitimate victim. The concept extends to other forms of violence in the family. Despite growing concern over child abuse, children continue to be considered legitimate targets for the use of physical force in the process of training and upbringing.

Even now, the unfaithful wife continues to exemplify the culturally legitimate victim in many cultures, and the husband who kills his adulterous wife is either exempted from punishment or treated with extreme leniency.

Impersonal Victims

Impersonal, non-specific, and intangible victims, such as the government, large corporations, organizations, and so forth, are considered by many as appropriate targets for victimization. Victimizing them is subject to fewer (if any) moral restraints and arouses less guilt than victimization directed against a personal, identifiable victim. The impersonal or diffuse character of the victim, its abstract nature, evokes little moral resistance in the person contemplating the victimization. As Sykes and Matza (1957:668) put it:

> Insofar as the victim is physically absent, unknown, or a vague abstraction (as is often the case in delinquent acts committed against property), the awareness of the victim's existence is weakened. Internalized norms and anticipations of the reactions of others must somehow be activated, if they are to serve as guides for behavior; and it is possible that a diminished awareness of the victim plays an important part in determining whether or not this process is set in motion.

The idea of stealing from or cheating the government or a large organization raises fewer moral scruples than the idea of cheating a person or stealing from a family. In his study of crime and custom of Hungarians in Detroit in the early 1930s, Beynon (1935) found that certain coal-stealing gangs received a sort of social approval in the Hungarian colony. The reason for approval had nothing to do with the material act or its perpetrators but with the victim. The coal was stolen not from some individual but from the property of an impersonal, unknown railroad company, which translated in their thinking to the absentee nobleman in their home country, from whose woods their parents used to gather firewood. The conversation between the researcher and the recording steward of a Hungarian church in Detroit illustrates well how impersonal victims are perceived as appropriate targets. In answer to a question about his fuel for the winter, the steward replied:

> We buy only stolen coal. It costs us $3.00 a ton which is less than half what we pay the coal dealers. The boys come and take our orders in the afternoon and then steal the coal at night from the cars on the railway tracks. Do you think it is wrong to steal coal or to buy stolen coal? No, of course not. You see, it is this way, stealing coal is different from other stealing. If I would take five cents of your money, that would be real stealing. You are a man just like me. I know you. I have never in my life stolen like that. No honest man would. Only the gypsies steal from other people that way. But coal stealing isn't like that at all. Why? The coal stands there on that

railroad tracks, and we never see the man who owns that railroad. It is an estate of some kind just like the estates in Hungary. Why should not the poor people get their coal from it? (pp. 763–4)

Henry (1978:53) offers the following quotation from 'Up against the Law Collective' (1974:33):

> It's important who we nick from. If we nick from our friends we deserve to get done. We certainly don't deserve to have any friends. If we nick from a big supermarket we're doing nothing wrong. It's a crime to steal from your brothers and sisters; it's a public service to help each other nick from millionaire companies.

Smigel and Ross (1970), who studied bureaucracies as victims, suggest that the size, wealth, and impersonality of big business and government are attributes that make it seem excusable, to many people, to steal from them. They add that such popular attitudes are behind a modern preventive technique used by certain American enterprises in an attempt to personalize the victim, thus evoking pity and compassion in the potential offender. Thus, in certain motels in the US a sign is placed in each room that reads: 'If any towels are missing when you leave, the maid cleaning the room will be responsible for them.' Smigel and Ross see such a notice as a device to deter theft by evoking sympathy for an individual rather than for a bureaucracy.

Disposable, Worthless, and Deserving Victims

What characterizes these three subtypes of culturally legitimate victims is society's attitude and reaction to their victimization. Normal public attitude to criminal victimization in which a fellow citizen and human being suffers tangible injury, harm, or loss is one of sympathy, compassion, and commiseration. The victimization of individuals belonging to these subtypes, however, does not evoke any of these positive feelings. In other words, nobody feels sorry for the victim. There is no outcry of indignation and little (if anything) is done to pursue those responsible for the victimization or to bring them to justice. When they are occasionally caught, the sentence of the court is, more often than not, an acquittal or extremely lenient.

Although these three subtypes of cultural victims are similar in many respects, they may still be distinguished from one another. The main differences between them lie in cultural stereotypes and social attitudes, in the way they are perceived and treated by the normative system of society.

Disposable victims. The attitude to 'disposable victims' or 'expendable victims' is one of hostility and antagonism bordering on hate, and their victimization is often welcomed with a sigh of relief. This is the lot that, in the past, was reserved for witches. At present, it is reserved for criminals and outlaws. Since they are disposable, they may be readily sacrificed and used as scapegoats to deter others or to show that society really means what it says when it threatens to punish those who commit crime. Whatever victimization they suffer, especially while they are behind bars, causes no uproar, or even concern, among the general public, who couldn't care less what happens to them. Their complaints, if ever aired, fall on deaf ears as if they are not entitled to the same kind of protection the rest of society enjoys.

Disposable victims are, to use a term coined by Spitzer (1975) in another context, 'social junk'. That is why whenever they are killed, whether legally executed or slain by other inmates, the general reaction is one of 'good riddance'.

Worthless victims. As a result of deeply anchored prejudices, our culture defines certain groups and the members of those groups as worthless. These are mostly people who are living in society but are not really part of it. They have chosen their own lifestyle, a different lifestyle that the majority does not approve of, and have decided to live on the margin. They have their own subcultures that neatly separate them from the rest of society. Social attitude to 'worthless victims' is one of contempt, and their victimization is usually met with tacit approval. They are society's outcasts: homosexuals, prostitutes, pimps, drug addicts, vagrants, skid row residents, and so on. The slang words used to describe them – 'faggot', 'queer', 'whore', 'narc', 'hobo', and so on – reflect well the way society despises them and shape the general reaction to their victimization. Their status as outcasts makes them reluctant to seek the protection of the police or even to report their victimization. They are therefore regarded by potential criminals and juvenile gangs as easy targets who may be victimized with impunity. The general perception that they are 'worthless' also explains the laxity in solving their cases once they are victimized.

Deserving victims. These are victims who through their dishonest, inconsiderate, deceitful, or reckless behaviour are seen as deserving their victimization. The popular judgment when they are victimized: 'He only got what he deserves' epitomizes society's attitude and reaction to this type of victim.

Deserving victims fit both the cultural type and the behavioural type, depending on the criterion one uses for typologizing them: the behaviour of the victim or society's attitude. The social attitude to deserving victims is indifference, coupled sometimes with secret admiration for their victimizer. Their victimization is not met with the proper action but rather with inaction and, occasionally, with inner satisfaction. The perfect example of the 'deserving victim' is the victim of a con game or some other type of swindle who was trying to steal, cheat, or realize some dirty profit but finally got fleeced.

Deserving victims are characteristically 'dirty hands' victims or 'guilty' victims. As a result rather than evoking pity, their victimization sometimes elicits this comforting but wicked feeling that the 'dirty bastard' finally got what he really deserved. In the Oscar-winning movie 'The Sting' with Paul Newman and Robert Redford, the elaborate con scheme revolves around a typically 'deserving victim', whose manners, arrogance, and dishonesty render him so unappealing to those watching the movie that his victimization is met not with sympathy for the 'sucker' but with applause.

Structural Types

Structural types designate groups who are more vulnerable than others to certain forms of victimization, criminal and otherwise, because of some structural variables. They are more exposed and less protected than other groups. The hierarchy created by the political and economic systems results in an unequal distribution of wealth and power and casts certain groups and classes in victim roles. Those who are at the bottom of the ladder of the social hierarchy are the ones who suffer the bulk of victimization. Their share of victims is often disproportionate to their numbers.

Structural vulnerability may also be related to the exercise of certain occupations, which render those who practise them particularly exposed to criminal attacks, such as taxi drivers, bank cashiers, pharmacists, operators of small grocery stores, and so on.

Behavioural Types: Provoking, Precipitating Victims

The existence of a provoking victim has been acknowledged for a very long time. Modern criminal codes recognize provocation by the victim as an extenuating circumstance that reduces a murder to manslaughter or makes a criminal homicide an excusable one.

Victims who fit this type are those whose behaviour precipitates, triggers, or acts as a catalyst for the attack against them. Wolfgang (1957) coined the term 'victim-precipitated' to refer to those criminal homicides in which the victim is a direct, positive precipitator in the crime. The role of the victim in such cases is characterized by his having been the first to show and use a deadly weapon or to strike a blow in an altercation – in short, the first to commence the interplay or resort to physical violence. A couple of cases cited by Wolfgang (1957) and Curtis (1975) will help illustrate this behavioural type. Among the victim-precipitated homicide cases Wolfgang encountered in his research is the case of a husband who accused his wife of giving money to another man. While she was making breakfast, he attacked her with a milk bottle, then a brick, and finally a piece of concrete block. Since she had a butcher knife in hand, she stabbed him during the fight. In another case, during a lover's quarrel, the male (victim) hit his mistress and threw a can of kerosene at her. She retaliated by throwing the liquid at him and then tossed a lighted match in his direction. He died from the burns.

Consenting, Willing, Inviting, Soliciting, and Participating Victims

Contrary to popular conceptions, criminal victimization does not always take place against the will or without the consent of the victim. Ever since crime came to be regarded as an offence against the sovereign (and later against the state/society), the non-consent of the victim has no longer been a prerequisite for the constitution of the offence, nor is the consent of the victim necessary to bring charges against the offender and to pursue the case to conviction. As a result, there are Criminal Code offences that may be committed even when the party who suffers the injury, harm, or loss is a willing, consenting partner. So why would the law criminalize an act to which the 'victim' does not object? Sometimes this is done to protect individuals judged incapable of giving free, enlightened consent or unable to protect themselves against victimization and exploitation. The typical example is 'statutory rape' where the consenting female is under age.

Other examples are violations of laws prohibiting the hiring of children under a certain age to do specific jobs, their use in the production of pornographic material, laws prohibiting the access of minors to certain places (racetracks, gambling casinos, adult movie theatres, and so on), or prohibiting the sale of or serving liquor to them. The prohibition is usually extended to other groups judged to be in need of protection, such as the mentally retarded, or even to individuals not suffering from any mental handicap but who are in the danger of being exploited as in the case of loan sharking. Other times, the criminalization of the behaviour in spite of the consent of the victim is done because the act is judged sufficiently injurious, harmful, or dangerous as to warrant its interdiction even when the parties involved are consenting. For example, causing a deliberate injury may qualify as wounding even when done with the consent or at the request of the victim and the same is true of assisted suicide.

Many of the willing, consenting, participating victims are in reality *legally created victims*, persons who are prohibited from doing things under the guise or pretext of their protection. Restriction of freedom and outright discrimination are sometimes couched in terms of 'protection.' A good example is the differential age specified by the law for consent to heterosexual and homosexual relations. It is clear that the higher age of consent required for homosexual acts is not meant to protect those who are homosexually inclined but to discriminate against them. Even laws that are really meant to protect certain vulnerable or exposed groups often fail to take into account the sexual and emotional needs of the members of these groups. What they do in fact is to impose restrictions on the behaviour of those judged in need of protection, thus preventing them from doing things that others are allowed to do. For example, the law that says a minor (under 16, 18, or 21 according to the jurisdiction) or a mentally retarded person cannot give free, enlightened consent to having sex amounts in practice to a prohibition against the 'protected' person having sex. All such paternalistic laws are problematic because they raise the question: to what extent should the criminal law try to protect people against their will and their wishes and to what extent should it restrict the freedoms of those who are under a certain (arbitrarily set) age.

What these paternalistic laws do is to create consenting and conniving victims. Offences committed against consenting, soliciting, and participating victims have an extremely high dark figure. Not surprisingly, these types of victims are generally unco-operative in their dealings with the criminal justice system and are naturally excluded from state compensation programs. But consenting, willing, or participating victims should not be confused with victims who co-operate with their victimizer under threat or duress or because of fear, such as victims of blackmail, extortion, or incest.

Negligent, Careless, Imprudent, and Reckless Victims[7]

People do not try to protect themselves or their property against criminal victimization with the same care, zeal, or diligence. Their attitudes, behaviour, and the precautions and protective measures they take (or do not take) make it possible to qualify them as prudent/imprudent, careful/careless, circumspect/reckless, cautious/negligent, and so forth. These adjectives or qualities denote extreme points at the far ends of a continuum with most people fitting somewhere in-between. Moreover, these are general traits describing the general attitude or behavioural patterns of a given individual; they do not describe the person's attitude or behaviour in all situations at all times.

One may be prudent in certain situations (for example, when on foreign turf) and imprudent in others (for example, when on familiar territory); circumspect on some occasions (for example, when sober) and reckless on others (for example, when drunk). Still, certain individuals may be designated as being generally the 'negligent or careless' type or as the 'reckless or imprudent' type. These attitudinal and behavioural traits are by no means static. It is known, for example, that reckless, imprudent people become prudent and less reckless with marriage, familial responsibilities, advanced age, and so forth. The traits are also dynamic in that they change according to the kind of interaction the person is engaged in and the person(s) with whom he/she is interacting. A person who may be very prudent and circumspect when dealing with strangers may be totally disarmed and thus lacking in prudence when interacting with members of the family or close friends.

The role these victim types play in property victimization has been empirically demonstrated. But the role is not limited to property offences and is equally important in some others (for example, hitchhike victimization). According to opportunity theory, many criminals are opportunists who take advantage of situations and environmental opportunities, many of which are created by the prospective victims' negligent, careless, imprudent, reckless, or facilitating behaviour.

Criminological Types: Recidivist and Chronic Victims

There is abundant empirical evidence from victim surveys indicating that certain individuals may suffer frequent and repeated victimization during the reference period. In other words, they are recidivist or repeat victims.

Actually, victims may be divided according to the frequency of their victimizations, into several categories or types: the one-timer, the occasional, the experienced or recidivist, the chronic, and so on. The one-timer is someone who has suffered only a single victimization. The occasional is someone who has suffered two or three isolated and unrelated victimizations over a lifetime or a very long period of time. The recidivist is someone who was subject to a frequent and persistent pattern of victimization within a relatively short period of time. The chronic victim is someone whose life is a continuing series of victimizations. The categorization of the one-timers does not pose a major operationalization problem. But the lines of demarcation between the other three categories: the occasional, the recidivist, and the chronic are somewhat arbitrary.

Victim surveys, without exception, found that while the majority of respondents do not report one single incident of victimization, a small top risk category seemed to be victimized almost incessantly. Ziegenhagen (1977) studied the repeated victimization of some individuals, and his findings suggest that recidivist victims can be distinguished from the general victim population by distinctive individual, social, and attitudinal orientations.

Recidivist and chronic victims are of particular importance to victimological research because they can shed light on the factors and variables associated with certain types of criminal victimization and can enhance our understanding of the notions of proneness and vulnerability.

NOTES

1. On the basis of an experimental study where prison inmates were shown videotapes of individuals and asked to rate the assault potential of these individuals on a scale, Grayson and Stein (1981) concluded that 'a non-verbal dialogue seems to exist between criminal and victim through which the victim communicates his or her vulnerability to the criminal in much the same way that releasor mechanisms operate in the animal world.'
2. For the importance of situational factors, see Wikström, P.O.H. (1985) *Everyday Violence in Contemporary Sweden: Situational and Ecological Aspects.* Stockholm:

The National Council for Crime Prevention. See also Mawson, A.R. (1978). *Transient Criminality: A Model of Stress-Induced Crime.* New York: Praeger.
3. For the impact of the victim on criminal justice decisions, see the following: Donald J. Hall (1975). The role of the victim in the prosecution and disposition of a criminal case. *Vanderbilt Law Review.* Vol. 28, No. 5, pp. 932–85 and Williams, K. (1976). The effects of victim characteristics on the disposition of violent crimes. In McDonald, W.F. (ed.), *Criminal Justice and the Victim.* Beverly Hills: Sage Publications.
4. Gottfredson (1984) analysed the 1982 British Crime Survey data and was struck by the relatively strong interrelationship between offending and victimization. For persons with at least one self-reported violence offence, the likelihood of victimization was 42 per cent, or seven times the likelihood of personal victimization for persons reporting no self-reported violent offences. When Gottfredson controlled for age, the relationship between self-reported delinquencies and self-reported violence and personal victimization persisted despite the controls. Gottfredson suggests that there is probably a lifestyle that, for some, includes high probabilities of misfortune, victimization, and offending, perhaps resulting from where they live, where they go, and with whom they associate. Gottfredson went on to test various hypotheses about these interrelationships using the British Crime Survey data. The data strongly suggested that lifestyles conducive to victimization of all forms are also conducive to offending.
5. See in particular, Hindelang *et al.* (1978), Gottfredson (1984), Braithwaite and Biles (1984), Mayhew and Elliott (1990).
6. Thornberry and Figlio (1972) examined victimization and criminal behaviour using a 10 per cent sample of individuals drawn from a 1945 Philadelphia birth cohort. The data revealed that arrest status was strongly and consistently associated with victimization.

   In the follow-up survey to the Philadelphia birth cohort, a study of self-reported victimization, Singer (1981) examined the extent to which victims are also guilty of serious assault. He reports that cohort members who were shot or stabbed were involved more frequently in official and self-reported criminal activity. Victims of serious assault had the highest probability of having a friend arrested, belonging to a gang, using a weapon, committing a serious assault, and being officially arrested.

   Johnson *et al.* (1973) followed up all victims of gunshot and stab wounds admitted to the City of Austin Hospital in Texas during 1968 and 1969. They found that 75 per cent of the male victims had a criminal record, and 54 per cent had a jail record. Savitz, Lalli, and Rosen (1977), using a Philadelphia cohort, also observed an association between official records of having committed assault and assault victimization. And in their London, England, survey, Sparks, Genn, and Dodd (1977), found victims of violent crime to be significantly more likely than non-victims to self report the commission of violent crimes.
7. The distinction between inviting/soliciting victims and careless/negligent ones is not always easy. Opportunities for criminal victimization may be deliberately created by the prospective victims. In her study of shoplifting in Chicago, Cameron (1964) points out that the lavish displays of merchandise that department stores exhibit to encourage 'impulsive buying' are, for the experienced pilferer, there for the taking. Gibbens and Prince (1962) report that a store in England sets out to achieve a certain level of shoplifting as a demonstration of the adequate lure of goods on display. If the shoplifting rate falls below the anticipated level, the store rearranges its shelves and counters on the assumption that they are not offering sufficient temptation for impulse buying and stealing. Naturally, department stores who act in this way fit more the inviting/soliciting type than the negligent type.

7 Criminology and Victimology

A HYBRID SCIENCE CALLED CRIMINOLOGY

Criminology is indeed a tremendously huge and hybrid science. For the criminologist must be equipped with knowledge of a considerable number of sciences: philosophy, sociology, psychology, psychiatry, legal science and perhaps many more.

Hermanus Bianchi (1956:208)
Position and Subject-Matter of Criminology

During the second half of the 20th century, criminology gradually established itself as a scientific discipline. The existing body of knowledge, the volume of research being carried out, the number of publications, the number of learned journals, and the number of colleges and universities offering courses and degrees in criminology, as well as the number of professional societies and associations, all reflect the solid position criminology has acquired among the social sciences. Still, the status of criminology as an autonomous social science is by no means undisputed.

Even scholars who identify themselves as 'criminologists' are reluctant to acknowledge the autonomy of criminology. Writing on criminology in the *Canadian Encyclopedia* James Hackler (1985:445), of the University of Alberta, starts by stating that 'criminology is a subfield of sociology'!

What is Criminology?

Criminology, from the Latin *crimen* and the Greek *logos*, is a global term used to designate a broad field of learning and a heterogeneous body of knowledge. Earlier we saw that there is no universal definition of either 'crime' or 'criminal', which is bound to lead to a divergence of opinion on how criminology, as a science, is to be defined. Early definitions gave a description of the subject matter or an enumeration of the areas of study covered by criminology or both. A good example of those definitions is the one given by Sutherland and Cressey (1960:3):

Criminology is the body of knowledge regarding crime as a social phenomenon. It includes within its scope the processes of making laws, of breaking laws, and of reacting toward the breaking of laws.

A similar definition, stressing both the theoretical and applied nature of a science of crime, is the one formulated by Johnson (1968:7), according to which:

> Criminology is the scientific study and practical application of findings in the areas of: a) crime causation and criminal behaviour and etiology, b) the nature of the societal reaction as a symptom of the characteristics of the society, and c) the prevention of crime.

Probably the most valiant attempt to define criminology is the one made by the Dutch criminologist Hermanus Bianchi, who in 1956 devoted a whole book to the definition of criminology, to a description of its subject matter, and to its position and relation to other scientific disciplines. Later, another Dutch criminologist, G. Peter Hoefnagels (1973:51), came up with the following definition:

> Criminology is an empirical science, related in part to the legal norm, which studies crime and the formal and informal processes of criminalization and decriminalization, the offense-offender-society situation, the causes and relations between the causes, and the official and unoffical reactions and responses to crime, criminals and society by others than offenders.

While Johnson's definition does not mention the process of law-making, Sutherland and Cressey as well as Hoefnagels see the sociology of law as an integral part of criminology. This is also Stan Cohen's view. According to Cohen (1988:9), the stuff of criminology consists of only three questions: Why are laws made? Why are they broken? What do we do or what should we do about this? Cohen claims that criminology has two sides: Causation and control. It is interesting to note that none of the definitions makes any mention of the victims of crime.

The dynamic nature of a relatively young discipline like criminology means that definitions of the discipline will change over time. Henry and Milovanovic (1994:110) offer the following outline of what they call 'constitutive criminology':

> Constitutive criminology is concerned with identifying the ways in which the interrelationships between human agents and their social world constitute crime, victims and control as realities. It is oriented to how we may deconstruct these realities and to how we may reconstruct less harmful alternatives.

Is Criminology a Normative Science?

Confusing criminology with the practical application of criminological knowledge to criminal policy often leads to the conclusion that criminology is essentially a normative science.

Theology and ethics are normative. They prescribe and proscribe. They define rules of behaviour and norms of conduct: how the individual ought to behave, what is good and what is evil, what is right and what is wrong. In short, they define what is desirable and undesirable in terms of individual and social behaviour. Theology and deontology are value laden. They are not and cannot be neutral or value free. They make value judgments concerning different types of human behaviour. The same could be said of criminal law.

Few would argue that criminal law is not a normative discipline. It is normative because it sets rules of behaviour and commands citizens to act or not to act in a certain way. Since criminology is indissolubly linked to the criminal law, it has been regarded by many scholars as a normative discipline. Michael Phillipson (1974), for example, argues that

> Crime and the criminal result from social definitions and social processes. The study of crime and the criminal, therefore, makes criminology a 'normative' discipline – that is, one that rests initially on the evaluation by non-criminologists of what 'the problem' is; its subject-matter is defined by particular social values.

Other scholars, like Hermann Mannheim (1965:13), have convincingly asserted the non-normative character of criminology:

> However, as the normative character of juridical laws has been questioned so has the non-normative character of criminology been doubted by other writers. H. Bianchi (1956) in particular has recently asserted that, since crime is a normative concept, this 'forces criminology to make a study of norms' and it is therefore a normative discipline. This, however, seems to betray a confusion between the study of norms, which is in itself non-normative, and the creation, establishment and use of norms, which characterize a normative discipline.

To argue that criminology is not a normative discipline is not to maintain that criminology is or can be value free. Like other social sciences, criminology cannot entirely exclude all value judgments. It is in a position analogous to that of sociology. The study of social norms constitutes an integral part of sociology, but this study does not make sociology a normative science.

Can Criminology Be Value-Free?

Criminology, like other social sciences, strives for objectivity and neutrality. It endeavours to become a value-free science. This is, however, a difficult, elusive, and almost impossible goal. Can criminology ever become value-free? Is there such a thing as a value-free social science? The majority of social scientists would no doubt answer in the negative. Myrdal (1958), among others, maintains that a value-free social science does not exist. Values enter into the research process through the selection of research problems, through the choice of methods, through the way data are conceptualized, through the concepts used, and finally in the interpretation of the data (Israel, 1972).

Probably the biggest obstacle in the way of value-free criminology is that it is quasi impossible for criminologists to free themselves from their own value systems, to rid themselves entirely of their biases and prejudices and take an ideology-free stand vis-à-vis society's norms and the laws incorporating those norms. Many criminologists do not see the quest for objectivity and neutrality as a worthwhile goal. Radical and critical criminologists, for example, are openly opposed to moral and political neutrality. They make no secret that they are ideologically committed and plead against an apolitical criminology. The following quotation from Taylor, Walton and Young's book, *The New Criminology* (1975:280–1), illustrates well this position:

> The new criminology must therefore be a normative theory: it must hold out the possibilities of a resolution to the fundamental questions, and a social resolution. It is this normative imperative that separates out the European Schools of Criminology from the eclecticism and reformism in professional American Sociology.... It should be clear that a criminology which is not normatively committed to the abolition of inequalities of wealth and power, and in particular of inequalities in property and life-chances, is inevitably bound to fall into correctionalism. And all correctionalism is irreducibly bound up with the identification of deviance with pathology.

Radical schools assign to the criminologist a role that goes far beyond mere study and observation, the formulation of theories and hypotheses. It is the role of a social and political activist. According to this view, the criminologist is no longer a scholar in an ivory tower taking a neutral and detached stand vis-à-vis the inequalities and injustices of society and the ensuing criminality. Nor should the criminologist take the role of a correctionalist, trying to modify and shape the behaviour of the lawbreaker to fit existing norms. He or she has to lead the fight against the existing power structure and against the present social and economic conditions that breed crime. The Norwegian criminologist Thomas Mathiesen is seen as a good example of the social scientist assuming this new engaged role. Here is how Mathiesen is viewed by Taylor, Walton, and Young (1975:381):

> For him, the problem, even in the relatively benign atmosphere of Scandinavia, was action; to change society 'as it is': not simply to describe 'The Defences of the Weak' but to organize them. The normative prescription

of the new Scandinavian criminology led to the formation of the K.R.U.M., a trade union for inmates of Scandinavian prisons, and a union which was able, two years ago, to coordinate a prison strike across three national boundaries and across several prison walls.

Despite such strong stands in favour of a normative, strongly committed criminology, there are scholars who remain attached to the idea of a non-normative, and non-partisan criminology. To them, criminology is and should remain apolitical. Such a stand, they argue, does not mean that criminologists should isolate themselves in an ivory tower or become socially apathetic. They can advocate reform and foster change on the basis of scientific rather than moral or ideological grounds.

Subject Matter of Criminology

Some years ago, criminology was the object of heated debates pertaining to its subject matter. Most of these debates focused on whether criminology should confine itself to the study of crime in the legal sense or whether it should extend its investigation to other deviant or anti-social behaviours that are not legally treated as crime. Sellin (1938) and Mannheim (1965) are both exponents of the broader view. Sellin argues that

A criminal law with classifications fully meeting the criteria of science is probably unthinkable, but the sociological analysis of criminal norms must delve below the labels of the law if it is to have any considerable scientific value . . . . The etiological study of conduct norms and their violations must be infinitely broader than the study of crime norms and must be relied upon to develop basic scientific units and categories (p. 38–9)

It was noted earlier that there is no intrinsic difference between behaviour designated by law as criminal and other behaviour not designated as such. It seems obvious, therefore, that criminology cannot limit itself to the study of crime in the legal sense but has to extend its scope to other norm violations and other types of human behaviour that share common characteristics with illegal behaviour.

The lines drawn by the criminal law are often arbitrary and artificial. Criminology, therefore, has to go beyond the categories of behaviour made criminal by the law and extend its scope to the broader category of social deviance. Confining the study to acts made criminal by the law would mean that the subject matter of criminology is not defined by its own intrinsic qualities but by legislators.

Criminology, as Phillipson (1974) points out, is a study of social processes, processes by which the criminal law is made and changed and by which the criminal law is maintained and enforced, and of the complex relationship between societal reactions to crime in the shape of the penal system and the quantity and quality of crime in a society. It is, in other words, a study of the processes by which only some people are selected for official labelling as delinquents or criminals, and so forth.

In the past, the subject matter of criminology was confined to the study of the causes of crime, the treatment of offenders, and the prevention of crime. In recent years, the study of the processes of criminalization and decriminalization, the process of labelling, has added new dimensions to this subject matter. At present, criminology comprises a politico-legal dimension, a behavioural dimension, and a social dimension.

Politico-Legal Dimension

The emphasis here is on the study of the law from sociological and political perspectives. What are the basic principles underlying the criminal law? What social values and social interests are protected by the criminal law? Who is influential in defining certain behaviours as criminal? Why are certain behaviours made criminal while others are not? In what way does behaviour defined as criminal differ from behaviours not defined as such? To what extent do legal definitions of crimes correspond to public views of behaviours so defined? Where should the boundaries of the criminal law be drawn; what are the limits of criminalization? To what extent is the criminal law ahead of, or lagging behind, social evolution and social change?

In other words, this dimension of criminology focuses upon the processes and procedures by which certain behaviours are defined as harmful or threatening to society and as warranting state intervention by means of criminal law and penal sanctions. It examines the role some interest groups (particularly those in positions of power) play in defining certain behaviours as criminal as well as the role of the public at large, grassroots movements, moral crusaders and moral entrepreneurs, pressure groups, and so forth in the criminalization and decriminalization processes.

Behavioural Dimension

The emphasis here is on the deviant behaviour itself. An in-depth analysis of the nature of the behaviour, its characteristics, the similarities and differences between the behaviour and other types of human behaviour, the trends and patterns of the behaviour, and so forth . The behavioural dimension embodies the study of two important processes:

The criminogenic process. The study of the origin and sources of criminal behaviour. What generates or favours the commission of crime? What are the motives behind various types of criminal behaviour? Why do some individuals engage in or persist in certain deviant behavioural patterns?

What are the characteristics of the perpetrator and of the victim? What types of relationships exist between offenders and victims? How do victim-offender interactions lead to the commission of certain crimes?

The criminal process. The study of the process of the commission of the crime. An analysis of the criminal or deviant acts, the temporal and spatial trends of such acts, the techniques of execution, the choice of targets, and so forth.

Social Dimension

The emphasis here is on the study of societal reaction to crime and deviance, the nature, forms, modes, and consequences of this reaction. What are the levels of tolerance of society to certain types of behaviour? Why does a given society react differently to similar types of behaviour? What form(s) does social reaction take, and why does it take the form(s) it does? What effect does societal reaction have on controlling and preventing criminal and deviant behaviour? Why do the mechanisms of social reaction operate in a differential and selective manner? What are the effects of labelling, ostracism, and stigmatization? The social dimension embodies the study of various processes including *the legal process* (that is the operations of the police and courts from arrest to trial), the *sentencing process*, the *penal or correctional process*, and the *labelling process*.

The Fragmentation of Criminology

Is it true, as some critics say, that criminology has no unified body of knowledge? It is true that criminological knowledge comes from other fields, such as sociology, psychology, psychiatry, law, history, and so forth. Yet the state of interdependence or 'subordination' that exists between criminology and these disciplines does not negate its status as an autonomous science. Such subordination applies not only to criminology but also to all so-called interdisciplinary sciences.

Claiming that criminology does not have a unified body of knowledge might have been true 50 or 40 years ago, but it is not true today. There now exists a unified body of knowledge regarding the crime phenomenon, and attempts to integrate knowledge derived from other disciplines into criminology have made enormous strides in recent years. It is true that until now there has been no integrated general theory of criminology, but this fact is equally true of many other social sciences. In sociology, for example, there is no general social theory but a multitude of specific theories about society. In criminology, there is no general theory of crime, but there is a multitude of specific theories of criminal and deviant behaviour.

What is important is that criminology is neither a cumulative science nor an auxiliary science. It is not, as some critics claim, a dependent science completely incorporated either by sociology or by psychology or by psychiatry. As Bianchi (1956:2) puts it:

> Criminology is indeed an *independent* science, not subject to the control of sociology, psychiatry or penal law or whatever science. It is even therefore, in fraternity with all further sciences that deal with man, maintaining its free position....

To claim that criminology has already attained a state of maturity that qualifies it for the status of an automonous social science is not to say that criminological theories are characterized by unity, harmony or integration. Criminology, as Ericson and Carrière (1994) maintain, is a fragmented field of enquiry and as such is subject to criticism and marginalization among academics. But this fragmentation is not limited to criminology. It characterizes many social science disciplines. Writing about 'the sociology of deviance'. Downes and Rock (1988:1) noted that it 'is not one coherent discipline at all but a collection of relatively independent versions of sociology'. They write:

> It is a common subject, not a common approach, which has given a tenuous unity to the enterprise.At different times, people with different backgrounds and different purposes have argued about rule-breaking,. The outcome has been an accumulation of theories which only occasionally mesh. Since deviance is strategic to all ideas of morality and politics, its explanation has been championed with great fervour. Writings tend to be factious, partisan, and combative.

Binder (1988:42) maintains that although criminology has had over one hundred years to assume a truly interdisciplinary nature, the dominant approach remains discipline-based. He also believes that the prospects for interdisciplinarity in the visible future are not great. So what leads Binder to such a conclusion? He insists that 'the intellectual heart of criminology is dominated by a single discipline (sociology) which has shown little proclivity toward incorporating, or even countenancing, other disciplinary perspectives.'

Referring to the tendency of researchers interested in the crime problem to look at the phenomenon in an *unidisciplinary* way, to the lack of an 'integrative synthesis', and the lack of convergence between the different schools of criminology, Binder (1988:44) makes no secret of his scepticism:

> ...it is difficult to be optimistic that criminology will achieve a substantial degree of interdisciplinarity in the foreseeable future, meaning something of the order of a 'fundamental epistemology of convergence' or 'an integrative synthesis.'

Theoretical and Applied Criminology

Like other social sciences, criminology has a theoretical and an applied component. Theoretical criminology is concerned primarily with the study of norms, violations and violators of norms for the purpose of finding general principles that would lead to the formulation of theory. Yet despite great strides forward in recent years, criminology has not yet developed a general theory of criminal behaviour.

Applied criminology, on the other hand, is primarily concerned with the practical applications of whatever theoretical knowledge is acquired about crime and criminals. Applied criminology does not directly aspire to the advancement of knowledge; it leans more toward the solution of concrete problems, such as treating offenders, reducing recidivism, and preventing crime. *Clinical criminology*, which uses and applies criminological, psychological, and psychiatric knowledge to the rehabilitation of offenders, is simply one of the branches of applied criminology. Criminological knowledge is also used and applied in other fields, notably in the areas of criminal policy and the administration of criminal justice.

Although the general distinction between the theoretical and applied fields of criminology is, in many ways, useful, it can never be absolute. Practice must have its base in theory, while data and knowledge needed for developing theories are generally obtained from practice.

According to Jayewardene (1973:21), the essential function of theory is to guide practice and the essential function of practice is to refine and reformulate theory. In Jayewardene's words 'practice without the support of theory is wasteful and theory without the support of practice is speculative.' Jayewardene believes that the need to integrate theory and practice in criminology is as great as the interdisciplinary integration of its theory. He sees the future viability of criminology as lying in 'a marriage between theory and practice – a marriage that would permit the practitioner to use the knowledge accumulated by research and impel the researcher to focus on the problems of the practitioner'. Another criminologist, Bianchi (1956:21), explains the continuous and inevitable interaction between theoretical and applied criminology:

> Pure science has to comprehend reality, to theorize it and to find its principles. Applied science serves to test theories and to employ them according to the purpose, if adequate to the subject-matter in question. We may exemplify this relation on the basis of criminology. Pure or theoretical criminology constitutes the theory and the apparatus of concepts and coordinates to be employed for the study of crime and man. It cooperates therefore with the findings and discoveries of applied criminology. Applied criminology uses the issues of theoretical criminology and tests their suitability.

Old and Modern Criminology

Scientific criminology is more than a century old. Since the publication of Lombroso's book *The Criminal Man* in 1876, criminological thinking has undergone fundamental changes. Over the years, several theories about crime, criminals, and punishment have been formulated only to be later rejected, abandoned, modified, or reformulated. Since current thinking in criminology is in many ways different from that of the 19th-or early 20th-centuries, it seems justifiable to distinguish between old and modern, between *past* and *contemporary* criminology. This distinction's primary aim is to compare the state of the discipline and the dominant ideas of its representatives at two distinct phases of its historical development. Other distinctions based on the differences in philosophy and ideology underlying the thinking of various criminologists may also be made. Along this line, one may distinguish between *conservative* (right wing), *liberal* (centrist), and *radical* (left wing) criminology. One can also differentiate between *conventional* or *mainstream criminology*, which is characterized by basic and general acceptance of existing laws and of the present criminal justice system, and *critical criminology*, which is characterized by its outright rejection of current laws and the present modes of dealing with crime and criminals.

In 1973, three British critical criminologists, Taylor, Walton, and Young published a book under the title *The New Criminology*. In this book the authors were highly critical of liberal, conventional criminology and made a strong plea for a radical, Marxist orientation. The title of the book was misleading and resulted in the words 'new', 'radical', and 'critical criminology' being used almost interchangeably. Obviously, there was nothing new about the authors' radical and critical orientation. They admit, in the revised edition (1975:278), that: 'This "new" criminology will in fact be an *old* criminology, in that it will face the same problems that were faced by the classical social theorists.'

The confusion created by the choice of *The New Criminology* as title for the first book was somewhat mitigated when the same authors called their second book *Critical Criminology*. It is, therefore, important to draw attention to the fact that old criminology was not necessarily or invariably conventional or conservative and that modern or contemporary criminology is not predominantly radical or critical. Some of the old criminological theories were radical in the full sense of the term, and many of the current theories may be safely qualified as conventional.

In compiling the following comparative table (Table 7.1) I have drawn upon the writings of several European and American criminologists, notably Törnudd and Anttila (Finland), Christie (Norway), Taylor, Walton, and Young (Britain), and Phillipson (Britain), Doleschal, Klapmuts and Miller (USA).

Table 7.1 Comparison between traditional/conventional criminology and critical/non-conventional criminology

Traditional/Conventional Criminology	Critical/Unconventional Criminology
Criminal behaviour Views criminal behaviour as qualitatively different from non-criminal behaviour.	Insists upon the temporal and cultural relativity of acts defined as criminal...sees no intrinsic difference between criminal and non-criminal behaviour... points out that behaviour that has a disapproved form (crime) also has objectively identical forms which are neutral or approved... different social groups are treated differently for behaviour which is objectively identical.
The criminal law Accepts the criminal law and the legal definitions of crime as givens...ignores the study of the social processes by which the criminal law is made and changed.	Questions the criminal law, the values and processes on which it is based..questions interests that are protected by the criminal law. Examines and criticizes the role of the public at large, pressure groups, interest groups, moral entrepreneurs, legislators, and so forth, in the criminalization process. Shifts the emphasis from the individual criminal to the definition of certain acts as criminal, from the stigmatized to the stigmatizer, from the labelled to the label itself and to the individuals who do the labelling, from the criminal to the system. Claims that problems of crime are aggravated or even created by the ways in which an offender is regarded and treated by persons in authority (the interactionist approach, labelling theory, etc.)
Explanations of crime Preoccupied mainly with the study of the causes of crime (etiological criminology). Draws heavily upon psychiatric and psychological studies of convicted offenders...characterized by individualistic explanations of the difference between criminals and conformists..attempts to show that those who commit criminal acts possess traits that differentiate them from non-criminals.	De-emphasizes the importance of the individual offender as an object of study while examining society itself and the individual's position in society, focuses on the role of society in creating and maintaining crime and criminals. Instead of asking the traditional questions 'why some individuals become criminals?' it asks why they are identified as criminal in a biased and selective process. Shifts the emphasis from the causes of crime to the legal norms that create crime. Draws heavily upon studies of the dark figure and hidden delinquency and criminality.

(cont'd)

Table 7.1 (*Continued*)

Traditional/Conventional Criminology	Critical/Unconventional Criminology
Crime and criminals	
Views crime as an aberration, as a form of maladjustment due to biological or psychological abnormality, abnormality that has to be treated and corrected.... Views criminals as a minority of ill, immoral, misguided or improperly socialized persons .... Places the blame for crime on the 'moral turpitude', lack of will power of the individual offender, on defective self-control, self-indulgence and on an undeveloped moral conscience.... Views crime as essentially a lower class phenomenon.	Views crime as an integral part of society, as a normal, not a pathological variety of human behaviour that serves useful functions, such as promoting social integration, norm reinforcement, and innovation. Views the criminal as serving a useful social function by acting as a scapegoat for the social system. Views criminality as a conflict situation and crime as the visible expression of a certain balance between differing social pressures. Attributes lower-class criminality and delinquency to a biased, selective and discriminatory process, to inaccurate and spurious labelling. Views lower-class criminality as a product of economic deprivation and of the weak position these classes have in society's power structure.
Societal reaction to crime	
Insists upon the value of punishment as a deterrent, as means of incapacitation and crime control.	Calls for the decriminalization of criminal acts that are based on outmoded or obsolete legal norms.... Insists upon deinstitutionalization and destigmatization (diversion). Advocates the control of physical crime opportunities and of the process by which acts and individuals are labelled deviant.
Emphasizes the role of treatment and correction as a way of changing the criminal and of preventing the repetition of criminal behaviour... equates or at least draws a parallel between the treatment of offenders and medical treatment.	Rejects the criminal-sick parallel, the equation of criminological treatment with medical treatment, criticizes the treatment ideology because of the threat it implies for legal safeguards and its tendency to sacrifice individual rights through the use of humane-sounding words (care, treatment, therapy) and by suggesting that no conflict of interest exists between the treater and the treated, between the therapist and the client.
Committed to the control of crime and deviance by means of law enforcement, punishment, and corrections.	Committed to the abolition of inequalities in wealth and power.

Criminology and Criminal Policy

Criminal justice in Canada is characterized by a startling absence of a set of well-defined objectives like those that guide legislators in other domains in their formulations of national policy and administrators in their implementation of such policy. It is not surprising, then, that while other systems in society are busily pursuing rational, compatible, and attainable goals, the system of justice is desperately struggling to achieve elusive, conflicting, or outright incompatible goals. In a speech to the Canadian Congress of Criminology (Calgary, 1977), Justice Antonio Lamer (who was at the time the Chairman of the now defunct Law Reform Commission of Canada and who is currently the Chief Justice of Canada's Supreme Court) deplored the lack of a coherent criminal policy and reminded the audience that Canadians have never cared to define the goals of the criminal justice system. He said:

> The fact remains, however, that never have we, as a nation, taken the time to decide what we want our criminal justice system to be all about, what should be its aims and purposes, or the restraints we want to impose upon ourselves in resorting to it. (1978:132)

Justice Lamer went on to give an example of the results of this absence of a clearly enunciated criminal policy:

> Judges were sending people to jail to denounce conduct or simply for reasons of retribution and the corrections and parole authorities were releasing them, in some form or fashion, because they were not dangerous. Society, through its judges, was trying to deter by punishing, and society, through its correctional agencies, was operating on an entirely different wave-length. (1978:136)

Justice Lamer (1978:129) suggested that 'the broad consensus and naïve optimism of the nineteenth century has been a disastrous foundation for our approach to the problems of criminality today.'

So where should the foundations of a criminal policy for the twenty-first century be sought? In the age of science and technology in which we live there seems to be little alternative to seeking scientific answers to the questions of crime and criminality, and to searching for scientific solutions to the many problems of the criminal justice system. Common sense and conventional wisdom are no longer an adequate basis for a policy aimed at dealing with such a complex phenomenon as crime. The science of criminology seems to be the logical source for the answers and solutions that are urgently needed.

In a broad sense, criminal policy should be concerned with reforming society itself, the laws and justice institutions. In a narrower sense, it is concerned, as Mannheim (1965) pointed out, with the modification of penal law and with the reform of the administration of criminal justice and the penalty system. Unfortunately, most criminologists tend to define criminal policy in a rather restrictive manner. For example, Lodge (1973), in a report to the Council of Europe, cited five aims for criminal policy, none of which deals explicitly with the social conditions that breed crime. These five aims are enforcement of criminal law, revision of criminal law, prevention of crime, administration of criminal justice (including the granting of discretionary powers to such services as the police), and treatment of offenders, including their rehabilitation.

Whether defined broadly or narrowly, it is evident that criminal policy is a primary area in which criminological knowledge can be used, in which criminological theory may be applied and tested. But is criminal policy an integral part of criminology? In 1938, Sellin suggested that the term 'criminology' be used to designate only the body of *scientific* knowledge and the deliberate pursuit of such knowledge. As to the technical use of knowledge in the treatment and prevention of crime, Sellin could not find a suitable term for it and hinted that it might be called '*crimino-technology*'. Mannheim (1965) also suggests that criminal policy be treated as a discipline apart rather than as an integral part of criminology. He finds it preferable that questions of what *ought* to be done to reform the criminal law and the penal system be treated as a separate discipline based upon the factual findings of the criminologist and penologist. Criminology, on the other hand, should remain a non-policy-making discipline which regards the 'ends' as beyond its province. Mannheim adds that this does not prevent the criminologist from advocating a certain measure of legal and administrative penal reform, but he or she has to do so as a politician or an ordinary citizen and voter rather than in the capacity of criminologist (1965:13).

It seems clear that the positions of Sellin and Mannheim to a large extent come from their conviction that criminal policy is inevitably an ideologically tainted field where the social scientist can hardly maintain objectivity and neutrality. This position is in sharp contrast with that advocated by radical and critical criminologists, who see criminology as being essentially a science of social policy. As may be seen from the definition given in the 1970–71 calendar of the former School of Criminology, University of California at Berkeley, criminology is 'concerned with rational social policies for dealing with crime and criminals – policies that will help enlargen freedom and increase justice in society'.

A PROMISING DISCIPLINE CALLED VICTIMOLOGY

A criminology which concentrates almost exclusively on the 'criminal,' and neglects almost entirely the causal role of the victim, is unlikely to establish a satisfactory theory: that is, one from which reliable predictions may be made.

Dennis Chapman (1968:166)
Sociology and the Stereotype of the Criminal

It is difficult to restrain the urge to dismiss victimology as the lunatic fringe of criminology.

Calvin Becker
quoted in Paul Rock (1994:xvi)

A Brief History of Victimology[1]

Early victimological notions were developed not by criminologists or sociologists but by poets, writers, and novelists among them Thomas de Quincey, Khalil Gibran, Aldous Huxley, the Marquis de Sade, and Franz Werfel. The first systematic treatment of victims of crime appeared in 1948 in Hans von Hentig's book *The Criminal and His Victim*. In the fourth part of the book, under the provocative title 'The Victim's Contribution to the Genesis of the Crime', von Hentig criticized the static unidimensional study of the offender which had dominated criminology and suggested in its place a new dynamic and dyadic approach that pays equal attention to the criminal and the victim. Von Hentig had earlier treated the topic in a paper published in the *Journal of Criminal Law and Criminology* in 1940. In it, he noted that

> It is true, there are many criminal deeds with little or no contribution on the part of the injured individual.... On the other hand we can frequently observe a real mutuality in the connection of perpetrator and victim, killer and killed, duper and dupe. Although this reciprocal operation is one of the most curious phenomena of criminal life it has escaped the attention of socio-pathology.

In his book, von Hentig (1948:438) is critical of the legal distinction between offenders and victims and the criteria used by the criminal law to make such attributions.

> Most crimes are directed against a specific individual, his life or property, his sexual self-determination. For practical reasons, the final open manifestation of human motor force which precedes a socially undesirable result is designated as the criminal act, and the actor as the responsible criminal. The various degrees and levels of stimulation or response, the intricate play of interacting forces, is scarcely taken into consideration in our legal distinctions, which must be simple and workable.

Elsewhere in the book von Hentig points out that

> The law considers certain results and the final moves which lead to them. Here it makes a clear-cut distinction between the one who does and the

> one who suffers. Looking into the genesis of the situation, in a consider-
> able number of cases, we meet a victim who consents tacitly, co-operates,
> conspires or provokes. The victim is one of the causative elements. (p. 436)

Von Hentig insisted that many crime victims contribute to their own victimization be it by inciting or provoking the criminal or by creating or fostering
a situation likely to lead to the commission of the crime. Other pioneers in
victimology, who firmly believed that victims may consciously or unconsciously play a causal role, outlined many of the forms this contribution can
take: negligence, carelessness, recklessness, imprudence, and so forth. They
pointed out that the victim's role could be a motivational one (attracting,
arousing, inducing, inciting) or a functional one (provoking, precipitating,
triggering, facilitating, participating) (Fattah, 1991).

Von Hentig's book was followed by a number of theoretical studies that
dealt with victim types, victim-offender relationships, and the role victims
play in certain kinds of crime. The book also provided an impetus for several
empirical studies that devoted special attention to the victims of specific
offences.

The term *victimology* was coined in 1949 by an American psychiatrist,
Frederick Wertham, who used it for the first time in his book *The Show of
Violence*. Wertham wrote:

> The murder victim is the forgotten man. With sensational discussions on
> the abnormal psychology of the murderer, we have failed to emphasize the
> unprotectedness of the victim and the complacency of the authorities. One
> cannot understand the psychology of the murderer if one does not under-
> stand the sociology of the victim. What we need is a science of victim-
> ology. (p. 259)

During the early years of victimology, literature on crime victims remained
relatively small when compared to that on criminology. During the 1980s,
however, a great spate of important books and articles marked the coming of
age of victimology (Rock, 1994). At present, it is fair to maintain that the
study of crime victims has become an integral part of criminology.

The need for criminology to thoroughly study the victims of crime may
today appear obvious, even axiomatic. And it may seem rather surprising
that such obvious need has escaped the attention of criminologists for over a
century. But it is not rare for social scientists to miss the obvious. This point
is well made by Rock (1994:xi) who points out:

> Even criminology and the sociology of deviance – disciplines concentrated
> most squarely on the analysis of crime, criminals and criminal justice –
> tended somehow to obliterate the victim for a very long while, failing to
> see what, in retrospect, should probably have been evident all along. Such
> omissions occur continually. They are an ineluctable part of any discipline,

> a consequence of the truth marked by Burke when he said that 'a way of seeing is always a way of not seeing.' The price of organizing, specializing and accumulating knowledge about any area is a systematic neglect of the other matters thrown out of focus and beyond the margins. Precisely because criminology is an empirically-driven discipline, it has tended to ignore those things that do not bear the name of crime, criminals and criminal justice.

Although victimology has firmly established itself as a major research area within criminology, its nature, importance and standing continue to generate a great deal of comments. Rock (1994:xi) describes victimology as a 'relatively amorphous discipline.' And at the *Fifth International Symposium on Victimology* (Zagreb, August 1985), Cressey openly declared that victimology is neither a scientific discipline nor an academic field. He called it instead 'a non-academic program under which a hodge-podge of ideas, interests, ideologies and research methods have been rather arbitrarily grouped.'

Be this as it may, the study of victims and victimization has the potential of reshaping the entire discipline of criminology. It might very well be the long awaited paradigm shift that criminology desperately needs.

The Controversy Surrounding the Subject-Matter of Victimology[2]

In their editorial introducing the *International Review of Victimology*, Freeman and Sebba (1989:1) posed some pertinent questions. They asked: 'is victimology a socio-political movement whose objective is the pursuit of victims' rights, or rather an academic activity concerned 'merely' with the pursuit of knowledge? Is victimology concerned exclusively with victims of crime, or also with other categories of victimization?' Not surprisingly, the editors did not attempt to answer these thorny questions. Should victimology confine its scope to victimization in a narrow sense, that is to victimization by crime, or should it extend its boundaries to general or global victimization?

A strong proponent of a global victimology (and by no means the only one) is Robert Elias, a political scientist at the University of San Francisco. Elias (1986) believes that victimology's most significant drawback might lie in its confining itself almost exclusively to criminological boundaries. Despite its broader origins, according to Elias, the discipline has rarely considered anything but crime victims and criminal victimization. He cites some critics who have challenged the scientific boundaries of victimology by suggesting 'that it has unnecessarily constrained itself within traditional criminology's boundaries and adopted the same conservative mentality'. (p. 22) Elias goes on to criticize victimological research for having accepted, either implicitly or explicitly, a role within criminology, which provides a convenient framework.

So what does Elias suggest? He pleads for victimology to move beyond criminology. He sees a broader role for victimology, a role that would fulfil not only victimology's now traditional tasks but also consider broader criminal definitions, the social and governmental sources of victimization and victim-producing cultures. This extension, in his view, would allow us to consider other kinds of victims, victimizers, and victimizations. It would promote a wider and more international victimology, that is, a 'new' victimology of human rights. As a political scientist, Elias argues against separating science and politics and claims that our politics inevitably give directions to our science but need not and should not preordain it. In the final pages of his book *The Politics of Victimization: Victims, Victimology and Human Rights*, Elias (1986:243) calls for a 'new' victimology embracing a broader definition of victimization that brings all victims, or at least many more victims, within its purview.

Elias's views, though shared by some others, do not represent those of mainstream victimology. The latter views are well represented by Edith Flynn. Flynn (1982) wonders if it would not be more productive for victimology to concentrate on the study of the behaviour of victims in crime situations. This approach would 'study victim behaviour during the commission of a crime, the victim's response to crime, and the provision of assistance, treatment, and services designed to overcome the harm done to the victim.'(p. 99) She believes that such a direction would not only be more feasible but would also reflect the mainstream of victimological endeavours. As a next step, it will probably be useful, she feels, for the field to differentiate conceptually the tasks of scientific study, research, and analysis of the phenomenon of victimization from professional activities focusing on victims in terms of services, treatment, or programs.

Advocates of a global victimology, a victimology encompassing all types and forms of victimization, are fond of drawing an analogy between this broader victimology and a criminology that does not confine itself to the study of criminal behaviour but extends its scope to social deviance. The parallel is attractive but defective. The field of social deviance, though broader than crime, is still a definable, identifiable, and delimitable subject. Social deviance is just a small part of social behaviour. As such, it lends itself to scientific inquiry and fits well as a subject for a scientific discipline. Global victimization, on the other hand, has no clear, precise, identifiable, or delimitable boundaries (Fattah, 1991). As Flynn (1982:98–99) points out 'if all pain and suffering (ranging, for example, from mental illness to neuroses) were to be defined as victimization, who would not be a victim?'

Should Victimology Be Restricted to Victimization by Crime?
Limiting the scope of victimology to criminal victimization may be faulted by some for being too restrictive and for confining the inquiry within the traditional boundaries of criminology. Some may claim, and rightly so, that

the boundaries between injurious and harmful behaviours made punishable by the criminal law and many other uncriminalized ones are artificial and arbitrarily drawn. Others may argue that several types of non-criminal victimization are no different from criminal ones. Both share similar characteristics and have the same effects and results. These arguments are not without merit. I believe, however, that the theoretical and practical advantages of limiting the study to criminal victimization far outweigh whatever drawbacks this limitation might have (Fattah, 1991).

In fact, the limitation is not just advantageous; it is essential. As a scientific discipline, victimology has to define, specify, and delineate its subject. It has to delimit the frontiers of its scientific inquiry. And as a branch of criminology, victimology is interested primarily, though not exclusively, in criminal victimization. Victimology has nothing to gain by cutting its ties to criminology and extending its scope of inquiry to every conceivable kind, type, form, and variety of human victimization. A breakaway from criminology and an extension of boundaries beyond the definable and the quantifiable present real dangers to the young and developing discipline of victimology. Were victimology to broaden its field to victimization in a generic sense, were it to choose such a loose and diffuse subject, its specificity would undoubtedly be lost. And by devoting itself to the unmeasurable phenomenon of global victimization, to the undefinable and unquantifiable phenomenon of human suffering, it risks losing its scientific character. The concepts of pain, suffering, victimization, and even harm are normative concepts. Deciding which types of suffering are worthy of study and which forms of victimization warrant denunciation would make victimology a norm-setting exercise. Victimology would be nothing more than a humanist movement.

The plea for theoretical victimology to maintain its scientific character and to circumscribe its subject matter within firm and clearly defined boundaries is in harmony with the goals of applied victimology. The ultimate goal of applied criminology, applied victimology, and of both criminal policy and victim policy is the prevention of criminal victimization as a way of alleviating human suffering and of improving the quality of human life. This goal can only be achieved through a rational, enlightened policy whose roots are anchored not in speculation but in empirical science (Fattah, 1991).

From Micro-Victimology to Macro-Victimology

In the 1970s individual studies of the victims of specific crimes were overshadowed by victimization surveys, which transformed the micro approach, characteristic of the early studies in victimology, into a macro approach aimed mainly at determining the volume of victimization, identifying the victim population, and establishing the sociodemographic characteristics of that population. While this macro approach is essential for studying the trends and patterns of victimization and the social and spatial distribution of some kinds of crime, it tells us very little about the social and personal settings in which those crimes take place. It is of limited value in understanding the psycho-and sociodynamics of criminal behaviour, the process of selecting the victim, victim–offender interactions, and the victim's contribution to the genesis of the crime. And although data from victimization surveys can be useful in understanding the correlates of fear of crime, they shed no light on the psychological and behavioural reactions to fear or on the social and personal consequences of criminal victimization for the victims.[3]

From Theoretical Victimology to Applied Victimology

In the last twenty-five years victimology underwent a major transformation. Early victimology was mainly theoretical concerned almost exclusively with causal explanations of crime and the victim's role in these explanations. The main focus was to examine the characteristics of victims, their relationships and interactions with their victimizers, and whatever contribution they might have made to the genesis of their victimization. This theoretical framework guided the pioneering research done in the early days of victimology by Ellenberger, Wolfgang, Amir, Normandeau, Curtis, Silverman, and Fattah among others. Concern for the plight of crime victims manifested itself primarily in the modest state compensation programs to victims of crime that were set up in some countries such as New Zealand, England, Canada, US, and others. The rediscovery of crime victims, spearheaded by the feminist movement, a movement that championed the cause of victims of rape and sexual assault and that of battered women, generated a great deal of empathy and sympathy for a largely disenfranchized group (Fattah, 1979, 1994).

Theoretical victimology became the object of increasing attacks and criticisms. It was portrayed by some (Clark and Lewis, 1977) as the art of blaming the victim. A new focus for victimology was taking shape: helping and assisting crime victims, alleviating their plight and affirming their rights. A political movement was born and victimology became increasingly defined and recognized by its applied component.

At the First National conference of Victims of Crime (Toronto, 1985), the victim movement was called the growth industry of the decade. In the United Kingdom it is considered the fastest developing voluntary movement.[4] Victims groups and associations are mushrooming all over North America and Europe. Inevitably, this growth has had a significant impact on victimology. Victimology meetings mirror the transformation of victimology from an academic discipline into a humanistic movement, the shift from scholarly research to political activism.

The recent transformation of victimology has not been without serious consequences. One of the consequences has been to refocus the notion of criminality on traditional crimes that have a direct, immediate, tangible victim. White-collar crime, corporate actions causing grievous social harms, whether they are legally defined as crimes or not, have once again been relegated to the background. Victim activists have focused their attention on, and directed their action to, the so-called conventional crimes. Corporate and business crimes, which may victimize millions of people (see Chapter 3), still go largely unreported and unprosecuted. Despite the scope of white-collar crime and although its depredations far exceed those of traditional street crime, it is totally left out of victim campaigns and so are other socially harmful actions, even the ones that qualify as legal crimes.

NOTES

1. For a more detailed history of Victimology see E.A. Fattah (1967) La Victimologie: Qu'est-elle et quel est son avenir? *Revue Internationale de Criminologie et de Police Technique.* Vol. 21, No. 2 (pp. 113–24) and No. 3 (pp. 193–202).
2. See Fattah (1991) *Understanding Criminal Victimization* Scarborough: Prentice-Hall Canada.
3. For a more detailed discussion on the contributions and limitations of victimization studies, see Fattah (1982).
4. See a report on the meeting published in the Ottawa Magazine, *Liaison* April 1985.

PART III
Criminology Past, Present and Future

*Criminology is a subject with a complicated past
and polemical present.*

Stan Cohen (1988:6)

Criminology Past:
The Historical Evolution
of Criminological Thought

8 Early Speculative Explorations

PRE-CRIMINOLOGICAL THINKING

> The criminal code under the *ancien régime* in France seemed 'planned to ruin citizens.' This was the dark side of successful despotism, of arbitrary authority in sovereign, church or aristocracy. It was the negation of the rights of the individual.
>
> Leon Radzinowicz (1966:1–2)
> *Ideology and Crime*

Throughout the Middle Ages, humans were perceived as selfish by nature and irremediably bad. The individual had to be severely contained and restrained, to be protected against natural selfishness, and preserved from temptation.

Crime was regarded not only as an offence against the victim and an affront to society but also as an offence against divinity that demands expiation and retribution. This conception of crime as a transgression against God inevitably led to harsh and cruel *punishments* against those guilty of criminal offences. Death was the penalty for dozens of offences, and was carried out by ingenious methods such as quartering, breaking on the wheel, and burning at the stake. For lesser offences, corporal punishments were widely and frequently used. These included whipping, lopping the ears, slitting the nostrils, piercing the tongue, branding on the forehead, cheek, or shoulder with hot iron, cutting off the hand, and various other kinds of bodily mutilations. *Criminals* were fitted with branks consisting of an iron frame surrounding the head and a sharp metal bit entering the mouth. They were attached to stocks. These wooden frameworks with holes for the offenders' feet alone or feet and hands were set up in public places. Criminals were also tied to ducking stools and intermittently immersed in water (Earle, 1972).

Suspects were tortured and tormented. A distinction was made between *preparatory* torture to extort a confession and *preliminary* torture to get the suspect to reveal the names of accomplices. In many cases, fiscal penalties, such as general confiscation of the property or estate of the accused, were pronounced as additional or complementary punishments. As laws were not codified, there was no sure way of knowing what was permitted and what was prohibited. *Justice* was arbitrary, and judges based their sentences not on earthly but on divine criteria. Judges enjoyed unbridled and unfettered discretion which led to flagrant disparities, inequalities, arbitrariness, and intolerable abuses. There were different courts, and consequently different justice, for the rich and the poor, noblemen and commoners, laymen and members of the clergy. Prosecution and conviction of animals and corpses were not uncommon (Evans, 1906; Dietrich, 1961). Since the offence had to be expiated, it made no difference whether the offender was a human being or an animal, alive or dead. Also common were trials by ordeals, in particular, by fire and boiling water. These trials made an appeal to the supernatural to reveal the guilt or innocence of the accused. Accusations and trials were often conducted in secrecy, but secrecy was by no means the only irregularity of criminal procedures. In sum, the system of justice was characterized by a total disregard for human rights or liberties, and the system of punishment was characterized by cruelty, barbarity, and lacked any respect for human dignity.

With the advent of the Age of Enlightenment (*Aufklärung*), there was a new sense of optimism as opposed to medieval pessimism, a passage from cruelty and severity to liberty and freedom. Philosophers of the 18th century, such as Montesquieu (1689–1755), Voltaire (1694–1778), and, especially, Jean-Jacques Rousseau (1712–76) propagated the belief in the original goodness of human beings and the notion that the state of nature was a state of innocence and moral purity. The Age of Enlightenment was characterized by a new conception of human nature. The individual was viewed as a rational and hedonistic being who should be left free to act, to choose between right or wrong, between good and bad. Faith in humanity's original goodness was bound to lead to the belief in unlimited human potential, in the possibility of correcting the individual who erred and did something wrong. The belief in the rationality of human beings was bound to produce drastic changes in the field of crime and justice. The most notable of these changes was to replace the theological notions of expiation and atonement by the utilitarian doctrine of deterrence, which gradually became the foundation of a new system of punishment.

PHILOSOPHICAL RUMINATIONS ON CRIME, CRIMINALS AND CRIMINAL JUSTICE

...a criminological doctrine which sees the sources of crime in the individual will advocate a programme including specific proposals for the reform of the criminal law and procedure and above all of the penal system.

Leon Radzinowicz (1966:58)
Ideology and Crime

Cesare Beccaria (1738–94)

One of the most influential books of the 18th century was a small mono-graph bearing the title *Dei Delitti e delle Pene*. The monograph was pub-lished anonymously in 1764 but it was written by an Italian philosopher, Marquis Cesare Beccaria. Beccaria's philosophy and ideas were not for the most part original. He was heavily influenced by French libertarianism and British utilitarianism. Beccaria's greatest contribution was to crystalize the ideas of the era and present them in a systematic, clear, and concise form and to integrate the various ideas of the new philosophy into a logical, coherent doctrine based on a hedonistic view of man and on a theory of society inspired by utilitarianism and Rousseau's notion of the social contract. Four grand principles seem to have guided Beccaria's recipies for reform.

Egalitarianism

Equality before the law is undoubtedly the *leit-motiv* in Beccaria's doctrine, and it is a natural reaction to the disparities and incongruities of the justice system of his era. Beccaria's deep concern for equality leads him to reject all that is subjective in law and justice and opt for an objectivism without limit. The visible abuses of the justice system made him believe that the only refuge lies in the safeguards of a legal formula that has general and equal applica-tion. Only an objective theory of justice can, in Beccaria's view, ensure equal justice and put an end to the despotism of judges.

There are two principal approaches to the determination of punishment. An *objective theory* of punishment places the greatest emphasis on the offence and the material circumstances surrounding it. It gives little or no attention to the personal characteristics of the offender or to the individual circumstances involved. It is concerned only with the material gravity of the offence and demands that the punishment be made to fit the crime. A *subjective theory* of punishment gives more consideration to the personal attributes, motives, and background of the offender than to the offence itself. It calls for an individualization of punishment and for a penal measure befitting not the crime but the individual being punished. Beccaria gives his unqualified support to an objective theory of criminal justice and advo-cates what he considered to be essential reforms needed to objectivize the system.

No individualization of punishment.　　Beccaria systematically rejects the prin-ciple that penalties should be individualized and should be adapted to each individual offender. He and the jurists of his era were convinced that equality and individualization are two incompatible principles. Even a century later, the French criminologist Gabriel Tarde was lamenting the same problem when he wrote 'The problem is, to individualize punishment is to inequalize it for equal faults' (*Le malheur est qu'individualiser la peine, c'est l'inégaliser pour des fautes égales*).

A rejection of individualization means that all those who perpetrate the same crime receive the same penalty whether they are young or old, recidivist or first-timers. Beccaria and the jurists of the Classical School viewed individualization of punishment as synonymous with disparity. This, however, is not necessarily true. Individualization could be used as a vehicle for fairness and equity. In the 'day fine system' applied in the Scandinavian countries fines are not meted out by the courts in absolute amounts but in units based on the daily income of the convicted offender. In this way, fines for the same offence are made proportional to the financial capabilities of each defendant.

No interpretation of the law. Not only did Beccaria call for the elimination of judicial discretion in the application of the law, but he also opposed judicial interpretation of it. Interpretation of the law is, by definition, a subjective exercise. If judges were allowed to interpret the laws, argued Beccaria, different interpretations of the same law would inevitably ensue. Drawing upon the principle of 'separation of powers' enunciated by Montesquieu, Beccaria argued that interpretation of laws is the prerogative of legislators, not judges. Beccaria insisted, however, that criminal laws be made simple and clear so that interpretation is unnecessary and so that they may be comprehensible to the citizens to whom they are addressed.

Punishment should fit the crime. Beccaria stipulates that the seriousness of various crimes be measured according to their material gravity and that punishment be made to fit the crime. According to this logic, a completed crime is more serious and deserves more punishment than a simple attempt even though criminal intent in the two cases is identical and although the non-completion of the crime is for reasons external to the offender's volition. Beccaria insists that there must be a proper proportion between crimes and sanctions and wants punishments to be of the same nature as the offences they punish.

Libertarianism

One of the main features of Beccaria's legal doctrine is the affirmation of citizens' rights, in particular, the right to be protected from the abuses of power by the state. He needed to find, therefore, (like other philosophers of the 18th century who were interested in the field of justice) a justification for the State's right to punish. Beccaria found this justification in Rousseau's theory of the *social contract*. According to this theory, an agreement was supposedly reached among individuals forming an organized society and between them and the ruler defining and limiting the rights and duties of each. In Beccaria's view, citizens sacrificed a part of their liberty so that they might enjoy the rest of it in peace and safety. But he then goes on to explain that according to the social contract, citizens yield only the *minimal* portion of their liberty to the state.

The principle of legality.   Beccaria's concern for the rights and liberties of all people logically leads him to consider legality as a fundamental principle of criminal justice. Liberty and human rights can only be protected by law, and only the law may set the minimal, but necessary, restrictions on those rights and liberties. Beccaria affirms in the strongest terms possible the two funda-mental principles of all criminal legislation: NO CRIME WITHOUT LAW (*nullum crimen sine lege*) and NO PUNISHMENT WITHOUT LAW (*nulla poena sine lege*).

Legal safeguards.   These two principles lead to yet another basic principle of criminal justice: *the non-retroactivity of criminal laws.* In a free society, criminal laws cannot be made retroactive and cannot be extended to acts committed before the laws were enacted.

Protection of people's rights and liberties requires that punishment be made personal and not extended to the offender's family or children. For this reason, Beccaria favoured servitude over fines and for the same reason, he was opposed to the sentence of general confiscation since it afflicted the innocent family more than the offender.

In recognizing people's inalienable rights, Beccaria had to acknowledge the individual's right to dispose of his/her own life. Under the influence of theological teachings, suicide used to be considered a serious crime. The possessions of the dead person were often confiscated, and vengeance was wreaked on the corpse in the name of the law. In England, for example, people who committed suicide were buried at a crossroad after having stakes driven through their bodies (Maestro, 1973:13). Beccaria called for the decriminalization of suicide.

Utilitarianism

For Beccaria, the major goal of government and legislation is a purely utilitarian goal: the greatest happiness shared by the greatest number (*La massima felicità divisa nel maggior numero*). Elsewhere, he affirms that com-mon utility is the foundation of human justice (1963:65).

In Beccaria's proposed system of justice the concept of utility replaces those of retaliation, expiation, and atonement as the justification for punishment inflicted by society on one of its members. For Beccaria, punishment is not a penalty that sanctions a moral fault; it is a necessity since it prevents a greater evil – crime. Not only does punishment have to be just; it must also be useful. For Beccaria the right to punish is based on *social utility* – preventing the criminal from committing further crimes (specific deterrence) and dissuading others from following the criminal's example (general deterrence). But this utilitarian goal has to be achieved without inflicting undue suffering on the criminal.

Certainty not severity of punishment is the best deterrent?   Despite Beccaria's unshakeable belief in the deterrent effect of punishment and his firm conviction in the utilitarian function of penalties, he is quick to note that it is the certainty of punishment not its severity that is apt to achieve maximum deterrence.

Beccaria seems to have been aware of some of the paradoxes of deterrence, for example, that severity and certainty of punishment cannot and do not go hand in hand. He realizes that there is an inverse relationship between the severity of any punishment and its certainty; the more the former is enhanced, the more the latter is reduced. He declared that '... impunity itself results from the atrocity of penalties.' (p. 44)

Celerity of punishment.   In his book, Beccaria insisted again and again that celerity of punishment is one of the most important factors in deterrence: 'promptness of punishment... is one of the principal checks against crime.' (p. 37)

Crime prevention.   Beccaria places great emphasis on crime prevention and feels that a punishment is not 'just' unless everything has been done to prevent the crime. One utilitarian aspect of his justice manifesto is that conformity can be achieved through incentives and that rewards are as effective in preventing crime as punishments are.

A call for decriminalization?   Beccaria recommends that criminalization be used very sparingly by the legislator. He realizes the difficulties in enforcing certain laws and feels that such laws should not be promulgated in the first place: 'A general rule: when a crime is of such a nature that it must frequently go unpunished, the penalty assigned becomes an incentive.' (p. 85) He also states that 'No law should be promulgated that lacks force or that the nature of the circumstances renders ineffectual.' (p. 81)

Humanitarianism

Beccaria's doctrine and his prescriptions for a fair and equitable justice system are not only utilitarian but also humanitarian. Beccaria's humanitarianism is clearly demonstrated in his strong opposition to torture, cruel punishments, general confiscation, and, above all, in his firm rejection of the death penalty. Despite Beccaria's great admiration for the French philosophers Montesquieu and Rousseau, when it comes to the issue of the death penalty, he finds no alternative but to take a stand different from theirs.

Principle of the least possible punishment.   Beccaria believes that severity defeats the utilitarian purpose of punishment, and he advises legislators to keep punishments at the lowest level necessary to achieve deterrence. The pain and suffering punishment promises the lawbreaker must slightly, only slightly, exceed the advantages and the pleasure from the crime. This is the optimal point; beyond this effective minimum, severity is both useless and unjust. It is unjust because it inflicts unnecessary pain and suffering and useless because it does not enhance punishment's effectiveness as a deterrent. Beccaria laid the foundations for a theory of punishment based on an arithmetic of pleasure, a notion that later inspired and influenced the British jurist Jeremy Bentham (1748–1832) in the formulation of his theory of punishments and rewards.

Opposition to the death penalty.   Beccaria finds the death penalty cruel and barbaric. He deplores the faulty logic inherent in the notion that to deter killing the state has to commit murder itself:

> The death penalty cannot be useful, because of the example of barbarity it gives men . . . . It seems to me absurd that the laws, which are an expression of the public will, which detest and punish homicide, should themselves commit it, and that to deter citizens from murder, they order a public one. (p. 50)

Opposition to torture.   Beccaria is also firmly opposed to torture because it is an infliction of pain on individuals who have not yet been convicted and who may, therefore, be innocent. He sees torture as the source of many judicial errors. If an innocent person is tortured 'either he confesses the crime and is condemned, or he is declared innocent and has suffered a punishment he did not deserve.' (p. 33)

Opposition to clemency, pardon, and legal excuses.   Beccaria is opposed to clemency and pardons, measures that were sometimes used to exempt some offenders from punishment or to reduce their penalty. He is also opposed to legal excuses, such as those offering impunity to accomplices in serious crime in exchange for denunciation of companions. This stand may at first glance appear in contradiction with Beccaria's humanitarianism, but, in fact, is not so. For Beccaria, such measures are in conflict with the principle of equality before the law. Besides, they are likely to weaken the deterrent effect of punishment by reducing its certainty and by fomenting the hope of impunity. Furthermore, pardons and mercy are only necessary when the laws are harsh and unjust. In a system similar to that advocated by Beccaria where laws are just, where sentences are fair, and where punishments are humane, he saw no need or place for clemency and pardon.

In his final conclusion, Beccaria summarizes in a single paragraph his theorem on punishment:

> In order for punishment not to be, in every instance, an act of violence of one or of many against a private citizen, it must be essentially public, prompt, necessary, the least possible in the given circumstances, proportionate to the crimes, dictated by the laws. (p. 99)

These conditions, which Beccaria saw as quite necessary for a system of just punishments, were at the time quite revolutionary. Twenty-five years later, at least two of these conditions were incorporated in the 'Declaration of the Rights of Man and of the Citizen' passed by the Revolutionary National Assembly of France on 26 August, 1789. Article VIII of the declaration stipulates that:

> The law ought to impose no other penalties but such as are absolutely and evidently necessary; and no one ought to be punished, but in virtue of a law promulgated before the offence, and legally applied.

Critique of Beccaria's Doctrine
At a time when there was a paucity of scientific knowledge about social phenomena and about human behaviour, Beccaria, the philosopher, succeeded in elaborating a logical, comprehensive and coherent doctrine regarding crime and punishment. Beccaria proved to be extremely perceptive both in his criticism of the existing justice system and in his suggestions for reform. Many of his statements were intuitive, but they proved correct and have since been confirmed by empirical research. His insistence that certainty of punishment rather than its severity ensures maximum deterrence, his affirmation of an inverse relationship between severity and certainty, and his emphasis on the celerity of punishment as an important deterrent influence, are all propositions supported two centuries later by the findings of criminological and behavioural research. While this is true of some of Beccaria's assertions, it is equally true that many of the logical foundations of his doctrine do not withstand scientific validation or empirical scrutiny. For instance:

1. His justification for society's right to punish is based on Rousseau's notion of the social contract which is a philosophical idea, not an empirical fact. Beccaria adopted the hypothesis without any attempt to check or to demonstrate its validity.

2. Probably the greatest weakness in Beccaria's logical construction is his abstract conception of human nature. His view of the individual as a rational, reasonable, and hedonistic being who strives for pleasure and carefully avoids pain, who has total control over his/her actions, who reflects and reasons before deciding to act, and who calculates the

advantages and disadvantages of his/her behaviour, bears little resemblance to real people. Debuyst (1969) notes that when the judges and
others engaged in the administration of justice began to function according to this abstract notion of human nature, they found themselves face
to face with the real delinquents and Beccaria's abstract conception
revealed its inherent weaknesses.

3.   Much of Beccaria's doctrine is based on unverified assumptions about
     the individual's knowledge, reason, and freedom to act. He presumes, for
     instance, that everyone is endowed with free will, that everyone is normal
     and responsible, and that it is possible to make every citizen knowledge-
     able about the law – hence, the legal presumption according to which
     nobody may be excused for ignorance of the law (*nul n'est censé ignorer
     la loi*).

4.   Beccaria's adherence to a purely objective theory of criminal justice and
     his rejection of all that is subjective (particularly his rejection of any
     individualization of punishment), though motivated by the desire to
     ensure equality before the law, transforms the system of justice into a
     rigid, inflexible, and ultimately unjust system. Such objectivity requires
     that no differentiation be made between those who commit identical
     offences, that all be uniformly punished. As soon as Beccaria's recom-
     mendations for fixed and uniform punishments were introduced in the
     law and put into practice, the rigidity of the system became evident and
     had to be remedied through a restoration of flexibility.

5.   Beccaria's belief in general and specific deterrence, his defence of punish-
     ment as means of crime prevention, and his arithmetic of pleasure are
     based on logic and common sense, not on observation or investigation.

6.   Beccaria advocates that crimes be ranked in seriousness according to the
     harm they cause to society. Yet, he leaves the concept of harm unde-
     fined, does not explain how this harm may be measured, how the various
     crimes may be graded or how punishments may be proportionalized to
     the seriousness of the offences they punish.

7.   Beccaria advocates that accomplices be punished less rigorously than the
     executor of the crime though in some cases the executor may be merely
     an instrument in the hands of the accomplice. Beccaria also advocates
     that attempted crimes be punished less severely than accomplished
     crimes. From a behavioural and criminological standpoint, aimed at
     adapting the penal measure to the personality and the dangerousness
     of the offender, such a distinction may be totally unjustified.

Despite these shortcomings, Beccaria's contribution to criminal law and
criminal justice is undeniable. Yet while Beccaria is generally regarded as a
luminous thinker and a great reformer he has not escaped criticism. Young
(1983:10) argues that Beccaria is essentially a retributivist and only second-

arily a utilitarian. In support of this claim, Young refers, among other things, to Beccaria's suggestion that seriousness of crimes be assessed only by their consequences, and Young sees this as commensurate with retributivism. But the major attempt to discredit Beccaria is made by Newman and Marongiu (1990). In their harsh, though often unjustified, attack they argue that Beccaria's adoration by penologists far outweighs the actual contribution he made to penology. They also claim that Beccaria was no great reformer and that his works are less profound than those of other great reformers of the 18th century, such as Voltaire or Bentham. They describe Beccaria as 'lazy, timid and reclusive.' In their view, Beccaria's Treatise is a document full of many obscurities and contradictions (p. 330) and that far from being a simple and clear document, the treatise is 'complicated, inconsistent, and disorganized' (p. 331). They equally maintain that the reform principles that are often ascribed to Beccaria and that made him famous were part of the general reformist approach and judicial enlightenment expounded by various thinkers before Beccaria published his Treatise (p. 333).

The unkind assertions that Newman and Marongiu (1990) put forward seem to be largely due to their attempt to judge Beccaria by today's standards and their failure to place his ideas and character in their social and historical context and to assess them according to the prevailing norms of his time. They try unconvincingly at the end of their article to address this weakness in their argumentation. They claim that since liberal values have been attached to Beccaria not only by his contemporaries but also by penologists of this century then it is fair to evaluate him in the light of modern ideas of reform (p. 343).

SCHOOLS OF EARLY CRIMINOLOGICAL THOUGHT: THE CLASSICAL AND THE NEO-CLASSICAL SCHOOLS

A school of criminological thought groups various scholars who share similar ideas, philosophies, and beliefs regarding law, crime, justice, and punishment.

The Classical School

The Classical School fits into the above category, and its most distinguished representatives are Carrara in Italy, Bentham in England, and Feuerbach in Germany.

The Doctrine
The doctrine of the Classical School is inspired by Beccaria's treatise 'On crimes and punishments' and by the teachings of other philosophers of the

Age of Enlightenment. It is essentially a rationalistic doctrine based on reason, and may be summarized as follows:

> Man is a rational, hedonistic creature, guided by reason and by consider-ations of pleasure and pain, of gain and loss. He is endowed with a free will and should therefore be held morally responsible and legally accountable for his actions. He may be controlled by fear and prevented from doing wrong by the threat of punishment.

The Concept of Free Will

Free will is a fundamental notion in the doctrine of the Classical School. It is an abstract concept not susceptible to definition, measurement, or empirical validation. Essentially, it is a philosophical belief that human beings are endowed with free volition, with an ability to choose freely between good and evil and between right and wrong. Free will is the power or, shall we say, the ability to make a free and equal choice between two different courses of action inspired by various motives but without being determined or condi-tioned by those motives. It is the ability to make a free and equal choice, either to act or to abstain without being pressured or influenced by external or internal forces (Saleilles, 1927).

The notion of free will logically leads to the principle of equal respons-ibility and equal guilt. Thus, it is not only compatible but also quite in line with the egalitarian philosophy of the Classical School. The doctrine of free will, as Saleilles (1929:55) points out, presupposes that in face of an identical act, be it theft, murder, or anything else, all those who have committed such act were equally free and consequently equally responsible. Such a doctrine, needless to say, is contradictory to a theory of causation which sees criminal behaviour, as subject to the influences of several factors leading to different degrees of motivation, varying levels of resistance to temptation, and so forth.

Moral Responsibility and Moral Guilt

Another basic principle underlying the doctrine of the Classical School is that of moral responsibility. Moral responsibility and moral guilt are the corollaries of the notion of free will. If one is free to choose, is able to distinguish right from wrong and still opts for the latter, that person is morally guilty and should be held accountable. As long as the ability to discern right and wrong is not affected, the individual is fully responsible for whatever crimes he/she commits. This leads to the exemption of only two classes of individuals: children under the age of discernment (usually fixed at seven years) and lunatics whose mental faculties are totally absent or grossly impaired. The doctrine, therefore, did not recognize any intermediate degrees of responsibility.

Crime and Punishment

Criminal law is a dogmatic system based essentially on rational, philosophical, and religious concepts. Crime is regarded not as an individual behaviour but as a legal entity. As one of the Italian representatives of the Classical School, Francesco Carrara, declared 'crime is not an action, it is an infraction.' 'It is not an entity in fact but an entity in law' (Radzinowicz, 1966:22). Crimes are graded according to their material gravity and are punishable by fixed penalties determined by law. Punishment is necessary to deter those who succumb to passions or temptations and for those who do not listen to the voice of reason. It has to be fixed in advance by the law to enable citizens to do a moral calculus: weighing the benefits of the crime against the pain and suffering of the penalty.

The Role of the Judge

Criminal judges, who during the '*Ancien Régime*' enjoyed unfettered discretion become mechanical distributors of punishments. The judge's role is merely to establish guilt or innocence and, in the former case, to pronounce the punishment prescribed and fixed in advance by the law.

The French penal code of 1791 reflects admirably the ideas and philosophy of the Classical School. Punishments are fixed, and no discretion is left to the judge. For any given crime, the penalty is so much time in prison, not one day more or one day less, or a fixed amount of fine, not a penny more or a penny less. All those who commit a certain offence were punished exactly in the same way. While these uniform penalties appeared to be very egalitarian, abolishing judicial arbitrariness and sentencing disparities, the apparent equality was the most unequal of all, treating offenders like digits and meting out the same punishment to all those who committed the same material act regardless of the human and social circumstances of the offender.

As Saleilles (1927:57) notes, it did not take long for the defects of the classical model to become evident, and in an attempt to remedy the rigidity of the law, the French penal code of 1810 re-established the elasticity of punishments, penalties within two fixed limits: a minimum and a maximum.

Critical Assessment of the Classical School

Merit

The Classical School made a substantial contribution to the reform of criminal laws and criminal justice in the 18th and 19th centuries. Among other things:

1. It was greatly influential in the abolition of torture, mutilations, and barbarous punishments, including the death penalty, in several European countries. One of its illustrious representatives in England, Sir Samuel

Romilly (1757–1818), played an important role in reforming and humanizing British law.

2. It affirmed the rights of citizens and the need to protect them against the abuses of power and the excesses of the criminal justice system. As Radzinowicz (1966:22) points out, one of the two main principles that guided Carrara's entire work is that 'the chief object of criminal law and criminal science is to prevent abuses on the part of the authorities.'

3. It fought relentlessly for the recognition of moral values, such as human dignity, reverence for life, and respect of individual freedom.

4. It limited, nearly eliminated, the discretionary power of the judge, a power that had led to intolerable abuses in the past. It also contributed to the abolition or reduction of judicial despotism, arbitrariness, and many of the injustices and irregularities of the old system of justice.

Criticism

The criticism made of Beccaria's doctrine applies as well to that of the Classical School. The whole system is based on a metaphysical notion, a philosophical fiction, the notion of *free will* and its corollary – moral responsibility. The doctrine is based on several questionable assumptions:

1. The belief that every person (except a young child or a lunatic) is endowed with a free will that is always present and unaffected by any internal or external pressure and is identical in all human beings.

2. The Classical School considers every act of volition an act of freedom. Just because an act was willful and deliberate does not mean that the actor was free. Impulsive, compulsive, and habitual acts are all acts of volition, but it is doubtful if the will of the perpetrator committing an offence under the influence of one of these pressures is totally free.

3. By denying that human behaviour is determined or conditioned or has natural causes and by stipulating that every act is a free act resulting from a free choice, the doctrine negates the principle of natural causation and dissociates the act from all the causal processes that led to its commission.

4. By eliminating discretion and by introducing the system of fixed punishments, the doctrine simply replaces the arbitrariness of the judge by the arbitrariness of the legislator.

5. One of the cornerstones of the doctrine is the belief in deterrence. Such belief is based on a series of doubtful assumptions: for example, the assumption that the individual is rational, is able to control his/her behaviour, learns from personal experience and the experience of others, and may be controlled by the fear of punishment. Moreover, deterrence raises moral and ethical objections because it treats the individual as a means rather than an end and advocates that someone be punished to instil fear in others or to be used as an example.

6. It does not recognize that human beings are not equal in their ability to resist temptations, to control their passions, impulses, and drives. The Classical School denies, therefore, the concept of differential responsibility or the existence of varying types or levels of responsibility.
7. It sees the act but ignores the actor and wants to make the punishment fit the crime with no consideration of the personality of the perpetrator or of his bio-psycho-social evolution.

The Neo-Classical School

The most distinguished representatives of this school are Rossi in Italy and Garraud and Joly in France. The Neo-Classical School maintains all the grand principles of the Classical School with two exceptions:

1. It introduces some flexibility into the rigid system of punishments advocated by the Classical School; and
2. It introduces some subjective elements into the totally objective view of responsibility promoted by the Classical School.

That the system of punishments advocated by the Classical School was rigid is beyond question. Radzinowicz (1966:123) explains the rigidity and its consequences in the following paragraph:

The rigidity of the Classical School on the Continent of Europe made it almost impossible to develop constructive and imaginative penal measures. Had our system of dealing with crime been confined within the pattern laid down in *Dei delitti e delle pene*, virtually all the reforms of which we are most proud would have been excluded because they would have conflicted with the principle that punishment must be closely defined in advance and strictly proportionate to the offence. There would have been no discharge, no adjustment of fines to the means of offenders, no suspended sentences, no probation, no parole, no special measures for young offenders or the mentally abnormal.

Saleilles (1929:63) also notes that as soon as the classical system was put into practice, it found itself in conflict with both public opinion and science. It ran against public opinion because it treated all those guilty of the same offence in the same manner and inexorably placed everyone upon the same footing. Yet, popular justice, exemplified in the decisions of the jury, judges the accused before the act. Faced with a fixed and invariable penalty, and stripped from all discretional power, the jury simply acquitted the accused in many cases. Saleilles (1927:64) points out that the system also ran counter to science because it was based on a fictitious concept contrary to all scientific notions – that of equal freedom – for every individual in face of the same act. When it comes to crime, freedom is the power and ability to resist evil, to control one's instincts, impulses, drives, passions, desires, and so forth. It is unscientific to maintain that this power is of equal strength for everyone or that it remains the same for each individual at all times, in all situations, and for all acts.

There were other innovations introduced into the criminal justice system as a result of ideas of the Neo-Classical School. Some of these innovations are given by Vold (1979:28):

i.   The Neo-Classical School introduced some modifications in the doc-
     trine of free will stipulating that the freedom of the will to choose could
     be affected by:
     a. pathology, incompetence, insanity, or conditions that make it im-
         possible for the individual to exercise free will;
     b. premeditation, which is introduced as a measure of the freedom of
         the will.
ii. Acceptance of the validity of mitigating circumstances: These might be
     physical (weather, mechanical, and so forth), environmental, or the
     mental condition of the individual.
iii. A modification of the doctrine of responsibility to provide for a mitiga-
     tion of punishment, with partial responsibility....
iv. Admission into court procedure of expert testimony on the question of
     the degree of responsibility, of whether the accused was capable of
     choosing between right and wrong.

The Neo-Classical School's admission that irresponsibility may be based not only on insanity but also on evidence of lack of freedom and its introduction of the theory of partial or limited responsibility leads to two conclusions (Saleilles, 1929:83):

– To exempt from punishment when it is established pathologically or
   psychologically that freedom of the will was absent; and,
– To reduce and lower the punishment when it is established that the
   defendant exercised only a partial freedom.

Saleilles (1927:85) sees these two conclusions as the first scientific attempt to apply the subjective position to criminology. However, the attempt, he affirms, was quite inadequate because it involved a practical difficulty and a scientific error: The practical difficulty is the absence of a criterion to determine the degree of freedom. The scientific error is that freedom is not open to demonstration and proof. How then could it be graded, even approximately?

9 Empirical Investigations and Naturalistic Explanations

CRIME AS A PRODUCT OF NATURAL CAUSES: ECOLOGICAL APPROACHES

> All observations tend likewise to confirm the truth of this proposition, which I long ago announced, that every thing which pertains to the human species considered as a whole, belongs to the order of physical facts; the greater the number of individuals, the more does the influence of individual will disappear, leaving predominance to a series of general facts, dependent on causes by which society exists and is preserved.
>
> Adolphe Jacques Quetelet (1842 and 1972:43)
> *Treatise on Man*

Since crime is as old as society, why is it that the scientific search for its causes did not begin until the 19th century? Prior to the 18th century human actions were attributed to a 'Divine Will', and it was generally believed that both natural and social phenomena obey 'Divine Laws.' Supernatural forces were held responsible for pushing people into sin and crime. These demonological explanations preclude any scientific search for the causes of criminal behaviour or for the earthly laws that govern social phenomena. It was not until the 18th century that scholars gradually accepted the idea that social phenomena constitute a natural order and that there exists a social nature subject to specific laws (Debuyst, 1969).

Debuyst (1969) points out that one of the essential conditions for the development of social science is the existence of cultivated groups interested in examining and analyzing in depth data acquired from observation and experience. Another requirement is the presence of a favourable intellectual climate allowing freedom of thought and expression. Without this creative intellectual environment, thinkers are subjected to 'compulsory conformity' and are unable to express any criticism of existing ideas or to formulate any new hypothesis. It is the absence of such freedom of thought and expression that explains why the social sciences are usually underdeveloped in theocratic and oligarchic societies. Social sciences are for free thinkers, and they can hardly flourish in an environment where those advancing new ideas or theories run the risk of being accused of heresy, blasphemy or of opposition to the regime. The intellectual milieu that prevailed in Europe during the

18th-century allowed the blossoming, acceptance, and diffusion of a great number of new ideas and made it possible for the social sciences to develop in the century that followed.

SCHOOLS OF CRIMINOLOGICAL THOUGHT: THE CARTOGRAPHIC SCHOOL

The best known representatives of the Cartographic School (also called the geographic, the statistical, or the ecological school) are *Adolphe Quetelet* and *André-Michel Guerry*. Guerry was a French lawyer, and Quetelet was a Belgian mathematician and astronomer. Guerry and Quetelet, as Garland (1985:113) points out, 'were concerned to show that crime is a social fact, with the regularities and social basis of all such phenomena.' Although Finland was the first country in Europe to publish criminal court statistics in 1754, it was the publication of the General Account of the Administration of Criminal Justice in France (*Compte Général*) in 1825 that led these two scholars to underake the first studies of scientific criminology. In his book *Essay on the Moral Statistics of France* (*Essai sur la statistique morale de la France*) published in 1833, Guerry analyzed the justice statistics of the first five years (1825–30) and used shaded ecological maps to represent different crime rates in relation to geographical facts and other variables. Three years later, in 1836, there appeared an elaborate analysis of crime and 'moral conditions' in France, Belgium, Luxembourg, and Holland written by Quetelet. Quetelet also dealt with crime in his other publications, notably in his *Treatise on Man*, the third chapter of which is concerned exclusively with the subject, and in his book published in 1848 under the title *Of the Social System and the Laws That Govern It* (*Du système social et les lois que le régissent*).

One finding that struck both Guerry and Quetelet was that crimes were remarkably constant in each department from one year to the next. This finding led to the conclusion that crime rates were the product of natural factors such as age, sex, and climatic conditions. This apparent constancy and unchangingness in crime rates led Quetelet to believe that criminal phenomena occur with 'mechanical regularity' and to declare that there is one tax which is paid each year more punctually than others and it is the tax of crime. He writes:

> Thus, as I have already had occasion to repeat several times, we pass from one year to another, with the sad perspective of seeing the same crimes reproduced in the same order, and bringing with them the same punishments in the same proportions. (1972:43)
>
> Also, I cannot repeat too often... that there is a budget which we pay with a frightful regularity – it is that of prisons, chains, and the scaffold. (1972:44)

André-Michel Guerry (1802–66)

Guerry examined the variables of sex, age, seasons, industrial and commercial developments, education, and so forth in relation to crime rates and came up with the following observations:

1. Women are more 'moral' than men, but as danger decreases, women become more aggressive and more undertaking.
2. There is a strong relationship between age and crime.
3. Criminality is subject to important seasonal variations. The high peak of crimes against the person and of sexual offences is reached during the summer.
4. Contrary to the widely held belief at the time that crime was the product of poverty, Guerry observed that the poorer the region, the less crime there is; and,
5. There is an inverse relationship between the number of homicides and suicides. Corsica, for instance, had the highest number of the former and the least number of the latter.

Adolphe Jacques Quetelet (1796–1874)

Quetelet may be regarded as the first scholar who tried to interpret social phenomena according to the law of great numbers, and although he believed that crime occurs with a consistency approaching mechanical regularity, he admitted that crime rates may be subject to certain fluctuations. He regarded such periodical fluctuations of criminality as a mathematical function dependent upon, and reflecting, the social and economic conditions of the period. He examined the possible relationship between crime and various natural and social factors, and came up with several conclusions.

Age, Gender and Crime
Quetelet (1972:38) declared that age is the factor that has the greatest impact on crime: 'Of all the causes which influence the development of the propensity to crime, or which diminish that propensity, age is unquestionably the most energetic.' With advancing age, cunning replaces force, and trickery replaces violence in the commission of crimes.

Female criminality is less than one-quarter of male criminality. Women commit more crimes against property than crimes against the person. In case of murder, they prefer poison. Quetelet (1972:37) explains the difference as follows:

> Now, the reason why females have less propensity to crime than males, is accounted for by their being more under the influence of sentiments of shame and modesty, as far as morals are concerned; their dependent state,

and retired habits, as far as occasion or opportunity is concerned; and their physical weakness, so far as the facility of acting is concerned. I think we may attribute the differences observed in the degree of criminality to these three principal causes.

The Thermic Law of Delinquency

Quetelet discovered that variations in temperature have a significant impact on the number of crimes. This led him to formulate what may be viewed as 'a thermic law of crime.' According to this law, crimes against the person reach their peak during the hot months while those against property have their maximum in the winter. Quetelet's explanation of these seasonal differences is that in winter misery and want are more especially felt and cause an increase of the number of crimes against property, whilst the violence of the passions predominating in summer excites more frequent personal collisions.

Furthermore, Quetelet observed that crimes against the person are more frequent in warmer regions, that is, southern regions, than they are in colder regions in the North, while the reverse holds true for crimes against property.

Crime and Poverty

Quetelet concluded that education and poverty are far from having as much influence on the 'propensity' to crime as is generally supposed. He found, as did Guerry, that several of the *départements* of France considered to be the poorest are, at the same time, the most 'moral'.

> Poverty is felt the most in provinces where great riches have been amassed...where...thousands of individuals pass suddenly from a state of comfort to one of misery. These rapid changes from one state to another give rise to crime, particularly if those who suffer are surrounded by materials of temptation, and are irritated by the continual aspect of luxury and of the inequality of fortune, which renders them desperate. (1972:35)

It was Quetelet, therefore, who drew attention to what later became known in criminology as the concept of 'relative deprivation'.

Alcohol and Crime

Quetelet noted a strong, positive relationship between alcohol consumption and crimes against the person, particularly homicide. He observed that out of 1129 murders committed in France during the space of four years, 446 have been in consequence of quarrels and contentions in taverns, a finding that would tend to show 'the fatal influence of the use of strong drinks'.

Crime and Opportunity

Quetelet also observed a strong relationship between crime and opportunity, a finding in concordance with the popular saying 'the occasion makes the thief' (*l'occasion fait le larron*):

> As we have already observed, to the commission of crime the three following conditions are essential: the will, which depends on the person's morality, the opportunity, and the facility of effecting it. (1972:37)

Cultural Heterogeneity, Industrialization and Economic Inequalities

One of Quetelet's most interesting findings is that countries where frequent mixture of people takes place, those in which industry and trade collect many persons and things together and possess the greatest activity and those where the inequality of fortune is most felt, all things being equal, are those that give rise to the greatest number of crimes.

Critical Assessment of the Cartographic School

At a time when physicians and psychiatrists (Jean Esquirol, Benedict Morel, James Pritchard, and others) were searching for the biological, morphological, and phrenological causes of crime, Guerry and Quetelet focused on the social conditions that breed crime. This emphasis can be easily seen in Quetelet's famous phrase:

> Society prepares crimes and the criminal is only the instrument that executes them...the criminal is then, in a way, the scapegoat of society.... Society contains the germs of all crimes that will be committed ...as well as the necessary facilities for their commission.
>
> (Quetelet, *Physique Sociale*, Lib IV)

Quetelet declared that an accurate investigation of all social factors would make it possible to discover the causes of crime and to eliminate or reduce them, a function that he saw as the first and foremost for legislators 'to whom belong the task of fixing the budget of crimes, in the same way as revenues and expenditures are fixed'.

Contrary to the individualistic and legalistic philosophy of the Classical School, emphasizing free will and denying the influence of external influences and pressures, the Cartographic School takes the position that crime, like other social phenomena, is caused by natural causes and is governed by natural laws. The Cartographic School regards crime as a social and mass phenomenon. It places the emphasis on the climatic, physical, social, and economic causes of crime. Needless to say, many of the observations made by Guerry and Quetelet in the first half of the 19th century are as valid today as they were when they were made.

Industrialized, wealthy, and prosperous countries have in general much higher rates of property crime than poor, underdeveloped ones. Male criminality remains qualitatively different from, and quantitatively higher than, female criminality. Criminologists have always been aware of the relationship between alcohol and violent crime, and they are rediscovering the strong positive association between crime and opportunity (see Mayhew *et al.*, 1976). The age group 15 to 25 commits much more than its numerical share of delinquency and crime. However, delinquency and crime reach their peak at present at a much earlier age than that observed by Quetelet (25 years) because the age of adolescence is now lower than it used to be.

Although most of Quetelet's observations are universally accepted, some of his explanations are not. Furthermore, his concept of a 'propensity to crime' in the sense of an inner tendency or inclination that goes up and down under the influence of demographic, economic, and climatic conditions is, on the whole, questionable.

Quantitative differences in crime rates between men and women, which Quetelet saw as a function of the inferior physical strength and superior morality of the female sex, might be better explained by differences in social roles assumed by men and women in Western societies. The narrowing of the gap between male and female criminality in recent years may be seen as a confirmation of this latter explanation. Yet, claims that the liberation of women and the growing similarity in the lifestyle of both males and females might be responsible for a lower male–female crime ratio have drawn sharp criticism from feminist criminologists, in particular, Carol Smart. In her book *Women, Crime and Criminology: A Feminist Critique* (1976), Smart strongly challenges the argument that female emancipation leads to increases in female crime rates.

Quetelet's explanations of the thermic laws of delinquency are also open to question. He attributes the high frequency of crimes against the person in warmer climates and in southern regions to the influence of heat on human passion and temper. Warmer climates and southern regions are characterized by a higher volume of social interaction, and this might well be the reason why crimes against the person are more common during the summer months and in the south.

The rise in property crime during the winter months, which Quetelet ascribes to increasing misery and to more pressing needs brought about by cold temperatures, might be explained in terms of the changing length of night and day. It is fair to assume that property crimes, at least the ones that are usually committed under a cloak of darkness, will increase with the increasing number of hours of darkness and decrease with the shrinking of nights during the summer months.

One should keep in mind, however, that Quetelet's remarks were made in the first half of the 19th century, and for that period they were innovative and insightful. Guerry and Quetelet should be given credit as the first scientific criminologists; Lindesmith and Levin (1937a) argued that they, rather than Lombroso, should be considered the founders of positivist criminology.

The studies of the Cartographic School generated fruitful discussions, and instigated further research based on criminal statistics. Ducpetiaux (1850) in Belgium and Von Ottingen (1867) and Von Mayr (1882) in Germany, examined variations in crime rates and correlated them with meteorological, economic and political factors. Von Mayr correlated the fluctuations in the price of rye with fluctuations in certain types of offences in Bavaria for the period 1836–61 and found a high positive correlation between theft and the price of rye.

In his assessment of Quetelet's work and contribution to criminology, Beirne (1987:1166) credits him with having opened the possibility of a sociological analysis of crime. In the view of many, the Cartographic School is the forerunner of what is now known as *ecological criminology* or *environmental criminology* (Brantingham and Brantingham, 1984). After being eclipsed by the appealing theories of criminal anthropology, the ideas and approaches of the School experienced a strong and lasting revival by the Sociology Department at the University of Chicago during the first half of the 20th century. Robert Park and his associates at Chicago, Clifford Shaw and Henry Mckay, used the groundwork of their 19th century European counterparts together with concepts borrowed from human ecology in a series of long-ranging studies examining the patterns of juvenile delinquency in large cities. One of the major findings of the Chicago School is that crime rates are closely linked to the geographic and physical environment. Not only did they find that rates of delinquency varied considerably in the different zones of the city, but more importantly that the high delinquency areas maintained those rates despite considerable changes in the ethnic and racial make-up of those who successively lived in the areas. This was interpreted as an indication that environmental variables are more important in determining crime rates than individual characteristics.

CRIME AS A PRODUCT OF INDIVIDUAL PATHOLOGY: MEDICAL AND PSYCHIATRIC APPROACHES

In the first place, all criminals are in one sense born criminals, in another, occasional criminals. All criminals possess a predisposition to crime, which is not the effect of external circumstances, but of something residing in the individual moral organization, in his manner of feeling and thinking.... And if he is without a predisposition to crime, he will never commit it, whatever be the occasion.

Raffaele Garofalo (1914:132–3)
Criminology

SCHOOLS OF CRIMINOLOGICAL THOUGHT: THE ITALIAN POSITIVIST SCHOOL

The most distinguished representatives of the Italian Positivist School (also called the *School of Criminal Anthropology*) are Cesare Lombroso, Enrico Ferri, and Raffaele Garofalo.

Just as Beccaria was deeply influenced by the writings of 18th-century philosophers, Lombroso's thinking was influenced by the phrenologists and evolutionist theorists. His ideas bear the marks of biological evolution (Charles Darwin) and social evolution (Herbert Spencer).

The Classical and Neo-Classical Schools were not concerned with the etiology of crime but with criminal law and criminal justice reform. The Italian Positivist School, on the other hand, was primarily concerned with the natural causes of crime. Its scholars were eager to provide an explanation of criminality and to use that explanation to draw the lines of a criminal policy grounded in the new science.

The Italian Positivist School had nothing in common with the Classical and Neo-Classical Schools. The latter schools firmly believed in freedom of the will, and viewed crime as the result of temptation's victory over reason. The Italian Positivist School, on the other hand, looked upon crime as a natural product, as a result of purely natural factors that leave no place for freedom (Saleilles, 1927:102). The Italian School's approach to the study of crime was positivistic in that it applied the logic and method of the natural sciences, in contrast to the speculative approach of the Classical School (Inciardi, 1978:97).

The basic ideas of the Italian Positivist School could be summarized as follows: *It studies criminality starting from the assumption that the natural causes of crime are to be found in the individual criminal. It believes that there are basic, fundamental differences between criminals and non-criminals. It claims that some individuals are born criminals and offers varying explanations for this natural defect. It replaces the notion of free will with the notion of determinism, being convinced that criminal tendencies are inherited and that born criminals are incorrigible.*

Cesare Lombroso (1835–1909)

The Notion of the Born Criminal
The notion of the *born criminal* is certainly the one for which Lombroso is best known and with which he is always identified. Over the years, Lombroso kept reducing the percentage these so-called born criminals constituted among the population of offenders, and continued to offer different causes for their anomaly.

Atavism

The idea that criminality is the result of a biological anomaly with which some individuals are born came to Lombroso like a revelation while, as a prison doctor, he was performing a post-mortem examination on the body of a notorious criminal named Villela. As he opened the skull he noticed an uncommon feature, a depression or a cavity, and was also struck by a greater anomaly in the cerebellum and a hypertrophy of the spinal cord. As a flash of lightning, the notion of 'atavism' sprang to his mind. Lombroso's daughter, Gina, (1911:xxiv-v) explains how her father came upon this idea:

> This was not merely an idea but a revelation. At the sight of that skull, I seemed to see all of a sudden, lighted up as a vast plain under a flaming sky the problem of the nature of the criminal – an atavistic being who reproduces in his person the ferocious instincts of primitive humanity and the inferior animals.

Atavism is an evolutionary concept. Literally, it means the hereditary transmission from remote ancestors. In Lombroso's theory, it is the tendency of some living beings to return to a distant type from which intermediate generations have made them deviate. Atavism is thus characterized by the reappearance of unusual traits in most recent representatives of the species, traits that were characteristic of that distant race. If, for example, a baby was born with a tail, he was considered an atavistic creature. In other words, the criminal, as Lombroso envisioned him, is a 'throwback', a reversion to the past, a relic of a vanished race. The idea that some people might be reversions to an earlier form of life was originally suggested by Darwin (1871, 1874, 2nd edn:137):

> With mankind some of the worst dispositions which occasionally without any assignable cause make their appearance in families, may perhaps be reversions to a savage state, from which we are not removed by many generations.

Epilepsy

Epilepsy is a brain disease. In the past, it used to be called 'morbus sacer' (the sacred disease), and was believed to be of divine origin. Lombroso noticed that the extreme excitability and irritability manifested by 'born criminals' are shared by epileptics and that contradictions and exaggerations of mood, humour, and sentiments are salient characteristics of both epileptics and 'born criminals'. He concluded that epilepsy and atavism form the substratum upon which the criminal world is based. Gina Lombroso (1911:72–3) cites her father as saying:

> The criminal is only a diseased person, an epileptic, in whom the cerebral malady, begun in some cases during prenatal existence, or later, in

consequence of some infection or cerebral poisoning produces, together with certain signs of physical degeneration in the skull, face, teeth, and brain, a return to the early brutal egotism natural to primitive races, which manifests itself in homicide, theft, and other crimes.

Degeneracy

Degeneracy is another evolutionary concept used by Lombroso to explain why certain individuals are born with criminal propensities. Degeneracy or biological regression was believed to be caused by certain diseases, such as syphilis, alcoholism, and epilepsy. The degenerate race was seen as a pathological variety of the normal species, a variety having its own distinctive biology, including such anomalies as an asymmetrical head, deformed ears, and everted lips.

Moral Insanity

Moral insanity is a term coined by the British psychiatrist James Pritchard (1835) who ascribed the absence of a moral sense to a pathological condition of the brain. Lombroso noticed a remarkable similarity between those he labelled 'born criminals' and the morally insane. Having observed that the same physical anomalies as well as the mental and moral qualities found in born criminals are also characteristic of the morally insane, he concluded that:

> The physical and psychic characteristics of born criminals coincide with those of the morally insane. Both are identical with those of another class of degenerates, known to the world as epileptics. (1911:58)

The Notion That Criminals Are Basically Different from Non-Criminals

Lombroso believed that the criminal man is a human being dominated by a pathological nature, and is governed by primitive, violent, and destructive instincts and impulses. He also believed that

1. The antisocial tendencies of criminals are the result of their physical and psychic organization, which *differs essentially* from that of normal individuals (1911:5).
2. The criminal constitutes a *specific type*, belongs to a particular species, and represents an anthropological variety that is biologically inferior.
3. There exists a close evolutionary link between the criminal and the 'savage' (*Crime: Its Causes and Remedies*, 1911:369).

Recognizable Features of Criminals

Lombroso claimed that born criminals exhibit numerous anomalies in the face and skeleton and in various psychic and sensitive functions. These characteristic traits may be grouped into four categories: *Morphological*

Features (stigmata); Physiological Traits; Psychological Traits; and Social Traits.

Heredity of Crime

Lombroso believed that crime is the issue of hereditary conditions and claimed that heredity is the principal organic cause of criminal tendencies. He makes a distinction between *indirect heredity*, that is heredity from a generically degenerate family with frequent cases of insanity, deafness, syphilis, epilepsy and alcoholism among its members. (1911:137); and *direct heredity*, that is heredity from criminal parentage.

Since crime is the product of atavism and degeneracy and since defective heredity leads to crime, then some races are more criminal than others. Lombroso believed that some races are more developed and are superior to others. He claimed that there are whole tribes and races more or less given to crime. As an example, he refers to the gypsies in Europe.

Biological Determinism

As mentioned above, Lombroso viewed crime as a necessary consequence of certain biological conditions that leave no place for freedom. Biological determinism is the logical conclusion to which the concepts of 'born criminal' and 'heredity of crime' inevitably lead. Criminals have no free will, are doomed even before birth to a career of crime, and all educational efforts fail to redeem them (1876:101).

Incorrigibility of Born Criminals

This is another conclusion to which the concepts of the 'born criminal' and 'heredity of crime' lead. The groups of born criminals or 'natural criminals' cannot be assimilated and made part of the social life. There is nothing to be done except to place them beyond the possibility of doing harm.

Enrico Ferri (1856–1928)

Ferri made a significant contribution to the theories and doctrine of the Italian Positivist School. It is Ferri, a lawyer and sociologist, who moderated many of Lombroso's exaggerations and who, in his book *Criminal Sociology* published in Italian in 1884, insisted that crime is not simply the product of biological and physiological factors, but of social, economic and environmental factors as well.

The Law of Criminal Saturation

The Italian Positivist School looked upon crime as a natural phenomenon produced by natural causes, hence the analogies made between crime and other natural phenomena. In formulating the law of criminal saturation,

Ferri (1917:209) draws a parallel between the state of crime and the saturation rule in chemistry. He writes:

> The level of crime each year is determined by the different conditions of the
> physical and social environment combined with the congenital tendencies
> and accidental impulses of individuals, in accordance with a law, which, in
> analogy to the law of chemistry, I have called the law of criminal satura-
> tion. As a given volume of water at a definite temperature will dissolve a
> fixed quantity of chemical substance and not an atom more or less; so in a
> given social environment with definite individual and physical conditions, a
> fixed number of crimes, no more and no less, can be committed.

Ferri adds that in chemistry an exceptional supersaturation may occur
through an increase of temperature of the solvent liquid. Also in criminal
sociology, beyond the regular and constant saturation, there is observable at
times an actual *criminal supersaturation* that results from extra conditions of
the social environment (war, revolution, and the like).

The law of criminal saturation reflects one of the fundamental differences
between the positions of the Italian Positivist School and the Classical
School. Crime, argues Ferri, is determined, and, therefore, its level may be
predicted. This is not possible according to the voluntaristic doctrine of the
Classical School in which crime is simply the outcome of unpredictable
individual choices.

Ferri draws two principal conclusions from the law of *supersaturation*:

1. The inaccuracy of speaking of the mechanical regularity of criminal
    phenomena, regularity that he feels has been greatly exaggerated since
    it was professed by Quetelet.
2. It scientifically proves that punishments have none of the efficacy attrib-
    uted to them. He asserts that crimes increase and decrease through a sum
    of causes that are very different from the penalties so easily promulgated
    by legislators and applied by judges and jailors.

The Multifactor Theory of Crime

Ferri insists that crime is the result of manifold causes, which, although
always found linked in an intricate network, can be detected by means of
careful study. He sees crime as the product of the interaction between
individual and environmental influences, between endogenous and exogen-
ous factors, and insists that 'without special individual inclinations, the
external impulses would not be sufficient' (quoted in De Quiros, 1911:21).
Crime-producing factors may be grouped into three categories:

1. *Individual or anthropological factors*: such as age, sex, civil status, profes-
    sion, domicile, social rank, instruction, education, and the organic and
    psychic constitution,

2. *Physical or natural factors*: such as race, climate, the fertility and dis-
    position of the soil, the relative length of day and night, the seasons,
    meteoric conditions, temperatures; and,
3. *Social factors*: such as density of population, emigration, public opinion,
    customs and religion, public order, economic and industrial conditions,
    agriculture and industrial production, public administration of public
    safety, public instruction and public education, public beneficence, and,
    in general, civil and penal legislation.

Classification of Criminals

Classifying criminals was a constant preoccupation of the scholars of the
Italian Positivist School, and it was an integral part of their proposed penal
policy. Since the purpose of punishment was no longer to expiate or atone
for a moral fault and since the penal measure had to be adapted to the
individual criminal, it was necessary to elaborate in advance typologies of
criminals that would assist judges in their choices of sanction and would
enable them to individualize the penal measure.

Ferri's classification of criminals contains five types: *Criminal Lunatics* or
insane criminals; *Born Criminals* or instinctive criminals; *Habitual Criminals*
or criminals by acquired habit; *Occasional Criminals*; and *Emotional Criminals* or criminals by passion.

Raffaele Garofalo (1852–1934)

The Natural Crime

One fundamental weakness in the theory of the born criminal is its incom-
patibility with the fact that crime is relative in time and space. Critics of the
Italian Positivist School, particularly Gabriel Tarde, were quick to point out
the inherent contradiction between the notions of the cultural variability of
crime and heredity of crime. In an attempt to prove that the two notions are
not incompatible, Garofalo took upon himself the task of showing that there
are certain acts that 'no civilized society can refuse to recognize as criminal
and repress by means of punishment.' They are offences against the fundamental altruistic sentiments of pity and probity in the average measure
possessed by a given social group (1914:33–4).

Garofalo considers the altruistic sentiment of *pity*, namely, the repugnance
to acts that produce physical pain, to be universal. He therefore considers
attacks upon human life as well as acts tending to produce physical harm to
human beings, such as the deliberate infliction of physical torture, to be
natural crimes. The other universal altruistic sentiment is the sentiment of
probity, a term expressive of respect for that which belongs to others. Attacks
upon the property of others are therefore natural crimes. Garofalo goes on
to dress a table of the so-called 'natural crimes' common to all people and of

'artificial' or 'positive crimes' that are relative to the special conditions of particular countries. Although he feels that the latter should also be punished, it is only the former that are of interest to the science of criminology. Garofalo's distinction between 'natural crime' and 'positive crime' is similar to the one between crimes that are *mala in se* and crimes that are *mala prohibita* (see Chapter 2).

Classes of Criminals

Garofalo is critical of Ferri's classification of criminals, which he claims is without scientific basis and is lacking in homogeneity and exactness. In its place, Garofalo proposes his own classification based upon moral anomaly, upon a particular kind of immorality. Garofalo suggests that criminals be classified into four categories:

1. *Murderers*: Garofalo regards murderers as the typical criminals in whom altruism is totally lacking.
2. *Violent criminals*: They are characterized by lack of benevolence or pity. Garofalo distinguishes two subcategories:
   (a) Violent criminals who commit *endemic crimes* or, in other words, such crimes as constitute the special criminality of a given locality, such as vendettas or political assassinations.
   (b) Violent criminals who commit *crimes of passion*: in some of those cases, the criminal may closely approach the normal person but a differential psychic element is always present.
3. *Criminals deficient in probity*. These are the ones who commit crimes against property. Social factors are much more influential here than in the preceding cases, but there is always a lack of probity. Their improbity may either be congenital or acquired.
4. *Lascivious criminals (Les Cyniques)*. These are the criminals who commit crimes as a result of sexual impulse and offences against chastity in general. They often suffer from some form of alienation.

Penal Philosophy of the Italian Positivist School

Negation of Free Will

The Classical School viewed people as masters of their own destiny, having total control over their own actions. The Italian Positivist School, on the other hand, viewed them as the product of natural (and social) factors over which they have little or no control.

Rejection of the Notion of Moral Responsibility

The negation of free will and the deterministic views of the Italian Positivist School logically lead to the denial of moral responsibility and to declare the criminal irresponsible. Consequently, another justification had to be found for whatever penal measures the state must take against criminals, and the Italian Positivist School declare them to be *socially* responsible. This social responsibility is explained by Ferri (1917:340–1) as follows:

> This moral responsibility [of the Classical School] is based on two conditions: free will and normal intelligence (or conscience) in the author of the crime. The Positivist School, on the contrary, maintains that as there is no free choice or free will, neither is there responsibility, culpability or moral imputability: and this does not involve as a consequence that there should also disappear all ... penal accountability of the wrongdoer. It maintains quite the reverse ... that physical imputability of crime is sufficient to constitute penal accountability, it being naturally at liberty to seek ... to adapt the practical forms of penalty or defense of society, to the different categories of criminals and crime.

Rejection of Punishment

By insisting upon determinism and predestination, the Italian Positivist School had to reject both retribution and deterrence as goals of penal measures. Both are contrary to the fatalistic theories espoused by the School. As Saleilles (1927:116–17) puts it:

> ... punishment can have no social status either as a penalty or as disapproval. Atonement can be exacted only for a wrong which one was free to avoid, and reproof can be demanded only for evil issuing from an act of free will. Punishment is only a means of public defense and security, analogous to the preventive measures taken against dangerous animals or insane men. Moreover there are no repressive measures; there are only measures of prevention to check the repetition and dissemination of crime. What is dangerous in the criminal and makes him a menace to society is not the crime once committed but the criminal himself: his personality, his temperament, ever leading him to further crime; the latent fundamental impulses which, when acted upon by circumstance, may break out into murder, theft, or offences against morality.

The Notion of Dangerousness (Temibilità or Pericolosità)

The Classical School was preoccupied with the seriousness of various crimes and with adapting punishment to the gravity of the offence. The Italian Positivist School sees the danger to society not in the crime but in the criminal and views this dangerousness as the proper criterion for social defence measures. The crime is something of the past, and it cannot be undone. It does not help to punish it after it has occurred. The only thing to do is to try to repair, if possible, the damage that it has caused (restitution, compensation to the victim, and so forth). What is really important is to prevent future crimes by controlling or neutralizing the dangerousness of the offender. Crime is merely a symptom of the criminal instinct or the criminal tendencies and propensities of its perpetrator. It is the revelator or indicator of his criminal nature.

Individualization of Social Defence Measures

The Italian Positivist School advocates true and total individualization of measures to be taken against criminals, individualization based on the dangerousness, the capacity for crime, and the social risk of the individual offender. Saleilles (1927:118–19) explains as follows the basis for individualization:

> Such individualization will no longer consider the crime committed; it will even disregard the degree of responsibility, for responsibility bears upon the accountability towards a particular action, which is not here pertinent. Such individualization will consider the true nature of the individual, his latent and potential criminality, and will seek to adjust the punishment to the requirements of moral improvement which each criminal presents.

Criminal Policy of the Italian Positivist School

The criminal policy advocated by the Italian Positivist School is geared toward prevention and social defence. Ferri summarizes the basic principle underlying this criminal policy in just one phrase: 'The punitive function is purely and simply a social defense function.' The measures advocated by Ferri (1917) may be divided into three categories: individualized measures fitting his five classes of criminals; penal substitutes; and measures of social defence.

Measures to Be Taken Against Criminals

1. *Born criminals* and *incorrigibles*: the first measure is in principle the death penalty. The only way of placing them beyond the possibility of doing harm is to eliminate them. Modern societies, however, may afford the luxury of keeping them in perpetual detention.
2. *Habitual criminals*: they should, in principle, be treated similarly to born criminals but with less rigour since their criminality is not as serious as that of the born criminals. They should therefore be placed in indeterminate detention with periodical review.
3. *Occasional criminals*: prison should not be used for this category. They should be sentenced to a high fine, be compelled to make restitution to the victim, and, if necessary, be forced to work but without detention.

4. *Emotional criminals* or *criminals by passion*: they should be forced to repair the damage they have caused. A special category of them, the political criminals, should be exiled.
5. *Insane criminals*: should be kept in special institutions set up for them.

Penal Substitutes

Ferri enumerates a large number of social, economic, and religious measures likely to reduce crime. He calls these measures *penal substitutes*. Among them are measures designed to improve production and to ensure a just division of wealth; measures for the reform of government, and changes in penal and civil laws; decriminalization of certain acts and their transfer from the domain of criminal to civil law; measures to improve the systems of detection and arrest and to improve police techniques and efficiency; protection of abandoned children through the creation of industrial schools or by placing the children on farms or on agricultural colonies; a struggle against the abuse of alcohol (such as the creation of an alcohol monopoly run by the state).

Measures of Social Defence

These include the elimination of criminals declared dangerous and those who confess their crimes, who have been caught *in flagrante delicto*, and in all cases where there is no chance of a judicial error. Ferri favours the extension of the right to self-defence since this will help society get rid of dangerous criminals. He is also in favour of publicity of criminal records, the abolition of pardon and statutes of limitation, and the abolition of the jury except in cases of political crimes and crimes of the press. The Italian Positivist School saw the judge as performing a scientific role that cannot be performed adequately by a jury composed of laymen. Furthermore, it feared that the jury might in some cases acquit dangerous criminals. In short, it felt that there is no place for the jury in a scientific system of justice.

Unlike the Classical School, which was renowned for its respect of human dignity and rights and for its continued efforts to humanize the criminal law and the penal system, the Italian Positivist School is pitiless in its attitude toward 'real' criminals, and the criminal policy it advocates is characterized by its extreme rigour. One aspect of this rigour is an extensive use of the death penalty as means of ridding society of dangerous criminals.

The criminal policy of the Italian Positivist School is also reactionary and regressive. because it calls for sacrificing, under the guise of protection of society, the legal safeguards acquired and recognized under the influence of the Classical School.

Critical Evaluation of the Italian Positivist School

Merit

In the history of criminology, there is probably no other figure that has been praised and attacked with as much vigour as that of Lombroso. Lindesmith and Levin (1937b:661) wrote that:

> What Lombroso did was to reverse the method of explanation that had been current since the time of Guerry and Quetelet and, instead of maintaining that institutions and traditions determined the nature of the criminal, he held that the nature of the criminal determined the character of institutions and traditions.

This criticism is similar to that of Sutherland and Cressey (1960:55), who claimed that by considering crime as an individual rather than a social phenomenon in contrast with previous schools (Guerry and Quetelet), the Italian Positivist School delayed by 50 years the progress of research started at the time it came into being without making any valid or lasting contribution of its own.

Mannheim's (1936), view is a more charitable one. He praises Lombroso for having 'saved criminal science from the shackles of merely academic abstractions and for having fertilized it with the rich treasure of the natural sciences.' And another German criminologist, Franz von Liszt, praised the trinity of the Italian Positivist School, Lombroso, Ferri, and Garofalo, for having:

> ... stirred us up from our metaphysical sleep and from our paralyzing theoretical jurisprudence; somewhat rudely and with unnecessary noise, but with lasting success. (Quoted in Mannheim, 1936:34)

Despite the ambiguity of many of the concepts and theories of the Italian Positivist School, the exaggerations of Lombroso, and the valid criticism made of its methodology, tenets, and criminal policy, there is little doubt that Lombroso's work constituted an important step in the evolution of criminology. It is not without reason or justification that Lombroso is considered by many as the father and founder of scientific criminology and that the year of publication of his book *The Criminal Man* (1876) is regarded as the birth year of positivist criminology.

The Italian Positivist School introduced the methods of the natural sciences in criminology, and focused the attention on the perpetrator, who was totally absent in the system of the Classical School, which, as Ferri said, recognized the act but ignored the actor. It showed that the causes of crime could be discovered by scientific inquiry. Its greatest merit, however, is that it generated a wealth of new and controversial ideas, ideas that led to criticism, discussions, and further research to validate or negate them, thus creating an enormous amount of interest and scientific curiosity in the field of crime.

In the field of criminal policy, the Italian Positivist School is to be credited with having launched the idea of a scientific system of criminal justice, with assigning to the judge (who under the Classical School was reduced to a mechanical distributor of punishment) a new scientific role, with having introduced the concept of individualization of punishment, and with having laid the foundations of the *Social Defence Movement*.

Enrico Ferri was asked by the Italian government to prepare a project for a new Italian criminal code based upon, and incorporating, the ideas and principles of the Italian Positivist School. However, the code he prepared was never implemented. Yet, it would be wrong to conclude that the teachings of the Italian Positivist School have had no influence whatsoever on criminal legislation in Italy or elswhere. The principle of individualization of punishment, the concept of dangerousness, the notion of social defence and its derivations (such as preventative detention of dangerous offenders, particularly sexual offenders) are firmly established in the criminal codes of many countries, including Canada. And in certain countries, such as Belgium (where there exists a special social defense law), and Italy (home of the trinity of the Italian Positivist School), the criminal codes bear visible marks of the doctrine of the school. For example, the Italian criminal code of 1931 recognizes in paragraph 108 the existence of criminals 'by tendency' or 'by disposition' and provides that:

> May be declared criminal by tendency he who, even without being recidivist, habitual, nor professional criminal, commits an intentional crime ...that reveals a special inclination to crime and which is caused by the particularly malevolent character of the offender.

Criticism
Use of deficient data and deficient methodology.   Lombroso and his disciples were severely criticized for using questionable data and defective methodology. (Wolfgang, 1973) He had no firsthand knowledge of the 'savage' whom criminals were supposed to resemble, and relied heavily upon measurements done by others without any knowledge of the techniques they used and the precision of their methods. He did not critically examine his sources of information, and approached individual physique as a static not as a dynamic phenomenon. Ferri himself admitted that one of the methodological weaknesses was to accept the measurement of crania of criminals without knowledge of the stature and age of the subjects despite a precise relationship between the various anthropological characteristics, such as between cranial capacity and age and stature.

With the exception of his study on the female offender, conducted jointly with his son-in-law Fererro, Lombroso did not try to check the validity of his findings or conclusions by studying adequate control groups. Even Hooton (1939), one of Lombroso's admirers, who tried to revive Lombroso's theories in the United States, had to admit that Lombroso's methodology suffered from the insufficient numbers and the ethnic and racial heterogeneity of the samples and populations studied as well as from the absence of any scientific statistical analysis.

Lombroso has also been criticized for his hasty and sweeping generalizations, particularly with regard to atavism, degeneracy, and epilepsy, for his defective use of analogy, and for correlating too many factors with crime without questioning the presence or absence of an underlying cause-and-effect relationship. An example of this criticism is given by Wolfgang (1973:265), who notes that after using questionable data from other countries regarding the proportion of prisoners who smoke, Lombroso concluded that 'It is clearly to be seen, then, that there is a causal connection between tobacco and crime, like that which exists in the case of alcohol.'

One of the devastating criticisms made of Lombroso's methodology was that of Charles Goring (1913:15)

> Since this belief [the born criminal, the criminal type] of Lombroso's was arrived at, not by methods of disinterested investigation, but, rather by a leap of the imagination, the notion thus reached then forming the basis upon which he conducted his researches, and constructed his theory – the whole fabric of the Lombrosian doctrine judged by the standards of science, is fundamentally unsound.

Critique of the Theory of the Born Criminal and the Criminal Type
Probably the fiercest attacks made against Lombroso were directed at his theory of the born criminal and his affirmation that there exists a specific criminal type. The critics, in particular Gabriel Tarde in France, pointed to the fact that crime is a relative phenomenon, which changes in time and space. Thus, it cannot be claimed that there is an 'anthropological type' that everywhere, at all times, had deserved the epithet 'criminal.'

Lombroso was further criticized for his varying explanations of why some individuals are born with the stigmata that predestine them to become criminals. Even Garofalo (1914:105–6) was highly critical of Lombroso's use of epilepsy as an explanation:

> In his later writings the same author [Lombroso] contended that epilepsy is always to be found in the born criminal. This theory I shall not stop to discuss since the fact is far from being established. Moreover, it is flatly contradictory of the theory of atavism, despite Lombroso's efforts to

reconcile the two theories. It seems hardly possible to conceive our first parents as unhappy epileptics.

Critique of Biological Determinism
Critics of Lombroso point to two initial errors in his assertion of biological determinism:
– To have denied the perfectibility of man. Lombroso's critics contended that an offender, even if abnormal, can be corrected and socialized. How could it be claimed, they argued, that it is impossible to change human beings when in nature the most savage animals can be tamed, trained, and have their tendencies transformed and changed?
– To have minimized the importance, in criminal etiology, of the social environment and to have placed the greatest emphasis on individual rather than social factors. As a result of this criticism, Lombroso in his later writings, Garofalo, and particularly Ferri did recognize the importance of environmental factors in crime causation. Nevertheless, they remained faithful to their belief in individual criminal propensities without which environmental stimuli would remain inoperative. Radzinowicz (1966:50) points out that Ferri maintained througout his entire career of teaching and research that an offender is always more or less abnormal.

Critique of the Criminal Policy of the Italian Positivist School
The criminal policy of the Italian Positivist School laid the emphasis on the protection of society even at the expense of human rights and civil liberties. The draconian measures the School recommended for the so-called 'real criminals' or 'true criminals' drew sharp criticism from many criminalists who have been struggling to humanize the system of punishment.

Moreover, believers in the religious, philosophical, and moral ideas of the era had great difficulty accepting the notion of determinism and remained attached to the basic concepts of the Classical School, such as 'free will', 'moral guilt', and 'moral responsibility'. As Saleilles (1927) points out, many viewed the Italian School not as an innovating and revolutionary school but as a reactionary movement, and they denounced the abuses of the policy of elimination the school advocated. They also found the notion of '*virtual criminality*' to be an extremely dangerous one since it allowed the most rigorous measures against simple suspects, thus sacrificing the basic principles of freedom.

The Demise of the Italian Positivist School: Charles Goring (1870–1919)

Goring (1913) performed careful measurements on thousands of inmates in English prisons and compared these measurements with those of the general population. He concluded that the only difference was a slight inferiority in stature and weight among the inmates. Here is Goring's conclusion:

> The preliminary conclusion reached by our inquiry is that this anthropo-logical monster has no existence in fact. The physical and mental constitu-tion (and intelligence) of both criminal and lawabiding persons, of the same age, stature, class and intelligence, are identical. There is no such thing as an anthropological criminal type. (p. 370)

Goring's study is generally considered the fatal blow to Lombroso's theory of the criminal type. But in his critical analysis of Goring's contribution, Beirne (1988) disagrees. Beirne points out that the same empirical criticism made by Goring had already been marshalled by French anthropologists and sociologists three decades before the appearance of *The English Convict*. Beirne also maintains that Lombroso himself had repudiated his initial position on the born criminal before Goring attempted to undermine that position.

Despite a steady, persistent and continuing criticism, the basic tenets of the Italian Positivist School, namely that criminals are abnormal and suffer from specific anomalies and abnormalities that differentiate them from normal law-abiding citizens are far from dead. They keep reappearing under modern scientific labels such as chromosomal aberrations, brain lesions, inadequate autonomic nervous system, glandular dysfunctions, chemical and hormonal imbalances, to name but a few. The everlasting appeal of this approach is not difficult to understand. For one thing, it reduces complex human behaviour to one single physical cause, and for another thing, its central premise, namely that offenders are biologically inferior or defective, allows ordinary citizens to view them as distinct individuals capable of committing the horrible crimes that they cannot conceive of themselves as capable of com-mitting. In a way, it is a self-assuring approach that makes it possible to dichotomize people into the normal and the abnormal, those who are crim-inally inclined and those who are not so inclined (Fattah, 1993c).

The Classical and Italian Positivist Schools Compared

Based on the arguments put forward in Chapters 8 and 9, there follows a comparison of the Classical school and the Italian Positivist School. For reasons of convenience this has been arranged in the form of a table (Table 9.1).

Table 9.1   A comparison between the Classical and Italian Positivist
Schools

The Classical School	The Italian Positivist School
The interest and attention are focused upon the act (crime).	The interest and attention are focused upon the criminal, the actor ... the act is only a symptom.
Crime is an immoral, an anti-ethical act, a legal infraction ... the emphasis is on the evil nature, the immoral aspects and illegal character of the act.	**Crime** is an act harmful to society ... the emphasis is on the anti-social character and the social aspects of the act.
Responsibility is a moral responsibility based on the notion of free will . the offender is assumed to possess free will and to be governed in his choices by considerations of pleasure and pain.	**Biological determinism** (+ Social): the individual is dominated by his or her physiological nature where the primitive instincts, violent and destructive, are masters. Crime is the fatal product either of a pathological temperament (Lombroso) or of the social environment and economic conditions (Ferri).
Free will is the power to choose equally between two courses of action inspired by different motives, but without being determined or conditioned by any of them. Criterion for responsibility is freedom.	Absolute rejection of moral responsibility and free will. The basis for society's intervention is the social responsibility of the delinquent. The criterion for responsibility is dangerousness and social risk (analogy with mental patients who are interned for the protection of society).
The criminal is presumed to be normal and responsible unless the contrary is proven.	**The criminal** is in principle an abnormal being (atavistic anomaly, pathological anomaly, etc.). Since the unique function of the penal measure is one of social defence, there is no reason to distinguish between those who are morally responsible and those who are not, but between those who are dangerous and those who are not. Rigorous measures are justified even if the offender is, morally speaking, irresponsible.
The method: logical, abstract.	**The method**: empirical, positivistic.
The penal law: an instrument of justice.	**The penal law**: an instrument of social defence.

(cont'd)

Table 9.1   (*continued*)

The Classical School	The Italian Positivist School
Punishment: no individualization (partial individualization with the Neo-Classical School)...prescribed in advance by the law...fits the crime measured by the objective gravity of the offence. Instrument of deterrence (special and general deterrence).	**Punishment**: rejection of punishment but individualization of the penal measures based on *a priori* classification of criminals. Advocates measures of social defence adapted to the nature of the criminal and level of dangerousness, as well as substitutes and alternatives to punishment.
The right to punish: is based on the theory of the social contract and on the concept of social utility.	**The right to punish**: is based on social reality. The need for society to protect itself against harmful acts and individuals who endanger its safety and security.
The role of the judge: establishing guilt ...once guilt is established, the judge becomes an automatic and mechanical distributor of punishment.	**The role of the judge**: to establish the criminal's type, to determine his or her dangerousness, and to pronounce the appropriate measure of social defence.
Criminal policy: humanitarian. Respects the liberty, freedom, and dignity of the human being, affirms inalienable human rights, and protects the individual against the abuses of the state.	**Criminal policy**: characterized by its extreme rigour...no respect for human rights nor for the legal safeguards. The interests of society have priority over the rights of the individual citizen.
Review measures: opposed to clemency, pardon, and statutes of limitation because – they are in conflict with the concept of equality. – they create the hope of impunity thus reducing the certainty of punishment and weakening the deterrent effect of punishment.	**Review measures**: opposed to these measures because they are likely to let free in society dangerous criminals and because they are in conflict with the goal of social defence.
Capital punishment: opposed to capital punishment.	**Capital punishment**: strongly for capital punishment.

10 Sociological, Sociocultural and Economic Explanations

CRIME AS A PRODUCT OF SOCIAL AND ECONOMIC CONDITIONS

From this point of view, the fundamental facts of criminality present themselves to us in an entirely new light. Contrary to current ideas, the criminal no longer seems a totally unsociable being, a sort of parasitic element, a strange and unassimilable body, introduced into the midst of society. On the contrary, he plays a definite role in social life. Crime, for its part, must no longer be conceived as an evil that cannot be too much suppressed. There is no occasion for self-congratulation when the crime rate drops noticeably below the average level, for we may be certain that this apparent progress is associated with some social disorder.

Emile Durkheim (1938:72)
The Rules of Sociological Method

SCHOOLS OF CRIMINOLOGICAL THOUGHT: SOCIOLOGICAL AND ECONOMIC APPROACHES

The French Sociological School: Gabriel Tarde (1843–1904)

Before devoting his entire time to teaching and writing, Tarde worked for several years as a magistrate, and was at one time head of the Statistics Service within the French ministry of justice. In addition to numerous articles, Tarde published many books, three of which are of particular interest to criminology. These are: *Comparative Criminality* (*La Criminalité comparée*, 1886), *Penal Philosophy* (*La Philosophie pénale*, 1890), and *The Laws of Imitation* (*Les Lois de l'imitation*, 1890).

During his years of public service as a magistrate, Tarde became interested in the psychosocial bases of crime. He was also one of the principal adversaries of the Italian Positivist School. In his book on comparative criminality, he takes up the task of refuting Lombroso's theories on the atavistic criminal and the criminal type. He effectively uses the notion of relativity of crime to denounce the concepts of the born criminal and the heredity of crime. Tarde flatly rejects the theory that attributes crime to genetic defects, to physical and biological causes, and elaborates his own explanation, which is a synthesis of sociology and psychology. His explanation has as its central focus the role of social environment in the etiology of criminal behaviour. Tarde's central idea is that every individual behaves according to the customs of his cultural environment. If someone steals or kills, he is simply imitating somebody else. It is not at all difficult to see the similarity between this notion, which Tarde later used to formulate his famous laws of imitation, and contemporary criminological theories, particularly the theory of differential association (Edwin Sutherland) and that of differential identification (Daniel Glaser).

For Tarde, there are two basic social processes: one is rare, and the other is quite common. The first is *invention*; the second is *imitation*. Inventive persons are a minority, and invention, particularly in the domain of human behaviour is not an everyday occurrence. Behaviour that may be considered a prototype is relatively infrequent. On the other hand, imitation, whose psycho-biological mechanism remains to be established, is, in Tarde's view, the typical element of social life.

The Laws of Imitation

Tarde affirms that social life is dominated by imitation. The members of a given society, because of their psychological individuality and through their actions, reactions, and interactions, continuously exercise multiple and repeated influences upon other members of their communities. In addition, by means of modern social processes (in particular, communication and education) communities act upon other communities, which results in continuous and infinite imitation. To explain how imitation takes place, Tarde formulated three principal laws that apply to crime as well as to all other aspects of social life.

The Law of Proportion

People imitate others in proportion to the frequency, the closeness, and stability of contacts they have with those others. With regard to stability, one has to distinguish between two environments. In cities and in crowded places, where contacts are close and multiplied and life is active and exciting, imitation phenomena will reach their maximum frequency, but they will not be stable and will change quite often. The pattern of imitation that dominates here is what Tarde calls 'fashion.' In the country and rural areas, on the other hand, contacts may also be frequent, but they are reduced to a limited number of persons. The groups are quite stable. Imitation will be less, and its dominant pattern will be respect for custom and tradition.

Applying this law to crime, Tarde notes that, like any other social behaviour, crime may become a fashion and result in what may be called a crime wave characterized by the contagious influence of the behaviour in question. For example, sociologists have noticed that committing suicide by an unconventional method does have contagious effects and may lead to a wave of similar suicides. If crime, on the other hand, becomes concentrated in certain closed environments, it may evolve into a custom or tradition that is culturally transmitted. The custom of vendetta in Corsica, Sicily, and Albania and the custom of theft among certain gypsy communities in central Europe are two examples.

The Law of Direction
This law concerns the direction in which imitations spread. Usually, the superior is imitated by the inferior; those who enjoy a certain prestige are imitated by those who are impressed and influenced by prestige. Members of the lower classes imitate the upper classes. When it comes to crime, imitation occurs in the same direction. Tarde noticed, for instance, that certain crimes, which previously were the prerogative only of royalty, were later imitated by other members of society and occurred at all social levels. In the same way, criminal fashions usually start in large cities (particularly the national capital) and spread afterwards to the country. Furthermore, the country that at the time was most admired for its vitality and strength was the United States of America. Tarde was quick to observe that delinquent behaviours that originate in the US (such as armed holdups in banks) were then imitated in Europe.

The Law of Insertion
Tarde explains this third and last law of imitation as follows: when two mutually exclusive fashions are in opposition, one tends to be substituted for the other. This law means that when one of these two fashions imposes itself, the second tends to decline and to disappear gradually. Infanticide and abortion are, for example, two mutually exclusive and opposed modes of disposing of an unwanted baby. Thus, when abortion becomes fashionable, infanticide declines and then disappears. There are, however, certain exceptions to this general rule. Tarde notes that if the new fashion increased a demand for the activity, there might be an increase in both.

Critique
Despite Tarde's important contribution to criminology and penology, he is much less known than some of his European contemporaries, such as Durkheim and Lombroso, and his work is not as widely or as frequently quoted as theirs. One of the reasons is probably the fact that most of Tarde's writings were never translated into English and remained, therefore, inaccessible to most American criminologists.

Beirne (1987:786), for example, points out that most recent histories of criminology ignore Tarde altogether. He also maintains that except for the considerable influence Tarde's writings posthumously exerted among American criminologists in the first two decades of the 20th century, there is little that could be traced directly to his intellectual legacy.

Tarde's major contribution is to have emphasized the role of the social environment in the genesis of criminality at a time when individual biological theories of criminal behaviour were in vogue. Like Durkheim, Tarde treated crime as a social phenomenon and stressed the importance of social factors in its causation. Contrary to Durkheim, who regarded crime as a normal and necessary aspect of social life, Tarde likened it to cancer that participates in the life of an organ but brings its death. It is the morbid and pathological nature of crime that leads Tarde to urge society to spare no effort in combatting it. Another difference between Durkheim and Tarde can be found in their respective approaches. Durkheim's approach is purely sociological. The individual has no existence independently of, or separately from, the society in which he lives. Tarde's long experience as a magistrate and his personal knowledge of individual criminals render his approach a psychosociological one. He recognizes the psychological individuality of each criminal even when talking about the common characteristics they exhibit.

Tarde is to be credited with having laid the foundations of a social learning theory of crime in which cultural influences predominate. As Wilson (1973:294) points out, it is a tribute to Tarde's originality and foresight that the ideas he expounded on crime causation last century became the working hypotheses of American criminologists several decades later.

Tarde's laws of imitation may be an oversimplification of social causation, but there is no question that imitation does play a major role in social life and particularly in the early learning stages of child development.

Tarde was unable to establish the psycho-biological mechanisms underlying the process of imitation, nor did he give adequate explanation of the mental processes that are at play when an individual imitates someone else. But in view of the underdeveloped state of the science of psychology in the latter part of the 19th century, he could hardly be blamed for such shortcomings. He will remain therefore a major figure in the annals of criminology and will be vividly remembered particularly by those who are able to read and enjoy his writings in his elegant and polished French.

Emile Durkheim (1859–1917)

Durkheim is one of the chief founders of modern sociology. He, like Auguste Comte, believed in and advocated the application of the methods of natural science to the study of society and social phenomena. There is hardly a sociology book in which Durkheim is not frequently mentioned and extensively quoted. But he is also well known in criminology for his theory of Anomie and for his original ideas about crime and punishment. Durkheim's writings that are of particular relevance to criminology are contained in *The Division of Labour in Society* (1893), *The Rules of Sociological Method* (1885), and *Suicide* (1897). His two laws of penal evolution were published not as a book, but as an article in 'L'année Sociologique' (1900–1901).

The Normality of Crime

Contrary to most criminologists of his era, who regarded crime as a symptom of social pathology, Durkheim finds nothing pathological in the crime phenomenon. To him, crime is a *normal* social fact since it is found not just in most societies but in every society of every type. There is no social life that is free from crime. It is true that crime changes forms, that is, the acts defined as crimes are not the same everywhere. But everywhere, in every society and at all times, there are individuals who behave in such a manner as to draw upon themselves penal repression. Even a society of saints would have its norms and norm-breakers:

> Imagine a society of saints, a perfect cloister of exemplary individuals. Crimes, properly so called, will be there unknown; but faults which appear venial to the layman will create there the same scandal that the ordinary offence does in ordinary consciousness. If, then, this society has the power to'judge and punish it will define these acts as criminal and will treat them as such. (pp. 68–9)

Durkheim concluded that no other phenomenon exhibits all the symptoms of normality more than crime since it is intimately linked to the conditions of collective life and since a society exempt from crime is utterly impossible.

Durkheim noted, however, that what is normal is simply the existence of crime, provided it attains and does not exceed, for each social type, a certain level. To admit that crime is a normal and integral part of social life does not mean it should not be hated. Durkheim notes that Pain too is quite undesirable. The individual hates pain in the same way society hates crime although pain is an aspect of normal physiology.

The Utility and Necessity of Crime

Crime is normal, but it is also necessary and useful. Its existence implies that the way to necessary social change remains open and in certain cases it directly prepares and paves the way for this change. Durkheim notes that it would never have been possible to establish the freedom of thought we now enjoy if the regulations prohibiting it had not been repeatedly violated before being solemnly abrogated. On the other hand, repressive law, which is society's reaction to crime, is useful because it promotes social solidarity and social cohesion by creating links that attach the individual to the group:

> Crime brings together upright consciences and concentrates them. We have only to notice what happens, particularly in a small town, when some moral scandal has been committed. They stop each other on the street, they visit each other, they seek to come together to talk of the event and to wax indignant in common. From all the similar impressions which are exchanged, from all the temper gets itself expressed, there emerges a unique temper... which is everybody's without being anybody's in particular. That is the public temper.
>
> *The Division of Labour* (1933:102).

In the light of the above, the criminal no longer seems a totally unsociable being, a sort of parasitic element, a strange and unassimilable body introduced in the midst of society. On the contrary, the criminal serves a useful function and plays a definite role in social life. Crime, for its part, must no longer be conceived as an evil that cannot be too much suppressed. On the contrary, if the crime rate drops noticeably below the average level, this is an indication of some social disorder. In *The Rules of Sociological Method*, Durkheim writes:

> Let us make no mistake. To classify crime among the phenomena of normal sociology is not to say merely that it is an inevitable, although regrettable phenomenon, due to the incorrigible wickedness of men; it is to affirm that it is a factor in public health, an integral part of all healthy societies.... (p. 67)

> Crime is, then, necessary; it is bound up with the fundamental conditions of all social life, and by that very fact it is useful. (p. 70)

Anomie

The word anomie comes from the Greek *anomia*, which originally meant lawlessness. The usage of the word was later expanded, and it was used to designate 'a total absence of a moral sense', 'disregard for divine law', 'lack of conformity', and so forth. De Grazia (1948) defines anomie as the 'disintegrated state of a society that possesses no body of common values or morals that effectively govern conduct'. Durkheim used the notion of anomie to explain the etiology of suicide. He saw certain types of suicides as closely linked to the sociocultural structure and concluded that these suicides are intimately related to the absence of norms, to an obscure perception of social values, and to the lack of social cohesion characteristic of modern industrial society.

Lunden (1973) believes that of the many contributions Durkheim made to the field of criminology, his advancement of the Theory of Anomie stands out above all others. Lunden writes:

In the process of social change (evolution) in society due to increased division of labour and heterogeneity the unifying forces of society tend to weaken. The standards and norms which had regulated society in the past become obsolete and inoperative or meaningless. When this occurs the restraints on passions no longer hold and a condition of 'deregulation or anomie' arises. The absences of restraints soon bring disorder and 'social chaos.' The end result is a smashing of the norms and society becomes 'atomised', fragmented and a 'disorganized dust of individuals.' As a result of this fragmentation and atomisation another serious condition arises in society – social isolation which brings about a decrease in social participation.' ... (p. 394)

> This is the milieu which produces crime and anti-social disorders. There are no constraints and the cult of individualism cuts away all inhibitions. . . . If social scientists desire an explanation of crime in high or low places, the real explanation lies in Durkheim's 'Anomie.' (p. 395)

A situation of anomie or normlessness may arise from a clash of aspirations and a breakdown of regulatory norms. This idea was reformulated by the American sociologist Robert K. Merton (1957:132) into a general principle: 'social structures exert a definite pressure upon certain persons in the society to engage in non-conforming rather than conforming conduct.'

The Two Laws of Penal Evolution
The article in which Durkheim presented what he describes as the two laws of penal evolution is probably the least known of Durkheim's writings on crime and punishment. The two laws served as topic for L. L. Robinson's (1972) doctoral dissertation. According to Durkheim, two laws seem to have dominated the evolution of systems of penal sanction. These two laws explain the quantitative and qualitative variations that characterize the history of punishment.
Durkheim formulates the *quantitative* law as follows:

> The intensity of punishment is greater in societies of a less advanced type and where centralized power has a more absolute character. (Robinson, 1972:2)

Durkheim tries to explain this law, which may be called the law of the progressive moderation of penalties, through a historical study of punishments. History shows that punishment has become milder throughout the ages, except where absolutism exists. This evolutionary sequence and this movement from harsher to milder penalties is largely explained by the transition from crime conceived as religious sin to a more modern conception of crime that views it as a secular infraction.

Durkheim also sees a close link between harsh penalties and absolutism. What makes the central power more or less absolute is the more or less radical absence of all countervailing power, systematically organized with the intent of moderating it. And he notes that the apogee of absolute monarchy marks the apogee of repression.

Durkheim warns that progressive moderation of penalties does not mean that punishment will gradually disappear or that it is on the way to extinction. While the catalogue of religious crimes, which usually invite the harshest punishment, is gradually diminishing, the number of secular crimes is simultaneously expanding.

The second law, the law of the *qualitative* variations in punishment, is formulated by Durkheim as follows:

> Deprivation of liberty and liberty alone for varying periods of time according to the gravity of the crime tends more and more to become the normal type of penal sanction. (Robinson, 1972:27)

Durkheim notes that less developed societies ignore imprisonment almost completely. This is in sharp contrast with more advanced societies where imprisonment is the sole form of punishment. Imprisonment was invented in early Christian times, but it was only in medieval Christian societies that prisons reached full development. At first, prison was considered only as a means of surveillance, but later incarceration or imprisonment became a punishment in itself. With the revolutionary French Code of 1791, prison became the base of a system of penal sanctions. While imprisonment was becoming more and more the dominant mode of punishment, the death penalty was being applied less and less frequently and was even disappearing completely from some codes. Gradually, the deprivation of liberty for a number of years or for life became the dominant mode of punishment.

From the two laws, examined together, Durkheim draws the following conclusion:

> In reality, therefore, there is no general weakening of the total system of penal sanctions. Taken alone a particular system is weakened but it was replaced by another which, being at least less violent and less harsh, continues to exhibit severities. It is not at all destined to undergo an uninterrupted decline.
>
> This explains the state of crisis in which penal law is to be found among all civilized peoples. We have arrived at the moment when penal institutions of the past have either disappeared or survived only by force of habit, but without others being born which respond better to the new aspirations of moral consciousness.
>
> Robinson's translation (1972:62–3.)

Critique

Durkheim's affirmation that crime is normal, necessary, and useful has not gone uncriticized. Ferri, for example, claimed that Durkheim has confused two separate notions: the constancy of crime, a statistical phenomenon brought to light by Quetelet, and the so-called normality of crime. These two notions, Ferri argues, have to be distinguished one from the other.

Bob Roshier (1977) took it upon himself to refute the argument that crime is necessary and functional. He criticizes Durkheim for having concluded that the inevitability of crime proves its necessity and argues that the former simply does *not* imply the latter. Roshier also addresses himself to Durkheim's claim that crime serves an adaptive function by enabling societies to adapt to changing conditions. He feels that Durkheim's examples of Socrates and liberal philosophy are insufficient to show that they were precursors of what eventually became 'necessary' changes, since it must also be shown that it was necessary for them to have formerly been defined as criminal. The fact that they *were* does not in every way demonstrate this. Roshier (1977:320–1) then concludes with the following criticism:

> ... the arguments purporting to show that crime is necessary because it performs vital functions for society are either fallacious or devoid of meaning. Needless to say, this does not rule out the possibility that some crimes sometimes have consequences that we may regard as beneficial. For example, it is often claimed that criminal activities involved with gambling, prostitution or pornography perform valuable functions for society. We may well agree with such arguments, but they are not arguments for the functions of crime, but for the functions of those activities, which happen to be defined as crimes. That is, they are not functional because they are crimes, but in spite of the fact that they are. Indeed, if they do perform the useful functions ascribed to them, they would presumably perform them even better if they were not so defined (and that is why they are usually areas where there are movements aimed at altering those definitions).

The debate on the functionality of crime continues. Downes and Rock (1988:108) argue that the effect of crime is often the reverse of that assumed in functional analysis, that is far from drawing together 'upright consciences', it all too often triggers off a retreat into isolationism.

In his critique of Durkheim's notion that crime is functional, Takala (1991:23) tries to show that Durkheim's version of the functional analysis of crime was based on doubtful premises. According to Takala (1991:220),

> Certain acts punishable as crimes may in a more profound view be indifferent or even beneficial to society. To understand this no doctrine of the usefulness of *crime* is needed. Certain other acts, also punishable as crimes, cause confusion, fear and isolation, and only their control and

prosecution create a social balance and confirms that the violated norms still are valid. To understand this one does not need a theory of how the social function of these crimes really is fulfilled through the action of the control system.

The Socialist School

There is no 'Marxist theory of deviance', either in existence, or which can be developed within orthodox Marxism. Crime and deviance vanish into the general theoretical concerns and the specific scientific object of Marxism. Crime and deviance are no more a scientific field for Marxism than education, the family or sport.

Paul Hirst
'Marx and Engels on Law, Crime and Morality'
In I. Taylor, P. Walton, and J. Young, *Critical Criminology*. (1975:204)

The Socialist School of Criminology is loosely based on the writings of Marx and Engels. Marx and Engels did not write a great deal on the subject of law and crime. They were interested in crime only as a sub-product of the capitalist system. The Socialist School sees economic structures as playing a decisive role in the causation of crime. It emphasizes economic determinism and attempts to explain criminality in terms of the dominant mode of production and the class nature of society. Workers are seen both as a product of circumstances beyond their control and as historical actors potentially capable of transforming these circumstances (see Peter Young, 1976). According to Young,

The working-class criminal is a man beset by material circumstances, existing in a social world where the sanctity of property and desirability of existing forms of behaviour are incessantly proclaimed whether it be in the school, the media or the workplace. He, within his own subculture, attempts to overcome his predicament albeit falteringly and with an inarticulate consciousness. That the 'delinquent solution' is no real solution, that it often merely exacerbates his own plight and that of his fellows, is obvious. (p. 14)

William Adriaan Bonger (1876–1940)

Bonger is a Dutch criminologist who, in the early years of the 20th century, succeeded in applying Marxist ideas to criminology and in translating socialist principles into criminological theory. His major work is *Criminality and Economic Conditions*, published in French in 1905 and translated into English in 1916.

Bonger, like the Italian socialist criminologists (Turati, Loria, Colajanni, and others), affirms that the abnormal element in crime is a social not a biological element. To him, the principal causes of crime are the pressures and abuses of the capitalist system, a system that leads to unlimited selfishness and egoism. In capitalist society, the social inequities and the inequal distribution of wealth are mainly responsible for crime. While much crime results from poverty, it is not the total amount of wealth but rather the manner of its distribution that bears most importantly upon criminality.

Austin Turk (1969:12) summarizes Bonger's theory with reference to the amount of criminal behaviour in a given population as follows:

1. Egoism implies the capability of committing criminal acts, while altruism implies the absence of this capability (in regard to virtually all crimes).
2. Capitalism promotes egoism, and therefore the capability of committing crime; socialism promotes altruism, and therefore the absence of this capability.
3. The proneness to commit crime actually results in criminal behaviour if
   a. The egoistic person perceives an opportunity to gain by illegal action an advantage at the expense of others, and/or
   b. Opportunities to achieve gratification legally are denied, i.e., the legal system is biased.
4. Capitalism is characterized by both (3a) and (3b), while socialism will ultimately remove both the need and the opportunity to seek gratification at the expense of others. Consequently,
5. Capitalism causes crime; socialism will ultimately eliminate crime.

In addition to these general principles, Bonger identifies a number of factors that he views as responsible for, or influential in, the commission of certain crimes. The following are some examples:

1. There is a relation between child labour and juvenile criminality. Although it is of smaller importance than the lack of care of the children among the proletariat, it is still one of the factors in the etiology of crime.
2. Long hours of immoderate labour are brutalizing and make the individual incapable of elevated sentiments. In general, the present method of production is an obstacle to the development of social instincts.
3. The housing conditions of the proletariat have also a significance as regards criminality, and for the special group of sexual offences their importance is very great. The disorder and squalor of the home communicate themselves to the inmates; the lack of room obliges the children to live, during a great part of the day, on the streets, with the result that they are brought into contact with all sorts of demoralizing

companions. Finally, the living together of a great number of unedu-
cated persons in one small dwelling is the cause of constant quarrels and
fights.
4. Ignorance and the lack of general culture must be ranked among the
    general factors of crime.

Another important concept in Marxist philosophy that bears great relevance
to socialist criminology is the concept of class struggle. Both the criminal law
and the criminal justice system are seen as instruments of oppression used
against the proletariat by the ruling class. Not only does the definition of
certain acts as crimes reflect the interests of the powerful classes, but also the
criminal justice system discriminates in a systematic fashion against the poor,
unprivileged, and powerless classes. Crime is concentrated in the lower
classes because the justice system criminalizes the greed of the poor while it
allows legal opportunities for the rich to pursue their selfish desires (Vold,
1979:165).

The conclusion of socialist criminologists is always optimistic. It is best
formulated by Zorli (quoted in De Quiros, 1911:69):

> When this environment is modified, when the iniquitous bourgeois society
> is overthrown and the socialistic ideal is realized, then misery will end, and
> the motives for crime will be wanting, education ending by turning men
> into angels.

The assumption that crime will disappear when socialism triumphs is
an assumption contradicted by experience and historical facts. The state
of crime and delinquency in present and former socialist countries, such
as China and Russia, speaks eloquently against this socialist utopian
dream.

Probably one fundamental weakness in Marxist thinking about crime is
the belief, shared by many criminologists (such as Taylor, Walton, and
Young, 1973), that 'a state of freedom from material necessity' ultimately
leads to 'a state of freedom from material incentive' and that once material
necessity has been eliminated property crimes will lose their *raison d'être* and
will rapidly disappear.

CRIME AS A PRODUCT OF PREDISPOSITIONS AND ENVIRONMENT

Societies have the criminals they deserve.

Alexandre Lacassagne (1885:167) in
*Actes du Premier Congrès International
d'Anthropologie Criminelle*, Rome

SCHOOLS OF CRIMINOLOGICAL THOUGHT: THE SCHOOL OF LYON AND THE AUSTRIAN SCHOOL

The School of Lyon

Among the schools that attempted to develop a synthesis of the theories of the Italian Positivist School and those of the Sociological School is the School of Lyon. The school is named after the French city where Alexandre Lacassagne (1843–1924), a forensic pathologist and a university professor, lived and worked.

The School of Lyon places a heavy emphasis on the influence of the social environment in the etiology of crime. Without denying the role of the biological and other endogenic factors, the school views crime as being primarily the product of the social milieu. It is the influence of the environment that can awaken and develop the latent antisocial tendencies in the criminal. Lacassagne claims that delinquency is produced by social excitations of individual states, and he cites as an example shoplifting from large department stores, which is triggered by the temptation created by the way the goods are displayed (see De Quiros, 1911:58).

Though the School of Lyon admits the influence of individual and physical factors, such factors are seen as being of limited importance in comparison with social and environmental ones. Individual factors are of primary importance only in the case of insane criminals or those who are in some way mentally defective.

The stigmata of degeneracy, held by Lombroso to be the visible marks of the born criminal, are interpreted by Lacassagne not as a result of atavism but as an inevitable consequence of the normal evolution of the human type under the bad influence of the criminogenic factors of the environment such as alcohol, malnutrition, disease, and so forth. However, while relating such factors to their social origin, Lacassagne admits that psychological and physical anomalies do influence organic, intellectual, and moral human functions.

The synthesis of individual and social factors is clear in Lacassagne's famous phrase pronounced at the first International Congress of Criminal Anthropology held in Rome in 1885:

> Social environment is the heat in which criminality breeds; the criminal is the microbe, an element of no importance until it meets the liquid that makes it ferment. (De Quiros, 1911:58)

His conviction that criminal propensities can have no effect outside of a criminogenic social milieu led him to declare that criminals are not born, but made by society and that the society that prepares and makes the criminals bears the sole responsibility for them. Hence societies have the criminals they deserve.

The Austrian School

Three branches of criminology owe their development to the Austrian School of Criminology. These are criminalistics, criminal psychology, and victimology. The name most often associated with the Austrian School is that of Hans Gross (1847–1915), an examining magistrate, public prosecutor, and later professor of criminal law. He is commonly regarded as the father of criminalistics, and his *Manual for the Examining Judge* and his *Criminal Psychology* have become classics. The work of Hans Gross was continued by Ernst Seelig in Graz and Roland Grassberger in Vienna.

According to the Austrian School, it is anti-scientific to dissociate the actor from the act or to study the offender in isolation from his criminal behaviour. Hence, the need to place criminalistics (which may be crudely defined as the scientific study of the criminal event) within the field of criminology.

To the Austrian School, criminal investigation is an integral part of criminological science. It is in this field that the investigator has to use what Seelig (1956) calls the golden rule of seven points: who, what, where, with what, why, how, and when? Criminalistics were so much a part of criminology in many countries in Europe that the title 'criminologist' was almost reserved for experts in police science, and books on criminalistics frequently used the word criminology in their titles. An example of these books is *The Great Adventure of Criminology* by Jürgen Thorwald, who traces the development of scientific methods of crime investigation over one hundred years. In Austria, criminalistics continue to be taught side by side with criminology at university institutes. One aspect of criminalistics, namely, the study of the criminal's '*modus operandi*', is seen as an important means of understanding the personality of the perpetrator, his or her motives and attitudes vis-à-vis the victim, and of measuring dangerousness, potential for rehabilitation, and so forth. It is not difficult to ascertain that victim/ target selection, a subject of growing interest in criminology, is but one aspect of the offender's *modus operandi*.

Gross also felt that criminal psychology should become a separate field within what he calls 'the science of the facts of criminal law' as it helps understand the nature of the human being who, Gross felt, was the most important object of criminal proceedings. He defined criminal psychology as a summary of all subjects of psychology that are necessary for the criminal investigator's work. However, much of Gross's treatise on criminal psychology deals with the psychic nature of the criminal, that is, the psychic motives leading to the crime. In addition, the book contains a part on the psychology of interrogation and a careful psychological treatment of sentencing by judges (see Grassberger, originally published 1956).

Contrary to the theories and hypotheses, which end up by organizing the whole science of criminology around the formation or the development of

Table 10.1   Criminological paradigms and the role of the criminologist

Type of criminology	Paradigm	Emphasis on	Key concepts	Criminal policy	Role of criminologist
Demonological and super-natural explanations	Spiritualism	Supernatural forces the devil, diabolical and satanic forces	Possession	Sacrifice Exorcism	Does not exist
Volitional criminology	Free will Hedonism Rationality	Mens rea, intention premeditation, malice, evil	Moral responsibility Moral culpability (the criminal is a malicious, evil being)	Punishment, Retribu-tion, deterrence, puni-tive, retributive justice	Law reform and re-form of institutions
Positivist criminology	Pathology Hard determinism Soft determinism	Predispositions Inclinations	Natural causation dangerousness (the criminal is an abnormal, sick, disturbed, deranged individual)	Social defence, incapa-citation, treatment, re-habilitation	Clinical treatment and rehabilitation
Structural criminology Critical criminology Radical criminology Feminist criminology	Social structures	Structural causes of criminality	Social injustice & inequal-ities, class struggle, patri-archal system	Social justice, equality, equitable distribution of wealth and oppor-tunities, social devel-opment	Social critic Social change agent
Victimology Peace-making Criminology	Conflict resolution Dispute settlement Prevention	Harm, injuries	Crime is a human conflict Crime is a social risk	Reconciliation Mediation Compensation Restitution Prevention	Mediation agent Reconciliation agent Prevention agent

the criminal's personality, the Austrian School places a strong emphasis not only on predisposing factors but also on actualizing or triggering factors, such as alcohol, temptation, provocation, and so forth. Predisposing factors are seen as insufficient by themselves to explain criminal behaviour.

Among the actualizing factors, special attention is given to the victims of crime, their interactions with the offender, and their role and contribution to the genesis of the crime. This leads to a new branch of criminology called victimology (see Chapter 7).

Table 10.1 (p. 245) is a compendium of the historical evolution of criminological thought citing different criminological paradigms, their key concepts, the criminal policy that flows from each paradigm and the corresponding role of the criminologist.

Criminology Present: Unsuccessful Endeavours, Unfulfilled Potential and Promising Trends

11 Recent Theoretical Developments

THE ETERNAL QUEST FOR THE ELUSIVE CAUSES OF CRIME

It might be suggested that even if this perspective is valid it is useless for the purpose of understanding and controlling criminal behaviour, that what we need is more research into causation to determine the etiology of particular criminal behaviours and patterns of behaviour, for ignorance about causation must inevitably result in impotence in relation to control or treatment.... But unfortunately it is not true that knowledge of causes invariably implies a corresponding ability to control or prevent. Moreover, there are a number of other reasons for thinking that to mount yet another costly safari to search for the source or sources of criminality would be a wasteful expenditure of scarce resources....

> Norval Morris and Gordon Hawkins (1969:50)
> *The Honest Politician's Guide to Crime Control*

In the 1930s criminology was the subject of a scathing critique by Michael and Adler (1933) (see Chapter 7). Half a century later, Albert Reiss Jr. (1981b:3) reminded criminologists that:

The body of knowledge that we think of as criminology owes more to models and theories from psychology and sociology than from any other discipline. Criminology, to be sure, has not lent itself to any single theoretical formulation within those disciplines, though there have been fashions in theories of crime.

Surely, there is no shortage of theories in criminology and the fashions alluded to by Reiss (1981b) are quite evident in the 'garden variety' of theoretical formulations. The diversity of approaches has been highlighted by McClintock (1988:253) as follows:

Criminologists have grouped themselves, with respect to the nature of their studies of criminality into: the ecological school; the functionalist-anomic school; those emphasizing the cultural and subcultural explanation of criminality; the labelling school and symbolic interaction; the socio-phenomenologists; the control theorists; and of course the so-called radical criminologists who emphasized the political nature of the definition and control of criminality. More recently crime has been studied in greater detail as regards the specific context in which it occurs and especially in relation to that of the victim.

The fact that none of these approaches, individually or combined, has yielded satisfactory results in terms of identifying the specific causes of crime has not dampened criminologists' enthusiasm and zeal. Despite past efforts and continuing endeavours, one is hard pressed to find a positive assessment of theoretical criminology. Few years ago, Australian criminologist John Braithwaite (1989:133) offered a non-flattering picture of the state of the discipline.

He wrote:

> The present state of criminology is one of abject failure in its own terms. We cannot say anything convincing to the community about the causes of crime; we cannot prescribe policies that will work to reduce crime; we cannot in all honesty say that societies spending more on criminological research get better criminal justice policies than those which spend little or nothing on criminology.

Braithwaite's lament is echoed by Weatherburn (1993:35) who maintains that criminology, like other social sciences, has not been successful in delivering 'theories of the same breathtaking scope as are routinely found, for example, in physics or chemistry.' Rather than continuing the futile attempts to develop a general theory that embraces all forms of crime, Weatherburn opts for detailed 'microtheories' of particular patterns of offending that possess some predictive ability and offer some guidance to policymakers.

Downes and Rock (1988:327) affirm that sociologists and criminologists 'have been chiefly effective in discrediting the work of their predecessors and contemporaries. Theirs have been destructive rather than constructive achievements.'

Complaints about the current state of criminology continue. Matthews and Young (1986:1) point to 'the theoretical bankruptcy of what purports to be "scientific" criminology' and insist that criminology, at present, is in a state of deep crisis. And a few years later, Gottfredson and Hirschi joined the chorus. In the preface to their book, Gottfredson and Hirschi (1990) express their unhappiness 'with the ability of academic criminology to provide believable explanations of criminal behaviour'. Many of their complaints sound familiar:

> One after another, the disciplines have staked a claim to crime, and each has ended up saying about crime what it says about nearly everything else. No explanation consistent with a disciplinary perspective seems to have the ring of truth .... . We have also been unhappy with the 'interdisciplinary' solution to this state of affairs. Within the university, criminology has

always been the prototypical *sub*-discipline, a derivative field of study hoping to achieve truth and status by accepting the insights of its parent disciplines. In fact, criminology shows that interdisciplinary attention is the road to theoretical and practical obscurity. (p. xiii)

Coming from two illustrious criminologists, this is, no doubt, a strong indictment of the discipline of criminology. But in view of criminology's longstanding obsession with finding the causes of crime, and in view of the negative assessment made below of etiological research (being based on faulty premises and therefore being largely unproductive, even futile), one cannot but agree with the essence of Gottfredson and Hirschi's critique.

It would not be an exaggeration to maintain that theoretical criminology has been essentially and predominantly an etiological criminology. Since its emergence as a social science in the second half of the 19th century, criminology has been preoccupied, almost obsessed, with the search for the causes of crime. This has produced a multitude of theories of the biological, psychological, and sociological variety. In the early decades of criminology, this zealous pursuit of the causes of crime might have been justified. Anxious to emulate the physical sciences and to use their methods, criminologists were convinced that to understand a phenomenon it is necessary to possess a thorough knowledge of the phenomenon's causes. The common analogy between crime and disease, which characterized many of the early writings in criminology, reflects a widely held belief that a good comprehension of the causes of crime is necessary for its control and prevention.

Having gone on for more than a century with no tangible or encouraging results, and in view of the strong and valid criticisms voiced at etiological research, one would have expected criminologists to reexamine their concepts and premises, and to move away from the endless pursuit of the elusive causes of crime to the more promising and less frustrating analyses of the phenomenon itself. Alas, there seems to be no end in sight to etiological research in criminology and the costly safaris that Morris and Hawkins (1969) warned against continue with little challenge. Those who called for an end to etiological research were vehemently denounced. Morris and Hawkins were, unfairly I think, lumped with conservative criminologists such as van den Haag, James Wilson, Issac Ehrlich, David Fogel and were labelled 'intellectuals for law and order' (Platt and Takagi, 1981:54). Don Cressey (1978) was highly critical of any attempt to abandon the search for the causes of crime. He wrote:

> The tragedy is in the tendency of modern criminologists to drop the search for causes and to join the politicians. Rather than trying to develop better ideas about why crimes flourish, for example, these criminologists – Wilson, van der Haag, Ehrlich, Fogel, Morris and Hawkins and hundreds

of others – seem satisfied with a technological criminology whose main concern is for showing policymakers how to repress criminals and criminal justice workers more efficiently.... If more and more criminologists respond – and they seem to be doing so – criminology will eventually have only "handcuffs 1A" orientation. (pp.179, 187)

And Cressey was not alone. In affirming the need for what he called 'radical realism', Jock Young (1986:4) decries criminologists' retreat from any discussion of causality and a criminology which has well 'abandoned its historical mission of the search for the causes of crime.' The nostalgia over the loss of etiology is echoed by Steven Box (1987:194) in his book *Recession, Crime and Punishment* which the author sarcastically describes as one that 'displays an oldfashioned, and therefore contemptible, concern with aetiology – the causes of crime'.

It seems that academic concerns, as Box (1987) points out, are not killed off too easily.

Critical Views on Etiological Research in Criminology

The cause of crime is still an intricate puzzle in social behavior, and no easy explanation will fit the observed facts.
                    Sykes, G.M. and Drabek, T.E. (1969)
                    Law and the Lawless: A Reader in Criminology
                    NY: Random House

'Why do people commit sin or violate God's commandments and divine laws despite the threat of eternal hell?' This question is not without relevance to criminology which for decades has been engaged in a relentless search for the causes of why people engage in proscribed behaviours. And yet, to my knowledge, this question has not been the subject of any scientific research or theorization. Probably, theologians who believed that sins are the doing of the devil did not feel a need to search any further for the causes or explanations of sinful behaviour. There has also been very little research into, or theorizing on, the causes of civil torts and harmful actions (see Morris and Hawkins, 1969:46). By contrast, violating the provisions of the criminal law has been the subject of endless and persistent causal research. One might ask: What makes violations of man-made laws more worthy of study and theorizing than violations of God-made laws? Although this eternal quest for the causes of crime has been denounced by many as fruitless, unproductive, and even futile, it continues to go on unabated and the vast majority of criminology textbooks continue to devote several chapters to the so-called 'theories of crime causation.' All this seems to suggest that 'crime' is a unique or at least a distinct category of human behaviour. More than half a century ago, Robert Maciver (1942), in his book *Social Causation* pointed out that 'it is

vain to seek the causes of crime as such, of crime anywhere and everywhere.'
He writes:

> Crime is a legal category. The only thing that is alike in all crimes is that
> they are alike violations of law. In that sense the only cause of crime as
> such is the law itself. What is a crime in one country is no crime in another;
> what is a crime at one time is no crime at another. The law is forever
> changing, adding new crimes to the catalogue and cancelling former ones.
> It may even, as not infrequently happens in times of crisis or revolution,
> designate as the most heinous of crimes certain forms of behaviour that
> were previously counted highly honorable. Since, then, crime varies with
> the law, the conditions that evoke it are equally variant. Moreover, the
> social conditions that increase the frequency of some categories of crime
> may diminish the frequency of others. Crime, then, is essentially relative. It
> has no inherent quality or property attaching to it as such, attaching to
> crime of all categories under all conditions. (p. 88)

Having noted that the question 'why crime?' has no more specific significance than the question 'why human nature?', Maciver (1942:88) continues his
criticism of the ongoing search for a general theory of crime:

> Since crime, as a category of social action, has no inherent universal
> property, we cannot expect to find, in the variety of persons who are
> convicted of crimes, any one psychological or physiological type, any
> character trait whatever that differentiates them all from other persons.
> The crime committer may be a maniac or a genius, a scoundrel or a
> patriot, a man without scruple or a man who puts his scruples above the
> law, a reckless exploiter or a man in desperate need. All attempts to find a
> physiognomy of crime have failed. The vaguer attempts to find a particu-
> lar mentality associated with lawbreaking are without warrant. The end-
> less vicissitudes of circumstances, opportunity, and personal history
> preclude the expectation of any simple inclusive formula.

A quarter of a century later, Morris and Hawkins (1969:45) added their voice
to those who were critical of the eternal quest for the causes of crime. They
insisted that:

> ...crime, like disease, is not a unitary phenomenon, and thus no single
> explanatory theory applicable to all crimes is feasible any more than a
> single theory can be found to explain all diseases. One of the best defini-
> tions of crime is Lord Atkin's statement, 'The domain of criminal juris-
> prudence can only be ascertained by examining what acts at any particular
> period are declared by the State to be crimes, and the only common nature
> they will be found to possess is that they are prohibited by the State and
> that those who commit them are punished.'

Morris and Hawkins go on to explain that crime consists of a great variety of human acts which in many cases have little more in common than that they are violations of the criminal law and they deplore that this simple fact is quite often ignored by many criminologists:

> This has not always been clearly recognized and the search for *the* cause of criminality was still being assiduously pursued.... Today, however, it is generally thought to have been an illusory quest, not unlike the eighteenth-century chemists' search for the elusive hypothetical substance, phlogiston, believed to be the principle of fire and the cause of combustibility of all inflammable bodies. The essential point is that the concept of tort, is a legal concept. Indeed very frequently the same act is both a crime and a tort. Yet – and this is significant – there is scant literature on the causation of tort. No research projects have been conducted to search for the primary cause of tort. Apart from problems of traffic safety, no one inquires what social or psychological pathologies underlie the incidence of tort in our society. No one has suggested that those who commit torts are biologically inferior to their fellows.... Equally, the search for *the causes* of crime is illusory, though recommended in some otherwise respectable criminological texts and pursued by many expensively outfitted criminological safaris. Shifts in the location of the causes of crime have varied with theoretical fashions in allied fields. Currently, psychiatric and sociological explanations have a wide following. (pp. 45–6)

More recently, Henry and Milovanovic (1994:120), called for abandoning the futile search for causes of crime since this search 'simply elaborates the distinctions that maintain crime as a separate reality, while failing to address how it is that crime is a part of society.'

Criticism of the long and ongoing search for the causes of crime has not been limited to North American criminologists. In an article entitled 'The futility of searching for causes of crime', Finnish criminologist, Patrick Törnudd (1971) is highly critical of criminologists' failure to consider the utilization problems in their preoccupation with a search for constant and identifiable 'causes' of crime. Törnudd's advice is that instead of searching for so-called 'causes' of crime, criminologists should formulate their research strategy and communicate their results in terms of estimates and predictions of: (a) fluctuations in the total level of criminality, or (b) the process determining the selection of offences and offenders to be punished (p. 23). Another Finnish criminologist, Raimo Lahti (1972), maintained that Scandinavian criminology no longer searches for the causes of crime or asks why some individuals become criminals. It is more concerned with finding out why certain individuals are identified as criminals in a selective process.

How Sound are the Premises Underlying Etiological Research?

Hopefully these lengthy quotations and these views, expressed by prominent scholars on both sides of the Atlantic, have alerted the reader that some of the fundamental premises underlying the assiduous pursuit of the 'causes' of crime are seriously flawed. What follows are *some* of the reasons why etiological research in criminology is not likely to be more successful, more fruitful and more productive in the future than it has been in the past.

1. As mentioned earlier, crime is a very heterogeneous, artificial and arbitrary category of behaviour (see Chapters 1 and 2). Crime, as Morris and Hawkins (1969:45) correctly point out, 'is not a unitary phenomenon, and thus no single explanatory theory applicable to all crimes is feasible any more than a single theory can be found to explain all diseases' (see above).

2. The atomization and fragmentation that are currently occurring in criminology, the emergence of new specialized criminologies, such as 'feminist criminology', 'black criminology', Australian 'Aboriginal criminology', reinforce the present scepticism regarding the possibility and feasibility of a general, unified causal theory of crime. Over-ambitious and presumptuous titles such as *A General Theory of Crime* (Gottfredson and Hirschi, 1990) notwithstanding, the growing acceptance of the doctrines of anti-essentialism and of cultural relativism seem to have watered down substantially any hopes that might have persisted regarding the prospects of a universal causal theory of crime.

3. The fact that what is defined as criminal behaviour is not inherently nor intrinsically different from non-criminal behaviour, and that for every behaviour defined as criminal and made illegal there are similar or even identical behaviours that are not so defined, seems to preclude any possibility of a causal theory that is *specific* to crime. It indicates that the causes of criminal behaviour are essentially the same causes of human behaviour in general, that crime does not have *specific* or *unique* causes. Causal explanations of criminal violence, for instance, can only be sought within the framework of a general theory of human aggression. Explanations of acquisitive crimes, whether of the street or white-collar variety, will have to be part of a general theory of human acquisitiveness. Explanations of sex crimes will have to be found in a general theory of human sexuality. Explanations of drug abuse cannot be limited to illegal drugs but have to be sought within a general theory of humans' search for altered states of consciousness. And so forth.

4. Another rather obvious, though often overlooked fact, is that the *causes* of human behaviour do not change from one era to another. Overlooking this fact often leads to what may be called *the etiological fallacy:* the assumption that a change in the definition of the behaviour is accompanied by a change in the causes of that behaviour. A simple example will suffice to illustrate this etiological fallacy. The causes of child beating or child abuse may well be the same now as they were 50 or a 100 years ago when such a behaviour was considered perfectly normal and desirable ('spare the rod and spoil the child'). What has changed are simply societal attitudes to, and society's definition of, the behaviour. But as soon as the phenomenon of child abuse was 'discovered' in the sixties, its 'causes' became the object of much research and theorizing. It mattered little to the researchers that the behaviour they were now analyzing as criminal had been for centuries, until it was recently redefined, a cultural norm, a normative requirement. It did not stop them from formulating theories and models stressing the psychopathology and the abnormality of the parents as the causes of child abuse! Related to this is another etiological fallacy, namely that an *external* definition of a behaviour is an indication of an innate abnormality in the perpetrator of that behaviour.

5. Criminal behaviour is dynamic behaviour and cannot therefore be explained by a static causal theory whether such theory focuses on the personal traits/attributes of offenders or their social or family background. As many criminal acts are situation- or context-specific and others are target-specific, their explanation has to be sought through a dynamic situational approach that focuses not on the *causes* of the behaviour but on the situational factors: facilitating, triggering, precipitating, catalytic factors (see Fattah, 1991, 1993c).

6. If it is true that criminals are not different from others (see Chapter 5) then any causal theory that has as its basic premise that criminals are 'abnormal', 'sick', 'peculiar', or 'different', is bound to fail. Crime, as Thomas Gabor (1994:6) points out 'is not the exclusive domain of abnormal individuals or occasioned by unusual circumstances unrelated to everyday life.' And since everyone has, at one time or another, committed acts that fit the legal definition of crime, a causal theory of offending that is unique, specific, or exclusive to those who are officially caught and punished cannot be a valid theory. Neither can be a criminological theory that is applicable only to dramatic and serious crimes such as murder and rape. Such theory, argues Vold (1958:201), is 'patently inadequate in that it fails to account for the criminal behaviour of the great bulk of the criminal population, i.e., those who become involved with crime'.

7. If committing crime is a deliberate choice, if criminal behaviour is a
    chosen activity, and if a criminal career is a chosen career (Fattah,
    1993c), then searching for the *causes* of this choice can be no more
    enlightening nor productive than searching for the causes of why people
    buy cars, go to university, or why some choose to become doctors or
    lawyers while others choose to become plumbers, electricians, bouncers
    or morticians. A theory of career or occupational choice is not a *causal*
    theory but a motivational theory. And it might well be that what is
    needed in criminology is not a *causal* theory but a motivational theory
    explaining the deliberate engagement in delinquent activities or the
    choice of a criminal career. Criminological research can benefit from a
    switch in focus, from the criminal to the crime: What makes crime
    attractive and appealing? The switch from causes to motives is currently
    taking place (see below). Katz (1988:3), for example, deplores positivist
    criminology's persistent 'preoccupation with a search for background
    forces, usually defects in the offenders' psychological backgrounds or
    social environment to the neglect of the positive, often wonderful attrac-
    tions within the lived experience of criminality'.
8. The largely neglected, though crucial, phenomenon of 'desistance from
    crime' or 'growing out of crime' is consistent with a motivational theory
    but inconsistent with the positivist causal theories of criminal behaviour.
    If crime is caused by a biological or psychological abnormality, how is it
    then that the majority of those who commit crime cease to do so at a
    relatively young age? How is it that the biological or psychological
    factors that push the individual into delinquency and crime suddenly
    become inoperational? Conversely, it is natural that the MOTIVES for
    committing crime weaken or even disappear with advancing age, that
    many crimes lose their attraction and their appeal, the older one be-
    comes. Matza (1964), for one, highlighted this paradox of positive
    criminology by insisting that if delinquents were as different from non-
    delinquents as positive theories portray them to be, then involvement in
    delinquency would be more permanent and less transient, more pervasive
    and less intermittent than is the case. He adds:

> Theories of delinquency yield an embarrassment of riches which seemingly
> go unmatched in the real world. This accounting for too much delinquency
> may be taken as an observable consequence of the distorted picture of the
> delinquent that has developed within positive criminology. (p. 22)

Recapitulation

Having summarized some of the questionable premises underlying
etiological research in criminology, it might be useful to end this critique
of the continuing search for the causes of crime by reiterating Morris

and Hawkins' (1969:52) conviction that 'attempts to fit all the phenomena of crime into a procrustean cause/effect framework are fundamentally misconceived'. Morris and Hawkins offer the following rationale in support of their rather unconventional conclusion:

> The use of the mechanical model derived from physical science in the behavioral and social sciences has in general proved notoriously unfruitful. We do not believe that this is because the type of causation involved is peculiarly complex (i.e., the multifactorial approach) but rather because the application of causal analysis in this field usually involves the same sort of logical error as the anthropocentric interpretation of animal behavior. The conceptual scheme does not fit the facts of experience. This is the basic reason for our refusal to commit scarce resources to this type of research. (pp. 52–3)

Despite all the warnings, the criticism, the convincing arguments, the causes of crime and delinquency continue to be an extremely popular research and teaching topic and to draw a substantial amount of research funds.[1] Not many criminologists seem to have heeded the advice or listened to the warnings given by scholars such as Robert Maciver, George Vold, Norval Morris, Gordon Hawkins, Patrick Törnudd, Raimo Lahti, to name but a few. The popularity of the continuing search for the causes of crime and delinquency, despite its disappointing results, is probably due to the belief, shared by many, that finding the causes is indispensable for an effective action to control and prevent crime. While it might be generally true that knowing the causes of a phenomenon might lead to better ways of dealing with it in the desired direction, this might not necessarily be the case with the phenomenon of crime, as has been pointed out by James Q. Wilson (1971) and more recently by Gottfredson and Hirschi (1990). To quote once more from Morris and Hawkins' (1969:52) highly inspired critique of etiological research:

> ...just as the understanding of causation does not entail a corollary capacity for control, so the control of phenomena is not always dependent upon the prior understanding of causation. Treatment cannot wait on the identification of causes. It is a vulgar error to assume that one needs to understand the etiology of a social condition before it can be controlled. In the field of mental health, treatment skills have far outdistanced etiological understanding, and diagnosis is related more to the prediction of the course and the most effective treatment of a condition than to its causation. The history of medicine is full of instances of the successful development and utilization of treatment and preventive methods which worked (e.g., lime juice for scurvy, quinine for malaria) long before the real nature of the illness involved was understood.

RECENT THEORETICAL DEVELOPMENTS IN CRIMINOLOGY

Changing Views of Crime

> If criminal behavior, by and large, is the normal behavior of normally responding individuals in situations defined as undesirable, illegal, and therefore criminal, then the basic problem is one of social and political organization and the established values or definitions of what may, and what may not, be permitted.

> George B. Vold (1958, p. 202)
> *Theoretical Criminology*

Crime as Normal Behaviour

Most criminological theories are predicated on the premise that crime is pathological or abnormal behaviour. But one can argue that a much better understanding of criminal behaviour could be achieved by regarding it as an illegal means of satisfying normal biological, psychological, or socioeconomic needs. Though not a novel approach, analyzing crime as a means to an end, as behaviour that fulfills a certain function for the perpetrator is a much more promising way of studying and analyzing crime. One of the research implications of this view is to shift the focus from the search for causes to an analysis of motives.

An analysis of motives can show, for example, that violence in many instances is a perfectly normal, even natural, response. Despite this, theories of violence and aggression fail to take into account the motive for the violence or to pay attention to what might have triggered the violent response. As a result, violence is invariably treated as abnormal or pathological behaviour, as an indicator of some psychopathology from which the perpetrator suffers. Treating violence as aberrant behaviour overlooks the fact that retaliatory violence, in particular, is a normal human reaction. Retaliation, as many (Westermarck, 1924; Jacoby, 1983) point out, is an 'ineradicable impulse' when harm is inflicted. Dautremer (1985:82) describes the desire for revenge as 'an innate sentiment in man' while Posner (1980:79) claimed that there is 'a vengeful component in our genetic make-up'.

Retaliatory violence is only one example of many to show that the general assumption of pathology that underlies individualistic theories of criminal and violent behaviour is a questionable assumption. Culturally-sanctioned violence, such as violent initiation rites, is neither abnormal nor pathological. Using violence to correct children's 'misbehaviour' is widely viewed as normal behaviour, is socially accepted and legally permissible (Section 43 of the Canadian Criminal Code), and yet the demarcation line between corporal punishment and child abuse is extremely blurred.

Criminological literature in recent years suggests a growing acceptance in criminology of the notion that crime is normal behaviour (Cusson, 1983; Cornish and Clarke, 1986; Katz, 1988; Fattah, 1993c).

Gottfredson and Hirschi (1990:xv) point out that 'nearly all crimes are mundane, simple, trivial, easy acts aimed at satisfying desires of the moment, as are many other acts of little concern to the criminal law.' The authors' definition of crime as 'acts of force or fraud undertaken in pursuit of self-interest' (p. 15) seems to indicate that the difference between crimes and non-crimes lies not in the nature of the behaviour but simply in the *means* used by the perpetrators of that behaviour.

Crime as Functional Behaviour

Durkheim's thesis that crime is necessary and functional (see Chapter 10) does not seem to have a wide following and has been challenged by criminologists like Roshier (1973) and Conklin (1975) among others.[2] The prevailing view among criminologists, as among the general public is that crime is a social evil that has to be eradicated. Some, however, insist that Durkheim was right in maintaining that crime is necessary (Törnudd, 1971) and functional (Morris and Hawkins, 1969). Morris and Hawkins point to the substantial evidence showing that social, industrial, and commercial progress is accompanied by an increase in criminal activity. They write:

> For as you expand the bounds of human freedom and economic and social potential, you equally expand the bounds of potentiality for nonconformity and delinquency and crime. As legitimate opportunities increase so also do illegitimate opportunities. As our economic insights now stand, industrialization seems to carry with it urbanization, which in turn carries with it the anonymity, isolation, frustration, discontent and the enormous criminogenic potential of the city.... In this sense juvenile delinquency and crime are functional and not dysfunctional; they are, at the present level of our knowledge, costs that must be paid for other socially valuable development processes in the community. (pp. 49–50)

Recent developments in the former socialist countries of Eastern Europe lend further support to this view. The rapid quantitative and qualitative changes in crime that took place almost immediately after the fall of the Berlin wall and the reunification of Germany, the quick increase in crime rates, documented by both official statistics and victimization surveys (Fattah, 1994c), were happening concomitantly with the transition from totalitarianism to democracy, the liberalization of society, the increase in freedom and mobility, the move from a controlled economy to a free market economy. In other words, crime was rising simultaneously with the positive changes that were occurring in the political, economic, and social spheres. Could it be, then, that rising crime rates are the price to be paid for democracy and freedom, for development, industrialization, and modernization?

Last century, the French sociologist Gabriel Tarde maintained that crime is the price we pay for 'our enlightenment and our discoveries' (quoted in Morris and Hawkins, 1969:48). The differences in crime rates between agrarian/rural and industrialized/urban societies lend credence to Tarde's claim and confirm Quetelet's earlier observation that the poorest regions in France had the lowest crime. The difference is not difficult to explain. Life conditions in poor, non-industrialized societies with economies of scarcity, are not conducive to the commission of property crimes that constitute the bulk of criminality in the modern industrialized world. There are few temptations and even fewer opportunities to perpetrate such crimes. The scarcity of goods, of material possessions and the sharing that inevitably takes place, dictated by the harsh realities of life, account for the lack of the motivation to steal.

Norval Morris (Morris and Hawkins, 1969) relates how, when he was director of the UN Asia and Far East Institute for the Prevention of Crime and Treatment of Offenders, he was asked by some of the trainees from poor developing Asian countries, with low but rising delinquency rates, how this trend could be stopped. He facetiously advised them to stop the development and the modernization:

> He urged them to ensure that their people remained ignorant, bigoted, and illeducated; that on no account should they develop substantial industries; that communications systems should be primitive; and that their transportation systems should be such as to ensure that most of the citizens lived within their own small, isolated villages for their entire lives. He stressed the importance of making sure their educational systems did not promise a potential level of achievement for a child beyond that which his father had already achieved. If it was once suggested that a child should be able to grow to the limit of his capacity rather than to the ceiling of his father's achievement, he pointed out, the seeds of the gravest disorder would be laid. He stressed the universal human experience that village societies are entirely capable of maintaining any discordance or human nonconformity within their own social frameworks and never need to call on centralized authority to solve their problems. (p. 49)

Crime as a Human Conflict

As mentioned earlier (Chapter 2), the criminal law as we know it today is a relatively new development in the history of legal institutions. It was also mentioned that prior to the emergence of the criminal law all disputes were civil disputes. As we have seen, there is no qualitative difference between the acts designated as crimes and civil torts. Theories of crime causation, however, treat crime as if it were a distinct, exceptional or unique category of behaviour. And the legal view of crime continues to regard it as an offence against the state, society or the sovereign.

Recent years have witnessed a growing criticism of these conventional views, and increasing calls for a return to the original notion of crime as a human conflict (Hulsman, 1986; Christie, 1977; Kennedy, 1990; Fattah, 1992, 1993d).

Christie (1977:3) has observed that the key element in a criminal proceeding is that the proceeding is converted from something between the concrete parties into a conflict between one of the parties and the State. Christie refers to two characteristics of modern trials: first, the parties are being *represented* and secondly, the one party who is being represented by the State, namely the victim, is so thoroughly represented that he or she for most of the proceedings is pushed completely out of the arena, reduced to the trigger – off of the whole process. These developments have resulted in the victim being a double loser; first, vis-à-vis the offender and secondly, by being denied the right to full participation in what might have been one of the most ritual encounters in life.

Jobson (1977:260) asserts that the criminal justice system has overextended itself into conflict situations that are not adequately solved by existing processes. He estimates that almost 50 per cent of crimes against persons and crimes against property prosecuted in the Canadian courts are characterized by an ongoing relationship between the offender and the victim. These crimes, argues Jobson, 'are not committed by strangers but by family members, neighbours, tenants or landlords, or within a customer seller relationship'. Jobson argues for treating these crimes as conflicts and dealing with them through mediation. He is critical of the adversary nature of the present trial process 'which must treat them as strangers in a duel to the finish'. He feels that mediation is a more satisfactory forum for settling these disputes which are characterized by an ongoing relationship.

The rediscovery of crime victims and the recent attempts in several countries such as Canada, Belgium, Germany to deal with criminal offences, even serious ones, through mediation and victim–offender reconciliation reaffirm the nature of crimes as human conflicts that could be dealt with effectively through a system of restorative justice, a system that places the emphasis not on punishment and retribution but on reconciliation, restitution, and compensation. Once the notion of restorative justice takes hold, the artificial boundaries and barriers between the criminal law and the civil law are likely to be removed and 'criminal' conflicts will be settled in a manner very similar or identical to that used for the settlement of civil disputes (Fattah, 1993d).

The move toward the privatization or the 'civilization' of 'criminal' conflicts is already underway. Some American States, California, for example, have made it possible for store owners/managers to deal with shoplifting incidents privately without involving the police or the criminal justice system. The move is simply a formal recognition of an informal but widespread practice that has been going on for many years.

Crime as Social Control

In an interesting article entitled *Crime as Social Control*, Donald Black (1983) suggests that conduct regarded as criminal is often quite the opposite. He believes that 'much crime is moralistic, and instead of being an intentional violation of a prohibition, it involves the pursuit of justice.' Black points out that 'while many citizens are entirely dependent upon legal officials such as the police to handle criminal offenders, others are prepared to protect themselves and their associates by any means at their disposal, including violence.' Black points out that violence is a mode of conflict management resembling the modes used in traditional societies which have little or no formal law.

The point is that when aggression is met with aggression, when violence is countered with violence, the roles are simply reversed. The initial aggressor becomes the victim and the initial victim is transformed into a victimizer. Labels are applied not on the basis of the original roles but the final outcome. The violent response, though defined as crime by the law, is perfectly legitimate in the eyes of the perpetrator who perceives his/her retaliation as an act of justice, as a rightful reprisal (Fattah, 1994d:4).

Black (1983:39) illustrates the conflict in the following manner:

> Here the State often imposes the categories of offender and victim upon people who were contesting the proper application of these labels during the altercation in question. Whether there was originally a crosscomplaint or not, however, in all of these cases the State defines someone with a grievance as a criminal. The offense lies in how the grievance was pursued. The crime is selfhelp...violence flourishes...and most of it involves ordinary citizens who seemingly view their conduct as a perfectly legitimate exercise of social control.

Crime as a Social Risk

As already pointed out, crime is not qualitatively different from civil torts or from many other harmful and injurious actions from which the citizens of a modern, technological, mechanized, and motorized society daily suffer. Modern life is a hazardous life. The risk of being victimized by crime is but one of the many risks to which people are daily exposed. Crime, as mentioned earlier (see Chapter 3), is not more harmful, more injurious, more serious, or more dangerous than a multitude of other behaviours in which people freely engage or to which they are knowingly or unknowingly exposed. There is no doubt that the deaths, injuries, and losses from victimization by crime are relatively minor when compared to those by other types of victimization (Fattah, 1991).

In Australia, for example, a comparison of causes of death for different age groups (James, 1992) reveals that, particularly for those over 55 years old, death rates by homicide are extremely low when compared to deaths in traffic accidents, by accidental falls, or by suicides and self-inflicted injuries.

Another study by the Law Reform Commission of the State of Victoria (1992) found the annual number of homicide victims to be far lower than the number of work-related traumatic deaths, let alone deaths from work-related illnesses. The average in Victoria of 74 homicide victims each year was far less than that of victims of suicide (421 for 1985), of fatal traffic accidents (678 in 1985), or of deaths from lung cancer (1551 in 1985).

In the province of Quebec, five times as many individuals lose their lives by their own hands committing suicide than by the hands of others committing homicide. And in 1991 more people died as a result of suicide than all traffic fatalities including those involving the death of pedestrians and snowmobilers (*Globe and Mail*, 16 December 1992).

The legal category of strict liability offences illustrates too vividly the fact that in the modern world, in one way or another, as much and more damage is done by negligence, or by indifference to the welfare or safety of others (pollution, second hand smoke, and so on), as by deliberate wickedness (Wootton, 1963). What intentional crime could have caused as much death, injury, harm and loss as did the Union Carbide incident in Bhopal, India; the Chernobyl nuclear disaster in Russia, or the *Exxon Valdez* oil spill off the coast of Alaska?

PARADIGM SHIFTS IN CRIMINOLOGY

From Determinism to Rational Choice

Within two centuries criminology seems to have gone a full circle. It moved from the voluntaristic notions propagated by the philosophers and legal scholars of the Classical School to the hard determinism espoused and defended by the Italian Positivist School, followed by the soft determinism characteristic of psychological and sociological criminology, only to come back to the notion of rational choice and of the reasoning criminal.

Over the same two centuries, views of the criminal underwent fundamental and radical changes. Criminological thinking shifted from the 'abstract man' of the Classical School to the 'average man' of Quetelet to the 'criminal man' of Lombroso. Now criminology seems to be slowly discovering the 'normal man', an offender who is neither diseased nor abnormal, who is not different from others. Beccaria's free agent gave way to the 'automaton' of the Italian Positivist School, the helpless puppet in the hands of natural (and social) forces. This reductionist and fatalistic view of the criminal was replaced by a probabilistic one that saw him as a creature constrained by his social antecedents and conditions, whose behaviour is not determined but is 'shaped' by the psychological and social baggage he is forced to carry. In recent years, Cornish and Clarke (1986) have again reintroduced the view of the criminal as a reasoning agent who makes a rational choice to commit crime or to engage in criminal activities.

Unlike positivist theories that view criminal behaviour as a distinct, unique, abnormal, pathological, irrational, purposeless, mindless, or senseless, and start with the premise that criminals are inherently different from noncriminals, the rational choice perspective (Cornish and Clarke, 1986) takes as its point of departure a set of radically different assumptions:

1. It recognizes the mundane, opportunistic, and rational nature of much offending, thus rejecting the view that depicts it as 'irremediably alien to ordinary behaviour – driven by abnormal motivations, irrational, purposeless, unpredictable, potentially violent, and evil' (Cornish and Clarke, 1986:v). Cornish and Clarke affirm that 'the leitmotif encapsulated in the notion of a "reasoning" offender implies the essentially nonpathological and commonplace nature of much criminal activity.' (p. 6)

2. Rather than emphasizing whatever differences may exist between criminals and non criminals, the rational choice perspective stresses some of the similarities. And rather than focusing on the irrational and pathological components in some crimes, it examines more closely the rational and adaptive aspects of offending. (p. vi)

3. Rather than viewing crime as a unitary phenomenon that could be explained by a general, far reaching theory, it calls for crime-specific analysis (*ibid*). 'Still, the approach is intended to provide a framework for understanding all forms of crime but without attempting to impose a conceptual unity upon divergent criminal behaviour.' (p. 6)

4. Rather than focusing attention solely on the criminal, his attributes, his traits, his background, and the factors governing his involvement in particular crimes, it draws attention to the criminal event itself and the situational factors that influence its commission (p. vi). Cornish and Clarke explain that 'whereas most existing theories tend to accord little influence to situational variables, the rational choice approach explicitly recognizes their importance in relation to the criminal event, and, furthermore, incorporates similar influences on decisions relating to involvement in crime.' (p. 6)

From Idealism to Realism, from Romanticism to Pragmatism

The 1960s and 1970s were the decades when romanticism and idealism in criminology reached their peak. The high point was attained with the publication of Taylor, Walton and Young's book *The New Criminology* (1973). In it, the three British criminologists, reformulated in a highly articulate form, the utopian assertions of early Marxist criminologists such as Zorli and Bonger. The harsh realities of the 1980s were bound to shatter the exaggerated optimism and romanticism of the two previous decades. The idealism of the 'new criminologists' gave way to what is now called 'left realism' or 'radical realism'. In 1986, in an edited book *Confronting Crime*, Matthews and Young articulated the new position, then followed a series of publications culminating in 1992 with three books on *realist criminology*, two edited by Matthews and Young and the third by John Lowman and Brian MacLean.

Realist criminology, according to Matthews and Young (1986:1), breaks 'with the romantic and idealist conceptions which have been conveyed by radical criminology.' Young (1986:21) explains that 'the central tenet of left realism is to reflect the reality of crime, that is in its origins, its nature and its impact.' This, according to Young, involves a rejection of tendencies to romanticize crime or to pathologize it, to analyze it solely from the point of view of the administration of crime or the criminal actor, to underestimate crime or to exaggerate it. And this realism, insists Young, is what informs and guides the practice in terms of what can be done about the problems of crime and social control. Young (1986:23) then traces the following direction for realist criminology:

> Realism...must neither succumb to hysteria nor relapse into a critical denial of the severity of crime as a problem. It must be fiercely sceptical of official statistics and control institutions without taking the posture of a blanket rejection of all figures or, indeed, the very possibility of reform.
>
> Realism necessitates an accurate victimology. It must counterpoise this against those liberal and idealist criminologies, on the one side, which play down victimization or even bluntly state that the 'real' victim is the offender and, on the other, those conservatives who celebrate moral panic and see violence and robbery as ubiquitous on our streets.
>
> To do this involves mapping out who is at risk and what precise effect crime has on their lives. This moves beyond the invocation of the global risk rates of the average citizen. All too often this serves to conceal the actual severity of crime amongst significant sections of the population whilst providing a fake statistical back drop for the discussion of 'irrational' fears.

In a later paper, Young (1992) explains what he calls the ten points of realism. These are:

1. *The principle of naturalism:* this principle, considered by Young to be the most fundamental tenet of realism, is that criminology should be faithful to the nature of crime...it should acknowledge the *form* of crime, the *social context* of crime, the *shape* of crime, its trajectory through *time*, and its enactment in *space*. (p. 26)

2. *The principle of multiple etiology:* crime rates, Young maintains, involve a fourfold etiology: the causes of offending, the factors which make victims vulnerable, the social conditions which affect public levels of control and tolerance, and the social forces which propel the formal agencies such as the police. (p. 30)

3. *The principle of specificity:* rejecting the generalizations of 'administrative criminology,' Young insists that it is central to a realist position that objective conditions are interpreted through the specific subcultures of groups involved. He argues that generalization is possible, but only given specific cultural conditions and social understanding. (p. 34)

4. *The principle of focusing on lived realities:* this means that realism is concerned with the material problem which particular groups of people experience in terms of the major social axes of age, class, gender, and race, and spatially with their locality. This principle, affirms Young, creates a close affinity between realism and subcultural theory. (p. 38)

5. *The principle of social control:* the control of crime, argues Young, must reflect the nature of crime. That is why it has to involve informal and formal interventions on both the level of the offender and the victim. To control crime from a realist perspective involves intervention at each part of the square of crime: the offender, the informal system, the victim, and the formal system. In realism, maintains Young, all points of intervention are possible and necessary. And although realism prioritizes structural intervention, it concedes that interventions at all levels, from target hardening to policing, are inevitably necessary. (p. 41)

6. *The principle of multiagency intervention:* multiagency social intervention is necessary and is one of the tenets of realism, because it corresponds both to the realities of crime and to the realities of social control. Multiagency intervention is the natural form of social control in industrial societies but it needs to be coordinated and to have an overall rationale. (p. 45)

7. *The principle of rational democratic input:* this principle requires taking people seriously because the public pay for community safety and they are the ones who empower the police and the local authority to make provisions for a safe environment. Social surveys are the instrument that gives voice to the experience of people and make it possible to differentiate the safety needs of different sectors of the community. (pp. 49–50)

8. *The principle of rational democratic output:* this principle has to do with the outcome of control measures. It is also the question of what crimes are being controlled, at what cost, and where do these crimes figure in public priorities. It is also a matter of connecting demand (crimes whose control is judged a priority for community safety) with supply (how effective the various agencies and initiatives are at their control with an eye to cost effectiveness). (p. 52)

9. *The principle of democratic measurement:* this principle pertains to realism and the criminal statistics, the question of what is the 'real' rate of crime and whether there is indeed such an entity. Realism maintains that crime rates are a product of the interplay of actors and reactors: of victims and offenders, on one hand, and of formal and informal control on the other. Rates of crime change as these interacting sectors change and any satisfactory theory of crime must, in the realist view, take cognizance of the totality of this process. (p. 56)

10. *The principle of theory and practice:* realism argues for merging theory and practice. It is critical of the divorce between theory and practice that is characteristic of traditional criminology and of criminologists who live in different areas than criminals and are socially distant from them. Realism is critical of the fact that most practice is divorced from theory on all but a rudimentary level and that a considerable part of criminological theory is, in fact, the critique by armchair theorists of other people's experience. (pp. 59–63)

Critique

In an attempt to respond to the critics of left realism, Young and Matthews (1992) summarize the various criticisms leveled at the new doctrine:

1. Left realist criminology has nothing new to say, it is simply a revamped version of traditional criminology with victimization statistics replacing police statistics, the traditional goal of the search for the causes of crime merely reelaborated, and the role of the criminal justice system criticized at a superficial rather than a fundamental level. (p. 1)

2. Realism constantly regresses to either neoclassicism or social positivism. The critics accuse realism either of merely reasserting the primacy of the police and the criminal justice system in tackling crime or of reverting to social positivism. (p. 3)

3. Realism merely reflects conventional definitions of crime. (p. 10)

4. Realism is merely pragmatism – interventions are pursued for opportunistic or contingent reasons, with little or no reference to any long-term strategies or principles. (p. 12)

5. Realism merely represents a new empiricism based on victimization studies; it replaces the uncritical acceptance of police figures with an equally uncritical use of victimization data. (p. 13)
6. Realism is a form of political populism; it merely moves from a public, 'common sense' attitude to one of policy. (p. 15)

Downes and Rock (1988:268, 272) view realist criminology as an attempt to create a middle position between the hysterical over-reaction of 'law and order politics' and the gross insensitivity to crime of the left in Britain. They see it as an approach that 'holds both analytic and political promise at a time when radical criminology was becoming increasingly scholastic, established and ritualistic.' They predict that, in its evolution, 'it is likely to become more and more a practical administrative criminology of the left, taking the problems of victimization seriously but giving a radical inflection to their solution, awarding prominence to special victims and seeking to control the police response to their needs.'

From Male-Centred Criminology to Feminist Criminology

Criminology has always suffered from a male bias. Until two or three decades ago it was male dominated and paid little or no attention to gender in its theoretical explanations or practical applications. The few early attempts to address female criminality (Lombroso and Ferrero, 1895; Pollak, 1961), or to explain why women commit less crime than men (Quetelet, 1842) were sexist and simplistic. The situation has changed dramatically in recent years thanks to a whole new generation of feminist criminologists. The focus on gender, characteristic of feminist research and writing on crime, has greatly enlivened criminological debates and enriched criminological knowledge. It provided new insights into the study of crime. Feminist critique of male-centered explanations and theories highlighted many of the shortcomings and inadequacies from which the old theories suffered.

Feminist criminology has been defined (Victoria Greenwood, 1981) as 'a collection of recent research, predominantly inspired and affected by influences from the women's movement, which illuminated the institutionalized sexism in the criminal justice process.' Downes and Rock (1988:273) describe it as

> ...a diverse body of work united by the critical view that the understanding of the criminality of women, and the role of gender in theories of deviance in general, have been ill served both by traditional and new criminologies.

The general lack of interest in female criminality that characterized criminology until the 1970s is usually attributed to women's lower crime rates when compared to those of men. It is the same reason that explains why elderly criminality is woefully understudied by criminologists. By ignoring the criminality of women, criminology was largely impoverished. As Jeanne Gregory (1986:59) points out:

> The general tendency to ignore female crime leads to a double failure. On one hand it fails to analyze the specific conditions through which female conformity and non-conformity are achieved. On the other hand it fails to recognize the critical comparative role that the analysis of female criminality provides in illuminating the 'peculiar' nature of male criminality. Indeed, it is only through the full elaboration of female crime and control that a coherent and consistent 'criminology' itself becomes possible... It is clear then, that criminologists ignore the sex variable at their peril.

It should be pointed out that what is commonly called feminist criminology is by no means a monistic theory. There are different streams within feminist criminology. Gregory (1986:64-5) identifies three branches of feminism: *radical feminists* (who have severed their connections with Marxism and who regard the break as permanent despite their frequent indebtedness to the methods and concepts of Marxism); *socialist feminists* (who retain the long-term goal of 'dissolving the hyphen' and so achieving theoretical and political integration between feminism and Marxism); and *bourgeois feminists* (whose goal is to obtain sexual equality within the economic and political framework of capitalism). Gregory points out that within feminist criminology, there is a tendency for the three strands to become entangled with bourgeois feminists being the easiest to identify.

From its beginnings, and until the present, feminist criminology has been and continues to be a 'critical criminology'. It is critical of the system of patriarchy and of the social structures responsible for women's powerlessness and for maintaining females in a state of economic dependency. It is critical of men's historical oppression of women. In its critique of gender inequality, the disparities in wealth and power between women and men, of gender-based oppression, feminist criminology has a lot in common with Marxist, socialist, and radical criminology. Its fight for women's rights and for social and gender equality is quite similar to Marxist criminologists' struggle for an end to class-based inequalities and oppression. Feminist criminologists, as Pat Carlen (1992:52) points out, are interested in providing a remedy to 'the gender-related wrongs done to women criminals by criminologists, police, courts and prisons.' Carlen praises feminist criminologists for having contributed to the demolition of certain sexist myths concerning women's lawbreaking and the regulation of deviant females. Carlen (1992) highlights the major contributions that feminist perspectives have made to the theoretical understanding of the meanings of women's lawbreaking and the differential social response to it. She credits feminist criminology with having:

1. highlighted the fact that women's crimes are committed in different circumstances to men's – that women's crimes are the crimes of the powerless;
2. shown that the response to women's lawbreaking is constituted within typifications of femininity and womanhood which further add to women's oppression;
3. engaged the debate about whether the development of a feminist criminology is a possible theoretical project, whether the focus on women lawbreakers is a 'proper' concern of feminism, and whether a 'feminist' jurisprudence is desirable and/or possible;
4. publicized conditions in the women's jails and of having conducted campaigns for a better deal for women in trouble, before the courts or in prison. (p. 52)

Karlene Faith's book *Unruly Women* (1993) is a good example of how criminology can be enriched by the writings of feminist criminologists.

Critique

Downes and Rock (1988:273) hail feminist criminology as 'the most notable development in the field of criminology during the 1980s, a decade that saw little that is original in theorizing about deviant behaviour.' They credit feminist criminology with having 'significantly reoriented the field of criminology and suggest that while it may not be a new paradigm, it has undeniably revitalized the exploration of existing perspectives'. (p. 292)

Male criticism of feminist criminology is likely to be dismissed as biased and to be blamed on misogyny, inadequate understanding of, and lack of sensitivity to, the feminist point of view. It seems appropriate, therefore, in an attempt to offer a valid and credible critique of feminist criminology, to refer to the writings of female criminologists who have pointed to certain weaknesses in the feminist position.

In 1988 Gelsthorpe and Morris declared that a 'feminist criminology' cannot exist. Instead, they prefer to talk of feminist criminologies, or better still, feminist perspectives within criminology. These perspectives are, in essence, anti-positivist and critical of stereotypical images of women, and the question of women is central. They share also an interest in using methodologies which are sympathetic to these concerns. (p. 227)

Pat Carlen (1992) shares Gelsthorpe and Morris's concern about the designation 'feminist criminology'. Carlen (1992) accepts the appellation 'feminist' but refuses to call herself a 'feminist criminologist'. She has problems attributing any meaning to the term 'feminist criminology' which would be either desirable or possible. Here is how Carlen explains her rejection of the term 'feminist criminology':

It would not be *desirable* because any universalizing theories of a taken-for-granted criminality inhering in biological female subjects must be as reductionist and essentializing as the much maligned biological ones. It is not possible for three reasons. First, present knowledge about criminal women and criminal justice has not developed via explanatory concepts which could be called distinctly 'feminist' – unless one counts as explanatory the usually descriptive use of the word 'patriarchy'; secondly, once the historically and socially specific discourses and practices within which women's lawbreaking and criminalization occur in Britain, the United States, Canada and Australia are investigated, a concern with gender constructions rapidly merges with questions concerning class, racism and imperialism. Thirdly, no single theory (feminist or otherwise) can adequately explain three major features of women's lawbreaking and imprisonment: that women's crimes are, in the main, the crimes of the powerless; that women in prison are disproportionately from ethnic minority groups; and that a majority of women in prison have been in poverty for the greater part of their lives. (p. 53)

Although Carlen does not believe that a 'feminist criminology' is either desirable or possible, she takes issue with those who do not believe that feminists should study 'women and crime' at all. While recognizing the benefits of such study, Carlen denies that there is a distinctly feminist theoretical conceptual system which might adequately explain (or call into question) the empirical phenomenon known as 'women and crime' (p. 54). She also finds the notion that there is a distinctly feminist *method* in criminology or sociology to be absurd (p. 55). Finally, Carlen declares herself against what she labels as 'theoreticist, libertarian, separatist and gender-centric tendencies in recent feminist writings on women's lawbreaking and criminal justice'. (p. 61)

One might add two points to Carlen's critique: First, it could be argued that feminist criminology is in reality a *'feminist victimology'* whose main concern is to emphasize, explain, and document the victimization of women at the hands of men, of the criminal justice system, and the patriarchal society. It is more interested in establishing the gender biases that permeate the operations of the criminal justice system and the general oppression of females, particularly those who are members of minorities and lower classes, than in finding the causes of crime per se or formulating general explanations of criminality.

Second, while it is undeniable that feminist criminology has offered invaluable insights and has made valuable contributions to the understanding of the role of gender in crime and social response to crime, it does not have the potential to provide a holistic explanation to the problem of crime. Just as Marxist and radical criminology has highlighted the class dimension and

272   *Criminology: Past, Present and Future*

has shown the discriminatory nature of the definitions of crime and criminal justice practices, so has feminist criminology succeeded in highlighting and documenting the gender biases. The gender-centrism of feminist criminology seems to preclude *a priori* the possibility of holistic or integrated explanations. It could be argued that feminist criminology is a 'separatist criminology' that promotes fragmentation rather than integration at a time when one of the major problems in theoretical criminology is the lack of integration or an integrative theory. Attempts at integration within feminist criminology have been limited to the variables of gender and class and to a lesser extent race. The question remains, of course, whether female criminality is so fundamentally different from male criminality that it could be explained by a specific, unique, or separate theory.

SOME PROMISING TRENDS IN CRIMINOLOGICAL RESEARCH

I propose that empirical research turn the direction of inquiry around to focus initially on the foreground, rather than the background of crime. Let us for once make it our first priority to understand the qualities of experience that distinguish different forms of criminality.

Jack Katz (1988:4)
Seductions of Crime

Paying Attention to Desistance from Crime

Since the beginnings of scientific criminology, the discipline has suffered from an intellectual obsession with the causes of delinquency and crime, why some individuals become delinquents and criminals. In other words, the search for causes has been devoted, almost entirely and exclusively, to the onset or the advent of delinquency. Very little attention was paid to why a large percentage of delinquents and criminals stop committing crime or give up criminal activity. And yet, understanding why many criminals desist from crime can enhance our understanding of why they start or why some persist. One of the critics of this preoccupation with onset and total neglect of desistance is David Matza. In his critique of positive criminology (1964), Matza notes that criminological theories' assumption that delinquent behaviour is constrained through compulsion or commitment imply that 'involvement in delinquency would be more permanent and less transient, more pervasive and less intermittent than is apparently the case.' Matza writes:

Given the assumptions of constraint and differentiation, the frequency with which delinquents more or less reform is most perplexing. Most juvenile delinquents outgrow their delinquencies. Relatively few become adult offenders. They grow up, come to terms with their world, find a job or enter the armed forces, get married and indulge in ... only an occasional spree. Anywhere from 60 to 85 percent of delinquents do not apparently become adult violators. Moreover, this reform seems to occur irrespective of intervention of correctional agencies and irrespective of the quality of correctional service. (p. 22)

Matza points out that the vast majority of criminological theories fail to account for 'maturational reform' and that the few that do fall into the trap of contradicting their own assumptions regarding the constrained delinquent. He writes:

Why and by what process do youngsters once compelled or committed to delinquency cease being constrained? Why and by what process is the easy continuity from juvenile delinquency to adult crime implicit in almost all theories of delinquency not apparent in the world of real events? Biological theories are hardest hit by the frequency of maturational reform if only because the compulsion of biological constraint has a more literal meaning than psychic or social constraint and has been so taken. What is it that happens to body type, endocrine balance, or neuropathic diathesis at approximately age 20 that is related to reform? (p. 22)

As mentioned repeatedly before, maturational reform, desistance from delinquency challenge the basic tenets of positive criminology. Whether the central explanatory notion is that of 'compulsion' (biological/psychological theories) or that of 'commitment' (sociocultural explanations), the theories fail to explain why the causes that are assumed to cause delinquency or to push the individual towards crime, lose their influence all of a sudden and become inoperational. Learning theories, whose central point of departure is that criminal behaviour is learnt, fail to explain how a behaviour that is learnt and practised in adolescence is suddenly 'unlearnt' or 'delearnt'. Even the labelling approach which rejects the notion of pathology was meant to explain persistence in crime and not desistance from crime. It tries to explain why some delinquents continue rather than why the majority do stop.

The formidable challenge posed to positive criminology by the concept of 'maturational reform' has led some criminologists (West and Farrington, 1977; Cusson and Pinsonnault, 1986) to start exploring the phenomenon of desistance from delinquency and to try to find out why it is that a large number of those who commit acts of delinquency or crime cease these activities once they have reached a certain age.

Attempts to Understand Conformity

The state of nature is a state of freedom from controls. Behaviour is directed to the satisfaction of basic needs, urges and drives. The process of 'socialization' is a process aimed at teaching and inculcating certain controls. Children's behaviour is natural behaviour. This is why they have to be taught how to control their impulses, their urges, their drives and how to satisfy their needs in a socially acceptable ways. They are ordered not to do this and not to do that, to behave in such and such a way, and to not conduct themselves in such manner. Social controls therefore are not natural but artificial and learned controls. This is why they have to be enforced by threatening and coercive means to counter the ever present tendency of human beings to revert to the state of nature. The endless search for the causes of crime overlooks the fact that most acts of delinquency and crime are actually reversions to a more natural state. If this is true then what needs to be explained is not why the controls fail but why they succeed, not delinquency but conformity.

Feminist criminologists are to be given credit for drawing attention to the importance of studying conformity and of explaining why it is that women are much more conformist than men are, why it is that females commit much less crime than men do. Heidensohn (1985) reports that in England approximately half the male population will be convicted of some offence at some time during their lives compared with only 15 per cent of the female population. This seems to be similar to Australian and North American trends (Allen, 1988). Heidensohn (1985:ix) points out that:

> Women have apparently no less capacity than men for committing criminal acts, nor do they face formally different rules and laws, but their official criminality tends to be lower, less frequent and less serious.

The need to explain women's conformity is a theme that is constantly referred to in feminist writings on crime. Leonard (1982:41) insists that 'the most challenging and unexplained issue is the astonishing absence of criminality within the female population.' Gregory (1986:58), quoted earlier, maintains that the very absence of crime amongst certain groups is no less important than its presence. She affirms that 'the lack of criminal activity within certain groups is as pertinent to the explanation as the high concentration of crime within other groups'.

It goes without saying that the study and analysis of conformity can yield great benefits for the policies of crime prevention and control. As Hart (1985:300) points out:

> If social and cultural factors have prevented the female half of the population from committing many crimes, the moral might be that we should reconsider as far as is within our power, the conventional forms of the upbringing and socialization of males.

With the exception of social control theories, few criminological theories (see for example, containment theory, Reckless, 1961:355) have paid attention to the factors that insulate many young people from crime, that prevent them from joining gangs, from engaging in criminal activities, and from choosing a criminal career.

In recent years, criminologists interested in elderly criminality (Fattah and Sacco, 1989) have tried to offer some explanations for the fact that the elderly are more conformist than the young, for why elderly criminality is only a fraction of young people's criminality.

From the Search for Causes to the Analysis of Motives

With notable exceptions (psychoanalytic theory, exchange theory, equity theory, rational choice, routine activities approach) the motives for the act are usually absent in the explanations of crime. Rejection of the voluntaristic, hedonistic notions of the classical school and the unqualified acceptance of the hard or soft determinism of positivism are probably responsible for criminologists seemingly deliberate omission of motives in their explanatory theories and models. One cannot but be surprised that the word 'motive' does not figure in the subject index of most criminology textbooks! Authors of these textbooks who devote entire chapters to the 'causes' of crime never care to explain to the reader the difference between 'cause' and 'motive.' One rare exception is Gwynn Nettler, who in his book *Explaining Crime* (1974:201) took the trouble of pointing out that causes and motives are neither identical nor interchangeable concepts:

> 'Reason,' 'motive,' and 'cause' are terms that are sometimes used interchangeably and sometimes distinctively. Our discussion illustrates good reasons for keeping the concepts separate. The reasons for an action may not be the motive for it; and the motive, as it is commonly understood, may not be operating as the cause of the action.

Cusson (1983:26) talks about the 'goals of the offence', the 'purpose of the crime', the 'meaning of the crime', the 'result that the author means to achieve by this act' and makes a clear distinction between these and the notion of cause as used in etiological research in criminology.

Until recently, most criminological theories have been concerned with the 'causes' of criminal behaviour. Whether the talk is about biological inferiority, glandular dysfunctions, mental disorder, psychological abnormality, anomie, differential association, differential opportunity, environmental influences, whether the talk is about strain, social bonds, or social control, the reference is to the causes *not* the motives of the behaviour. Motives such as need, greed, profit, gain, revenge, jealousy, lust, rage, love, hate, excitement, pleasure, fun, thrill, power, and so on are not taken into account and do not constitute part of the explanations. This is surprising since human behaviour is purposeful behaviour and the key to understanding it is unquestionably the motive or the need the perpetrator is trying to satisfy by engaging in that behaviour. In view of this rather axiomatic observation, the theories' deliberate omission of any reference to the motives is rather perplexing.

It appears that criminologists are somewhat unable to free themselves from the early positivist belief that crime is a 'natural occurrence' that has 'natural causes'. While this is true of accidents, (whose causes should be the subject of thorough inquiries and analyses), the case of criminal behaviour is rather different. Crime, with the exception of offences of negligence (which incidentally are not the ones aimed by the causal explanations), is a deliberate, purposeful, motivated behaviour. If the violent behaviour, to use one example, is an instant retaliation or an act of self-defence then its explanation lies not in some psychopathology or family background but in the MOTIVE for the violence, what is to be achieved by the violence.

Some criminologists have gone as far as denying that motives are key ingredients in criminal behaviour. In their summary of Hirschi's social control theory published in 1969, Williams and McShane (1994:188) make the following statement:

> While not all social control theorists have done so, Hirschi expressly rejected the idea that any motivation is necessary for deviant behaviour to occur.

His association with Michael Gottfredson, with whom he has been publishing jointly in recent years, must have led Hirschi to revise his earlier position. Thus, in their book *A General Theory of Crime* (1990:256), they declare that:

> ... our theory suggests that the motive to crime is inherent in or limited to immediate gains provided by the act itself. There is no larger purpose behind rape, or robbery, or murder, or theft, or embezzlement, or insider trading. Therefore policies that seek to reduce crime by the satisfaction of theoretically derived wants (e.g., equality, adequate housing, good jobs, self-esteem) are likely to be unsuccessful... . Because offenders do not have overwhelming impulses to commit crime, our theory suggests that some limited benefit can accrue to programs that focus on variables necessary to the commission of particular criminal or deviant acts.

Recently, Hirschi seems to have reversed his earlier view altogether because in a paper published four years after the book (1994:423), he and Gottfredson make an unambiguous statement. They categorically declare that 'causal theories must be motivational theories'.

Gottfredson and Hirschi's rediscovery of motives is characteristic of a new trend in criminology, a shift of emphasis from causes to motives. This new emphasis is quite visible in the work of Katz (1988), Cornish and Clarke (1986), Cohen and Felson (1979), Clarke and Felson (1993) among others.

Glenn Walters's (1990) theory of the criminal lifestyle is also particularly worth noting because of the heavy emphasis it places on the offender's motives. The ninth postulate of the theory affirms that 'criminal events can be understood as incorporating a complex interlinking of thoughts, motives, and behaviours.' Walters (1990:94) explains this particular postulate in the following manner:

A primary tenet of the lifestyle theory of criminality is that cognition, motive, and action are meaningfully connected. It is reasoned further that the convergence between certain thoughts, motives and behaviours is stronger in some instances than in others. Stated somewhat differently, there appear to be several clusters of behaviours that correspond more closely with certain thoughts and motives than others.

What is most surprising is that it took criminologists so long to rediscover the vital importance of studying and analyzing the motives of delinquency and crime despite findings of delinquency research suggesting how important these motives are in explaining the phenomenon (Downes, 1966; Cusson, 1983). Downes's (1966) observations of delinquency among adolescent boys in East London in the early 1960s illustrate well the importance of motives. 'Status frustration', 'alienation', and 'delinquent subculture' were concepts that did not seem to fit descriptions of boys involved intermittently in offences of the fighting/joy-riding/theft/vandalism variety. Typically, they were not members of structured gangs (see Downes and Rock, 1988:147).

Downes and Rock (1988:148) point out that the most frequent of the reasons quoted by the boys themselves for delinquency was boredom. To them delinquency is a means of alleviating boredom, an exciting behaviour. Downes and Rock (1988:149) identify three linkages between delinquency and excitement: delinquency is the *means* to buying excitement; delinquency is the raw material of excitement; and delinquency is a *by-product* of the pursuit of actions that are exciting in themselves.

The emphasis in Cusson's (1983) study *Why Delinquency?* is also on the motives for the delinquent behaviour, or what Cusson calls 'goals of the offence' (p. 25). Having noted that delinquent behaviour is fairly widespread among young people of all classes and backgrounds, Cusson's thesis is that 'delinquent activities allow adolescents to satisfy many desires, to solve some real problems, to live intensely, and to enjoy themselves thoroughly. It is one means of obtaining what most people are searching for: excitement, possessions, power, and the defence of essential self-interests.'

To understand delinquent activity Cusson (1983:25) suggests that one should start by looking for the objective, the goal, what the delinquent wanted to achieve by his act: revenge? the victim's money? This type of answer is the opposite of the one formulated in causal studies, for example: 'he killed because he was a psychopath'. Cusson is critical of criminologists who for a long time have rejected this goal-orientated approach 'because it is one that allows no distinction between the delinquent and non-delinquent.' Cusson insists that the arguments of the rejectionists are inspired by the 'differentialist' obsession which, since Lombroso, has never ceased to haunt criminology. In Cusson's words:

> There has been a preoccupation with nothing other than what constitutes the difference between the criminal and the non-criminal. Like the alchemists who were ever seeking the philosopher's stone, criminologists continue to look for the difference in nature between the delinquent and the non-delinquent. Obviously their research will be in vain. For criminals belong to the human species, and their behaviour can be understood with the same logic as that used in the case of all men. And if we agree that delinquents are men before being delinquents, crime must be studied the same way any 'normal' behaviour would be studied. (p. 29)

From Dispositional Theories to Situational Theories

Fifty years ago, Sutherland (1947) suggested that explanations of deviance and crime are either situational or dispositional, and that of the two, situational explanations might be the more important. Commenting on Sutherland's statement, Birbeck and La Free (1993:113) state that despite Sutherland's remark, sociologists focused for the following four decades, with a few notable exceptions, on dispositional theories to the near total exclusion of situational variables. Birbeck and La Free (1993:114) offer three reasons that help explain this total neglect of situational variables: (1) they refer to the sociological training of most criminologists which leads them to think of the setting for crime in terms of broader social phenomena, for example, subcultures and parenting styles rather than situations; (2) the fact that individuals sometimes respond differently to the same situation has encouraged criminologists to relegate situational experience to a status dependent on dispositions; (3) they suggest that the systematic examination of situational variables is theoretically and methodologically complex, requiring the definition of key concepts, the development of conceptual models of the interaction between actors and situations, and the design of appropriate empirical research.

Extensive research on violence, vandalism, and other forms of antisocial behaviour led Zimbardo (1978:157) to challenge the prevailing stereotypes which locate the source of evil in people. He insists that 'we have been programmed by our socialization process and basic institutions to accept doctrines of *individual* guilt, sin, culpability, and failure, as well as to accept the cult of the ego, the strength of character, and the stability of personality.'

According to Zimbardo, contemporary social psychology maintains that we all *overestimate* the extent to which behaviour – be it evil, good, or neuter – is *dispositionally controlled*, while at the same time we systematically *underestimate* the degree to which it is *situationally controlled* (p. 59).

Criminal behaviour is dynamic behaviour and cannot therefore be adequately explained by the static theories that have dominated the discipline of criminology for over a century. The manifest and generally acknowledged failure of these theories (see above) points to the need for a new, dynamic approach that shifts the focus from predisposing factors to environmental, situational, triggering, and catalytic factors; from the notion of propensities and inclinations to the concept of opportunity. Such a dynamic situational approach pays great attention to the contexts in which violent confrontations occur and analyzes these confrontations as situated transactions (Luckenbill, 1977). It maintains that many crimes are situation-specific, context-specific, and target-specific. And in contrast to the dispositional perspective which postulates that the impulses for crime come from within the individual and are manifestations of the psychopathology of the offender, the situational approach looks upon criminal behaviour as a response to environmental stimuli, stimuli that ineluctably include the characteristics and the behaviour of the potential victim (Fattah, 1991).

The situational approach pays also great attention to victim-offender interactions. As Felson and Steadman (1983:59-60) point out:

> Outcomes of an aggressive interaction are not determined by either the characteristics or the initial goals of the participants; rather, they are at least partly a function of events that occur during the incident. In other words, violence is, in part, situationally determined – the result of events and circumstances that cause a conflict to escalate.

The situational approach posits that many crimes of personal violence, particularly spontaneous, impulsive, unplanned, and unpremeditated ones, are outcomes of long or brief interactions between two or more individuals. As such, these crimes cannot be adequately explained by static theories of criminal behaviour that focus on offender characteristics but give no consideration to the dynamic forces unique to each situation. It is these dynamic forces that determine, condition, shape, or influence the offender's behaviour in that particular situation. Theories attempting to explain criminal behaviour by referring to the biological or psychological characteristics or social background of the offender ignore the crucial role played by situational and triggering factors in the etiology of crime. In contrast to the dispositional approaches, the situational approach is a dynamic one. One of the underlying premises of this approach is that character attributes and personality traits, such as aggressiveness, callousness, and dishonesty, are neither constant nor absolute and thus, alone, have very little explanatory value. Some individuals become aggressive only when they have consumed alcohol or when they are provoked. Others may use violence only when their vanity is hurt. Some men become violent only in situations where they feel the need to assert their maleness. Some individuals may be shy and withdrawn without peer support only to become extremely mean when in the presence of, and under pressure from, their peer group. People may be scrupulously honest in one situation and shamelessly dishonest in another.

The situational approach highlights the inherent weaknesses of dispositional theories of criminal behaviour by showing that everyone is capable of committing a crime in certain situations, when under certain pressures, in the presence of certain triggering factors.

Violent behaviour, for example, could hardly be understood without a thorough analysis of the transaction that occurs between the participants prior to the perpetration of violence (Hepburn, 1973). Although this might seem axiomatic, and despite the obvious dynamic and interactionist nature of violent crime, criminological research, with only a few exceptions, has focused on the perpetrator's characteristics and background and has ignored the verbal exchanges between the participants prior to the use of physical force.

The situational approach also pays great attention to the problems of communication in confrontational encounters, such as rape and robbery situations. It analyses the subjective definitions and interpretations of the participants and see this as a key to understanding and explaining their actions and their responses. It also examines how victims respond to face-to-face victimization and the impact of the response on the final outcome of the victimization event (Fattah, 1984; 1991). The findings of this type of research could be used to provide potential victims with some guidelines on how to behave in specific victimization situations to minimize the chances of physical injury and of the crime being completed.

One situational theory that is rapidly gaining acceptance in criminology is *opportunity theory*. The idea that opportunity shapes and influences people's behaviour is not new. The old proverb, used by Rossini as the title of one of his operas, 'the opportunity makes the thief', is a crude formulation of the theory. The concept of opportunity carries different meanings in criminology and the relationship between opportunity and crime is manifold (Fattah, 1993c). Opportunity theory places the emphasis not on the characteristics of the offender but on the characteristics of the situation. The notion of opportunity links environmental criminology (Brantingham and Brantingham, 1984), to the rational choice perspective (Cornish and Clarke, 1986), and to victimology (Fattah, 1991). Opportunities for victimization are not evenly present in time or space and they are greatly influenced by the behaviour of potential victims/targets. The rational choices offenders make, particularly with regard to target selection, are strongly influenced by opportunities and victims' behaviour.

NOTES

1. A few years ago in the USA, the National Institute of Justice together with the MacArthur Foundation launched a major multimillion dollar research program aimed at finding the causes of criminality. The research program has a distinguished advisory board chaired by Yale sociologist/criminologist Albert J. Reiss, Jr.
2. Downes and Rock (1988:89) maintain that Durkheim's argument that crime is a normal, functional and even healthy social phenomenon put functionalism in bad odour with criminology (as distinct from sociology) and they quote John Mays (1964) who remarked that, taken literally, it was a 'morally repugnant' argument.

Criminology Future: What Does the Future Hold for Criminology?

12 The Future of Criminology and Criminology of the Future

...a criminology liberated from its scientific individualism and blinkered empiricism has a future potential that is full of challenge and far from pessimistic.

> A. Keith Bottomley (1979:150)
> *Criminology in Focus:*
> *Past Trends and Future Prospects*

Criminals of the future will probably have many of the same motives as today's crooks... greed, lust, revenge... but the ways in which they carry out their crimes may be radically different. With technology now into development, a criminal will be able to invade your home using computer links, telephone and two-way video taps. He or she may attack you with psychological harassment or mind manipulation techniques, demanding protection money to stay out of your brain. New technology will make all these things possible, even likely.

> Tom Keenan (1984:12)
> Transcript of the CBC programme 'Ideas'

THE FUTURE OF CRIMINOLOGY

In his introduction to the edited book *The Futures of Criminology*, Nelken (1994:2) has this to say about the future of criminology:

> ...if futurology were the aim, the safest prediction of the immediate future of the discipline (as in the prediction of recidivism) would be that it would see more of the same sort of work which currently represents the mainstream. Outside of feminism, for example, the attempt to produce a postmodern criminology has still hardly begun.

The Finnish criminologist Patrick Törnudd (1985) is probably right: 'There will never be a Nobel prize in criminology.' In physics, in astronomy, in biology, in chemistry, in archeology, there is, and there will always be, place and opportunities for startling, spectacular, and far-reaching discoveries. By their very nature social sciences do not lend themselves to earth-shattering revelations. This comment is not meant to denigrate the disciplines that study this or that aspect of society. It is simply a reminder of the basic differences between the natural and the social sciences. Galileo's principles of isochronism, of inertia, Newton's law of gravitation, Einstein's theory of relativity will probably survive and withstand the test of time. Social science theories, on the other hand, are impermanent, changeable, replaceable, and often untestable.

Because of its specific subject matter, criminology, more than other social sciences, is subject to serious limitations. Awareness of these limitations should not be cause for pessimism but for realism; it should not be reason for resignation but for perseverance. As Törnudd (1985:67) points out,

> The permanent feature of all criminological research is that its subject-matter, crime, is a manifestation of counteracting social forces. This precludes quantum leaps in the organization of criminological knowledge or in the art of applying this knowledge. The self-regulative mechanisms may make even real improvements in the understanding of crime or in the art of dealing with crime difficult to discern.

Yes, there might never be a Nobel Prize for criminology. However, in the age of insecurity in which we live, criminologists' positions and status are safe and secure. At the risk of stating the obvious, one can say that as long as there is crime, there will be a need for a science of crime. An academia free of criminology is only possible if we can have a crime-free society. The more changes occur in the forms and patterns of crime and the more crime there is, the stronger will be the need for research on crime, if not to find its elusive causes, then at least to understand its manifestations, its context, its seductive appeal and to find effective means for its prevention or its reduction.

Predicting the future, particularly in the social sciences is, at best, a hazardous exercise. But social studies would not be complete unless they included a significant historical component and some reflection on the society of the future. The ideal social science curriculum is one that examines and analyzes where we were, where we are, and where we are heading.

For criminologists, like myself, who have no crystal ball, the only available option is to try to make a realistic appraisal of the future of criminology based on a careful reading of its history, its evolution, and its present state. Such a reading and such an analysis lead to the conclusion that the future of criminology is a bright one. Despite the absence of a unified conceptual framework and the diversity of paradigms, despite the apparent lack of success in the fields of etiology and crime prevention, despite the recent setbacks and the current sombre mood, there are ample reasons for optimism about the future of criminology. Certainly I disagree with Taylor, Walton, and Young's (1973) claim that radical analysis is bound to make criminology peripheral and marginal. Quite the contrary, I have no doubt that criminology will, in the future, occupy a prominent place among the social sciences, though it is undeniable that it will be different from criminology as we know it today. Rather than being in a state of crisis; criminology is currently going through a specific stage of development and is suffering from the pains of maturation and growing up.

Criminology is a very dynamic discipline. It lacks the stability of the natural sciences and undergoes dramatic changes within short periods of time. The marked differences between criminology of the 1990s and criminology of the 1920s or 1950s should alert us to the perils of long-term predictions. And because funds for criminological research come mainly from governments, criminology is susceptible to changes in the political climate and fluctuations in the public mood. This factor explains the fads and fashions that appear now and then in criminological research and that are largely the result of research priorities set by funding agencies. Research conducted in the coming decades will shape and mold criminology of the future. The advances made and the branches of criminology in which they will occur will be determined to a large extent by future research priorities. These priorities will be greatly influenced by the interests of politicians and policy-makers.

There are sufficient indications that the years to come will witness a continuing and even an accelerated shrinkage in the funds allocated by governments for independent research. As a result, policy-makers will have an ever-growing say in, and an increasing influence upon, the areas to be researched and the directions research will take. Inevitably, this will lead to a decline of basic and theoretical research in criminology and to the proliferation of narrowly focused applied studies. Politicians and policy-makers have a clear preference for research that has concrete and preferably instant practical applications, research with immediate pay-off, whose results could be translated quickly into policy and political action or that could provide empirical support to politically made decisions. Criminal justice research, for many years to come, is likely to be increasingly pragmatic, atheoretical, and policy-orientated.

Future Changes in Crime

Since criminology by definition is the science of crime, criminology of the future will be greatly influenced by future changes in the nature and forms of crime. The structure of criminality in future decades, its dimensions, and its trends will have a strong bearing on the orientation criminology will take.

Crime is a dynamic phenomenon. And while some traditional crimes are likely to persist for centuries, many present-day crimes will eventually disappear only to be replaced by new forms that have emerged. I personally believe that the most important single factor responsible for the fundamental changes in the nature of crime in the 20th century has been the automobile. Yet surprisingly, there are very few criminological studies examining and analyzing the role the car has played in transforming many types of crime and in producing new forms of criminality.

It is more than likely that the 21st century will witness even greater transformations in criminality. This time, the technology responsible for the change will be computer technology. The computer will become as a vital feature of life in the 21st century as the automobile has become in the second half of this century. It will drastically change every aspect, every facet of life in most parts of the world. It is bound to produce profound changes in the nature and forms of crime. The branch of criminology that holds the greatest promise right now is, no doubt, the one dealing with the infinite variety of present and future computer crime as well as the future implications of computer technology to many types of property crime.

Thanks to computer technology, crime in the 21st century will be very different from crime today. And future generations of delinquents might bear little resemblance to past or present generations of criminals. Many are likely to be bright, well-educated, and well-to-do. And while differences according to age might not totally disappear, gender and racial differences are likely to become less pronounced. The lack of identification with criminals in present-day society and the current dichotomy dividing the population into two distinct groups – we, the law abiding and they, the law breaking – might change. If it does, it is likely to bring about a positive change in attitudes towards criminals, who will no longer be regarded as those against us but as those amongst us.

Whether all this happens or not remains to be seen, but one thing is almost certain: it is that most contemporary criminological theories will be obsolete. The changing nature of crime and the changing make-up of the criminal population will deal the fatal blow to theories of crime that equate deviance with pathology and take as their point of departure the presumed fundamental differences between criminals and other citizens. The new forms of crime, the characteristics of the future generations of delinquents will reveal the inherent inadequacies and the shortcomings of most contemporary theories, especially those of the biological and psychological variety. The demise of these theories will be hastened by a likely increase in political violence and a decline in acquisitive violence. Such developments will greatly emphasize the need for new criminological theories with a strong political dimension, theories that may succeed where present ones have failed.

Future Changes in the Criminal Law

The state of interdependence between criminology and the criminal law means that criminology of the future will be greatly influenced by the changes that will take place in the criminal code. Although it is certain that criminal codes of the future will be substantially different from current ones, it is difficult to tell what their basic philosophy will be.

Norval Morris (1973) believes that the criminal law of the future will be predominantly administrative, reserving punishment for a persistent flouting of regulatory controls. Whatever the philosophy and orientation of future criminal codes may be, one can fairly predict that they will not be dominated, like present ones, by an obsession with the right of property, a right termed by Beccaria as 'a terrible and perhaps unnecessary right'. In the 20th century, North American society achieved a great deal of affluence, and it is likely that the trend will continue in the coming century. There is every reason to believe, therefore, that North American society in the 21st century will be characterized by even greater prosperity, by an abundance of goods and services. In an extremely affluent society the right of individual property is bound to lose the central importance it now enjoys. The relative seriousness of property offences, which constitute about 70 per cent of all crime, will undoubtedly decline. Other things that are now taken for granted, privacy and freedom, for example, will become more fragile and hence much more precious commodities than material goods, which will be abundant.

The primary function of the criminal code will be to protect these valuable and vulnerable commodities. More so because the same technological advances that will make it easier to protect whatever material possessions one has will pose greater and greater threats to human rights and freedoms. This is not say that property crime will disappear, but only that it will cease to be the dominant mode of criminality that it is today. There are two kinds of society where property crimes are neither dominant nor prominent: societies with very few goods and societies with too many goods. The capitalist system is, by its very nature, an inequitable system. Increasing affluence is not likely to eliminate or even reduce the inequalities in wealth and power. Affluence will simply mean that the have nots of the future will be living far above the subsistence level, that the vast majority of the population will be free from material need. But since freedom from material need does not mean freedom from material incentive (and the experience of socialist countries provides solid empirical evidence confirming this), property offences, in newer forms but lesser numbers, will continue to be committed. It is almost certain that many of the current forms will be depenalized; others might even be decriminalized. Many will probably be transferred from the domain of the criminal law to that of civil and administrative law.[1]

The 21st century is likely to witness a tremendous expansion of the above laws at the expense of the criminal law, which in all likelihood will be used less and less as a means of conflict resolution. Future changes in the modes of social control, the end of imprisonment as we know it today, the introduction of new sanctions based on the notions of compensation and restitution, will render the division between the law of crime and the law of torts much less important than it is right now. The boundaries between the criminal law and civil law will become even more blurred in the future than they are at present (Fattah, 1992).

Future changes in the criminal code will likely deprive radical criminologists of one of their most popular arguments. They will no longer be able to claim that the code is an instrument designed to protect the interests of the powerful and to ensure the continuing domination and oppression of the proletariat. It might be true that present criminal codes, whose origins can be traced to an era when class differences were much more pronounced, do reflect the moral values of the elites and do protect the material interests of the upper social strata. But criminal codes of the future will likely be different. The values they will be designed to protect will not be those of any given social class but will be the values and norms of a higher order, of a more universal nature.

In a society obsessed with a never-ending pursuit of wealth and material goods, protection of property becomes one of the most important functions of the criminal code. The major threat to the society of the future will not be, as it is now, the violation of property rights. This threat will pale in comparison to the threats posed by nuclear and other technologies. People's fears in the future will not be that their property will be stolen or their houses broken into; sophisticated security systems and comprehensive public insurance schemes will take care of that. Their major fear will be of major environmental catastrophes, nuclear or biological terrorism, or genetic technologies that could wipe out the human race.

There will be other, lesser fears than those created by the advances in genetic technology, genetic engineering, and the manipulation of the human embryo. A major part of future criminal codes will have to be devoted to the regulation of previously unregulated areas, such as organ transplants, organ sales, artificial insemination, test tube fertilization, gene and sperm banks, uterus rental, and many other issues related to the technical manipulation of human reproduction. And it is easy to imagine how difficult it will be to try to explain the new forms of criminality by using obsolete and antiquated criminological theories developed during the 20th century. What is important to mention here is that the material interests, which are currently the focus of the criminal code, will surrender their place to superior moral values. The interests of humanity at large, not the interests of any particular class, will provide the guiding principles for the criminal code of the future.

Criminology may be expected therefore, as Wollan (1980) predicted, to become somewhat more concerned for values and, hence, to shift slightly from the empirical, scientific end of the spectrum toward the normative, philosophical end.

Future Changes in Social Reaction to Crime

Since the study of societal reaction to crime and deviance constitutes an important component of criminology, it seems logical to expect that changes in this reaction would have a significant impact on criminology of the future. Societal reaction to crime is a global term encompassing several components, such as society's attitude to crime and deviance, society's penal philosophy, modes of formal and informal social control, criminal sanctions used against those who break the laws, and so on.

Attitudes to deviance depend on one's interpretation of it and the causes believed to be behind it. Interpretation of deviance is a function of the frame of reference in a given society at a given era. The history of social attitudes to deviance reveals three distinct phases: the mystification of deviance, the criminalization of deviance, and the medicalization of deviance.

The *mystification of deviance* corresponds to the era when demonological or other-worldly interpretations prevailed. Deviance was explained with reference to some 'other-world' power or an Omnipotent spirit. In primitive and preliterate animistic societies, it is believed to be the work of evil spirits or evil forces. In the theological age, it was blamed on Satan or the Devil. The purpose of punishment, as Pfohl (1985:25) points out, 'was to purge the body of the sinner of traces of the Devil and thereby restore the body of the community as a whole to its proper relation to God'.

The Age of Enlightenment brought about a fundamental change in the frame of reference and consequently in attitudes to deviance. The view of humans as reasonable, rational hedonistic beings endowed with free will meant that they could be deterred by the fear of punishment. The logical outcome of this thinking, namely, the *criminalization of deviance*, is intended to force potential deviants into conformity through the threat of criminal sanctions.

Positivism and advances in medicine and psychiatry were bound to bring yet another change in the explanation of, and attitudes towards, deviance. Deviance would no longer be regarded as a legal entity but as sickness, and deviant behaviours would be given medical meanings. The view of deviance as pathology also meant a shift from punishment to treatment, the divestment of criminal justice and the coming of the therapeutic state (Kittrie, 1971;1).

The *medicalization of deviance* and the advent of treatment could be easily seen from the following quotation from George Ives (1914:335):

> In the future, when the courts convict a prisoner, he will not merely disappear from view, to undergo a senseless, indiscriminating punishment. He will not, in fact, be punished more than any other patient; but he may have to undergo a course of treatment varied according to his special need, which may, or may not, be painful in its operation.

What is the next phase? I believe we are moving slowly into an age that is characterized by the *toleration of deviance*. Homogeneous, monocultural societies are something of the past. Industrialization, urbanization, modern means of transportation, and mass communication have resulted in a breakdown of cultural, if not geographic, boundaries. They have led to unprecedented waves of migration and to unparalleled population mobility and heterogeneity. The declining birth rate in Western industrial societies will make it imperative in future decades, despite an ever growing use of robots, to import huge numbers of foreign workers. So the society of the future will be even more ethnically and culturally heterogeneous than it is today. Its main feature will be its extreme human and cultural diversity, the multiplicity of religions, mores, customs, and moralities.

In such a society, deviance will not be too conspicuous, it will not evoke a forceful reaction nor strong demands for conformity. Diversity will enhance the levels of tolerance to deviance. Furthermore, one of the basic rights that will be demanded and ultimately recognized in the society of the future will be the right to be different. And, ultimately, Taylor, Walton, and Young's (1973:282) dream of 'a society in which the facts of human diversity, whether personal, organic or social, are not subject to the power to criminalize' may come true. The toleration of deviance will lead to mass decriminalization and depenalization of many behaviours that are still governed by anachronistic laws. This, however, is a long-term development. In the near future, social attitudes to crime and deviance will continue to oscillate between harshness and mildness, between punitiveness and leniency, as a function of politics and the state of the economy. And we do know what negative impact economic insecurity and economic crises can have on public attitudes towards criminals and punishments.

Attitudes will also be influenced by the media and by a variety of social movements, such as populism and feminism. Whether populism will be a major political force in the 21st century is difficult to tell. There are no antecedents to instruct us about the role ordinary people play in a highly technological, post-industrial society. Feminism, on the other hand, is here to stay. In a relatively short period of time, feminists have succeeded in bringing about important changes in social attitudes towards sex crimes, particularly rape, family violence, discrimination against women, and so on. The change in attitudes paved the way to changes in the criminal code and in criminal justice practices in many areas.

Grassroots movements have contributed either to restoring, reinforcing, or changing certain attitudes. The victim movement has been successful in focusing attention on the plight of victims of crime and in forcing changes in the law and the justice system. It was influential in the creation of victim services. One group, MADD (Mothers Against Drunken Drivers) can be credited with legal, judicial, and attitudinal changes towards the particular behaviour of impaired driving.

Other groups, on the other hand, have been responsible not for change but for blocking, hindering, or delaying change. The pro-life movement has consistently opposed any attempt aimed at modernizing the laws related to the termination of pregnancy. In the US, the gun lobby has resisted and successfully prevented many attempts towards effective gun control. Religious fundamentalists have been trying very hard, sometimes successfully, sometimes unsuccessfully, to reverse the liberalization trend of the 1950s and the 1960s and have gone as far as demanding a return to censorship.

Radical theories that have as one of their central components the concept of power will need to be revised to take into account the shift in the balance of power from the elites to the grassroots. The notion of economic interest needs also to be re-examined. The economic interests of the National Rifle Association are too visible to be ignored. It is doubtful, however, that economic interests alone are the mobilizing force behind victim groups, pro-life lobbies, and feminist associations, to name but a few.

Future Changes in the Punishment of Offenders

The evolution of punishment is a sad but fascinating subject not only because it documents man's cruelty and inhumanity to man but also because it confirms Durkheim's claim that the history of punishment is a history of constant abolition. It is always reassuring to learn that punishment has only a past but no future. History teaches us that no punishment is permanent, transcendental, or indispensable. All punishments seem to disappear once they have served their presumed purpose and once society has found more suitable substitutes. With the exception of the death penalty, old-time punishments have disappeared in modern, civilized societies. The bilboes, the ducking stool, the whipping post, the brank, the stock, the pillory, and the scarlet letter can only be found in history books, novels and in horror museums.

Somehow, the death penalty has defied social evolution and still remains in the criminal codes of many countries as an anachronism, as a relic from the past, a vestige from a bygone era. Despite its persistence, social and penal evolution dictate that its days are numbered. Total abolition will come when respect for human life reaches such a point that it becomes too abhorrent to use death as a means of punishment. It was the growing respect for the human body in the 18th and 19th centuries that led to the removal of corporal punishments, maiming, and body mutilations from the arsenal of penal sanctions.

The abolition of prisons will probably take longer than that of the death penalty, but it will inevitably come. Several factors, the least important of which will be the ever-accelerating costs, will contribute to bringing about an end to imprisonment. Continuing research on the effectiveness of prisons as a deterrent is likely to yield solid empirical evidence showing their failure to perform their primary function. And at some point in the future, respect for liberty and freedom will be such that society will find it too abominable to punish people by depriving them of one of their fundamental and inalienable rights. But above all, imprisonment will hardly be necessary in the society of the future. As Nils Christie (1968:172) predicted some three decades ago:

> In the age of electronics, it will be possible to exercise effective control over criminal offenders outside prisons. Cheaper, simpler, and, in the opinion of many, more humane substitutes for prison walls will be provided by radio transmitters fastened to criminal offenders, by radio-locaters, by telephone reports from criminal offenders to a controlling apparatus with facilities for voice analysis, etc., etc. The enforcement of an order to stay within a defined geographical area will be carried out so effectively that a stay in prison can be avoided.

What sounds like an Orwellian scenario is already with us. Many of these electronic prison substitutes are now in use in the United States and Canada and are being introduced in European countries such as the Netherlands. This development signals the dawn of a new era in the history of social control, an era where the technological control of human beings and their behaviour will become a popular and widespread practice. In the highly technological society of the future, the temptations to use such methods of control will be overwhelming, and the costs will be very modest compared to the costs of imprisonment. The social dangers are likely to be minimized and the ethical objections will probably be overcome. Depriving people of their liberty was rationalized in the eighteenth century as more humane than corporal punishments, and the technological control of human beings will be rationalized in the 21st century as more humane than imprisonment.

The image of the state control apparatus of the future is rather frightening. New forms of both incumbent and insurgent terrorism will undoubtedly emerge, the latter being fomented by the persistence of the political and social injustices that breed violence. Insurgent terrorism invariably generates a forceful reaction from governments because of the threat it creates to the authority of the state and the challenge it poses to the legitimacy of power. Recent events are very instructive in this respect. The risk of victimization by a terrorist act for a British, Canadian or American citizen, when measured objectively and compared to other risks of modern life or to the risk of conventional criminal victimization, is very small and very remote. Yet, thanks to the sensationalized reporting by the media, the risk is magnified into an eminent danger. This fear, in turn, is used by politicians to create a climate of mass hysteria in order to justify all kinds of suppressive, oppressive, and repressive measures undertaken under the guise of fighting terrorism. The end result is a colossal expansion of the state control apparatus. The serious threats this expansion poses to human rights and freedoms are too obvious to need any elaboration. One of the dangers is the extension of counterinsurgency measures from political crime to conventional crime, from political violence to ordinary violence, from subversive groups to organized crime, from political activists to drug smugglers or traffickers.

One frightening scenario for the future is one that portrays 'a society so concerned with physical security that it is in grave danger of undermining the social democracy it wishes to protect.'[2] According to this scenario, Western democracies will slowly and gradually be transformed into 'big brother police states' as a result of the gradual removal of the constitutional limits on the exercise of power by the state, limits that distinguish a constitutional state from a police state (Cobler, 1978:143). According to Cobler such big brother police states will be characterized by an intrusion of police attitudes into all areas of social life and the generalization of an attitude dominated by ideas of 'security' and 'order'. Cobler (1978:146) paints the following picture of such a police state:

> Concepts deriving from police theory and methods are employed in an attempt to channel or quell political confrontations; they include 'order', 'orders', 'subordination', 'security' and 'prevention.' Police strategies of conflict management are used to defend 'normality' against any deviant political behaviour. Police institutions, following exclusively the logic of a campaign against an enemy, define what 'order' is and who 'disrupts' it.

The advent of the big brother police state will be facilitated by the great advances in computer and surveillance technology, which will offer previously undreamt of techniques of political control. This whole issue has hardly been examined, even by radical criminologists. A treatise on the place and role of computers in the technology of repression remains to be written.

The prospect of Western democracies being transformed into big brother police states does not hold great promise for radical or liberal criminology. The future of the social sciences in such a gloomy scenario would be bleak. Political protest would be harshly punished, political dissent would be severely repressed, and radicalism in academia would not be tolerated. As already mentioned (Chapter 9), social sciences need a favourable intellectual climate allowing freedom of thought and expression.

CRIMINOLOGY OF THE FUTURE

There is no such thing as a monolithic social science. It is impossible to speak of *the* future orientation of any social discipline since there are always multiple perspectives. Naturally, one may try to speculate on the dominant orientation of any discipline, for example, on what will be characterized as mainstream criminology 50 or 100 years from now.

The changes outlined above in crime, in the criminal code, in social attitudes to crime and deviance, in the methods of social control, mean that criminology of the future will be very different from contemporary criminology. Few of the current assumptions and hypotheses of traditional or radical criminology are likely to be confirmed; most will probably be proven wrong. Neither positivist criminology with its emphasis on individual pathology, on the abnormalities and peculiarities of criminals, nor radical criminology with its emphasis on class conflict and upper-class oppression of the proletariat will be able, at least in their present form and without major modifications, to provide satisfactory explanations for the dominant forms of crime in the mechanical, computerized, robotized society of the future.

The current criticisms that have been or are being leveled at the two major contending paradigms in criminology offer the best clues to criminology's future development. It seems logical to expect that as criminology moves into the 21st century, it will, as a result and in the light of these criticisms, modify its assumptions and hypotheses, re-examine its fundamental paradigms and theoretical perspectives, and reformulate its theories.

CURRENT DEFICIENCIES AS INDICATORS OF FUTURE ORIENTATIONS

Three somewhat different perspectives can be identified in contemporary criminology (see Chapter 7):

1. A *conservative*, correctionally oriented criminology also called *administrative criminology*, whose two basic premises are: the identification of deviance with pathology and the belief that law-breakers are fundamentally different from law-abiding citizens. Conservative criminology is pro-establishment. It accepts and helps maintain the official ideology. Not only does it accept the legitimacy of the legal order, it takes its legitimacy for granted, as a given, and sees it as inherent and absolute.

2. A *liberal* sociology of deviance leaning heavily on a labelling or interactionist approach. It is critical of the establishment and advocates changes in the law and the criminal justice system to reduce the biases and injustices inherent in the system. It questions the legitimacy of the legal order, sees legitimacy as relative, and believes that there is a legitimacy crisis. The law *per se* is seen as good, but many existing laws are bad and in need of reform.

3. A *radical*, Marxist criminology, which is neither correctionalist nor reformist. It is rejectionist, anti-establishment, and its aim is to change the economic and social orders. It demystifies and exposes the 'false' ideology that capitalism benefits the workers. Existing legal order is regarded as illegitimate, and the illegitimacy is viewed as inherent and absolute because the criminal law is used by the state and the ruling class to secure the survival of the capitalist system.[3]

As may be seen from this very crude division, there are three identifiable perspectives. Still, it is quite common in current criminological literature to divide criminology into two orientations: traditional or mainstream criminology and critical criminology. Traditional criminology is variously labelled conventional, administrative, correctionalist, reformist, positivist, clinical, applied, pragmatic, and so on. Critical criminology is labelled Marxist, socialist, materialist, new, anticorrectionalist, and so on. The labels 'critical' and 'radical' are often used interchangeably, which is misleading. It is true that one cannot be radical without being critical, but one can be critical without necessarily being radical.

The tendency to polarize criminology into two camps is unfortunate because it tends to ignore the plurality of perspectives within both traditional and critical criminology and tends to lump criminologists with substantially different views, and even different ideologies, into the same camp.

Since the emergence of the *new criminology*, radical criminologists have been quite vocal in their attacks on, and their criticism of, conventional, orthodox criminology. They criticized it for being unimaginative, ahistorical, and apolitical, even for depoliticizing criminological issues. They accused it of correctionalism and intellectual eclecticism and of advocating peacemeal reform. They deplored its narrow approach to the issue of crime and its failure to deal with the wider (or indeed the immediate origins) of crime and deviancy. These wider origins, they claim, could only be understood in terms of the rapidly changing economic and political contingencies of advanced industrial society (Taylor, Walton, and Young, 1973). They further deplored conventional criminology's refusal to deal with society as a totality and, indeed, for placing people apart from society. Conservative criminologists are criticized for ignoring the structure of power, for paying little or no attention to the sociology of law, and for their failing to address the 'provocative basic questions' posed by the persistence of crime, deviance, and dissent.

The critics struck back. The 'heavy-hitters' like Klockars (1980) and Mankoff (1980), a conflict theorist himself, criticized radical criminologists for their 'poor scholarship, embarrassing empirical failures, for their strident moral and political imperialism' (Klockars), 'for intellectual shoddiness bordering on anti-intellectualism' (Mankoff). The soft-hitters criticized radical criminology for being 'historically naive' and 'empirically shallow', for being 'emotionally based', 'intellectually biased', and 'scholastically bankrupt' (quoted from Inciardi, 1980:8).

Others cited 'radical criminology's metafunctionalism, instrumentalism, and romanticism of illegality' (Spitzer, 1980) and pointed to radical criminologists' neglect of crime in socialist countries, their deep political commitment and 'praxis', their shunning of empirical research, their 'religious' devotion to Marxist ideology and total belief in the 'goodness' of socialist society, and their 'overpoliticization' of crime (Shichor, 1980).

Paul Hirst (1975), a Marxist sociologist himself, criticized radical criminologists for seldom questioning their own theoretical–ideological point of departure and its relation to Marxist theory and for rarely questioning their own position, assumptions, and interests. He claimed that a true Marxist approach would abolish the field of crime and deviancy as a coherent object of study.

Another Marxist criminologist, David Greenberg (1976), charged that radical theorists have ignored the existence of a substantial consensus among members of the general public concerning many categories of crime. He also took them to task for failing to acknowledge that members of the working class are frequently the victims of crimes carried on by other underprivileged individuals from low income backgrounds, so that they have a stake in current laws and their enforcement (see Gibbons, 1979:190).

Predictions about the future of radical criminology abound. They vary from the dire, gloomy predictions of Karl Klockars (1980) to the reasoned, realistic prophecies of Don Gibbons (1979). Klockars predicts that the most visible and celebrated variety of radical criminology, namely, the one which draws its inspiration from Marx, will not survive the rigours of scholarly scrutiny. He believes its total bankruptcy will soon be declared and affirms that we are witnessing the late phase of Marxist criminology. Despite the demise of socialism in Europe, this extreme view seems unwarranted especially when one keeps in mind Pelfrey's survey of academic criminologists in which 57 per cent of the respondents indicated that the 'new criminology' is a viable alternative to traditional criminology. Pelfrey (1980) reports that the respondents were inclined toward the new criminology as a perspective with definite potential and one that is seen to be capable of transposing traditional criminology.

Huff's (1980) predictions regarding the conflict perspective are more moderate. He doubts that the conflict perspective could evolve into a grand theory of criminality and deviance although it has the potential of being much more systematically linked with general sociological theory.

Friedrichs (1980) offers two possible scenarios for the evolution of radical criminology: one negative and the other positive. The former stresses the potential splintering of the different streams within radical criminology as well as the ever-present dangers of co-optation. This pessimistic scenario echoes what Rock (1979:83) expressed just a year earlier when he wrote:

> It is conceivable that radical criminology will shatter into a host of subordinate criminologies, each veering towards a parent world view.

Friedrichs' second scenario considers the possibility that the emerging varieties of radical criminology will complement and strengthen each other and that by the 1990s the radical framework, being, in his view, the most responsive to the economic chaos of the 1980s, will have become the dominant criminological paradigm.

In Gibbons' (1979) opinion, such development is very unlikely. The probability that mainstream criminology will be declared dead and that a new radical or Marxist criminology will be ushered in as the dominant paradigm seems to him quite remote because as he points out,

> Radical criminologists are too few in number to be able to bring about such a result. Even more important...many of the major themes of radical criminology are ambiguous, overly simple, or inchoate, so that Marxist criminological theory is not sufficiently robust to capture the allegiance of most criminologists. (p. 195)

According to Gibbons (1979:195), the most likely development in the criminology of the future is one in which a modified brand of mainstream criminology will develop, informed by many of the themes that have appeared in recent years in the social labelling, and deviance literature, in conflict versions of criminological thought, and in radical-Marxist analysis.

It has been pointed out (Longmire, 1982) that there are barriers to the development of perspectives and methodologies critical of the dominant criminological practice. In a given society, the mainstream of any social science appears to be shaped by, and dependent upon, the existing social and economic orders. If this is true, then it follows that in a capitalist system mainstream social science cannot be Marxist and in a Marxist system it cannot be a traditional conventional one. It seems reasonable to assume, therefore, that half a century from now mainstream criminology in North America, whatever its underlying paradigms may become, will be in harmony with the social order, the politico-economic system in place. One need not stretch the imagination to the limit to predict what the future holds for North American society. It would be sheer naïvety to think or to expect that in 20, 30 or 50 years, socialism will replace capitalism as the dominant mode of production or that there will be a radical change in the way the relations of economic production are organized. Recent political changes in Eastern Europe suggest that such possibility is extremely unlikely. There is no question that North American society in the year 2050 will be a highly advanced capitalist society, a prototype of a post-industrial society.

Future Orientations of Criminology

If these assumptions are correct then the dominant paradigm for North American criminology in the future cannot, and will not, be a radical or Marxist paradigm. This does not mean that the current paradigms for conservative and liberal criminology will continue unchallenged or unchanged. On the contrary, they are likely to undergo a thorough transformation. The content and orientations of criminology of the future will not only be influenced and shaped by the changes in crime, the criminal law, societal reaction to deviance, the methods of social control outlined above, but they will also depend largely on the success of mainstream criminologists in correcting the deficiencies, inadequacies, weaknesses, and shortcomings identified and decried by radical criminologists. As intellectuals, whether academics or researchers, they cannot remain oblivious or indifferent to the strong and serious criticisms that have been levelled at traditional, conventional criminology. It is to be expected, therefore, that mainstream criminologists, whether conservative or liberal, correctionalist or reformist, will take into account at least some of the valid criticisms that have been made. This should make it possible to draw the basic lines along which mainstream criminology is likely to develop in the coming decades.

Mainstream criminology of the future will pay more attention to history. The historiography of crime remains one of the most neglected areas in criminology. And yet, crime cannot be understood unless it is examined and analysed in its historical context. But somehow historians have neglected the study of legal history while criminologists have ignored the social history of crime. The explanation lies, no doubt, in traditional criminology's focus on individual pathology, an emphasis that leads to the dismissal of history as irrelevant to the explanation of crime. Even in recent years, historical studies in criminology have been relatively few and far between. In the seventies, Gibbons (1979:199) noted that although American criminology is more than eight decades old, by and large, criminological inquiry in the US has rarely looked backward to law-breaking in the 1800s or before and has thus suffered from historical impoverishment.

Foucault's study, *Discipline and Punish* (1979), and his account of how penal institutions and the power to punish became a part of our lives not only revived the dying interest in penological history but also showed the vital role history can play in enhancing our understanding of criminal and criminal justice phenomena. It is to be expected, therefore, that criminologists will pay increasing attention to history in coming years and that history will become an important dimension of the analysis of crime, of social reaction to deviance and of criminal justice institutions.

Mainstream criminology of the future will pay more attention to the sociology of law. Writing in 1964, Chambliss deplored the severe shortage of sociologically relevant analyses of the relationship between particular laws and the social setting in which these laws emerge, are interpreted and take form. Sociology of law, as Aubert (1969) points out, has an important critical function as an aid in enhancing the legal profession's awareness of its own function in society.

The sociology of deviance, the labelling perspective, made it abundantly clear that sociology of law is an integral part of criminological inquiry. The historical evolution of criminology shows that the sociological study of law is a necessary and logical step in the pursuit of knowledge about crime. Thus, the focus of criminological inquiry shifted from rule breaking (the Classical School) to rule breakers (the Italian Positivist School) to include rule-making and rule-makers (sociology of law) and rule-enforcing and enforcers (the labelling perspective).

Mainstream criminology of the future will be politically orientated. Criminology in the future will be characterized by a heightened awareness of the political dimensions of crime and the political roles of the criminal law and the criminal justice system.

Mainstream criminology has been justifiably criticized for being apolitical. Prior to the mid-1960s it was characterized by the unquestioning acceptance of the definitions of crime. Moreover, as Allen (1974) points out, the political dimensions of criminal justice were not of primary concern to most of those professionally or academically involved in the study and administration of criminal justice. Sociologists of deviance, labelling theorists, and radical criminologists should be credited with having sensitized mainstream criminologists to the fact that the definition of behaviours as criminal is inherently a political decision, that the criminal law and the criminal justice system do protect certain political interests and do perform political functions. As Allen (1974:22) puts it,

> Because of the nature of penal sanctions, the interests that the system of criminal justice is called on to protect, and because of the system being an arm of government and a channel for the exercise of state power, criminal justice is inherently and inescapably political. It was the failure to perceive these facts that rendered much prior scholarship in the field irrelevant and sometimes perilous to the maintenance of essential political values. Basic human interests are today, as in the past, threatened by the exertion of state power through the agencies of penal justice; in consequence, it is of first importance that this realization be reflected in the scholarship.

It is doubtful that future criminology could ignore these political dimensions particularly since state repression is likely to assume a more political character. The demarcation line between political crime and conventional crime (or common-law crime) will become increasingly blurred as a result of criminals becoming more politicized and of governments insisting that political insurgents are nothing but common criminals. The future politicization of mainstream criminology does not necessarily mean that scientific criminology will be used as a vehicle for the dissemination of a particular political ideology.

Mainstream criminology of the future will be more normative.   In the future, it is more than likely that the illusion of a value-free criminology will be hard to maintain or to defend.

Weber maintained that sociology must be value-neutral if it is to be genuinely scientific, and his advice is heeded by many sociologists, who maintain that sociology is an objective and value-free science (see Gibbons, 1979:133). Several mainstream criminologists have adopted a similar posture and have deliberately abstained from addressing issues of criminal policy. They were following the advice of highly regarded criminologists such as Sellin (1938) and Mannheim (1965) who advocated a separation of criminal policy from criminology (see Chapter 7).

For criminologists who cherish an objective, neutral, value-free criminology the issue has been a thorny one, and their attempts to maintain a so-called value-free stand have not succeeded in camouflaging their biases in favour of the status quo. For obvious reasons, radical and critical criminologists have not been haunted by the same dilemma since they entertain a declared bias against a value-free social science.

As the ideal goal of mainstream criminology, namely, a value-free and ideologically neutral discipline, becomes less and less attainable (and perhaps less desirable), criminology will become more normative, concerned not only with what has been and what is but also with *what ought to be*. While mainstream criminologists of the future might not be as ideologically and politically committed as contemporary radical criminologists are, it seems certain that mainstream criminology of the future will not be an ivory tower discipline and that most criminologists will find it increasingly difficult, maybe impossible, to remain aloof from the heated ideological and political debates that will be raging around them. The separation between 'scientific criminology', on the one hand, and 'criminal policy', on the other, will also be difficult to maintain. Direct government funding of research is bound to generate demands for investigations which have explicit relevance to policy issues (Wiles, 1976:5).

Mainstream criminology of the future will integrate criminological theory with a broader theoretical framework.   The approach mainstream criminology has taken to explain crime has been criticized on several grounds. Schur (1969) deplored 'the common tendency to see crime as an alien, asocial phenomenon and to think of it as somewhat existing outside of organized society.' This attitude, he insists, leads to 'compartmentalizing crime problems and ignoring their close relations to the other conditions of our society, out of which criminals as well as conformists emerge.'

Commenting on various crime theories, Vold (1958:11) noted that:

> ...crime will be explained differently, depending on which frame of reference is the point of departure. Each approach usually regards itself as self-sufficient; no view falls back on any of the others for confirmation or verification; each considers its explanations most nearly adequate, and none welcomes or accepts the criticism of another point of view.

In the state of affairs described by Vold, it is not difficult to understand why theoretical criminology has not been successful in its primary task: 'explaining crime.' Because behaviour defined as criminal is not qualitatively different from other behaviour it does not seem very fruitful to try to explain it independently of, or differently from, non-criminal behaviour. Yet, individualistic explanations have failed to situate criminal behaviour within a general theory of human behaviour and have treated it as if it were a separate and distinct entity. It is true that as long as there is no satisfactory or completely adequate theory of human behaviour in general, there will be no entirely adequate or generally accepted theory of criminal behaviour (Vold 1958:305).

Since crime is not a unitary phenomenon, Vold (1958:314) believes no single theory will emerge to provide the explanations for the many varieties of behaviour involved. He also does not expect criminological theory to develop wholly adequate and acceptable explanations of criminal behaviour until the whole group of 'the behaviour sciences' reaches a corresponding adequacy of theoretical explanation of human behaviour in general.

Sociological explanations of the mainstream variety have failed, on the other hand, to locate the sociology of crime within the focal concerns of mainstream sociological theory and have failed to link crime more closely to history, economics, and political science.

Gibbons (1979:212) predicts that crime levels and responses to law-breaking will be influenced by the economic changes underway in American society in ways that will need to be divined by a new generation of criminologists:

> The American economy can no longer be treated as a given that needs no special attention. As criminologists go about ferreting out the causal dimensions of crime, they must include economics in their study of social factors.

Mainstream criminology will take a broader orientation toward social problems in general not just the crime problem.   Traditional criminology has not taken a holistic approach to crime and has treated criminality independently of, and in isolation from, other social problems. Robinson (1985) points out that in today's world, it is impossible to explain crime by studying crime or the institutions that combat crime. Likewise, it is wrongheaded to study independently the myriad problems that plague modern societies. He provides a list of no less than 34 social problems found in current social problems texts. Many of the problems on the list are related in one way or another to criminal justice, and most of them are undoubtedly interrelated. Yet, many criminologists still believe that the problem of crime can be studied separately and independently. Robinson's mctaphoric illustration of our traditional approach is enlightening:

> Our approach, assuming as criminal justice researchers we are at all interested, is to select one problem and find its cause: 'the cause of juvenile delinquency, of drug abuse, or gang warfare.' We perceive our society as if it were a doll factory turning out huge percentages of 'defective' dolls. As researchers, we sit outside the factory in little, individual, separated, and sealed houses, one house for fixing defective fingers, another for ears, another for right feet, left feet, hair, and so forth. No one deals with the whole doll and certainly few ask what's wrong with the factory. If we do not ask the right questions, we cannot set out in the right direction to find the answers. (p. 111)

Mainstream criminology of the future will have to deal with social problems, crime being only one of them, as interrelated rather than independent phenomena and will have to take as a departure point the hypothesis that many of them have common roots and are produced by the same socio-political-economic-cultural conditions.

Mainstream criminology of the future will pay more attention to comparative research.   The word comparative research or comparative criminology hardly appears in any of the subject indexes of American textbooks in criminology. And it is not surprising that both radical and mainstream criminologists have been criticized for not doing comparative research. The issue has surfaced in debates between the two sides. Mankoff (1980) admits the importance of criminologists and other social scientists engaging in comparative studies, the most valuable of which is that within a particular society when it changes its social structure in some fundamental way. He sees comparisons between nations having different levels of economic development and distinctive political and cultural traditions as problematic because too many confounding variables are brought into play.

Mankoff (1980) further suggests that studies of 'crime and conflict in preliterate societies, feudal societies, and socialist societies may exhibit certain distinctive features that can lead to valuable sociological generalizations.' He explains:

> If one finds that Marxist categories are not helpful in organizing social patterns, one can try 'industrial versus agrarian', or 'Christian versus Moslem' societies for purposes of comparison. (p. 147)

Shichor (1980:195) points to radical criminologists' lack of sensitivity to the fact that there are differences among various capitalist societies. He argues that taking the US as the embodiment of capitalist society does not contribute to the understanding of the crime problem. It does not explain why in countries like England, France, Sweden, Norway, or New Zealand violent crimes are not as frequent as in the US and in some they probably do not exceed the crime level of socialist regimes.

Mainstream criminology of the future will rely more on social and cultural anthropology. As Reiss (1980) points out, criminologists have borrowed heavily from sociology and psychology. Criminology (see Chapter 11) has been dominated by the search for the causes of crime. Criminologists believed all along that these causes are to be found either in the individual or in society, that they are the product of nature or nurture. It was natural, therefore, for them to turn to psychology and to sociology to seek the answers to many of the questions about the etiology of crime, especially since most criminologists had been trained in these two disciplines. Few criminologists (for example, D. Szabo, 1993) were interested in the potential contribution anthropology could make to the understanding of crime and social reaction to crime. As a result, there has been little crossfertilization between anthropology and criminology.

Criminologists' ethnocentrist views of crime and the widespread acceptance of the doctrine of universalism have made it difficult for anthropological insights to have an impact on criminological theory. In view of what was said (Chapter 1) about 'crime' being a matter of definition rather than an intrinsic or inherent quality of the behaviour so labelled and what was said in Chapter 2 about the cultural relativity of crime and of victimization, there seems to be little doubt that knowledge in criminology could be greatly enhanced and enriched by the findings and insights of research in social and cultural anthropology. For example, the anthropological perspectives on violence and aggression presented in Signe Howell and Roy Willis's edited book (1989) *Societies at Peace*, Aster Akalu's (1985) anthropological study of morality among the Ethiopian Nuer, and Renteln's well-documented defence of the theory of cultural relativism (1991) cast serious doubts on many of the ethnocentric premises that underlie most theories of positivist criminology. A critical assessment of these latter theories cannot ignore the questions raised by these anthropological, ethnographic and cross-cultural studies.

Developments in criminology that are taking place at present in non-Western and Third World countries will certainly create a great challenge to West European and North American criminologists and will force them to re-examine, re-evaluate, and eventually to revise their current views and theories about crime, criminals and social reaction to crime.

CONCLUSION

This bird's eye view and these possible scenarios of criminology in the 21st century are not meant to be a comprehensive analysis of what criminology in the future will be like. They are simply meant to provide some futuristic and thought-provoking ideas that would create controversy and hence stimulate discussion and debate. The future of criminology will naturally depend on its willingness and its ability to confront not only the problem of crime but also other general and pressing problems of our society. After all, crime is intimately linked to social, economic, political and cultural conditions. No action against crime will be effective as long as the present injustices, inequities, and disparities persist, as long as poverty, unemployment, gender and racial discrimination, and so on continue unabated. The reform of the criminal code, the reform of the criminal justice system, would be meaningless unless undertaken within the context of global social reform.

NOTES

1. Already in the 1970s a government commission is Sweden recommended that minor property offences be depenalized (See Asplin, 1975).
2. Anonymous blurb on Sebastian Cobler's (1978) book cover.
3. These three perspectives correspond roughly to three identifiable political ideologies. But they are, by no means, the only perspectives. Others include feminist criminology and realist criminology discussed in the previous chapter. There is also the *abolitionist perspective* championed by Louk Hulsman and Nils Christie, which in the description of Stanley Cohen (1988:27), deals with reaction rather than behaviour.

Bibliography

Akalu, A. (1985). *Beyond Morals? Experiments of living the life of the Ethiopian Nuer*. Lund: CWK.

Albanese, J. (1985). *Organized Crime in America*. Cincinnati: Anderson Publishing Company.

Allen, F.A. (1954). Raffaele Garofalo. *Journal of Criminal Law, Criminology and Police Science*. 45:4, pp. 373–90.

Allen, F.A. (1974). *The Crimes of Politics: Political dimensions of criminal justice*. Cambridge, MA: Harvard University Press.

Allen, J. (1988). The 'masculinity' of criminality and criminology: Interrogating some impasses. In M. Findlay & R. Hogg (eds), *Understanding Crime and Criminal Justice*. Melbourne: The Law Book Company Ltd.

Amnesty International (1975). *Prisoners of Conscience in the USSR: Their Treatment and Their Conditions*. London: Amnesty International.

Amnesty International (1977). *Annual Report 1977*. London: Amnesty International.

Amnesty International (1981). *Disappearances*. London: Amnesty International.

Amnesty International (1983). *Political Killings by Governments*. London: Amnesty International.

Amnesty International (1984). *Torture in the Eighties*. London: Amnesty International.

Amnesty International (1993). *Getting Away with Murder – Political Killings and Disappearances in the 1990s*. London: Amnesty International.

Anderson, D.C. (1995). *Crime and the Politics of Hysteria: How the Willie Horton Story Changed American Justice*. New York: Random House.

Angiolillo, P.F. (1979). *The Criminal as Hero: Angelo Duca*. Lawrence: Regents Press of Kansas.

Anttila, I. (1964). The criminological significance of unregistered criminality. *Excerpta Criminologica*. 4, p. 411.

Anttila, I. (1971). Conservative and radical criminal policy in the nordic countries. In *Scandinavian Studies in Criminology*. 3, pp. 9–21. Oslo: Universitetsforlaget.

Anttila, I. (1974). Victimology: A new territory in criminology. In *Scandinavian Studies in Criminology*. 5, pp. 7–10. Oslo: Universitetsforlaget.

Anttila, I. & Jaakkola, R. (1966). *Unrecorded Criminality in Finland* (Series A: 2). Helsinki: Institute of Criminology.

Appleby, T. (1992, October 26). Giving crime a bad name. *Globe and Mail*.

Aromaa, K. (1974). Victimization to violence: A Gallup survey. *International Journal of Criminology and Penology*. 2:4, pp. 333–46.

Aromaa, K. (1974). Our violence. In *Scandinavian Studies in Criminology*. 5, pp. 35–46. Oslo: Universitetsforlaget.

Aromaa, K. (1984). Three surveys of violence in Finland. In Richard Block (ed.), *Victimization and fear of crime: World perspectives*. pp. 11–21) Washington, DC: U.S. Dept. of Justice, Bureau of Justice Statistics.

Aschaffenberg, G. (1913). *Crime and its Repression*. Boston: Little, Brown.

Aspelin. E., Bishop, N. Thornstedt, H. & Törnudd, P. (1975). *Some Developments in Nordic Criminal Policy and Criminology*. Stockholm: Scandinavian Research Council for Criminology.

Aubert, V. (1969). *Sociology of Law: Selected Readings*. Harmondsworth: Penguin.

Australia (Victoria). (1992). *Homicide*. 40. Melbourne: Law Reform Commission of Victoria.

Barak, G. (1994). *Media, Process, and the Social Construction of Crime: Studies in Newsmaking Criminology*. NY: Garland Publishing.

Barker, T. & Roebuck, J.B. (1973). *An Empirical Typology of Police Corruption: A Study in Organizational Deviance*. Springfield, Ill.: Charles Thomas.

Barnes, H.E. & Teeters, N.K. (1959). *New Horizons in Criminology* (3rd edn). Englewood Cliffs, NJ: Prentice-Hall.

Bassiouni, M.C. & McCormick, M. (1996). *Sexual Violence: An Invisible Weapon of War in the Former Yugoslavia*. Occasional Paper No. 1. Chicago: De Paul University Institute of Law.

Beccaria, C. (1963). *On Crimes and Punishments*. (Henry Paolucci, Trans.). The Library of Liberal Arts. Indianapolis: Bobbs-Merrill Company (Original work published 1764).

Becker, H. (1963). *Outsiders*. London: Free Press of Glencoe.

Beirne, P. (1987). Adolphe Quetelet and the Origins of Positivist Criminology. *American Journal of Sociology*. 92:5, pp. 1140–69.

Beirne, P. (1988). Heredity versus Environment. *British Journal of Criminology*. 28:3, pp. 315–39.

Beirne, P. (1987). Between Classicism and Positivism: Crime and Penalty in the Writings of Gabriel Tarde. *Criminology*. 25:4, pp. 785–819.

Belson, W.A., *et al.* (1970). *The development of a procedure for eliciting information from boys about the nature and extent of their stealing*. London: London School of Economics – Survey Research Centre.

Betenson, L.P. (1975). *Butch Cassidy – My Brother*. Provo: Brigham Young University Press.

Beynon, E.D. (1935). Crimes and customs of Hungarians in Detroit. *Journal of Criminal Law, Criminology & Police Science*, 25, pp. 755–74.

Bianchi, H. (1956). *Position and subject-matter of criminology: Inquiry concerning theoretical criminology*. Amsterdam: North Holland Publishing.

Biderman, A.D. (1967). Surveys of population samples for estimating crime incidence. *Annals of the American Academy of Political and Social Science*. 374, pp. 16–33.

Biderman, A.D. (1981). Sources of Data for Victimology. *Journal of Criminal Law and Criminology*. 72:2, pp. 789–817.

Biderman, A.D. & Reiss, A.J. Jr. (1967). On exploring the dark figure of crime. *Annals of the American Academy of Political and Social Science*. 374, pp. 1–15.

Biderman, A.D. & Lynch, J.P. (1991). *Understanding Crime Incidence Statistics – Why the UCR Diverges from the NCS?* New York: Springer Verlag.

Bilsky, W. & Wetzels, P. (1994). Victimization and crime. Normative and individual standards of evaluation. *International Annals of Criminology*. 32:1/2, pp. 135–52.

Binder, A. (1988). Criminology: Discipline Or And Interdiscipline? *Issues in Integrative Studies*. 5, pp. 41–67.

Birbeck, C. & La Free, G. (1993). The Situational Analysis of Crime and Deviance. *Annual Review of Sociology*, Vol. 19, pp. 113– 137.

Black, D. (1970). Production of crime rates. *American Sociological Review*. 35:4, pp. 733–48.

Black, D. (1983, February). Crime as social control. *American Sociological Review*. 48, pp. 34–45.

Block, R. (ed.). (1984). *Victimization and fear of crime: World perspectives*. Washington, DC: US Dept. of Justice, Bureau of Justice Statistics.

Blumenthal, M., Kahn, R.L., Andrews, F.M. & Head, K.B. (1972) *Justifying Violence: Attitudes of American Men*. Ann Arbor: Institute for Social Research.

Bohn, G. (1983, 21 September). Japanese Canadians and the war. *The Vancouver Sun*. p. B1.

Bonger, W.A. (1916). *Criminality and Economic Conditions*. Boston: Little, Brown and Co. (Original work published 1905).

Bosworth-Davies, R. & Saltmarsh, G. (1995). Definition and Classification of Economic Crime. In J. Reuvid (ed.). *The Regulation and Prevention of Economic Crime Internationally*. London: Kogan Page.

Bottomley, K.A. (1979). *Criminology in Focus: Past Trends and Future Prospects*. Oxford: Martin Robertson.

Box, S. (1971). *Deviance, Reality and Society*. London: Holt, Rinehart & Winston.

Box, S. (1983). *Power, Crime, and Mystification*. London: Tavistock Publications

Box, S. (1987). *Recession, Crime and Punishment*. London: Macmillan.

Braithwaite, J. (1989). The state of criminology: Theoretical decay or renaissance? *Australian and New Zealand Journal of Criminology*. 22:3, pp. 129–35.

Braithwaite, J. & Biles, D. (1979). On being unemployed and being a victim of crime. *Australian Journal of Social Issues*. 14, pp. 192–200.

Braithwaite, J. & Biles, D. (1980). Overview of findings from the first Australian national crime victims survey. *Australian and New Zealand Journal of Criminology*. 13, pp. 41–51.

Braithwaite, J. & Biles, D. (1984). Victims and offenders: The Australian experience. In R. Block (ed.), *Victimization and fear of crime: World perspectives*. Washington, DC: US Dept. of Justice (NCJ-93872).

Braithwaite, J. & Pettit, P. (1994). Criminalization, decriminalization and republican theory. *International Annals of Criminology*. 32:1/2, pp. 61–80.

Brantingham, P.J. & Brantingham, P. (1984). *Patterns in Crime*. New York: Macmillan.

Browning, C. (1992). *Ordinary men: Reserve Police Battalion 101 and the Final Solution*. New York: Harper Collins.

Bunyan, T. (1977). *The History and Practice of the Political Police in Britain*. London: Quartet Books.

Cameron, M.O. (1964). *The Booster and the Snitch*. London: Free Press of Glencoe.

Canada: Government of Canada (1982). *The criminal law in Canadian society*. Ottawa.

Canada: Law Reform Commission of Canada (1974). *The meaning of guilt*. Working Paper No. 2, Ottawa: Information Canada.

Canada: Law Reform Commission of Canada (1974). *The Principles of Sentencing and Dispositions*. Working Paper No. 3, Ottawa: Information Canada.

Canada: Law Reform Commission of Canada (1974). *Restitution and Compensation/Fines*. Working Papers Nos. 5 & 6, Ottawa: Information Canada.

Canada: Law Reform Commission of Canada (1976). *Our criminal law*. Ottawa: Information Canada.

Canada: Law Reform Commission of Canada (1976). *Dispositions and Sentences in the Criminal Process*. Ottawa: Information Canada.

Canada. Ministry of the Solicitor General (1981). Victims of crime. *Canadian urban victimization survey bulletin*, No. 1. Ottawa.

Canada. Ministry of the Solicitor General (1984a). Reported and unreported crime. *Canadian Urban Victimization Survey Bulletin*, No. 2. Ottawa.

Canada. Ministry of the Solicitor General (1984b). Crime prevention: Awareness and practice. *Canadian Urban Victimization Survey Bulletin*, No. 3. Ottawa.

Canada. Ministry of the Solicitor General (1985). Female victims of crime. *Canadian Urban Victimization Survey Bulletin*, No. 4. Ottawa.

Canada. Ministry of the Solicitor General (1985). Cost of crime to victims. *Canadian Urban Victimization Survey Bulletin*, No. 5. Ottawa.

Canada. Ministry of the Solicitor General (1985). Criminal victimization of elderly Canadians. *Canadian Urban Victimization Survey Bulletin*, No. 6. Ottawa.

Canada. Ministry of the Solicitor General (1986). Household property crimes. *Canadian Urban Victimization Survey Bulletin*, No. 7. Ottawa.

Canada. Ministry of the Solicitor General (1987). Patterns in violent crime. *Canadian Urban Victimization Survey Bulletin*, No. 8. Ottawa.

Canada Ministry of the Solicitor General (1988). Patterns in property crime. *Canadian Urban Victimization Survey Bulletin*, No. 9. Ottawa.

Canada. Ministry of the Solicitor General (1988). Multiple victimization. *Canadian Urban Victimization Survey Bulletin*, No. 10. Ottawa.

Canadian Centre for Justice Statistics (1994). Trends in Criminal Victimization: 1988–1993. *Juristat*, Vol. 14, No. 13.

Canadian Centre for Justice Statistics (1994). Canadian Crime Statistics, 1993. *Juristat*, Vol. 14, No. 14. (August).

Canadian Centre for Justice Statistics (1994). Homicide in Canada, 1993. *Juristat*, Vol. 14, No. 15.

Canadian Centre for Justice Statistics (1995). Homicide in Canada – 1994. *Juristat*, Vol. 15, No. 11. (August).

Canadian Centre for Justice Statistics (1995). Canadian Crime Statistics, 1994. *Juristat*, Vol. 15, No. 12. (August).

Canadian Committee on Corrections (1969). *Toward unity: Criminal justice and corrections*. Ottawa: Information Canada.

Carlen, Pat. (1992). Criminal women and criminal justice: The limits to, and potential of feminist and left realist perspectives. In R. Matthews and J. Young (eds), *Issues in Realist Criminology*. London: Sage.

Chagnon, N. (1983). *Yanomamo. The Fierce People*. New York: Holt, Rinehart and Winston.

Chambers, G. & Tombs, J. (eds). (1984). *The British crime survey: Scotland*. A Scottish Office Social Research Study. Edinburgh: HMSO.

Chambliss, W. (1964, Summer). A sociological analysis of the law of vagrancy. *Social Problems*, 12:46–77, 335–52.

Chambliss, W. (1981). The criminalization of conduct. In H. Lawrence Ross (ed.), *Law and Deviance*. Beverly Hills, CA: Sage.

Chambliss, W. (1989). State-Organized Crime. *Criminology*. Vol. 27:2, pp. 183–208.

Chambliss, W. & Mankoff, M. (1976). *Whose Law, What Order? A Conflict Approach to Criminology*. New York: Wiley.

Chapman, D. (1968). *Sociology and the Stereotype of the Criminal*. London: Tavistock.

Chermak, S.M. (1995). *Victims in the News: Crime and the American News Media*. Boulder: Westview Press.

Chomsky, N. (1987). *Pirates and Emperors*. Montreal: Black Rose Books.

Christie, N. (1952). Fangevoktere i Konsentrasjonsleire. *Nordisk Tidskrift for Kriminalvidenskap*. 41, 439–58. (Also published as a book in 1972.)

Christie, N. (1968). Changes in penal values. In N. Christie (ed.), Aspects of Social Control in Welfare States. *Scandinavian Studies in Criminology*. 2, pp. 161–72. London: Tavistock.

Christie, N. (1971). Criminologist: Technician or poet? *Scandinavian Studies in Criminology*. 3, pp. 140–45. Oslo: Universitetsforlaget.

Christie, N. (1977). Conflicts as property. *British Journal of Criminology*. 17:1, pp. 1–19.

Christie, N. (1986). The ideal victim. In E.A. Fattah (ed.), *From Crime Policy to Victim Policy*. London: Macmillan.

Christie, N. (1993, March 10, 17, 24). Crime control as industry. *CBC IDEAS Transcripts*. Toronto.

Christie, N., *et al.* (1965). A study of self-reported crime. In K.O. Christiansen (ed.), *Scandinavian Studies in Criminology* (Vol. 1). London: Tavistock.

Clark, L. & Lewis, D. (1977). *Rape: The Price of Coercive Sexuality*. Toronto: Women's Press.

Clarke, R.V. (1981). The prospects of controlling crime. *Home Office Research Unit Research Bulletin*. 12, pp. 12–19. London: HMSO.

Clarke, R.V. (1992). *Situational crime prevention. Successful case studies*. New York: Harrow and Heston.

Clarke, R.V. & Felson, M. (1993). Routine activity and rational choice (Vol. 5 in *Advances in Criminological Theory*). New Brunswick: Transaction Publishers.

Clinard, M. (1978). *Cities with little crime: The case of Switzerland*. Cambridge: Cambridge University Press.

Cobler, S. (1978). *Law, order and politics in West Germany*. Harmondsworth, England: Penguin.

Cohen, L.E. & Felson, M. (1979). Social change and crime rate trends: A routine activities approach. *American Sociological Review*. 44, pp. 588–608.

Cohen, M.R. (1971). Moral aspects of criminal law. In A.S. Goldstein & J. Goldstein (eds), *Crime, Law and Society*. pp. 35–59. New York: Free Press.

Cohen, S. (1988). *Against Criminology*. New Brunswick: Transaction Books.

Comfort, A. (1970). *Delinquency and Authority: A Study in the Psychology of Power*. London: Sphere Books.

Congalton, A.A. & Najman, J.M. (1974). *Who are the Victims?* Sydney: New South Wales Bureau of Crime Statistics and Research.

Conklin, J. (1975). *The Impact of Crime*. New York: Collier-Macmillan.

Conklin, J. (1977). *Illegal but not Criminal*. Englewood Cliffs, NJ: Prentice-Hall.

Cooper, H.H.A. (1977). Terrorism: The problems of the problem of definition. *Chitty's Law Journal*. 26:3, pp. 105–8.

Cornish, D.B. & Clarke, R.V. (1986). *The Reasoning Criminal: Rational Choice Perspectives on Offending*. New York: Springer Verlag.

Corrado, R., Roesch, R., Glackman, W., Evans, J.L. & Legen, G.J. (1980). Life styles and personal victimization: A test of the model with Canadian Survey Data. *Journal of Crime and Justice*. 3, pp. 129–39.

Corré, A. (1891). *Crime et suicide*. Paris.

Corré, A. (1868). *Essai sur la criminalité*. Journ. des Econ. (Janvier) p. 76 [quoted by G. Aschaffenberg, 1913, p. 5].

Cressey, D.R. (1969). *Theft of the Nation: The Structure and Operations of Organized Crime in America*. New York: Harper and Row.

Cressey, D.R. (1978). Criminological theory, social science, and the repression of crime. *Criminology*. 16, pp. 171–91.

Cressey, D.R. (1985). Research implications of conflicting conceptions of victimology. In Z.P. Separovic (ed.), *Victimology: International Action and Study of Victims*. pp. 43–54. Zagreb: University of Zagreb.

Cressey, D.R. & Ward, D.A. (1969). *Delinquency, Crime and Social Process*. New York: Harper and Row.

Cretney, A. & Davis, G. (1995). *Punishing Violence*. London: Routledge.

Curtis, L. (1975). Victim precipitation. *The Aldine crime and justice annual 1974*. Chicago: Aldine Publishing Co.

Cusson, M. (1983). *Why Delinquency?*. Toronto: University of Toronto Press.

Cusson, M. & Pinsonneault, P. (1986). The decision to give up crime. In D. Cornish and R. Clarke (eds), *The Reasoning Criminal: Rational Choice Perspectives on offending*. New York: Springer Verlag.

Darrow, C. (1902). *Resist not evil*. Montclair, NJ: Patterson Smith. (Reprinted 1972.)

Darwin, Charles. (1874). *The Descent of Man* (2nd edn). Chicago: Rand McNally.
Dautremer, J. (1985). The vendetta or legal revenge in Japan. *Transactions of the Asiatic Society of Japan.* 13, pp. 82–9.
Davis, J.F. (1952). Crime news in Colorado newspapers. *American Journal of Sociology.* 57, pp. 325–30. (Reprinted in S. Cohen & J. Young (eds). (1973). *The Manufacture of News.* London: Constable).
Debuyst, C. (1969). *Introduction à la criminologie.* Cahiers de l'Université Catholique de Louvain.
Del Frate, A.A., Zvekic, U. & Van Dijk, J.J.M. (1993). *Understanding Crime – Experiences of Crime and Crime Control.* Rome: UNICRI, Publication No. 49.
De Grazia, S. (1948). *The Political Community – A Study in Anomie.* Chicago: The University of Chicago Press.
Dietrich, G. (1961). *Les Procès d'Animaux du Moyen-Age à nos Jours.* Lyon.
Dion, R. (1982). *Crimes of the Secret Police.* Montreal: Black Rose Books.
De Quiros, C.B. (1911). *Modern Theories of Crime.* Boston: Little, Brown.
Ditton, J. & Duffy, J. (1983). Bias in the newspaper reporting of crime news. *British Journal of Criminology.* 23, 159 65.
Doleschal, E. (1970). Hidden crime. *Crime and Delinquency Literature.* 2:5, pp. 546–72.
Doleschal, E. & Klapmuts, N. (1973). Toward a new criminology. *Crime and Deliquency Literature.* 5:4, 607–26.
Dollard, J., Doob, L.W., Miller, N.E., Mourer, O.H. & Sears, R.R. (1939). *Frustration and aggression.* New Haven: Yale University Press. (Reprinted 1957.)
Doob, A.N. (1991). The many realities of crime. In R.A. Silverman, J.J. Teevan & V.F. Sacco, (eds), *Crime in Canadian Society.* pp. 29–36. (4th edn). Toronto: Butterworth.
Downes, D. (1966). *The Delinquent Solution: A Study in Subcultural Theory.* London: Routledge and Kegan Paul.
Downes, D. & Rock, P. (1988). *Understanding Deviance – A Guide to the Sociology of Crime and Rule – Breaking.* (2nd. edn). Oxford: Clarendon Press.
Driver, E.D. (1961). Interaction and criminal homicide in India. *Social Forces.* 40, pp. 153–58.
Durkheim, E. (1900) Deux Lois de L'évolution Pénale. *L'Année Sociologique.* Vol. IV, pp. 65–95.
Durkheim, E. (1933). *The Division of Labor in Society.* New York: Free Press. (Reprinted 1965.)
Durkheim, E. (1938). *The Rules of Sociological Method.* New York: Free Press.
Earle, A.M. (1972). *Curious Punishments of Bygone Days.* Rutland, Vermont: Charles E. Tuttle Company.
Economist, The. (1994, 15 October). 'Measuring crime. A shadow on society.' pp. 21–3.
Edelhertz, H. (1970). *The nature, impact and prosecution of white-collar crime.* Washington, D.C: US Dept. of Justice Law Enforcement Assistance Administration.
Elias, R. (1986). *The Politics of Victimization: Victims, Victimology, and Human Rights.* New York: Oxford University Press.
Ellenberger, H. (1955). Psychological relationships between criminal and victim. *Archives of Criminal Psychodynamics.* 2, pp. 257–90.
Ellickson, R.C. (1991). *Order Without Law: How Neighbours Settle Disputes.* Cambridge, Mass.: Harvard University Press.
Ellis, D. (1987). *The Wrong Stuff.* Canada: Collier Macmillan.
Elmhorn, K. (1965). Study of self reported delinquency among children in Stockholm. In K.O. Christiansen (ed.), *Scandinavian Studies in Criminology.* 1, pp. 117–46. London: Tavistock.

Ennis, P.H. (1967, June). Crime, victims and the police. *Trans-Action*. pp. 36–44.

Ennis, P.H. (1967). *Criminal victimization in the United States: A report of a national survey*. Washington, DC: U.S. Government Printing Office.

Ericson, R.V. (1991). Mass Media, Crime, Law and Justice: An Institutional Approach. *British Journal of Criminology*. 31:3, pp. 219–49.

Ericson, R.V., Baranek, P.M. & Chan, J.B.L. (1987). *Visualizing Deviance: A Study of News Organizations*. Toronto: University of Toronto Press.

Ericson, R.V., Baranek, P.M. & Chan, J.B.L. (1991). *Representing Order: Crime, Law and Justice in the News Media*. Toronto: University of Toronto Press.

Ericson, R.V., Carriere, K. (1994) The Fragmentation of Criminology. In David Nelken (ed.) *The Futures of Criminology*. London: Sage.

Ermann, M.D. & Lundman, R.J. (1982). *Corporate Deviance*. New York: Holt, Rinehart & Winston.

Evans, E.P. (1906). *The Criminal Prosecution and Capital Punishment of Animals*. London: Heinemann.

Evans, J., Leger, G. (1979). Canadian victimization surveys: A discussion paper. *Canadian Journal of Criminology*, 21:2, pp. 166–83.

Faith, K. (1993). *Unruly Women: The Politics of Confinement and Resistance*. Vancouver: Press Gang Publishers.

Farner, J.A. (1880). *Crimes and Punishments*. London: Chatto and Windus.

Fattah, E.A. (1967). La victimologie: Qu'est-elle et quel est son avenir? *Revue Internationale de Criminologie et de Police Technique*, 21:2, pp. 113–24, and 3, pp. 193–202.

Fattah, E.A. (1976). The use of the victim as an agent of self-legitimization: Toward a dynamic explanation of criminal behavior. *Victimology: An International Journal*. 1:1, pp. 29–53.

Fattah, E.A. (1979). Some recent theoretical developments in victimology. *Victimology: An International Journal*. 4:20, pp. 198–213.

Fattah, E.A. (1980). *Crime and the abuse of power*. pp. 69–92. Final general report. Document submitted to the 5th Joint Colloquium (Bellagio 21–24 April, 1980). Milan: Centro Nazionale di Prevenzione e Difesa Sociale.

Fattah, E.A. (1981). Terrorist activities and terrorist targets: A tentative typology. In Y. Alexander & J.M. Gleason (eds), *Behavioral and Quantitative Perspectives on Terrorism*. pp. 11–32. New York: Pergamon Press.

Fattah, E.A. (1982). Les enquêtes de victimisation: Leur contribution et leurs limitations. *Déviance et Société*, 4, pp. 423–40.

Fattah, E.A. (1984). Victim's response to confrontational victimization: A neglected aspect of victim research. *Crime and Delinquency*. 30:1, pp. 75–89.

Fattah, E.A. (1986). On some visible and hidden dangers of victim movements. In E.A. Fattah (ed.), *From Crime Policy to Victim Policy*. London: Macmillan.

Fattah, E.A. (1989a). Victims and victimology: The facts and the rhetoric. *International Review of Victimology*. 1:1, pp. 43–66.

Fattah, E.A. (1989b). Victims of abuse of power: The David/Goliath syndrome. In E.A. Fattah (ed.), *The Plight of Crime Victims in Modern Society*. pp. 29–73. London: Macmillan.

Fattah, E.A. (1991). *Understanding Criminal Victimization*, Scarborough, Ont: Prentice-Hall Canada.

Fattah, E.A. (1992). Beyond metaphysics: The need for a new paradigm – On actual and potential contributions of criminology and the social sciences to the reform of the criminal law. In R. Lahti and K. Nuotio (eds), *Criminal law theory in transition*. Helsinki: Finnish Lawyers Publishing Company.

Fattah, E.A. (1993a). Crime prevention between chaos and reason. In Clive Begg (ed.), *Chaos or reason, community safety in the twenty-first-century.* pp. 17–31. Lutwyche: Australian Crime Prevention Council.

Fattah, E.A. (1993b). La relativité, culturelle de la victimization. *Criminologie.* 26:2, 121–36.

Fattah, E.A. (1993c). The rational choice/opportunity perspective as a vehicle for integrating criminological and victimological theories. In R.V. Clarke & M. Felson (eds), *Routine activity and rational choice* (Vol. 5, in *Advances in criminological theory*). New Brunswick: Transaction Publishers.

Fattah, E.A. (1993d). From a guilt orientation to a consequence orientation. A proposed new paradigm for the criminal law in the 21st century. In W. Kuper & J. Welp (eds), *Beiträge zur Rechtswissenschaft.* Heidelberg: C.F. Müller Juristischer Verlag.

Fattah, E.A. (1994a). Victimology: On some problematic concepts, unjustified criticism and popular misconceptions. In G.F. Kirchhoff, E. Kosovski, & H.J. Schneider, (eds), *International debates of victimology.* Mönchengladbach: WSV Publishing.

Fattah, E.A. (1994b). Violence against the elderly: Types, patterns, and explanations. *International Annals of Criminology.* 32:1/2, pp. 113–34.

Fattah, E.A. (1994c). From victimization by the state to victimization by crime. A side effect of transition to democracy? In U. Ewald (ed.), *New definitions of crime in societies in transition to democracy.* Godesberg: Forum Verlag.

Fattah, E.A. (1994d). *The Interchangeable Roles of Victim and Victimizer.* Helsinki: HEUNI. 26 pages.

Fattah, E.A. (1995). Restorative and Retributive Justice Models – A Comparison. In H. H. Kühne (ed.) *Festschrift für Koichi Miyazawa.* Baden-Baden: Nomos Verlagsgesellschaft. pp. 305–15.

Fattah, E.A. & Raic, A. (1970). L'alcool en tant que facteur victimogène. *Toxicomanies.* 3:2, pp. 143–73.

Fattah, E.A. & Sacco, V.F. (1989). *Crime and Victimization of the Elderly.* New York: Springer Verlag.

Felson, M. (1994). *Crime and Everyday Life.* Thousand Oaks: Pine Forge Press

Felson, R.B. & Steadman, H.J. (1983). Situational factors in disputes leading to criminal violence. *Criminology.* 21:1, pp. 59–74.

Ferri, Enrico. (1917). *Criminal Sociology.* Originally published by Little, Brown and Company. (Reprinted in 1967 by Agathon Press.)

Fiselier, J.P.S. (1978). *Victims of crime: a study of unreported crime* [in Dutch]. Utrecht: Ars Aequi Libri.

Fishman, M. (1978). Crime waves as ideology. *Social Problems.* 25, pp. 531–43.

Flynn. E.E. (1982). Theory development in victimology: An assessment of recent progress and of continuing challenges. In H.J. Schneider (ed.), *The Victim in International Perspective* (pp. 96–104). Berlin: de Gruyter.

Forward, S., Buck, C. (1983). *Betrayal of Innocence: Incest and its Devastation.* New York: Penguin.

Foucault, M. (1979). *Discipline and Punish: The Birth of the Prison.* New York: Vintage.

Freeman, J. & Sebba, L. (1989). Editorial. *International Review of Victimology.* 1:1, pp. 1–2.

Friedrichs, D.O. (1980). Radical criminology in the U.S.: An interpretive understanding. In J.A. Inciardi (ed.), *Radical Criminology – The Coming Crises.* pp. 35–60. Beverly Hills, CA: Sage.

Gabor, T. (1991). Crime by the public. In M.A. Jackson & C.T. Griffiths (eds), *Canadian Criminology: Perspectives on Crime and Criminality.* Toronto: Harcourt Brace Jovanovich.

Gabor, T. (1994). *Everybody Does It! Crime by the Public*. Toronto: University of Toronto Press.

Garland, D. (1985). The Criminal and his Science. *British Journal of Criminology*. 25:2, pp. 109–37.

Garofalo, J. (1977). *Local Victim Surveys: A Review of the Issues*. Washington, D.C: US Dept. of Justice (Analytic Report SD-VAD-2).

Garofalo, J. & Hindelang, M. (1977). *An introduction to the national crime survey*. Washington, DC: US Government Printing Office.

Garofalo, R. (1885/1914). *La criminologie*. Paris: Alcan. [French edition: 1888].

Garofalo, R. (1914). *Criminology*. Little, Brown and Company. (Reprinted in 1968 by Patterson Smith, Montclair, New Jersey.)

Garret, P. (1954). *The Authentic Life of Billy the Kid*. Norman: University of Oklahoma Press.

Gartner, R. & Doob, A.N. (1994). Trends in Criminal Victimization: 1988–1993. *Juristat*, Vol. 14, no. 13 (June).

Geis, G. & Meier, R.F. (1977). *White-collar Crime: Offenses in Business, Politics, and the Professions* (revised edition). New York: Free Press.

Gelsthorpe, L. & Morris, A. (1988). Feminism and Criminology in Britain. *British Journal of Criminology*. Vol. 28:2, pp. 223–40.

Genefke, I. (1995). Evidence of the Use of Torture. In N. Gordon and R. Marton (eds.). *Torture – Human Rights, Medical Ethics and the Case of Israel*. London: Zed Books.

Gibbens, T.C.N. & Prince, J. (1962). *Shoplifting*. London: Institute for the Study and Treatment of Delinquency.

Gibbons, D.C. (1965). *Changing the Law Breaker*. Englewood Cliffs, NJ: Prentice-Hall.

Gibbons, D.C. (1971). Observations on the study of crime causation. *American Journal of Sociology*. 77, pp. 262–78.

Gibbons, D.C. (1979). *The Criminological Enterprise: Theories and Perspectives*. Englewood Cliffs, NJ: Prentice-Hall.

Gillin, J.L. (1926). *Criminology and Penology*. New York: Century Co.

Glueck, S. & Glueck, E. (1956). *Physique and Delinquency*. New York: Harper Row.

Goddard, H.H. (1920). *Human Efficiency and Levels of Intelligence*. Princeton: Princeton University Press.

Goff, C.H. & Reasons, C.E. (1978). *Corporate crime in Canada: A critical analysis of anti-combines legislation*. Scarborough, Ont: Prentice-Hall Canada.

Goode, W.J. (1969). Violence among intimates. In D.J. Mulvihill, M.M. Tumin & L.A. Curtis (eds), *Crimes of violence*. A staff report submitted to the national commission on the causes and prevention of violence. pp. 941–77. Washington, DC: United States Government Printing Office.

Gordon, D. (1990). *The Justice Juggernaut*. New Brunswick, NJ: Rutgers University Press.

Goring, C.H. (1913). *The English Convict*. London: HMSO.

Gottfredson, M.R. (1984). Victims of crime: The dimensions of risk. Home Office Research and Planning Unit Report No. 81. London: HMSO.

Gottfredson, M.R. & Gottfredson, D.M. (eds). (1988). *Decision-making in Criminal Justice* (2nd edn). *Law, Society and Politics* (Vol. 3). London: Plenum Press.

Gottfredson, M.R. & Hindelang, M.J. (1977). A consideration of memory decay and telescoping biases in victimization surveys. *Journal of Criminal Justice*. 5, pp. 202–16.

Gottfredson, M. & Hirschi, T. (1990). *A General Theory of Crime*. Stanford: Stanford University Press.

Graber, D. (1980). *Crime News and the Public*. New York: Praeger.

Graber, D. (1984). *Processing the News*. New York: Longman.

Grassberger, R. (1973). Hans Gross. In Mannheim,H. (ed.). *Pioneers in Criminology*. (2nd edn., 1st edn. published in 1956), pp. 305–17.

Grayson, B. & Stein, M.I. (1981, Winter). Attracting assault: Victims' nonverbal cues. *Journal of Communication*. pp. 68–75.

Green, G.S. (1990). *Occupational Crime*. Chicago: Nelson Hall.

Greenberg, D. (1976). On one-dimensional criminology. *Theory and Society*. 3, pp. 610–21.

Greenwood, V. (1981). The Myths of Female Crime. In A.M. Morris & L.R. Gelsthorpe (eds) *Women and Crime*. Cropwood Conference Series No. 13, Cambridge: Cambridge Institute of Criminology.

Gregory, J. (1986). Sex, class and crime – Towards a non-sexist criminology. In R. Matthews & J. Young (eds), *Confronting Crime*. London: Sage.

Gross, H. (1968). *Criminal Psychology: A Manual for Judges, Practitioners and students*. Montclair, NJ: Patterson Smith.

Guerry, A.M. (1833). *Essai sur la statistique morale de la France*. Paris: Chez Crochard.

Hackler, J. (1985). Criminology. In *Canadian Encyclopedia*. Edmonton: Hurtig Publications.

Hahn, R.G. (1977). *Deterrence and the death penalty: A critical review of the econometric literature*. Ottawa: Ministry of Supply and Services.

Hall, A.C. (1902). *Crime in its relations to social progress*. New York: Columbia University Press. (Reprinted in 1968 by AMS Press, New York.)

Hall, D. (1975). The role of the victim in the prosecution and disposition of a criminal case. *Vanderbilt Law Review*. 28:5, pp. 932–85.

Harris, M. (1975). *Culture, People, Nature*. New York: Crowell.

Hart, J. (1985, August 30). Why do women commit less crime? *New Society*. pp. 298–300.

Hart, M.H. Jr. (1971). The aims of the criminal law. In A.S. Goldstein & J. Goldstein (eds), *Crime, Law and Society*. pp. 61–7. New York: Free Press.

Haskell, M. & Yablonsky, L. (1974). *Criminology, Crime and Criminality*. Chicago: Rand McNally.

Hauge, R. & Wolf, P. (1974). Criminal violence in three Scandinavian countries. In K.O. Christiansen (ed.), *Scandinavian Studies in Criminology*. 5, pp. 25–33. Oslo: Universitetsforlaget.

Heald, S. (1986). The ritual use of violence: Circumcision among the Gisu of Uganda. In D. Riches (ed.), *The Anthropology of Violence*. Oxford: Basil Blackwell.

Heelas, P. (1989). Identifying peaceful societies. In S. Howell & R. Willis (eds), *Societies at Peace: Anthropological Perspectives*. London: Routledge.

Heidensohn, F.M. (1985). *Women and Crime*. London: Macmillan.

Henry, S. (1978). *The Hidden Economy – The Context and Control of Borderline Crime*. London: Martin Robertson.

Henry, S. & Milovanovic, D. (1994). The Constitution of Constitutive Criminology: A Postmodern Approach to Criminological Theory. In David Nelken (ed.) *The Futures of Criminology*. London: Sage.

Hentig, H. von. (1940/41). Remarks on the interaction of perpetrator and victim. *Journal of Criminal Law and Criminology*. 31, pp. 303–09.

Hentig, H. von. (1948). *The criminal and his victim*. New Haven: Yale University Press. (Reprinted in 1967 by Archon Books.)

Hepburn, J.R. (1973). Violent behaviour in interpersonal relationships. *Sociological Quarterly*. 14, pp. 419–29.

316   *Bibliography*

Herdt, G.H. (1982). *Rituals of manhood: Male initiation in Papua New Guinea.* Berkeley: University of California Press.

Herman, E.S. (1982). *The Real Terror Network: Terrorism in Fact and Propaganda.* Boston: South End Press.

Hewitt, P. (1982). *The Abuse of Power: Civil liberties in the United Kingdom.* Oxford: Martin Robertson.

Hills, S.L. (1987). *Corporate Violence: Injury and Death for Profit.* Totowa: Rowman and Littlefield.

Hindelang, M.J. (1976). *Criminal Victimization in Eight American Cities: A Descriptive Analysis of Common Theft and Assault.* Cambridge, MA: Ballinger.

Hindelang, M.J., Gottfredson, M.R. & Garofalo, J. (1978). *Victims of Personal Crime: An Empirical Foundation for a Theory of Personal Victimization.* Cambridge, MA: Ballinger.

Hinrichs, R. (1987). *Das Chronische Opfer.* Stuttgart: Georg Thieme Verlag.

Hirschi, T. & Gottfredson, M. (1983). Age and the Explanation of Crime. *American Journal of Sociology.* 89:3, pp. 552–84.

Hirschi, T. & Gottfredson, M. (1990, October). Substantive positivism and the idea of crime. *Rationality and Society.* 2:4, pp. 412–28. (Reprinted in Francis T. Cullen & Velmer S. Burton, Jr. (eds). (1994). *Contemporary criminological theory.* Aldershot: Dartmouth.)

Hirst, P.Q. (1975). Marx and Engels on law, crime and morality. In I. Taylor, P. Walton, & J. Young, (eds), *Critical Criminology.* pp. 203–32. London: Routledge & Kegan Paul.

Hobbes, T. (1651). *Leviathan.* New York: Dutton. (Reprinted in 1965.)

Hoefnagels, P.G. (1973). *The Other Side of Criminology: An Inversion of the Concept of Crime.* Deventer: Kluwer.

Hogg, R. (1988). Taking crime seriously: Left realism and Australian criminology. In M. Findlay & R. Hogg (eds), *Understanding Crime and Criminal Justice.* Melbourne: The Law Book Company Ltd.

Holstein, J.A. & Miller, G. (1990). Rethinking victimization: An interactional approach to victimology. *Symbolic Interaction.* 13:1, pp. 103–22.

Honderich, T. (1957, December 7). Why Red Ryan's shadow still hangs over every prison yard? *Maclean's.*

Hood, R. & Sparks, R. (1970). *Key Issues in Criminology.* London: Weidenfeld and Nicolson (World University Library).

Hooton, E. (1939). *Crime and the Man.* Cambridge, Mass.: Harvard University Press.

Hough, M. (1986). Victims of violent crime: Findings from the British crime survey. In E.A. Fattah (ed.), *From Crime Policy to Victim Policy.* pp. 117–32. London: Macmillan.

Hough, M. (1995). Anxiety About Crime: Findings from the 1994 British Crime Survey. *Research Findings* No. 25. London: Home Office Research and Statistics Department.

Hough, M. & Mayhew, P. (1983). *The British crime survey.* Home Office Research Study No. 76. London: HMSO.

Hough, M. & Mayhew, P. (1985). *Taking account of crime: Key findings from the 1984 British crime survey.* Home Office Research and Planning Unit Report No. 85. London: HMSO.

Howell, S. & Willis, R. (1989). *Societies at peace: Anthropological Perspectives.* London: Routledge.

Hubbard, J.C., DeFleur, J.L. & DeFleur, L.B. (1975). Mass media and social problems. *Social Problems.* 23, pp. 22–34.

Huff, C.R. (1980). Conflict theory in criminology. In J.A. Inciardi (ed.), *Radical Criminology – The Coming Crises*. pp. 61–77. Beverly Hills: Sage.

Hulsman, L.H. (1986). Critical criminology and the concept of crime. In H. Bianchi & R. van Swaaningen (eds), *Abolitionism: Towards a Non-repressive Approach to Crime*. Amsterdam: Free University Press.

Hume, S. (1994). Article. The *Vancouver Sun*, 15 October, 1994.

Huxley, Aldous. (1947). *Point Counter Point*. London: Chatto & Windus.

Inciardi, J.A. (1978). *Reflections on Crime: An Introduction to Criminology and Criminal Justice*. New York: Holt, Rinehart and Winston.

Inciardi, J.A. (1980). *Radical Criminology: The Coming Crises*. Beverly Hills: Sage.

Israel, J. (1972). Is a non-normative social science possible? *Acta Sociologica*. 15:1, pp. 69–89 .

Ives, G. (1914). *A History of Penal Methods*. London: S. Paul & Co.

Jacoby, S. (1983). *Wild Justice: The Evolution of Revenge*. New York: Harper and Row.

James, M.P. (1992). The elderly as victims of crime, abuse and neglect. *Trends and Issues*, 37. Canberra: Australian Institute of Criminology.

Jaywardene, C.H.S. (1973). Criminologist: Theoretician or Practitioner. *Criminology Made in Canada*, Vol. 1, No. 1, pp. 11–31.

Jeffrey, C.R. (1956). The structure of American criminological thinking. *Journal of Criminal Law, Criminology and Police Science*. 46, pp. 658–72.

Jensen, G.F., Brownfield, D. (1986). Gender, lifestyles, and victimization: Beyond routine activity. *Violence and Victims*. 1:2, pp. 85–99.

Jobson, K.B. (1977). Dismantling the system. *Canadian Journal of Criminology*. 19:3, pp. 254–72.

Johnson, E.H. (1968). *Crime, Correction and Society* (revised edn). Homewood, IL: The Dorsey Press.

Johnson, J.A., Kerper, H.B., Hayes, D.D. & Killinger, G.G. *et al.* (1973). The recidivist victim: A descriptive study. *Criminal Justice Monographs*. 4:1. Huntsville, TX: Sam Houston State University.

Kappeler, V.E., Blumberg, M. & Potter, G.W. *et al.* (1993). *The Mythology of Crime and Criminal Justice*. Prospect Heights, IL: Waveland Press.

Katz, J. (1987). What makes crime 'news'. *Media, Culture and Society*. 9, pp. 47–75.

Katz, J. (1988). *Seductions of Crime*. New York: Basic Books.

Keable, J. (1981). *Rapport de la Commission d'enquête sur des opérations policières en territoire québecois*. Québec: Ministère de la Justice.

Keenan, T. (1984). *Crimes of the Future*. Transcript of CBC program IDEAS (Oct. 15–29). Toronto: Canadian Broadcasting Corporation.

Kennedy, L.W. (1990). *On the Borders of Crime – Conflict Management and Criminology*. New York: Longman.

Killias, M. (1989) *Les Suisses face au crime*. Lausanne: Grüsch/Ch.

Kinberg, O. (1960). *Les problèmes fondamentaux de la criminologie*. Paris: Cujas.

Kittrie, N.N. (1971). *The Right to be Different: Deviance and Enforced Therapy*. Baltimore, MD: Penguin.

Klecka, W.R. & Tuchfarber, A.J. (1978). Random digit dialing: A comparison to personal surveys. *Public Opinion Quarterly*. 42, pp. 105–14.

Klockars, C.B. (1980). The contemporary crises of Marxist criminology. In J.A. Inciardi (ed.), *Radical Criminology – The Coming Crises*. pp. 92–123). Beverly Hills, CA: Sage.

Knapp, W. (1972). *The Knapp Report on Police Corruption*. New York: Braziller.

Köchler, H. (1988). *Terrorism and national liberation*. Frankfurt: Peter Lang.

Koenig, D. (1974). *Correlates of self-reported victimization and perceptions of neighbourhood safety*. Victoria, B.C.: University of Victoria, Dept. of Sociology (mimeographed). (Also printed in L. Hewitt and D. Brusegard (eds) *Selected papers from the social indicators conference*. Edmonton: Alberta Bureau of Statistics (1977)).

Kooistra, P. (1983). American Robin Hoods: The criminal as social hero. *Criminal Justice Abstracts*. 15:2, pp. 214–27.

Kooistra, P. (1989). *Criminals as Heroes: Structure, Power and Identity*. Bowling Green: Bowling Green State University Popular Press.

Kutchinsky, B. (1970). *Studies on pornography and sex crimes in Denmark*. Copenhagen: New Social Science Monographs.

Kutchinsky, B. (1971). *Perceptions of deviance and criminality*. Council of Europe, Ninth Conference of Directors of Criminological Research Institutes, Strasbourg.

Kutchinsky, B. (1973). The effect of easy availability of pornography on the incidences of sex crimes: The Danish experience. *Journal of Social Issues*. 29, pp. 163–81.

Lahti, R. (1972). On the Reduction and Distribution of the Costs of Crime: Observations on the Objectives and the Means of Criminal Policy. *Jurisprudentia*, 1, pp. 298–313.

Lamer, A. (1978). Criminal justice – A total look. *Canadian Journal of Criminology*. 20:2, pp. 126–41.

Lauritsen, J.L., Sampson, R.J., & Laub, J.H. (1991). The link between offending and victimization among adolescents. *Criminology*. 29:2, pp. 265–92.

Lea, John. (1992). The analysis of crime. In J. Young & R. Matthews (eds), *Rethinking criminology: The Realist Debate*. London: Sage.

League of Nations (1937). *Convention for the prevention and punishment of terrorism*, Geneva.

Leblanc, M. (1975a). Middle class delinquency. In R. Silverman & J. Teevan (eds), *Crime in Canadian Society*. pp. 213–22. Toronto: Butterworths.

Leblanc, M. (1975b). Upper class vs. working class delinquency. In R.A. Silverman, J.J. Teevan & V.C. Sacco (eds), *Crime in Canadian Society*. pp. 102–18. Toronto: Butterworths.

Leblanc, M. (1977). *La délinquance juvénile au Québec*. Québec: Ministère des Affaires Sociales.

Lee, G.W. (1984). Are crime rates increasing? A study of the impact of demographic shifts on crime rates in Canada. *Canadian Journal of Criminology*. 26:1, pp. 29–41.

Lemert, E. (1951). *Social Pathology – A Systematic Approach to the Theory of Sociopathic Behavior*. New York: McGraw Hill.

Lemert, E. (1967). *Human Deviance, Social Problems and Social Control*. Englewood Cliffs, NJ: Prentice-Hall.

Lemert, E. (1974). Beyond Mead: The societal reaction to deviance. *Social Problems*. 21, pp. 457–68.

Leonard, E.B. (1982). *Women, Crime and Society: A Critique of Criminological Theory*. New York: Longman.

Levy, R., Perez-Diaz, C., Robert, P., & Zauberman, R. (1986). *Profils sociaux de victimes des infractions: Premiers résultats d'une enquête nationale*. Paris: Centre de recherches sociologiques sur le droit et les institutions pénales.

Lindesmith, A. (1940, July–August). Dope fiend mythology. *Journal of Criminal Law and Criminology*. 31, pp. 199–208.

Lindesmith, A. & Levin, Y. (1937a). English ecology and criminology of the past century. *Journal of the American Institute of Criminal Law and Criminology*. 28.

Lindesmith, A. & Levin, Y. (1937b). The Lombrosian myth in criminology. *American Journal of Sociology*. 42, pp. 653–71.

Lombroso, C. (1876). *L'homme criminel* [The Criminal Man]. Paris: Alcan.

Lombroso, C. (1968). *Crime, its causes and remedies*. Montclair, NJ: Patterson Smith. (Original work published 1911.)

Lombroso-Ferrero, G. (1911). *Criminal man according to the classification of Cesare Lombroso.* G.P. Putnam's Sons. (Reprinted in 1972 by Patterson Smith, Montclair, New Jersey.)
Longmire, D.R. (1982). The new criminologist's access to research support: Open arms or closed doors. In H. Pepinsky (ed.), *Rethinking Criminology.* Beverly Hills: Sage.
Lotz, R.E. (1991). *Crime and the American Press.* New York: Praeger.
Lowman, J. & Maclean, B. (1992). *Realist criminology: Crime Control and Policing in the 1990s.* Toronto: University of Toronto Press.
Lukenbill, D.F. (1977). Criminal homicide as a situated transaction. *Social Problems.* 25, pp. 176–86.
Lunden, W. (1958). Emile Durkheim. *Journal of Criminal Law, Criminology and Police Science.* 49:1, pp. 2–9.
Lynch, J.P. (1993). The Effects of Survey Design on Reporting in Victimization Surveys – The United States Experience. In W. Bilsky; C. Pfeiffer & P. Wetzels (eds) *Fear of Crime and Criminal Victimization.* Stuttgart: Ferdinand Enke Verlag.
Lynch, M.J. & Groves, W.B. (1989). *A Primer in Radical Criminology.* (2nd edn). New York: Harrow and Heston.
Maciver, R. (1942). *Social causation.* Boston: Ginn.
Maestro, M.T. (1973). *Cesare Beccaria and the Origins of Penal Reform.* Philadelphia: Temple University Press.
Mankoff, M. (1980). A tower of Babel: Marxist criminologists and their critics. In J.A. Inciardi (ed.), *Radical Criminology – The Coming Crises.* pp. 139–48). Beverly Hills, CA: Sage.
Mann, E. & Lee, J.A. (1979). *RCMP – The RCMP vs. The People.* Don Mills, ON: General Publishing.
Mannheim, H. (1936). Lombroso and his place in modern criminology. *Sociological Review.* 28.
Mannheim, H. (1965). *Comparative Criminology.* London: Routledge and Kegan Paul.
Marongiu, P. & Newman, G. (1987). *Vengeance: The Fight Against Injustice.* Totowa, NJ: Rowman and Littlefield.
Mathiesen, T. (1990). Contemporary Penal Policy – A Study in Moral Panics. In N. Bishop (ed.) *Scandinavian Criminal Policy and Criminology 1985–1990.* Stockholm: Scandinavian Research Council for Criminology.
Matthews, R. & Young, J. (1986). *Confronting Crime.* London: Sage.
Matthews, R. & Young, J. (eds). (1992). *Issues in Realist Criminology. London: Sage Publications.*
Matthews, R. & Young, J. (eds). (1992). Questioning left realism. In *Issues in Realist Criminology.* London: Sage.
Matthews, R. & Young, J. (eds). (1992). Reflections on realism. *Rethinking Criminology: The Realist Debate.* London: Sage.
Matza, D. (1964). *Delinquency and Drift.* New York: John Wiley.
Mawson, A.R. (1978). *Transient Criminality: A Model of Stress-induced Crime.* New York: Praeger.
Maxwell, J. (1914). *Le concept social du crime et son évolution.* Paris: Alcan.
Mayer, J. (1933). Toward a science of society. *American Journal of Sociology.* 39, pp. 159–79.
Mayhew, P., Clarke, R.V.G., Sturman, A.K. Hough, J.M. (1976). *Crime as Opportunity.* Home Office Research and Planning Unit Report No. 34. London: HMSO.
Mayhew, P. & Elliott, D. (1990). Self-reported offending, victimization, and the British crime survey. *Violence and Victims,* 5:2, 83–96.

Mayhew, P., Maung, N.A., & Mirrlees-Black, C. (1993). *The 1992 British Crime Survey*. Home Office Research Study 132. London: HMSO.

Mays, J. (1964). *Crime and Social Structure*. London: Faber and Faber.

McCabe, S. & Sutcliffe, F. (1978). *Defining Crime: A Study of Police Decisions*. Oxford: B. Blackwell for the Oxford University Centre for Criminological Research.

McClintock, F. (1988). Criminology perspectives. In *Actes du XI Congrès International de Défense Sociale*. Buenos Aires.

McDonald, D.C. (1978). Commission of inquiry concerning certain activities of the RCMP. *Freedom and Security: An Analysis of police issues*. Ottawa.

McIntosh, Mary. (1975). *The organization of crime*. London: Macmillan.

Mendelson, B. (1956). Une nouvelle branche de la science bio-psycho-sociale: La victimologie. *Revue Internationale de Criminologie et de Police Technique*. 10, pp. 95–109.

Menninger, K. (1966). *The Crime of Punishment*. New York: Viking.

Menninger, K. (1973). *Whatever Became of Sin?* New York: Hawthorn Books. (Reprinted by Bantam Books in 1978.)

Merton, R.K. (1957). *Social Theory and Social Structure*. New York: Free Press. (Revised and Enlarged Edition.)

Michael, J. & Adler, M.J. (1933). *Crime, Law and Social Science*. Montclair, NJ: Patterson Smith. (Reprinted 1971.)

Mickleburgh, R. (1996). China Executes Crackdown on Crime. The *Globe and Mail* (Saturday, 29 June: A10).

Milgram, S. (1969). *Obedience to Authority: An Experimental View*. New York: Harper and Row.

Mill, J.S. (1859). *On Liberty*. New York: Bobbs-Merrill. (Reprinted 1956.)

Miller, W. (1973). Ideology and criminal justice: Some current issues. *Journal of Criminal Law and Criminology*. 64:2, pp. 141–54.

Mirrlees-Black, C., Mayhew, P. & Percy, A. (1996). The 1996 British Crime Survey – England and Wales. *Home Office Statistical Bulletin*, Issue 19.

Mitford, J. (1974). *Kind and Usual Punishment. The prison business*. NY: Vintage.

Morris, A. (1941). Criminals' Views on Crime Causation. *The Annals*. Vol. 217, Sept. pp. 138–44.

Morris, N. (1973). *The law is a busy body*. Copyright by the New York Times Co. (Reprinted by World Correctional Service Centre.)

Morris, N., Hawkins, G. (1969). *The Honest Politician's Guide to Crime Control*. Chicago: University of Chicago Press.

Myrdal, G. (1958). *Value in social theory: A selection of essays on methodology* (ed. P. Streeten). NY: Harper.

National Opinion Research Centre (NORC) (1967). *Criminal Victimization in the United States: A Report of a National Survey*. By Philip H. Ennis. Washington, D.C.: US Government Printing Office.

Nelken, D. (1994). *The Futures of Criminology*. London: Sage Publications.

Nettler, G. (1974). *Explaining Crime*. NY: McGraw-Hill.

Nettler, G. (1984). *Explaining Crime*. 3rd edn. NY: McGraw-Hill.

Newman, D.J. (1977). White Collar Crime: An Overview and Analysis. In G. Geis and R.F. Meier (eds) *White-Collar Crime*. New York: The Free Press.

Newman, G. & Marongiu, P. (1990). Penological Reform and the Myth of Beccaria. *Criminology*. 28:2, pp. 325–46.

Nsereko, D.D.N. (1983). *Group victims of crime and other illegal acts linked to abuse of public power with special reference to Africa*. Paper prepared for the UN Secretariat.

O'Brien, R.M. (1985). *Crime and Victimization Data*. Beverly Hills: Sage.

Orwell, G. (1969). The Fascination of crime. In G.M. Sykes & T.E. Drabek, (eds); *Law and the Lawless: A Reader in Criminology*. pp. 50–2. New York: Random House.

Paolucci, H. (1963). Translation of C. Beccaria's *On crimes and punishment*. Library of Liberal Arts.

Parker, G. (1977). *An introduction to criminal law*. Toronto: Methuen.

Parker, L. (1983, September 21). Internees in US lost a way of life. The *Vancouver Sun*, B3.

Parmelee, M. (1918). *Criminology*. New York: Macmillan. (Reprinted 1926.)

Pelfrey, W.V. (1980). The new criminology: Acceptance within academe. In J.A. Inciardi (ed.), *Radical Criminology – The Coming Crises*. pp. 233–44 Beverly Hills, CA: Sage Publications.

Penick, B.K. & Owens, M.E.B. (eds). (1976). *Surveying crime*. Washington, DC: National Academy of Sciences.

Pepinsky, H.E. & Jesilow, P. (1984). *Myths that Cause Crime*. Cabin John, MD/ Washington, DC: Seven Locks Press.

Pfohl, S.J. (1985). *Images of Deviance and Social Control*. New York: McGraw-Hill.

Phillipson, M. (1974). *Understanding Crime and Delinquency: A Sociological Introduction*. Chicago: Aldine Publishing.

Platt, T. & Takagi, P. (eds). (1977). Intellectuals for law and order: A critique of the new realists. *Crime and Social Justice*, 8:1–16.

Pollak, O. (1961). *The Criminality of Women*. New York: A.S. Barnes Pennsylvania Press.

Posner, M. (1995, January). The allure of the accused: Why do some women fall for notorious men? *Chatelaine*. 68:1, pp. 46–8, p. 80.

Posner, R.A. (1980). Retribution and related concepts of punishment. *Journal of Legal Studies*. 10, pp. 71–92.

Postman, N. (1985). *Amusing Ourselves to Death: Public Discourse in the Age of Show Business*. New York: Viking.

Punch, M. (1985). *Conduct Unbecoming: The Social Construction of Police Deviance and Control*. London: Tavistock Publications.

Quetelet, A.J. (1842). Treatise of man. In S.F. Sylvester. (1972). *The Heritage of Modern Criminology*. pp. 25–44. Cambridge, MA: Schenkman Publishing.

Quinney, R. (1970). *Social Reality of Crime*. Boston: Little, Brown.

Quinney, R. (1972). Who is the Victim? *Criminology*. 10:3, pp. 314–23.

Quinney, R. (1974). *Critique of Legal Order*. Boston: Little, Brown.

Quinney, R. (1977). The Study of White-Collar Crime: Toward a Reorientation in Theory and Practice. In G. Geis & R.F.Meier (eds) *White Collar Crime – Offenses in Business, Politics and the Professions*. (revised edition). NY: Free Press, pp. 283–95.

Radzinowicz, L. (1966). *Ideology and Crime*. London: Heinemann.

Reckless, W.C. (1961). *The Crime Problem*. (3rd edn). New York: Appleton-Century-Crofts, Inc.

Reed, J. (1978). *From Private Vice to Public Virtue: The Birth Control Movement and American Society since 1830*. New York: Basic Books.

Reiman, J.H. (1979). *The Rich Get Richer and the Poor Get Prison: Ideology, class, and criminal justice*. New York: John Wiley.

Reiman. J.H. (1984). *The Rich Get Richer and the Poor Get Prison*. (2nd edn) Toronto: John Wiley.

Reiman, J.H. (1990). *The Rich Get Richer and the Poor Get Prison*. (3rd edn) Toronto: John Wiley.

Reino, S. (1980). *Victims of violence: Results of the 1976 national surveys.* Helsinki: Research Institute of Legal Policy. Publication No. 40.

Reiss, A.J., Jr. (1980). Sociological and psychological influences on criminology. In H.J. Schneider (ed.), *The Psychology of the·Twentieth Century.* Weinheim: Beltz Verlag.

Reiss, A.J., Jr. (1981a, Summer). Foreword: Towards a revitalization of theory and research on victimization by crime. *Journal of Criminal Law and Criminology.* 7:2, pp. 704–10.

Reiss, A.J., Jr. (1981b). Soziologische Enflüsse auf die Kriminologie. In H.J. Schneider (ed.), *Kriminalität und Abweichendes Verhalten* (Band 1). Weinheim: Beltz Verlag.

Reiwald, P. (1949). *Society and its Criminals.* New York: International Universities Press.

Renteln, A.D. (1990). *International Human Rights: Universalism versus Relativism.* Newbury Park: Sage.

Robin, M. (1976). *The Bad and the Lonely: Seven Stories of the Best – and Worst – Canadian Outlaws.* Toronto: Lorimer.

Robin, M. (1982). *The Saga of Red Ryan and Other Tales of Violence from Canada's Past.* Saskatoon: Western Producer Prairie Books.

Robinson, C. (1985). Criminal justice research: Two competing futures. *Crime and Social Justice.* 23, pp. 101–28.

Robinson, L.L. (1972). *Durkheim's 'Two laws of penal evolution'* (Trans. and annotated). Ann Arbor: University Microfilms.

Rock, P. (1979). The sociology of crime, symbolic interactionism and some problematic qualities of radical criminology. In D. Downes & P. Rock (eds) *Deviance and Interpretations.* pp. 52–84. London: Martin Robertson.

Rock, P. (1988). *A History of British Criminology.* Oxford: Clarendon Press.

Rock, P. (1994). *Victimology.* Aldershot: Dartmouth.

Roshier, B. (1973). The selection of crime news by the press. In S. Cohen & J. Young (eds) *The Manufacture of News.* pp. 28–39. London: Constable.

Roshier, B. (1977). The function of crime myth. *Sociological Review.* 25, pp. 309–23.

Rubin, S. (1971). Developments in correctional law. *Crime and Delinquency.* 17:2, p. 213.

Rummel, R.J. (1994). *Death By Government.* New Brunswick: Transaction Publishers.

Rusche, G. & Kirchheimer, O. (1939). *Punishment and Social Structure.* (Reprinted in 1968 by Russell and Russell, New York.)

Ryan, P.J. (1995). *Organized Crime – A Reference Handbook.* Santa Barbara: ABC-CLIO, Inc.

Sacco, V.F. (1982). The Effects of Mass Media on Perceptions of Crime. *Pacific Sociological Review.* 25, pp. 475–93.

Sacco, V.F. & Kennedy, L.W. (1994). *The Criminal Event.* Scarborough, ON: Nelson Canada.

Sack, F. (1994). Conflicts and convergences of theoretical and methodological perspectives in criminology. In U. Ewald (ed.), *New Definitions of Crime in Societies in Transition to Democracy.* Bonn: Forum Verlag Godesberg.

Saleilles, R. (1927). *L'individualisation de la peine*, Paris: Félix Alcan. Trans. as *The Individualization of punishment*, Boston MA: Little, Brown and Company. Reprinted 1968, Montclair NJ: Patterson Smith.

Samuel, Y. (1939). *Les amoureux des criminels* (L'enclitophilie). Paris: Librarie Maloine.

Sarbin, T.R. (1969). *The Myth of the Criminal Type.* Paper read at Russell House, University of California on 24 February 1969.

Sasson, T. (1995). *Crime Talk: How Citizens Construct a Social Problem*. New York: Aldine de Gruyter.

Savitz, L., Lalli, M. & Rosen, L. (1977). *City life and delinquency – Victimization, fear of crime, and gang membership*. Washington, DC: U.S. Government Printing Office.

Sawatsky, J. (1980). *Men in the Shadows – The RCMP Security Service*. Toronto: Doubleday Canada.

Schauss, A. (1981). *Diet, Crime and Delinquency*. Berkeley, CA: Parker House.

Scheingold, S.A. (1991). *The Politics of Street Crime – Criminal Process and Cultural Obsession*. Philadelphia: Temple University Press.

Schiller, Friedrich von. (1781). The robbers. In Henry G. Bohn (Trans.) *The works of Frederick Schiller: Early dramas and romances*. (Vol. 4 of Bohn's Standard Library). London: G.G.I. & J. Robinson. (Original work published 1792.)

Schlesinger, P. & Tumber, H. (1993). *The Media Politics of Criminal Justice*. Oxford: Clarendon Press.

Schmidt, R. (1895). *Die Aufgaben der Strafrechtspflege*. pp. 182–83. Published in Leipzig.

Schrager, L. & Short, J.F. (1977). Toward a Sociology of Organizational Crime. *Social Problems*. 25, pp. 407–19.

Schur, E.M. (1965). *Crimes without Victims: Deviant Behavior and Public Policy*. Englewood Cliffs, NJ: Prentice-Hall.

Schur, E.M. (1969). *Our Criminal Society: The Social and Legal Sources of Crime in America*. Englewood Cliffs, NJ: Prentice- Hall.

Schur, E.M. (1971). *Labelling Deviant Behavior: Its Sociological Implications*. New York: Harper Row.

Schur, E.M. (1980). *The Politics of Deviance: Stigma Contests and the Uses of Power*. Englewood Cliffs, NJ: Prentice-Hall.

Seelig, E. (1956). *Traité de criminologie*. Paris: Presses Universitaires de France.

Seidman, D. & Couzens, M. (1974, Spring). Getting the crime rate down: Political pressure and crime reporting. *Law and Society Review*. 8, pp. 457–93.

Sellin, T. (1938). *Culture conflict and crime*. New York: Social Science Research Council.

Sellin, T. (1951, October). The significance of records of crime. *Law Quarterly Review*. 67, pp. 489–504.

Shaw, G.B. (1946). *The crime of imprisonment*. New York: Philosophical Library.

Shearing, C.D. & Stenning, P.C. (1982). *Private security and private justice: The challenge of the 80s*. Montreal: The Institute for Research on Public Policy.

Sheley, J.F. (1985). *America's 'Crime Problem' – An Introduction to Criminology*. Belmont, CA: Wadsworth.

Sheley, J.F. & Ashkins, C.D. (1981). Crime, crime news, and crime views. *Public Opinion Quarterly*. 45, pp. 492–506.

Sherman, L.W. (1974). *Police Corruption*. New York: Anchor.

Sherman, L.W. (1978). *Scandal and Reform: Controlling Police Corruption*. Los Angeles: University of California Press.

Sherman, L.W. (1992). *Policing Domestic Violence: Experiments and Dilemmas*. New York: Free Press.

Shichor, D. (1980). Some problems of credibility in radical criminology. In J.A. Inciardi (ed.), *Radical Criminology – The Coming Crises*. pp. 191–212. Beverly Hills, CA: Sage.

Short, J.F. & Nye, F.I. (1958). Extent of unrecorded juvenile delinquency. *Journal of Criminal Law, Criminology and Police Science*. 49, pp. 296–302.

Silberman, C. (1978). *Criminal Violence, Criminal Justice*. New York: Random House.

Silverman, R.A. (1980). Measuring crime: A tale of two cities. In R.A. Silverman and J.J. Teevan, Jr. (eds), *Crime in Canadian Society*. pp. 78–90 (2nd edn). Toronto: Butterworth.

Simon, D.R. & Eitzen, D.S. (1986). *Elite Deviance* (2nd edn). Boston: Allyn and Bacon.

Singer, S. (1980). *Victims in a subculture of crime: An analysis of the social and criminal backgrounds of surveyed victims in the Birth Cohort Follow-up*. (Unpublished dissertation, Univ. of Pennsylvania, Dept. of Sociology.)

Singer, S. (1981, Summer). Homogeneous victim-offender populations: A review and some research implications. *Journal of Criminal Law and Criminology*. 72:2, pp. 779–88.

Singer, S. (1986). Victims of serious violence and their criminal behavior: Subcultural theory and beyond. *Victims and Violence*. 1:1, pp. 61–70.

Skogan, W.G. (1975). Measurement problems in official and survey crime rates. *Journal of Criminal Justice*. 3, pp. 17–32.

Skogan, W.G. (1976). Crime and crime rates. In W.G. Skogan (ed.) *Sample Surveys of the Victims of Crime*. Cambridge, MA: Ballinger.

Skogan, W.G. (1981). *Issues in the measurement of victimization*. Bureau of Justice Statistics – U.S. Dept. of Justice. Washington, DC: U.S. Government Printing Office.

Skogan, W.G. (1984). Reporting crime to the police: The status of world research. *Journal of Research in Crime and Delinquency*. 21, pp. 113–137.

Skogan, W.G. (1986). Methodological issues in the study of victimization. In E.A. Fattah (ed.) *From Crime Policy to Victim Policy*. pp. 80–116. London: Macmillan.

Skogan, W.G. & Maxfield, M.G. (1981). *Coping with Crime – Individual and Neighborhood Reactions*. Beverly Hills: Sage.

Smart, C. (1976). *Women, Crime and Criminology: A Feminist Critique*. Boston: Routledge & Kegan Paul.

Smigel, E.O. & Ross, H.L. (1970). *Crimes Against Bureaucracy*. New York: Van Nostrand.

Snider, L. (1993). *Bad Business: Corporate Crime in Canada*. Scarborough, Ontario: Nelson Canada.

Sparks, R. (1992). *Television and the Drama of Crime – Moral tales and the Place of Crime in Public Life*. Milton Keynes: Open University Press.

Sparks, R.F. (1981). Surveys of victimization – An optimistic assessment. In M. Tonry and N. Morris (eds), *Crime and justice: An annual review of research*. 3, pp. 1–60. Chicago: University of Chicago Press.

Sparks, R.F., Genn, H.G. and Dodd, D.J. (1977). *Surveying Victims: A Study of the Measurement of Criminal Victimization*. London: John Wiley.

Spitzer, S. (1975). Toward a Marxian theory of deviance. *Social Problems*. 22, pp. 638–51.

Spitzer, S. (1980). Leftwing' criminology – An infantile disorder? In J.A. Inciardi (ed.), *Radical Criminology – The Coming Crises*. pp. 169–90. Beverly Hills, CA: Sage Publications.

Statistics Canada (1981). *Homicide statistics – 1980*. Catalogue 85–209 Annual. Ottawa: Minister of Supply and Services.

Statistics Canada (1970–1984). *Crime and traffic enforcement statistics*. Annual Report (Catalogue No. 85–205). Ottawa.

Statistics Canada (1976). *Homicide in Canada: A statistical analysis*. Ottawa: Ministry of Industry Trade & Commerce.

Steffensmeier, D.J. & Terry, R.M. (1973). Deviance and respectability: An observational study of reactions to shoplifting. *Social Forces*. 51:4, pp. 417–26.

Steiner, J.M., Hadden, S.C. & Herkomer, L. (1976). Price Tag Switching. In C.W.G. Jasperse *et al.* (eds) *Criminology Between the Rule of Law and the Outlaws.* Deventer: Kluwer.

Steinmetz, S.K. (1986). The violent family. In Mary Lystad (ed.) *Violence in the Home: Interdisciplinary Perspectives.* New York: Brunner/Mazel.

Summers, A. (1994). *The Secret Life of J. Edgar Hoover.* New York: Pocket Books.

Sumner, G.W. (1906). *Folkways. A Study of the Sociological Importance of Usages.* New York: Ginn.

Surette, R. (1992). *Media, Crime and Criminal Justice: Images and Realities.* Pacific Grove, CA: Brooks/Cole Publishing.

Sutherland, E.H. (1940). White-collar criminality. *American Sociological Review.* 5:1, pp. 1–12.

Sutherland, E.H. (1949). *White Collar Crime.* New York: Dryden.

Sutherland, E. & Cressey, D. (1960). *Principles of Criminology* (6th edn). New York: Lippincott.

Sutherland, E. & Cressey, D. (1978). *Principles of Criminology* (10th edn). Philadelphia: Lippincott.

Svalastoga, K. (1956). Homicide and social contact in Denmark. *American Journal of Sociology.* 62, pp. 37–41.

Sykes, G. (1978). *Criminology.* NY: Harcourt Brace Jovanovich.

Sykes, G. & Drabek, T.E. (1969). *Law and the Lawless: A Reader in Criminology.* NY: Random House.

Sykes, G. & Matza, D. (1957). Techniques of neutralization: A theory of delinquency. *American Sociological Review.* 22, pp. 664–70.

Szabo, D. (1993). *De l'anthropologie à la criminologie comparée.* Paris: Librarie Philosophique J. Vrin.

Szasz, T. (1965). *Psychiatric Justice.* New York: Macmillan.

Takala, J-P. (1991). *The functions of crime: a critique – Part I: Durkheim.* Paper presented at the American Society of Criminology meeting in San Francisco. 25 pages.

Tannenbaum, F. (1938). *Crime and the Community.* NY: Ginn.

Tappan, P.W. (1947). Who is the criminal? *American Sociological Review.* 12, pp. 96–103.

Tappan, P.W. (1960). *Crime, Justice and Correction.* NY: McGraw-Hill.

Tarde, G. (1886). *La criminalité comparée.* Paris: Alcan.

Taylor, I., Walton, P. & Young, J. (1973). *The New Criminology: For a Social Theory of Deviance.* London: Routledge and Kegan Paul. (Third Impression with Revisions, 1975.)

Taylor, I., Walton, P. & Young, J. (1975). *Critical Criminology.* London: Routledge and Kegan Paul.

Thackeray, W.M. (1869). On being found out. In *Collected Works.* 20, pp. 125–32. London: Smith, Elder.

Thorwald, J. (1965). *La grande aventure de la criminologie* (French translation of the original *Das jahrhundert der detektive* published by Droemersche Verlaganstalt, Zurich).

Thornberry, T.P. & Figlio, R.M. (1972, November). *Victimization and criminal behavior in a birth cohort.* Paper presented at the meetings of the American Society of Criminology, Caracas, Venezuela.

Törnudd,, P. (1971). The futility of searching for causes of crime. *Scandinavian Studies in Criminology.* 3, pp. 23–33. Oslo: Universitetsforlaget.

Törnudd, P. (1985). A more sombre mood. *International Annals of Criminology.* 23, pp. 67–80. Paris.

Tsutomi, H. (1991, November). *Reformulating Cloward and Ohlin's differential oppor-tunity theory into rational choice perspective: Occupational orientation of Japanese institutionalized delinquents.* Paper presented at the American Society of Criminol-ogy annual meeting in San Francisco.

Tuchfarber, A.J. & Klecka, W.R. (1976). *Measuring crime victimization: An efficient method.* Washington, DC: The Police Foundation.

Tuchfarber, A.J. & Klecka, W.R. (1976). *Random digit dialing: Lowering the cost of victimization surveys.* Washington, DC: The Police Foundation.

Turk, A.T. (1969). Introduction. In W.A. Bonger's *Criminality and Economic Condi-tions.* Bloomington: Indiana University Press.

Turk, A.T. (1982). *Political Criminality: The Defiance and Defense of Authority.* Beverly Hills, CA: Sage.

Turner, J. (1974). *The Structure of Social Theory.* Homewood, IL: Dorsey.

Ujimoto, K.V. (1976). Contrasts in the prewar and post-war Japanese community in B.C. *Canadian Review of Sociology and Anthropology.* 13:1, pp. 80–9.

Up Against the Law Collective (1974). *Police Corruption.* Vol. 2, pp. 21–35.

US Department of Justice (1981). *Victims of Crime.* Bureau of Justice Statistics Bulletin. Washington, DC: US Government Printing Office.

US Department of Justice (1985). *The risk of violent crime.* Bureau of Justice Statis-tics. Washington, DC: US Government Printing Office.

US Department of Justice (1986). *Crime and Justice Facts,* 1985. Bureau of Justice Statistics, Washington, DC: US Government Printing Office.

US Department of Justice (1993). *Highlights from 20 Years of Surveying Crime Victims – The National Crime Victimization Survey,* 1973–92. Bureau of Justice Statistics. Washington, DC, US Dept. of Justice.

US Department of Justice (1995). *Violence Against Women: Estimates from the Re-designed Survey.* Bureau of Justice Statistics Special Report. Washington, DC: US Dept. of Justice.

US President's Commission on Law Enforcement and Administration of Criminal Justice (1967). *The challenge of crime in a free society.* Washington, DC: US Government Printing Office.

US President's Commission on Law Enforcement and Administration of Criminal Justice (1967). *Task Force Report: Organized Crime.* Washington, DC: US Govern-ment Printing Office.

United Kingdom, Home Office (1983). *The British Crime Survey.* By M. Hough and P. Mayhew. London: HMSO.

United Kingdom. Scottish Office (1984). *The British crime survey – Scotland.* (eds) G. Chambers & J. Tombs. A Scottish Office Social Research Study. Edinburgh: HMSO.

United Nations (1979, July). *Report of the inter regional meeting held in New York.* In preparation for the 6th UN Congress on the Prevention of Delinquency and the Treatment of Offenders.

Van Dijk, J.J.M., Mayhew, P. & Killias, M. (1990). *Experiences of Crime Across the World. Key Findings of the 1989 International Crime Survey.* Deventer: Kluwer.

Van Dijk, J.J.M. & Mayhew, P. (1993). *Criminal victimization in the industrialized world: Key findings of the 1989 and 1992 international crime survey.* The Hague: Directorate of Crime Prevention, Ministry of Justice.

Van Dijk, J.J.M. & Steinmetz, C.H.D. (1984). The burden of crime in Dutch society, 1973–1979. In Richard Block (ed.), *Victimization and fear of crime: World perspectives.* pp. 29–43. Washington, DC: U.S. Dept. of Justice, Bureau of Justice Statistics.

Vaz, E.W. (1965). Middle-class adolescents: Self-reported delinquency and youth culture activities. *Canadian Review of Sociology and Anthropology.* 2:1, pp. 52–70.

Vaz, E.W. (1966). Self-reported delinquency and socio-economic status. *Canadian Journal of Corrections.* 8, pp. 20–7.

Vaz, E.W. (1967). *Middle class Juvenile Delinquency.* New York: Harper and Row.

Vold, G.B. (1958). *Theoretical Criminology.* New York: Oxford University Press.

Vold, G.B. (1979). *Theoretical Criminology* (2nd edn prepared by Thomas J. Bernard). New York: Oxford University Press.

Walker, S. (1985). *Sense and Nonsense About Crime. A Policy Guide.* Monterey, CA: Brooks/Cole Publishing Company.

Walklate, S. (1990). Researching Victims of Crime: Critical Victimology, *Social Justice,* 17:25–42.

Waller, I. & Okihiro, N. (1978). *Burglary: The Victim and the Public.* Toronto: University of Toronto Press.

Wallerstein, J.A., & Wyle, C.J. (1947). Our law-abiding lawbreakers. *Federal Probation.* 25, pp. 107–12.

Walmsley, R. (1986). *Personal violence.* Home Office Research and Planning Unit Report No. 89. London: HMSO.

Walters, G.D. (1990). *The criminal lifestyle: Patterns of serious criminal conduct.* Newbury Park: Sage.

Wardlaw, G. (1982). *Political Terrorism.* Cambridge: Cambridge University Press.

Weatherburn, D. (1993). On the quest for a general theory of crime. *Australian and New Zealand Journal of Criminology.* 26, pp. 35–46.

Weihofen, H. (1956). *The Urge to Punish.* New York: Farrar, Straus.

Weiss, K., & Borges, S. (1973). Victimology and rape: The case of the legitimate victim. *Issues in Criminology.* 8:2, pp. 71–115.

Wertham, F. (1949). *The Show of Violence.* New York: Doubleday.

West, D.J. (1967). *The Young Offender.* New York: International University Press.

West, D., & Farrington, D. (1977). *The Delinquent Way of Life.* London: Heinemann.

Westermarck, E.A. (1924). *The Origin and Development of the Moral Ideas* (2 volumes). London: Macmillan.

Wikström, P.O.H. (1985). *Everyday violence in contemporary Sweden: Situational and ecological aspects.* Stockholm: The National Council for Crime Prevention.

Wilber, G.L. (1949). The scientific adequacy of criminological concepts. *Social Forces.* 28, pp. 165–74.

Wiles, P. (1976). The new criminologies: Introduction. In *Crime and Delinquency in Britain.* 2, pp. 1–35. London: Martin Robertson.

Wilkins, L.T. (1964). *Social Deviance.* London: Tavistock.

Williams, F.P. & McShane, M.D. (1994). *Theories in Criminology* (2nd edn). Englewood Cliffs: Prentice-Hall.

Williams, K. (1976). The effects of victim characteristics on the disposition of violent crimes. In McDonald, W.F. (ed.), *Criminal Justice and the Victim.* Beverly Hills: Sage.

Wilson, J.Q. (1971, January). Crime and the liberal audience. *Commentary.* 77.

Wilson, J.Q. (1975). *Thinking about Crime.* New York: Basic Books.

Wilson, J.Q. & Herrnstein, R.J. (1985). *Crime and Human Nature.* New York: Simon and Schuster.

Wilson, M.S. (1973). Gabriel Tarde. In H. Mannheim (ed.), *Pioneers in Criminology.* pp. 292–304, 2nd edn. (1st edn published in 1954). Montclair, NJ: Patterson Smith.

Wilson, P.R., & Brown, J. (1973). *Crime and the Community.* Brisbane: University of Queensland Press.

Wilson, P., Lincoln, R. & Chappell, D. (1986). Physician Fraud and Abuse in Canada: A Preliminary Examination. *Canadian Journal of Criminology.* Vol. 28:2, pp. 129–46.

Wines, F.H. (1895). *Punishment and Reformation: An Historical Sketch of the Rise of the Penitentiary System.* New York: B. Blom. (Reprinted 1971.)

Wolfgang, M.E. (1957). Victim-precipitated criminal homicide. *Journal of Criminal Law, Criminology and Police Science.* 48:1, pp. 1–11.

Wolfgang, M.E. (1958). *Patterns in Criminal Homicide.* Philadelphia: University of Pennsylvania Press.

Wolfgang, M.E. (1973). Cesare Lombroso (1835–1909). In H. Mannheim (ed.), *Pioneers in Criminology.* Montclair, NJ: Patterson Smith.

Wollan, L.A. Jr. (1980). After labeling and conflict: An aspect of criminology's next chapter. In J.A. Inciardi (ed.), *Radical Criminology – The Coming Crises.* pp. 287–98. Beverly Hills, CA: Sage.

Wootton, B. (1963). *Crime and the Criminal Law: Reflections of a Magistrate and Social Scientist.* London: Stevens.

Wright, K.N. (1985). *The Great American Crime Myth.* London: Greenwood Press.

Yochelson, S. & Samenov, S. (1976). *The Criminal Personality.* New York: Jason Aronson.

Young, D.B. (1983). Cesare Beccaria: Utilitarian or Retributivist? *Journal of Criminal Justice.* 11, pp. 317–26.

Young, J. (1986). The failure of criminology: The need for a radical realism. In R. Matthews & J. Young (eds), *Confronting Crime.* London: Sage.

Young, J. (1992). Ten points of realism. In J. Young & R. Matthews (eds), *Rethinking Criminology: The Realist Debate.* London: Sage.

Zedner, L. (1994). *Victimology.* Aldershot: Dartmouth.

Ziegenhagen, E.A. (1977). *Victims, Crime and Social Control.* New York: Praeger.

Zimbardo, P.G. (1972). Pathology of punishment. *Trans-Action.* 9, pp. 4–8.

Zimbardo, P.G. (1978). The psychology of evil: On the perversion of human potential. In L. Krames, P. Pliner, & T. Alloway (eds) *Aggression, Dominance, and Individual Spacing.* New York: Plenum.

Subject Index

Rehabilitation, 4, 175, 180, 244
Relative deprivation, 68, 210
Relativity of victimization, 59–61
Restitution, 33, 45, 146, 221, 222, 261, 289
Restorative justice, 146, 261
Retaliation, 258, 262, 276
Retribution, 5, 179, 192, 221
Retributive justice, 146, 261
Revenge, 258, 275, 277, 284
Reverse record checking, 107–8
Rites of passage, 60, 258
Routine activities approach, 275

Schools of criminological thought
  Austrian School, 244, 245
  Cartographic/Ecological
    School, 208–13, 248
  Chicago School, xi, 213
  Classical School, 195, 201–5, 211, 214, 218, 220, 221, 223, 225, 227, 228–30, 263, 275, 300
  French Sociological School, 231–40, 243
  Italian Positivist/Positive
    School, 132, 214–31, 243, 263–4, 300
  Neo-Classical School, 205–6, 214, 230
  Psychiatric School, 132, 140–1
  School of Lyon, 243
  School of Mental Testers, 132
  Socialist School, 240–2
Self-report studies, 97, 129
Shoplifting, 117, 153, 166, 243, 261
Sin, 37–8, 237, 251, 278
Situational approach, 145, 146, 278–80
Situational factors/variables, 129, 145, 147, 156, 165, 255, 264, 278–80
Situational theories, xiv, 278–80
Social contract, The (Rousseau), 194, 195, 199, 230
Social control theories, 275, 276
Social defence, 221–3, 225, 229, 230
Social ecology, xi
Social learning theories, 234, 273
Socialization, 274, 278
Statutory rape, 50

Strict liability, 52, 263
Subcultural theory, 248, 266, 277, 278
Suicide/assisted suicide, 35, 39, 64, 138, 196, 209, 233, 235, 236, 263
Summary executions, 70
Symbolic interaction, 248

Techniques of neutralization, 129
Technological control of human beings, 293
Technology of repression, 294
Telephone interviews, 106, 107, 110
Telescoping, 108–9
Terrorism, 57, 86, 289
  definition of, 57–9
  incumbent, 58, 293
  insurgent, 58, 293–4
Tests of criminality, 42
Thermal Law of Delinquency
  (Quetelet), 210, 212
Three Mile Island nuclear plant, 80
'Three strikes and you are out' Laws, 6
Torts (*see* Civil torts)
Torture, 72, 74–5, 94, 192, 198, 203
Transient criminality, 166

Uniform Crime Reports, 9, 96, 99, 104
Union Carbide disaster (*see* Bhopal)
United Nations Asia and Far East
  Institute for the Prevention of
  Crime, 260
United States
  Bureau of Justice Statistics, 10, 13, 25, 35, 147, 152, 153
  Central Intelligence Agency
    (CIA), 59, 72–3, 76–7
  crime clock, 23
  President's Commission on Law
    Enforcement and
    Administration of Justice, 12, 29, 90, 103
  Senate Select Committee on
    Intelligence, 72–3
  Violent Crime Control and Law
    Enforcement Act of 1994, 5
  Watergate Affair, 129
Universalism, 44, 304
Utilitarianism, 194, 196–7

Name Index